MAY – – 2017

MAXIMUM HARM

MICHELE R. MCPHEE

MAXIMUM

HARM

THE
TSARNAEV
BROTHERS,
THE FBI, AND
THE ROAD TO
THE MARATHON
BOMBING

ForeEdge

ForeEdge

An imprint of University Press of New England

www.upne.com

© 2017 Michele R. McPhee

All rights reserved

Manufactured in the United States of America

Designed by Mindy Basinger Hill

Typeset in Minion Pro

For permission to reproduce any of the material in this book,

contact Permissions, University Press of New England,

One Court Street, Suite 250, Lebanon NH 03766;

or visit www.upne.com

Library of Congress Cataloging-in-Publication Data

Names: McPhee, Michele, author.

Title: Maximum harm : the Tsarnaev brothers, the FBI, and the road to the
    Marathon Bombing / Michele R. McPhee.

Description: Lebanon, NH : ForeEdge, [2017] | Includes bibliographical refer-
    ences and index.

Identifiers: LCCN 2016049146 (print) | LCCN 2017007836 (ebook) | ISBN
    9781611688498 (cloth : alk. paper) | ISBN 9781512600728 (epub, mobi & pdf)

Subjects: LCSH: Tsarnaev, Dzhokhar. | Tsarnaev, Tamerlan. | United States. Fed-
    eral Bureau of Investigation. | Terrorists—United States. | Informers—United
    States. | Terrorism—United States—Prevention. | Boston Marathon Bombing,
    Boston, Mass., 2013.

Classification: LCC HV6432.8 .M33 2017 (print) | LCC HV6432.8 (ebook) |
    DDC 363.325/97964252—dc23

LC record available at https://lccn.loc.gov/2016049146

5 4 3 2

CONTENTS

AUTHOR'S NOTE

When two bombs were detonated on Boylston Street, 550 feet away from the finish line of the Boston Marathon on April 15, 2013, a familiar sense of dread came over me. There was no cell phone service. Loved ones were unreachable. At 2:49 P.M., the place just yards from where I'd had coffee hours earlier was a war zone. There were body parts, pools of blood, broken glass—it was a scene of inexplicable mayhem. Boston was under attack.

That day I began investigating the marathon bombings for ABC News, and I have not stopped since. I was there as crime scene detectives and federal agents collected evidence and when the FBI released photographs of the suspects referred to as "Black Hat" and "White Hat" four days after the bombings. Just hours after that release, I raced to Cambridge when those same suspects were believed to have murdered an MIT police officer in cold blood and then carjacked a getaway vehicle. The carjacking victim escaped but left his cell phone behind in his Mercedes SUV. Police used its GPS device to track it to Watertown, my next stop. There, reporters ringed the streets until, in unison, we dove behind cars when we heard bullets being fired and explosives going off during a wild battle between the suspected bombers and the police.

At 1:01 A.M. on April 19, the bullets stopped. More than two hundred spent rounds littered the streets and were recovered from nearby homes. One suspect was dead. The other was on the run. And they had been publicly identified by the FBI as Tamerlan Tsarnaev, twenty-six, and his brother, Dzhokhar, nineteen, two Russian immigrants who had been living in a subsidized apartment in Cambridge. I remained in the paralyzed city of Watertown for the next sixteen hours as SWAT teams searched door to door, telling terrified residents to stay put. Many people were forced to plug bullet holes in their homes. One family had the surreal experience of seeing a round pierce their television set as it was broadcasting news of the insanity going on outside their house. Just after 6:00 P.M., a Watertown man went out for a smoke and found drops of blood that led to his boat, the *Slip Away II*, dry-docked in his yard. When he pulled back the tarp covering the boat, he saw a bleeding man in the bottom of the boat and scrambled for his phone. Within minutes, cops had ringed the boat, and after one of them seemed to see movement, they fired on it. The first shot was followed by a twelve-second barrage of gun blasts fired by police into the side of the boat accompanied by flash-bang grenades whose hum could be heard blocks away. Then there came the order to cease fire. Dzhokhar Tsarnaev was captured alive—just barely alive. Grateful residents of Watertown lined the streets to cheer the cops as they pulled out of the city later that night. I know a lot of police officers who didn't have to pay for a round of beers that night.

Since then I have attended every arraignment and court appearance of the accused bomber, Dzhokhar Tsarnaev, and four other men charged in the attacks, his college friends who were imprisoned for lying to investigators in a terrorism case.

Tragically, the Boston Marathon attack was not the first time I had been on the scene of a terrorist attack on American soil.

When two planes were hijacked from Boston's Logan Airport and flown into Manhattan's World Trade Center Towers on September 11, 2001, I was the police bureau chief for the New York *Daily News*, working out of One Police Plaza and on the scene at Ground Zero when the towers collapsed.

The very same homeland security flaws that I investigated as a *Daily News* reporter were partly to blame for the Boston attacks. In a Congressional hearing weeks after the deadly attack in 2013, former Boston Police Commissioner Ed Davis told federal lawmakers that the lack of information sharing between the FBI and Boston Police Department detectives assigned to work with the FBI on the Joint Terrorism Task Force in Boston, all of whom had top security clearance, hindered his officers from investigating the allegations made by counterterrorism counterparts in Russia. In other words, the FBI didn't share intelligence with their BPD counterparts on the task force—not exactly the spirit of cooperation that had been pushed by counterterrorism experts in the aftermath of 9/11.

Similar laments were made after 9/11 by New York Police Department Commissioner Ray Kelly, who repeatedly warned me and other reporters who worked out of One Police Plaza that it was "not if, but when" the United States would be attacked by Islamic extremists again. The biggest threat, Kelly said, would be homegrown terrorists. He was right. Researchers with the George Washington University Program on Extremism released a report on the Islamic State of Iraq and Syria (ISIS) in America in 2015 that included startling numbers: more than 900 Americans were under investigation in the United States for connections to terrorism; 250 had traveled abroad to join the jihad; and 56 had been arrested for terrorism-related activities in 2015 alone.[1] Sadly, four of those arrests took place in Massachusetts in under one year. One of the four, Alexander Ciccolo, is the son of a venerable Boston Police Department captain who was part of the department's response to the marathon attacks in 2013.[2]

The Tsarnaev brothers, their parents, and two sisters—all of whom had fled Russia in 2002 and settled in Massachusetts—were certainly among the many people who had benefited from the generosity of Americans. They had been granted political asylum and given housing, public assistance, and free education. Dzhokhar even became an American citizen, sworn in alongside other immigrants on September 11, 2012, in the auditorium commonly known as the Boston Garden. Ironically, on the same day four Americans were murdered at the hands of Islamic extremists in Benghazi, Libya. Despite all that the United States had given the Tsarnaev family, the two brothers became the very sort of men that counterterrorism officials have been so afraid of since 9/11: homegrown terrorists.

But this time, I believe, the federal government played a direct role in creating the monster that Tamerlan Tsarnaev became—a murderer whom his little brother looked up to and a man so desperate to become an American citizen that he was willing to do anything, even betray his friends and relatives.

I spent three years researching this book, and in it I have outlined my theory that the FBI recruited Tamerlan as an operative in late 2010, months before the Federal Security Service of Russia (FSB) warned the FBI's Boston field office that he had become radicalized and planned to obtain training from "bandit groups" in his native Russia.[3] In fact, Dzhokhar's defense attorneys have stated that the FBI attempted to recruit Tamerlan to inform on fellow Muslims, writing: "We base this on information from our client's family and other sources that the FBI made more than one visit to talk with Anzor, Zubeidat and Tamerlan, questioned Tamerlan about his internet searches, and asked him to be an informant."[4]

It is no secret that the FBI has relied heavily on Islamic informants to thwart terrorist plots, a practice that has been condemned by the American Civil Liberties Union and other organizations. Tamerlan would have been the perfect recruit, a handsome multilingual Muslim with ties to both the drug world and a controversial mosque in Cambridge blocks from his house, one that was started and built by a man now serving a federal sentence for terrorism and that counted several convicted terrorists among its congregants. And it was certainly not a secret that Tamerlan was motivated to become a US citizen. In 2009 he participated in an online photo essay titled "Will Box for Passport." In 2010 he was barred from fighting in the National Tournament of Champions, even though he had twice won the title of heavyweight champion of New England, because he was not a citizen. Then there was the issue of money: Tamerlan didn't have any, at least not on paper. For occupation on his death certificate the medical examiner wrote, "Never Worked."[5] Yet he drove a Mercedes without holding a job. He also got married and had a little girl. History has shown that working for the federal government as an informant can be lucrative. Tamerlan got away with so much villainy that only a hands-off policy formulated at the local level by one or more agencies responsible for national intelligence could have engineered it. His probable situation with such agencies is eerily similar to the former relationship of James "Whitey" Bulger and the Boston office of the FBI.

Evidence suggests that in 2011 Tamerlan secretly worked on an investigation that dismantled a ring of crack cocaine dealers who moved the drug from Boston to Portland, Maine. Federal investigators called the investigation Operation Run This Town, and its targets were Eritrean gang members including one of the eventual defendants, Hamadi Hassan, a native of Cambridge who had grown up with Tamerlan. In fact, the Bureau of Alcohol, Tobacco, Firearms and Explosives (ATF) would trace the gun used to murder

Sean Collier, an MIT police officer, four days after the Tsarnaevs detonated the bombs back to that crew of Eritrean drug dealers, who loaned the gun to Dzhokhar along with the bullets, which he called "food for the dog."[6] Tamerlan's assistance in Operation Run This Town is the only plausible reason he was never investigated for a grisly triple homicide later in 2011, in which he was clearly implicated.

Four months after the brutal murders, on January 21, 2012, Tamerlan traveled to Russia for six months without a valid US passport, even though he was on two terror watch lists. (He did have a passport issued in his birthplace of Kyrgyzstan.) There is evidence that while there he acted at the behest of both American and Russian intelligence to finger Chechen rebels, some of whom were quickly killed. On his return, he was guided through customs at John F. Kennedy International Airport, still on the watch lists and still without a US passport.

The *9/11 Commission Report* made tightening border security a key recommendation.[7] Apparently that recommendation did not apply to Tamerlan. There may be a reason—perhaps a deal was made, with promises of mutually advantageous cooperation—that goes beyond lax security, however.

This book lays out the evidence that I collected over more than three years of reporting, using court documents and police interviews and tracking down dozens of people connected to both the investigation and the Tsarnaev clan. It is now up to the reader to decide if US authorities made Tamerlan a promise: *If you help us, we will help you.* And if that promise was reneged on, leading him to change sides.

Tamerlan wanted to be an American so badly that he killed for the chance.

MAXIMUM HARM

PROLOGUE
PATRIOTS' DAY

Steve Woolfenden was excited. It was the first time his wife, Amber, was running in the Boston Marathon, a milestone she had worked toward since joining the Wicked Runners Club in Salem, Massachusetts. He maneuvered their three-year-old son, Leo, in his stroller—the three-wheeled carriage specially designed with bicycle motocross (BMX) tires for hard-core runners—toward the finish line.

The crowd up and down Boylston Street near the finish line grew even bigger after the Red Sox game ended at 2:08 P.M. Leo was happy in his stroller, and Steve found a decent spot near the Marathon Sports store so that Amber might actually see them, even though there were roughly 27,000 runners on the course that had left the starting line in Hopkinton, Massachusetts, in several waves since 9:00 A.M. The mobility-impaired athletes took off first, followed by the wheelchair racers and then the racers on hand cycles. Then the elite women were launched at 9:22, followed by the elite men at 9:32. At 10:00 am the first wave of 9,000 regular runners took off; twenty minutes later, the second wave of 9,000 took off, and then the final wave of 9,000 left Hopkinton at 10:40 A.M.[1] By 12:36 P.M. the winners had been declared: Ethiopia's Lelisa Desisa won the men's race, with a time of 2:10:22, and Rita Jeptoo of Kenya won the women's race with a time of 2:26:25. But hundreds of runners were still on the course at 2:49 P.M., including Amber Woolfenden.

Steve had planned to meet some friends at M Bar, but that wasn't going to happen. It was on the other side of Boylston Street, and there was no way he could cross. So he pulled out his phone, sent them an update via text, and pushed Leo from the store's doorway toward the international flags that lined the last leg of the 26.1-mile race and settled in closer to the finish line. Focused on the runners and waiting for Amber, he didn't notice the backpack on the sidewalk just to the left of Marathon Sports. Then came the boom. It sounded like one of the cannon blasts that exploded on the Esplanade on the Fourth of July or at the start of a New England Patriots' game. No one knew what it was at first.

Boston Police Department (BPD) Sergeant Dan Keeler knew it wasn't good. He transmitted an urgent message over his police radio: "Stop the race! Stop the race! Send me everything you have to Boylston."[2] The runners were stopped in Brookline, before they made their way into Boston's Back Bay. Amber Woolfenden was one of them.

"I was in shock and disbelief," Steve would later recall. "It registered that we needed to get out of there. The most logical choice would be to take a one-eighty and go the other way. And we didn't get that opportunity."[3]

Steve spun around and hustled away from the first explosion, headed north on Boylston toward the Forum restaurant. He made it exactly 183 yards—moving right into the zone of the second bomb, which detonated thirteen seconds after the first one. This bomb produced an ugly orange fireball more deadly than the first because of the way it was detonated: it was inside a backpack that had been set down sideways, so that the explosive device inside, improvised from a pressure cooker, blew outward instead of upward. The first bomb was placed upright, but it would still create the maximum harm intended when it was detonated with a device fashioned from a remote controller for a toy car, such as one that a little boy like Leo might have used.

A video would later reveal that in the seconds before the second bomb was detonated, Steve was jostled by a skinny man in a white baseball cap who had been standing near a tree in front of the Forum restaurant and behind a row of children lined up along a metal barricade. Some leaned on it. Others, like Martin Richard, put their feet between the grates and hoisted themselves higher. With that blast Steve was hit with an intense heat, a pressure that made him feel like "every part of my body was being punched," he recalled. He thought he was still standing because he was holding fast to the stroller.

But he soon realized he had been blown to the ground. He yanked back the stroller's cover and saw Leo bleeding. The toddler was screaming over and over again: "Mommy! Daddy! Mommy! Daddy! Mommy! Daddy! Mommy! Daddy! Mommy! Daddy!"

"Leo was conscious. He was alive. He was bleeding from the left side of this head," Steve recalled. He was nauseated by the smell of burning hair and flesh and by the smell of sulfur that enveloped him—a smell like rotten eggs, which cops all around him recognized from their days at a firing range. He could hear screams and sirens and saw body parts littered like puzzle pieces all around him. The air around him was so hot that he felt like he was in front of a pizza oven. Terrified, Steve had only one thought: get his son the hell off Boylston Street.

Steve reached for his Leo, his fingers numb. Later, he remembered thinking: "Well. Let's get out of here. And that's when I discovered my leg had been severed off." He recognized his boot on the ground next to him, with his sheared-off limb inside it. He realized that a glob of what looked like bloodied Scotch tape was in fact his Achilles tendon and knew he had to stop the bleeding. He ripped off his belt and tied it tightly around his thigh.

He was completely helpless. The buckles on the stroller were mangled, and he couldn't unstrap Leo. A stranger knelt down next to him, and Steve implored him to help Leo, saying: "My son's bleeding from his head. You need to get him out of here. Please get my son to safety." And the man said, "I will do that but first I'm going to put another tourniquet on your leg."

Then another man, also a stranger, came to Steve's side. Leo was gone, and Steve had no idea whether or not he was going to die right there on the sidewalk. The stranger got in his face, Steve remembered, and kept him conscious. "You're going to fucking make it," the man said. "You're going to fucking make it."

Across the street stood BPD Officer Tommy Barrett, stunned. He didn't know where to start. "There was so many people that were hurt seriously that it was hard to choose who to begin helping first. So that's what I was doing, just trying to pick who, maybe who was hurt the worst, in my view. Everybody was hurt really bad, but I was trying to pick who I could help first," he remembered.[4] Barrett ran toward the toppled metal barricade, where the most seriously maimed people—those directly in the blast zone—were fighting for their lives. The Boston cop used his gloved hands to beat out the flames around a man on fire in front of him. Another man helped by dousing smoldering remains with the contents of a beer bottle that had been abandoned on an outside table, as a woman tried to use a cloth napkin as a tourniquet around a critically wounded man's upper thigh. Three strangers were all desperately trying to keep one man alive. The man on fire was Marc Fucarile. His flesh was festooned with scalding hot BB pellets, shrapnel from the bomb. Barely conscious, his body engulfed in flames, he grabbed for his belt and got third-degree burns on his hands as he pulled it off in desperation, knowing he had to stop the bleeding from his severed leg.

When the fire was out, Barrett's attention turned toward someone yelling, "There's a kid over here!"

The kid was Leo. Barrett ran toward the child, pulled him to his chest, and carried him like a football across Boylston Street toward Dartmouth Street, where a medical tent had been set up to treat any runners who might be in need of care. Within minutes it went from a site for massages and treatment for heat stroke and sprains to a mass casualty response site staffed by a team of doctors, nurses, and volunteers so skillful that every one of the 264 patients—many of them critically injured—who would eventually be evaluated and transported to area hospitals survived, including the 17 who had suffered traumatic amputations.[5] Boston Emergency Management Services (EMS) Chief James Hooley set up a system for tagging the wounded: 30 people received red tags, indicating that they were in critical condition and therefore were the first to be transported; 25 patients who were seriously wounded but not at risk of dying immediately got yellow tags, and another 35 who were badly hurt got green tags. In all, 118 people were raced to Boston-area hospitals, most within a two-mile radius of the bomb blasts.[6]

A block before Barrett made it to the tent, one of the seventy-three ambulances that would eventually flood the bloodstained street stopped. "I have a young boy," Barrett told the paramedics with the ambulance and handed Leo to them before running back toward the boy's father and the mess of charred flesh and congealing blood around him.

"It was brutal," Barrett recalled. "I stepped on somebody's leg. People were missing legs, and you know, the legs were ripped off. It wasn't anything clean or neat. A lot of people had, you know, clothes that were torn, shredded."

He saw a woman sitting up, desperately trying to keep her eviscerated insides within her body. She screamed, her arms desperately flailing, before she went limp. A medical examiner would later determine that she had been conscious for only a minute between being injured and dying. Her name was Lingzi Lu, a 23-year-old Boston University student from China and her entire body was ripped apart by bomb shrapnel. A jagged, twisted piece of metal was lodged in her leg, another piece of the bomb would later be found in her purse. Lingzi went to the marathon with another Chinese student, Danling Zhou, who would recall holding her own intestines in, her stomach a gaping messy hole of burning flesh, while trying to comfort her friend. "Everyone is panicked. Everyone is asking what's happening. I never think it's a bomb. I tried to calm Lingzi down. Lingzi is holding my arm. I'm about to tell her it's okay, let's go. I never get to say that," Danling recalled, crying.[7]

Observing the young woman in her death throes, Barrett told himself, "There's nothing I can do for her. There were other things I could help people with. Those are the people I had to move to."[8]

Those people included Steve Woolfenden, who at this point had no idea whether he was going to live or die or where his son had been taken. For that matter, Steve had no idea where his wife was. But he was distracted from his own panic by the cries of Denise Richard, who was keening "Please Martin. Please Martin," over her little boy, a piece of shrapnel still embedded in her right eye. Steve would later learn that Martin was only eight and, as Mayor Martin Walsh—who succeeded Thomas M. Menino, mayor at the time of the blasts—would come to say repeatedly, had a smile "that could light up Fenway Park."

Martin's entire fifty-three-inch-tall body had been blasted with small nails, tiny pieces of black plastic, round metal pellets, small fragments of wood, and metal pieces of the bomb. He was wearing a Boston Celtics jersey over a New England Patriots T-shirt. Both garments were charred, stained with smoke, ripped, peppered with holes, and stiff with blood.

Martin's father, Bill Richard, was also in a bad way. His sneakers had been blown apart and his pants shredded. A large piece of metal was imbedded in his leg. Bill couldn't hear the screams of his family over the ringing in his ears. He could smell the vile odor that covered the street like a wet shroud, the combined smell of spent gunpowder and burning hair. The hair of seven-year-old Jane Richard, Bill's youngest child and only daughter, was burning. Bill watched, horrified, as Jane tried to get up but fell right back down. Her leg was gone. A firefighter would later recall, horrifyingly, that the little girl's limb looked like it had been put through a meat grinder. It was then that Bill made the extraordinarily difficult decision to leave Denise with their dying son to get Jane and their oldest boy, Henry, to a hospital.

"When I saw Martin's condition I knew he wasn't going to make it. I just knew from what I saw that there was no chance, the color of his skin," Bill would recall later, on the stand in the trial of the man who killed his son.[9] "I knew in my head that I needed to act quickly or we might not only lose Martin, but we might lose Jane too." He shielded Jane's eyes as he carried her, Henry clinging to his side with eyes shut tight. Shock had drained the color from Henry's face.

Steve Woolfenden winced as he watched Martin's eyes roll into the back of his head, which was singed: "I saw a little boy and his mother . . . I saw Martin's face. And I could see a boy that looked like—he was fatally injured." Steve was close enough to reach out and put a comforting hand on Denise Richard's back. She turned to him in a moment of pure humanity to ask: "Are you okay?" He nodded. Denise turned back to Martin as he died.

Not far away Adrianne Haslet-Davis's husband, Adam, was holding his wife's severed lower leg. His own calves were missing chunks of flesh as big as scoops of ice cream, which had been seared away. He was in shock. Adrianne crawled over shattered glass to reach him and began to shout his name, her arms shredded and bleeding. "I screamed Adam! Adam!" she remembered. "I thought that because I couldn't hear myself scream I was dead."[10]

The first bomb, detonated at 2:49 P.M., was not as powerful as the second, the FBI would determine, because—as explained above—when it was detonated the force went upward instead of outward. Still, it was powerful enough to kill twenty-seven-year-old Krystle Marie Campbell, her daddy's "princess, every father's dream," who—with her best friend, Karen Rand-McWatters— was among the throngs of people who pushed their way down Boylston Street after leaving the Red Sox game. Before she left home, she had given her father a hug, their daily ritual, and then set off for the game with her girlfriend, before meeting the men they were dating.

Sometime around 2:00 P.M. the girlfriends had stopped on a bridge in the Boston Public Garden and let a stranger snap a picture of them. "It was a beautiful day. We were being silly and touristy," Karen later recalled.[11] Less than an hour later came the blast that hurled both women to the ground. "I remember lying on the ground wondering if I was a dreaming, if I had really made it to the marathon." The force of the explosion snapped Campbell's femur. Her body was covered in burns, and her hair was singed and smoking. She had a BB pellet embedded in the back of her ear, cuts and scrapes on her neck, and contusions on her tongue. Internally, she suffered thermal injuries. Her entire body was hit with pellets, and they were also found in her clothes.

Krystle was moaning, and when Karen tried to move closer to her friend she found that her own leg was gone. She pulled herself closer to Krystle using her cut, burned hands, dragging herself over the shattered glass and white-hot BB pellets that littered the ground. "I got close to her head, we put our faces together," Karen remembered. "She said very slowly that her legs hurt. Her hand went limp in mine and she never spoke again." A marathon volunteer was photographed at that moment standing over both women, with her rubber-gloved hands pressed against their hearts, a tragic photo that would be shown to the jury, but horrifying enough to be kept from the public.[12]

Leo Woolfenden wasn't the only child crying for his mother. All Rebekah Gregory could hear, over the incessant ringing that filled her head, was her son, Noah, screaming for her. "I looked down and I couldn't see my legs. My bones were literally on the sidewalk next to me. I thought that was that day I would die," Rebekah would remember.[13] Her eardrums were perforated. She barely felt the skin on her arms being ripped apart by shards of glass on the sidewalk as she tried to crawl to her bleeding son. "I could hear Noah. I don't know how. I could hear my little boy. 'Mommy! Mommy! Mommy!' Over and over again."

Nicole Gross was a tourist, a physical therapist from North Carolina who had come to cheer her mother across the marathon's finish line. She didn't notice the man in the black baseball cap who was behind her right before she fell back in "slow motion." On the ground, she propped herself on her elbows and looked down. It was eerily silent. She could see people's mouths opened in horror, but she couldn't hear anything: "I just screamed for somebody to save me, hear me!"[14] Her eardrums had burst, her left leg was shattered, her right leg had been blown apart, and her right ankle was mangled, her shoe dangling from her severed Achilles tendon. She was in terrible, unimaginable pain. She wasn't alone.

When the first bomb went off, Gillian "Ginny" Reny, an eighteen-year-old high-school student, was blown back and saw the "bodies everywhere, blood everywhere." She tried to get up to run but couldn't. "My leg was completely torn apart," she remembered. "I had nothing to stand on. I was one hundred percent sure I was going to die."[15]

Celeste Corcoran later wished that she could block out what she experienced at 2:49 P.M. on that Patriots' Day. "I, unfortunately, remember every single detail," she would later say. "I remember being thrown into the air. Landing hard. Not being able to breathe. I remember this thick, thick black heavy smoke. I was choking. There was this deafening silence. My eardrums got blown out."[16] Her husband, Kevin, was terrified but also furious. He held his wife's hand tight, not telling her both of her legs were gone. "This is a terror attack," he said.

He caught himself and began to comfort her: "I love you. You are going to live. I'm not leaving your side. Hold on. Hold on. It's going to be okay." With what little breath she had left, Celeste began to scream.

Kevin was right. People at the Boston Marathon had been attacked in an act of premeditated bloodletting not seen since 9/11—only the atrocities in 2013, investigators would discover, were committed by homegrown *jihadi* who had been given a life much better than the one they had fled courtesy of their adopted countrymen. However, on that terrible spring afternoon, no one knew who the perpetrators were. Certainly not Steve Woolfenden, who was transported to Boston Medical Center with a woman he had never met before. They held hands in the ambulance, and she told him her name was Gina DiMartino. "I wanted to hold someone's hand," Steve would explain.

The emergency room at Boston Medical Center was filled with a gruesome cacophony of screams, including some from Steve. Then he heard a voice saying, "I'm looking for my husband Steve," he remembered. "It was my wife's voice. Amber's voice. Amber came and grabbed my head and said, 'Leo is at Children's Hospital. He's okay. He's alive.'"

It would be one of the two last things he remembered before being raced into surgery; the other was his wedding ring being tugged from his hand. He woke up in a recovery room, having had his lower left leg amputated.

Leo was across town at Boston Children's Hospital with a skull fracture, a head laceration, and a perforated left eardrum. Steve wouldn't see his son for four days

Things like this didn't happen in Boston. This is not a city where the amputated limbs of seventeen people should be scattered on sidewalks alongside the lifeless bodies of a child and two young women. This was a scene made familiar only from watching BBC footage taken after suicide attacks in Middle Eastern markets or Israeli cafes. They didn't belong in the City on a Hill, the birthplace of liberty in America. But unlike the perpetrators of most of those bloody attacks chronicled in faraway places, the terrorists who attacked people at the Boston Marathon were very much alive. Alive and at large.

9

PART ONE

THE HUNTERS

*The Five-Day
Search for the
Boston Marathon
Bombers*

1

THESE MOTHERFUCKERS ARE HERE

The bombs detonated along the finish line left behind "a river of blood," as Assistant US Attorney Steve Mellin would later say.[1] The fireballs came from weapons designed and built to cause maximum harm, intended "not to just kill but destroy," Mellin said. And destroy they did. Business in the Back Bay came to an immediate and abrupt halt. Hundreds of bartenders, waitresses, and retailers were temporarily put out of work because stores, restaurants, and other businesses were damaged or shuttered as a large swath of Boylston Street became a crime scene. Citizens of the Commonwealth of Massachusetts were afraid to leave their homes. Bomb technicians from the Massachusetts State Police (MSP) and the BPD searched the sixty-one bags that had been left at the scene and detonated a suspicious backpack found under the grandstand seating at the finish line. Crime scene technicians solemnly processed the thousands of BB pellets and pieces of bomb that covered the street. Technicians from the Massachusetts Medical Examiner's Office recovered the body parts. Witnesses were interviewed. Video footage was secured. MBTA buses were called in to get the terrified runners and spectators away from the bomb site and to the Castle at Park Plaza to be reunited with their loved ones. The FBI commandeered an entire hangar at South Boston's Black Falcon Cruise Terminal to set up a makeshift lab to process the evidence. More than twenty different agencies were involved in the hunt for the marathon bombers, and investigators took over two floors of the Westin Copley Place hotel to set up a command post.

The city was frantic, and the uncertainty about what would happen next was written in the "terror on the faces of the people of Boston," remembered BPD Superintendent Billy Evans.[2]

Evans had been among the 30,000 runners on Patriots' Day, the eighteenth time he had participated in the Boston Marathon and his forty-seventh marathon. He left Hopkinton that morning and sprinted the 26.2-mile course, hearing the cheers of his officers who whooped for him along the entire route until he made his way to the finish line, where his wife, Terry, and their son, Will, welcomed him with hugs and congratulations. And he had made good time, he noted, smiling—three hours and thirty-four minutes. Not bad for a beat-up old guy from Southie whose fifty-four-year-old wiry frame had taken plenty of abuse when he had been a patrolman chasing bad guys on the streets of Boston. Evans liked to say that he was more runner than cop. Today, his office at One Schroeder Plaza—which serves as BPD headquarters and is named for two murdered police officers (the brothers Walter and John Schroeder, both of whom were shot and killed on the job)—is decorated with his marathon medals, dozens of them in frames on the wall. Not a day goes by when Evans isn't reminded of the Schroeder brothers, and the terrorist attack on Boylston Street was a gruesome reminder of how Walter Schroeder had died at the hands of another domestic terrorist group.

To this day in the BPD the Schroeder name is legendary, synonymous with police work. In 1973 John Schroeder was shot dead when he interrupted a pawnshop robbery in the Roxbury section of Boston. It was a horrible loss for his family and the entire city, whose residents knew all too well the story of Walter Schroeder, a Boston patrolman who had been murdered by the notorious group of anarchists known as the Weather Underground.

The FBI described the group this way in a 2004 press release about its history: "The Weather Underground—originally called the Weathermen, taken from a line in a Bob Dylan song—was a small, violent offshoot of the Students for a Democratic Society (SDS), created in the turbulent '60s to promote social change. When the SDS collapsed in 1969, the Weather Underground stepped forward, inspired by communist ideologies and embracing violence and crime as a way to protest the Vietnam War, racism, and other left-wing aims. 'Our intention is to disrupt the empire . . . to incapacitate it, to put pressure on the cracks,' claimed the group's 1974 manifesto, Prairie Fire. By the next year, the group had claimed credit for 25 bombings and would be involved in many more over the next several years."[3] Those bombings were expensive, and in the late 1960s and early 1970s, many members took to bank robberies to fund attacks.

Walter Schroeder's killers were two women from wealthy families who attended Brandeis University, a male classmate of theirs studying social work, and three other men, career criminals, who had met at the state prison in Walpole and then been paroled. Together they would become a terror cell that killed a Boston cop. In 2013, Islamic extremists had the same goal—attacking the United States. The radicals in the Weather Underground used bombs and bullets to protest the Vietnam War; Islamic extremists used bombs and bullets to protest US interventions in the Middle East. In both cases, their actions caused innocent people to die.

On September 23, 1970, Schroeder, a World War II veteran with nineteen years on the police force and a wife and nine kids at home, responded to a silent alarm at the State Street Bank and Trust, in the Brighton neighborhood of Boston. Schroeder arrived at the bank minutes after Katherine Powers and Susan Saxe, both twenty-one, and their Brandeis classmate Michael Fleisher, twenty-two, along with the parolees William "Lefty" Gilday, forty-one; Robert Valieri, twenty-one; and Stanley Bond, twenty-six, had broken in and stolen $26,000 from a bank vault. Gilday had been a minor league baseball player from Amesbury when he went to the Walpole state prison for bank robbery. When he was behind bars, he met Bond, a Vietnam War helicopter pilot with a lengthy rap sheet for petty crimes; and Valieri, a small-time hood from Somerville. The three crooks entered a program that helped convicts get into prestigious universities—which is how they met their wealthy co-conspirators. Together, they were going to fund a revolution. The Brighton bank robbery, prosecutors would learn, was not their first.

When Schroeder climbed out of his cruiser just before midnight, Gilday fired his rifle, a shot that proved fatal to the officer. His murder sparked an unprecedented police response involving every law enforcement agent and National Guardsman in the vicinity. Bond, Fleisher, and Valieri were apprehended within days. Saxe was on the lam for five years before she was arrested and sentenced to seven years in prison; Power eluded authorities until 1993, when she turned herself in and served six years in prison.

Gilday's bullet-riddled time on the lam has been described as the largest manhunt in New England history.[4] After a wild firefight and a long police chase using MSP helicopters, Gilday was captured. He was later convicted and sentenced to death, a sentence that would be overturned only when Massachusetts abolished the death penalty in 1982.

More than three decades later, Superintendent Billy Evans, who was called "Mousy" by his closest peers, would be involved the same sort of hunt that his predecessors had undertaken for Gilday, one that—like the 1970 hunt—would end in a wild firefight with a domestic terrorist.

———

When the first bomb was detonated at 2:49 P.M., Evans was soaking in the hot tub at his neighborhood gym, the South Boston Athletic Club (known as the BAC). He had earned the indulgence after running the marathon and was looking forward to having a few beers after it. Thirteen seconds later came the second blast, and within minutes one of his men, Detective Cecil Jones, ran into the gym to break the news: "Superintendent, I think two bombs just went off in Copley Square." Evans jumped out of the hot tub, showered, double-parked in front his South Boston home, kissed his wife, put on his uniform and raced back to the finish line he had crossed just hours earlier. But now the scaffolding with the massive blue and yellow emblem for the Boston Athletic Association was shredded. The windows of businesses were blown out. There were body parts strewn on the street he had run down a short time before. Bomb parts were everywhere. The entire street stank of burned flesh and rotten eggs. It looked more like a scene from Baghdad, Iraq, than from Boston. "It was unbelievable. Surreal. I could see the terror on people's faces, the fear," Evans remembered thinking. "Stuff like this only happens in a movie."

But there was work to do. An invisible enemy had attacked the city. At that time no one knew why. They knew only the names of the dead: Martin Richard, Lingzi Lu, Krystle Marie Campbell. The victims' bodies remained on Boylston Street for hours, part of the very active FBI crime scene, but the remains were not left alone, not even for a moment. "They were ours," BPD Captain Frank Armstrong, who had been a street cop and commander in Dorchester, would say.[5] He stood guard over Martin's body, making sure that the FBI forensic experts were respectful of the smallest bombing victim and, more importantly, that his body was not left alone for even a second.

Armstrong would not stand guard alone. As investigators from the FBI and the BPD crime scene squad analyzed the carnage and looked for the attackers around the clock, chasing down every lead and even using overhead drones, BPD Officers James Scopa and William Zubrin honored little Martin alongside their captain, staying with the body all night. Lingzi had her own sentry: BPD bomb technician Frank Geahry stood by her body near the ruins of the Forum restaurant, which was an eerie sight with blood-splattered lunches and melted drinks still set up on the white tablecloths covering patio tables. Not far away—near Marathon Sports, the site of the first blast—BPD Officer Paul Downing watched over Krystle's body. The uniformed Boston cops were joined by other police officers as they waited until after midnight, when the medical examiner's staff members could finally move the victims from Boylston Street to the morgue in Albany Street.

As his officers watched over the dead, Evans met BPD Commissioner Ed Davis and Deputy Superintendent Dan Linskey, and they went to work taking care of the city and its panicked residents, tourists, and the officers under them. Evans had been up since 5:00 A.M. on Monday for the race and was afraid to stop moving. "As long as my legs were active, my mind was active," he would later say.

The FBI took over Boylston Street, but it was still the BPD's job to secure the crime scene. "That means nobody gets into it. No one touches evidence," Evans commanded his 2,100 police officers. It wasn't easy. Main roads through Boston such as Newbury Street and Huntington Avenue had been shut down. The hotels near Boylston Street had to be evacuated, along with many of the homes in the Back Bay. "It had to be emptied out to preserve the integrity of all that evidence."

The last thing anyone needed was more people in the city. The Boston Bruins canceled Monday night's hockey game at the TD Garden, although some players had already arrived. All Boston police officers were ordered to start working twelve-hour shifts, which they were happy to do. Everyone wanted to catch whoever was responsible. By 4:54 P.M. Monday Mayor Menino had checked himself out of Brigham and Women's Hospital, where he had been getting cancer treatments (he had also undergone surgery just days earlier for a broken leg) and made his way to the ballroom at the Westin that was serving as a makeshift command center. Even that command center was chaotic.

The ballroom only had one hard-wired landline, which was commandeered by Richard DesLauriers, the FBI special agent in charge of the Boston field office, so he could talk to people in Washington. There were also calls from President Barack Obama to Menino and Governor Deval Patrick to express his condolences. By 8:50 P.M. Monday, the last patient injured in the blasts had been tended to. But the bloody aftermath was far from over.

The next four days would be a blur of evidence collection, asking anyone with pictures or video footage of the marathon to turn those items over to the FBI, and dealing with the belongings that runners and others had left behind in their panic. So many cops and federal agents flooded into the city that many of them were forced to sleep in their cars in the FBI garage at One Center Plaza. By late Monday night a charity, the One Fund, had been set up and donations from all around the world began pouring in.

On Tuesday the FBI searched a Revere Beach apartment belonging to a young Saudi they initially called a "person of interest" and agents were photographed by multiple members of the news media as they carried large bags out of the Ocean Avenue apartment building, sparking wild speculation about the apartment's occupant. In fact, twenty-two-year-old Abdulrahman Ali Alharbi was in the Boston suburb on a full scholarship from Saudi Arabia to study in America. The second blast had blown him into the street, and he had arrived at the hospital covered in other victims' blood. There he had been grilled by Boston police officers and the FBI, and overnight he had uniformed police officers outside of his hospital room. By the end of the day authorities announced that he was a witness and not a suspect. Homeland Security Secretary Janet Napolitano would testify to Congress that the Ali Alharbi had been put on a watch list by her department but then been removed. "He was never a subject. He was never really a person of interest," she said.[6]

Also on Tuesday the FBI announced that the bombers had carried heavy black bags or black backpacks that had contained bombs made out of pressure cookers. Agents had recovered a vital piece of evidence: the bottom of one of the converted pressure cookers, which had been found on the rooftop of a hotel on the race route. It had been blasted a hundred feet into the air by the bomb's force. Stamped onto the bottom of the six-quart container was its brand name, Fagor. The pressure cooker was made in Europe and sold at only one department store in the United States, Macy's. That night, the NBA cancelled the Boston Celtics basketball game at the TD Garden.

On Wednesday Mayor Menino returned to Brigham and Women's Hospital for cancer treatment, and his cabinet held a meeting there to discuss recovery priorities for the city, including getting people back to work. Napolitano announced that the FBI wanted to speak with individuals seen in at least one video recovered from the Boylston Street crime scene, but she did not elaborate. Then, around 1:00 P.M. CNN reported, erroneously, that a suspect was in custody, which sparked a rush to the John Joseph Moakley United States Courthouse in South Boston. As the media surrounded the building, a bomb threat was called in, and the courthouse was evacuated. Once the threat was determined to be unfounded, the building was reopened—but by then all proceedings had been canceled.

By Thursday, Evans hadn't stopped moving for four days. He had no idea that the Boston Marathon bombers would strike again in a matter of hours, with the murder of a police officer, the carjacking of a young businessman, and a wild firefight in a blue-collar suburb of Boston.

———

At 5:20 P.M. that Thursday the FBI held a press conference at the Westin. FBI agents had identified two men wanted in connection with the horrific blasts. "We consider them to be armed and extremely dangerous," DesLauriers told reporters.[7] As he spoke, grim-faced agents flanked two massive posters of the wanted terrorists—with "Armed and Dangerous" written at the bottom. "No one should approach them," DesLauriers said. "No one should attempt to apprehend them except law enforcement. Let me reiterate that caution. Do not take action on your own."

The release of the suspects' photos did nothing to soothe frayed nerves. In fact, in some ways the pictures just heightened existing fears. The bombers, captured in a grainy still images taken from a security camera feed at Whiskey's Bar on Boylston Street, looked like a thousand other Boston college kids in frat-boy weekend wear. The suspects were white boys with baseball caps and black backpacks jostling through a crowd of other white boys with baseball caps enjoying the spring sunshine and cheering friends and relatives toward the finish line. They could be anywhere. They could be anyone. Nerves had been frayed before DesLauriers's announcement, but after the press conference, strangers were eyed with additional suspicion. Unattended vehicles were seen as potentially explosive-packed weapons of mass destruction.

Not surprisingly, residents of Cambridge began calling 911 to report suspicious idling vehicles near their homes. The first call came at 6:02 P.M. from a woman who told a Cambridge police dispatcher that a green Ford Explorer SUV was parked near her home at Hamilton and Magazine Streets. The license plate was obstructed, meaning that a police officer was not able to run the registration to get a name and address for the vehicle's owner. After making the call she stood in the street and flagged down Sergeant Rob Lowe.

The last thing any police officer wanted to do that night was spend the shift following up on unsupported tips from terrified Cambridge residents. Even before the pictures were released, there had been nonstop calls about unattended bags and tips about innocent Muslims. It had been an exhausting four days, and the FBI's press conference was a clear signal that no one in the law enforcement community was anywhere close to getting some rest. Every police radio was crackling nonstop with calls to 911, reports of suspicious vehicles, transmissions from fellow officers, and orders from dispatchers—all becoming a confusing stream of white noise. One of those calls had sent Lowe.

"This car has been parked in front of my house forever. It looks suspicious. There was another one earlier. Can you come check it out?" the woman who made the call asked Lowe, pointing to a Ford Explorer with a man behind the wheel. A Cambridge Police Department report of the dispatch details the actions Lowe took.

"We got a report of a suspicious vehicle," Lowe told the driver. "Can I ask why you are parked here?"

"Just waiting for somebody. I'll be leaving in a little bit," the driver said. He then drove off. The person he was "waiting for" was apparently not going to show up.

At 6:15 P.M., after the Ford Explorer had pulled away, Lowe spotted another SUV around the corner on Erie Street. This one was a Chevy Tahoe with smoked-out, or intentionally dark tinted, windows. He called the information in to the dispatchers. The rear window on the passenger side slid down as Lowe got close, Congressional investigators would later learn when they interviewed multiple Cambridge police officials who had concerns about what had happened that night.

"Sir," Lowe said, "can I ask why you are parked here?"

The driver didn't turn around. Instead he twisted his upper body toward the sergeant at his passenger side window and grunted: "I'm with the FBI."

"Okay, I need to see some ID?"

The driver fumbled in the vehicle's console next to him and pulled out a wallet, flipping it open and holding it out to Lowe with the ID extended.

"Can you hand it to me?"

"No."

The sergeant was taken aback. "Sir. I need to see your ID."

"I'm with the FBI. Can you please leave?"

"I need to see your ID," Lowe repeated.

"I'm not giving it to you dude," the driver said.

Lowe climbed back into his cruiser and reported in, according to the Cambridge Police Department report. "STOPPED A VEHICLE. PARTIALLY OBSTRUCTED PLATE. PERSON INSIDE ID'ED SELF AS FED AGENT. WOULD NOT PRESENT ID TO CAR 18." As Lowe spoke with the dispatcher, the SUV took off.

Then, at 6:35 P.M., Cambridge Police Officer Peter Vellucci spotted the vehicle that Lowe had called in near Allston and Brookline Streets. He followed it, calling his location in to the dispatch officer. According to the report, ten minutes later another SUV with a "sketchy guy" began to follow Vellucci's cruiser. The two SUV license plates were obstructed. That meant only one thing to local police: the drivers were feds.

That kind of outright disrespect was unnerving, even given the fact that the FBI and law enforcement agencies in Massachusetts had hardly had a courtesy-filled relationship. There had been the James "Whitey" Bulger debacle, in which leaders of the FBI's Boston field office had put a murderous drug dealer on their payroll as a way to advance their own careers. There had also been the Congressional investigation into an FBI's informant unholy alliance that had been made public months earlier, despite the bureau's efforts to keep the deal agents had made with the East Boston mob boss a

21

secret from the MSP, the Essex County District Attorney's office, and even the attorney general of Massachusetts.

Something was clearly going on in Cambridge that night that the feds did not want to share with local law enforcement officials. All week there had been whispers about arguments at the Black Falcon Cruise Terminal evidence center. There ten separate viewing stations with computer terminals had been set up along three rows to review the 655 videos that the FBI would later say had been collected as part of the investigation. Cops and agents sat side by side looking for anyone in the footage who looked out of place or nervous, or who was carrying a black backpack—the pieces of which had been found in the flesh of some of the marathon bombing victims and collected by FBI forensic examiners at hospitals all over the city. Off to one side, remembered one veteran BPD homicide investigator, two FBI agents sat alone. They didn't introduce themselves. They didn't mingle. Instead they compared photos in their laps with photos on their computer screen, a detail corroborated by other witnesses who requested anonymity. The FBI had sent an expert from its Forensic Audio, Video, and Image Analysis Unit, Special Agent Anthony Imel, from his lab at Quantico, Virginia, to Boston to oversee the data collection. Imel did not appear to have any oversight of the FBI agents sitting by themselves, the witnesses said. A local FBI special agent, Kevin Swindon, who supervised the Boston division's Computer Analysis Response Team, didn't either. He was too busy analyzing a security tape taken from inside the Forum restaurant, which in a clear and horrifying way showed the second blast. "We had numerous amounts of employees watching this video over and over and over again," he would later tell ABC News. "We couldn't see anything that stuck out."[8]

One man from the Drug Enforcement Agency (DEA) finally could not take it any longer. He stood up and confronted the duo: "What are you guys looking at?" There was no response. A retired investigator who was there later recalled in an interview conducted on background that the DEA agent said: "Fuck you guys. You know who these mutts are and you're not sharing!" The agent stormed out. But his words stuck with the other officers and agents still looking at the videos. Those FBI agents were not seen at the evidence center again.

Multiple police officers assigned to work at the Black Falcon Cruise Terminal but not authorized to speak on the record have told me: "They knew. They held it [the information] for days. They knew."

———

The story about the strange encounters between the Cambridge Police Department and the FBI would be repeated over and over again, reaching police officers in Cambridge by Thursday (and eventually being recounted to investigators from Senator Charles Grassley's office). Seeing the vehicles in Cambridge with obstructed plates after the photos of "Suspect Black Hat" and "Suspect White Hat," as the two perpetrators were now labeled, led Cambridge cops to surmise that the FBI had a lead on the identities of the bombers, and that the lead had led them to Cambridge—without alerting the city's police department, their purported law enforcement partners.

Among the cops concerned about what the FBI knew was Rob Lowe, who called his lieutenant, Chris Bertolino, on the Cambridge Police Department's primary dispatch line and asked him to switch over to a supervisory channel, according to radio transmissions.

"Do you know anything about the FBI being around here?" Lowe asked. Bertolino didn't. Neither did anyone else.

The Cambridge officers raised their eyebrows at one another. There was nothing that mattered more than catching the marathon bombers, and if the FBI knew the bombers might be in Cambridge, they should have taken advantage of the eyes, ears, and expertise of the uniformed personnel in the city. Even if FBI agents didn't want to share their information, they didn't need to be belligerent.

At roughly 9:30 P.M. on Thursday, traffic on Brookline Street, which was used as a way to get from Memorial Drive to Central Square, was at a standstill. Even the police couldn't get through. The game had gone on too long. Another Cambridge police supervisor, who asked not to be identified, drove the wrong way down Brookline Street to find an MBTA bus stopped in the middle of the street. Cambridge detectives were standing nearby.

"What the hell is going on?" the supervisor remembers demanding.

"We have no fucking idea," a Cambridge police officer answered. "The FBI asked us to stop the bus."

An MBTA bus stopped in the middle of a main drag was a problem.

"Tell that fucking bus driver to move the fucking bus," another Cambridge police supervisor barked. That's when a man approached the group of Cambridge officers, several witnesses recalled, and introduced himself as John Foley, the assistant special agent in charge of the FBI's Boston field office.

Foley was apologetic. He tried to smooth things over and explained that there were agents from all over the country working in Cambridge and he couldn't control some of them. There was nothing to worry about, Foley said.

Cambridge Police Commissioner Robert Haas arrived on the scene. Rank-and-file cops watched as the men talked excitedly in the street. There was mass confusion in Cambridge. Agents from the FBI's mobile surveillance team scowled at police officers and vice versa. Tensions were high and getting higher. Someone was going to get hurt.

"These motherfuckers are here," cops began to muse aloud to one another. It was clear to the Cambridge police officers on duty that the FBI had likely identified the two baseball-cap-wearing lunatics who had left the bombs on Boylston Street. They just weren't sharing the information—as usual.

Lowe drove home, but he didn't have a chance to change out of his uniform or talk to his wife or four kids before the next tragedy was broadcast over every police radio in the vicinity of Cambridge. The voice of MIT Police Sergeant Clarence Henniger, recognized by many of his police partners in the city, screeched: "Officer down! Officer down!" The very danger that Cambridge police officers and supervisors had been predicting had came to fruition: Sean Collier, an MIT police officer, had been murdered in cold blood, shot in the head as he sat in his cruiser on campus by the very men the FBI had been searching for, Suspect Black Hat and Suspect White Hat. Only that would not become clear until the end of a two-day crime spree initiated by the suspects in the hours after Collier's murder. To this day many people believe the violence of that spree could have been prevented.

If in fact the FBI had known the identity of the baseball-cap-wearing bombers and had shared that information with local law enforcement agents, would Sean Collier be alive today?

That was a question that would eventually be asked on Capitol Hill by federal lawmakers—in particular, Senator Grassley. After meeting with multiple MIT police officers and Cambridge police officials, Grassley fired off a letter to FBI Director Robert Mueller that contained some pointed questions.

Grassley wrote that "uniformed members of the Cambridge Police Department encountered multiple teams of FBI employees conducting surveillance. It is unclear who the FBI was watching." He then asked Mueller, "was the FBI conducting surveillance in the area of Central Square in the City of Cambridge on the night MIT Officer Sean Collier was shot dead?"[9]

To this day the FBI categorically denies knowing who the bombers were before one of them was killed in the gun battle. On October 18, 2013, the FBI's Boston field office released a strongly worded statement after Grassley's letter became public: "There has been recent reporting relating to whether or not the FBI, Boston Police, Massachusetts State Police, or other members of the Joint Terrorism Task Force knew the identities of the bombers before the shootout with the alleged marathon bombing suspects and were conducting physical surveillance of them on April 18, 2013. These claims have been repeatedly refuted by the FBI, Boston Police, and Massachusetts State Police. To be absolutely clear: No one was surveilling the [bombers], and they were not identified until after the shootout. Any claims to the contrary are false."[10]

No one really believed the FBI's denials, especially local law enforcement officials. The night of Collier's death, the question became not just what the FBI was trying to hide, but also who. And of course, why?

Cambridge police officers would not be the only ones asking. Privately BPD officials and MSP brass began to speculate that all along FBI agents had known much more about the bombers than what they had shared with local law enforcement agents. That speculation became more urgent at 12:51 A.M. on Friday, April 19, when two of their own, BPD Detective Ken Conley and MSP Trooper Dan Wells were nearly shot to death by friendly fire when the unmarked MSP pickup truck they were driving in was mistaken for a vehicle that had been erroneously reported as stolen. Both men were assigned to the FBI's Joint Terrorism Task Force (JTTF) in Boston, and they had been assigned to be in the area of Cambridge the night before in plainclothes. They heard the "officer down" call and responded to it. Then came another urgent message of "shots fired" from a Watertown police officer. As they made their way toward Watertown a "be on the lookout" (BOLO) warning was issued for "an unmarked black MSP pickup truck."[11]

An MSP trooper spotted an unmarked black MSP pickup truck traveling on Adams Street and opened fire. The trooper's twenty-one shots pierced the vehicle, but miraculously the two cops inside were not hit. One of the bullets was lodged in the headrest on the driver's side, just inches from where Conley was sitting (both men were later honored at the White House by President Barack Obama, albeit quietly, almost secretly). Still, no explanation was ever given of how the two members of the JTTF made it to Watertown so quickly. And multiple law enforcement agents noted that on Thursday night the same vehicle had been in the same area of Cambridge where the other FBI vehicles had been spotted, an area that police would soon learn was the bombers' neighborhood.

Commissioner Davis would soon raise his own questions about the FBI very publicly at a Congressional hearing, at which FBI agents steadfastly refused to show up to provide answers. And Davis's Superintendent Evans would soon find himself in a Watertown backyard yelling, "Hold your fire! Hold your fire!" as bullets rang out around him.

2
GET ON IT

April 18 started early and ended late for all Massachusetts law enforcement officials. President Barack Obama was in town that morning for an interfaith service to honor the bombing victims at the historic Cathedral of the Holy Cross in Boston's South End, the mother church for Boston Catholics. More than two thousand people crowded the pews—many of them dignitaries and politicians, including the current governor, Deval Patrick, and his predecessor Mitt Romney. Secretary of State John Kerry, a Bostonian, and Massachusetts Senators Elizabeth Warren and Ed Markey were there, along with most of the Congressional delegation from the Commonwealth and officials from every Massachusetts police agency. The politicians sat among relatives of the victim of the first bomb, Krystle Marie Campbell, and teachers from the Neighborhood House Charter School where the marathon bombing's youngest victim, Martin Richard, had been a beloved student.

Both the president and First Lady Michelle Obama had spent time in Boston as Harvard University students, a point that the president referred to in his remarks from the altar: "Boston is your home town, but we claim it a little bit too."[1] At that point, the president looked at Boston Mayor Thomas Menino, whose longtime friend BPD Deputy Superintendent Dan Linskey had wheeled him into the service, his broken leg in a cast. He had repeatedly checked himself out of Brigham and Women's Hospital, where he had been getting cancer treatments, as the wounded and the maimed began filling the hospital, to attend briefings at the makeshift command center at the Westin Copley Place hotel. Officers told me on background that the mayor refused to take painkillers for his broken leg or the cancer that was moving quickly through his body—a disease that would take his life in October 2014—so he could be clearheaded. During the service he hoisted himself out of his wheelchair, his face twisted with pain, and talked about his beloved city. "We are one Boston. Nothing can tear down the resilience of this city."[2]

As uplifting as the service proved to be, it had been a security nightmare for police department heads who had already put in long hours in the days since the deadly blasts. To make matters worse, there was the awkward matter of disinviting Suhaib Webb—the imam of the Islamic Society of Boston Cultural Center, a conglomerate that includes a large mosque in Roxbury and the smaller mosque on Prospect Street in Cambridge where the Tsarnaev brothers worshipped—because he could not pass a Secret Service background check. Webb publicly complained on his Twitter page about having first been invited to be on the dais with the president at the service and then being disinvited, telling his followers that he had been replaced but not explaining why. In the previous days Webb had been an outspoken critic of the Boston Marathon attack and had condemned the cowards who dropped the bombs as "criminals and enemies of society" on his Twitter page. The Islamic Society of Boston Cultural Center offered trauma counseling services and urged congregants to cooperate with the FBI if agents came calling. Still, Webb could not shake off some of his past associations with radicals like Lady Al Qaeda Aafia Siddiqui (discussed in a later chapter) and convicted terrorists who had prayed at his mosque.[3]

In fact, Siddiqui had been an MIT student, and that fact led to some additional nagging concerns for MIT Police Chief John DiFava. It was clear that the bombings had been an act of terrorism, and DiFava knew that Webb, an imam familiar on the MIT campus because of the Cambridge mosque's proximity for Muslim students, had just been disinvited from a position near the president of the United States. DiFava was also receiving demands about every fifteen minutes from MIT administrators for updates on the investigation, and calls from panicked parents of students (both Americans and foreigners) were flooding his department's phone lines. When DiFava finally pulled out of the Stata building's parking garage just after 9:35 P.M. on Friday, expecting to head home for the night to care for his ailing mother, he was tired. That's when he saw one of his officers, Sean Collier. DiFava pulled alongside Collier's cruiser to say hello.

Collier was a born cop. When he was three years old, he told his mother that he was going to be a police officer. When he played cowboys and Indians, he was always the sheriff, the good guy. Even as a little boy, one of six children in a blended family, he would squeal when he saw a police car and make whooping siren noises until one of his siblings begged him to shut up. By the time he graduated from high school he was already on his way toward achieving that goal, working as a volunteer auxiliary police officer in his hometown of Somerville, Massachusetts. He would become the youngest Somerville Police Department auxiliary officer ever to be promoted to sergeant. He paid his own way through the MBTA's Transit Police Academy, knowing that despite his high score on the civil service test, veterans received preference on civil service hiring lists, and he had not served in the armed forces. With veterans on the list ahead of him, Collier knew that going through the academy on his own dime would help him with police commanders doing the hiring. He was right. His dedication paid off, as did his self-funded police academy training—which saved the MIT Police Department from having to pay for it. To this day he holds the record for the highest grade point average of any graduate of the academy, an accomplishment that led to his hiring by the MIT Police Department.

DiFava liked Collier. Sure, he was a go-getter, willing to jump into any fray, but he managed to do it without being a hothead. He was the type of cop who would quietly let homeless people into a warm basement on campus. Against the rules? Sure, but it was still the right thing to do. He was good at bantering with the college kids and had solid relationships with other officers. DiFava would be sorry to lose him, though he was happy on Collier's behalf: the cop was just three weeks away from realizing his childhood dream of becoming a full-time Somerville police officer, and DiFava was sure he would be an asset to the entire city.

DiFava and Collier chatted in their cars for about three or four minutes about the bombers, whose photos had been released hours earlier. Then DiFava said goodbye.

"Be safe," the chief called out his window.[4] Collier nodded.

Earlier Collier had been in the dispatch area with his buddies David Sacco and Joe West, watching the press conference the FBI held at 5:20 P.M. A video of the suspects had been released and posted on the FBI's website. The video had been found among the hours and hours of footage viewed at the Black Falcon Cruise Terminal. Within hours of its release, the video had been viewed twelve million times. It showed a taller man in a black hat walking down Boylston Street, with a shorter man in a white hat behind him. The FBI said that the two men were the bombers, and they were armed and dangerous.

At roll call that night, MIT officers would later recall, Collier pointed to Suspect Black Hat and remarked: "This guy looks familiar. I think I have seen him around campus." Other officers looked at the image and shrugged. Both suspects looked like typical MIT students, most of whom were white guys who tended to wear baseball caps and carry backpacks.

Collier was assigned to sector 1–2, two sections of the east part of MIT's campus. The assignment included walking a route around some of the main buildings. He climbed into cruiser 285 and started the routine business of the night: having improperly parked cars towed and making sure suspicious characters weren't lurking around the campus. Sacco was working the desk, monitoring 911 calls and radio traffic from nearby police departments.

"This lady's not too happy her car's gone," Collier texted Sacco not long after he and DiFava parted company. Everything seemed mundane, routine—just another night as a campus cop. Collier and Sacco made plans about meeting after their shift ended and waited for 11:00 P.M. to come.

Then came a 911 call to Sacco at the desk. Sacco responded: "MIT Police. Call recorded. Officer Sacco."[5]

"Hi. Umm . . . we're in the Koch Institute," postdoctoral student James Van Deventer said. "We're hearing a lot of loud noises outside of our window. They don't sound exactly like gunshots but they're sharp quick noises. There is a police officer who seems to be, umm, seems to be in the vicinity in a car but we really don't know what's going on. So yeah, do you have any information?"

Sacco asked for more information. "On the Stata side or the Main Street side?"

"On the Stata side."

"And you're hearing—how do you describe the noises?"

"It sounds like somebody's hitting a trash can really loud. Something along those lines."

"There's an officer in a cruiser near there?"

"There's a cruiser that's right by there," Van Deventer answered.

"Okay, we will check it out."

The Stata side of the building was in Collier's patrol area. Sacco picked up the radio to dispatch him to the scene. "Sector 1–2 respond to suspicious noises or loud noises near Koch building, Stata side."

There was no response. He tried again. Silence. Sacco then tried calling Collier's cell phone. Ever since the most recent construction to expand the campus had begun, the radio had been acting up. The call went right to voice mail. Sacco sent Collier a text. No response again. Another call over the radio. Still no answer.

"Other units, I am trying to raise Sector 1–2. No response."

Sergeant Clarence Henniger keyed his radio microphone. "What is the nature of the call?"[6] He had worked with Collier since the latter joined the MIT police force. It wasn't like Collier not to answer. He was not the type of cop "to take a slide"—leave early, hoping the bosses wouldn't notice. Nor was he the type to chat up a young coed and ignore the radio.

"We just got a call about loud noise, drums, some sort of loud noise coming from the direction where Collier was," Sacco responded.

"Use the emergency alert button," Henniger instructed Sacco and turned his cruiser around to head back to Vassar and Main Streets, sure that Collier was already answering the call. He dialed Collier's cell phone, twice, and got voice mail both times. And Collier made no response to the emergency alert tone. That was odd, especially for a cop like Collier. Henniger's stomach twisted as he got the feeling that something was wrong, and that gut instinct was proved right seconds later as he pulled into the area where Collier's cruiser was parked.

Collier's cruiser's lights were on, the driver's side door and window were open, and the engine was still running. Henniger threw his own cruiser into park and ran up to the driver's side of Collier's car. Collier had been shot three times in the head and three times in the right hand. His body was leaning toward the passenger seat, which was soaked with blood. The blood was everywhere in the car: splattered all over Collier's radio and shining slickly on his gun belt, pooled in the front seat, and even spotted on the can of sugar-free Red Bull in the cruiser's cup holder. A 9-millimeter shell casing sat in a pool of congealing blood on Collier's seat, and there was another on the passenger seat and a third lodged under the carpeting. Copper projectiles littered the cruiser floor. Collier's hand-held microphone had been ruined by gunfire. His police hat was on the passenger seat.

"Oh my goodness! All units respond!" Henniger shouted into his own radio. "Officer down! Officer down! *All units*, officer down!"

He checked for a pulse and knew that Collier wasn't going to make it. He screeched his last order for an ambulance. "Get on it!"

West responded, sickened: "Sarge, we got everything on it."

Henniger noticed a gunshot wound in Collier's left temple and another one in his neck. Clearly Collier had been shot as he reached for his microphone, because there was a hole through his right hand. Henniger looked around, panicked. The scene might still be hot—whoever was responsible for executing a cop, his friend, might still be near the murder site, could even be in a bush somewhere, waiting to ambush another police officer.

Henniger reached over and took Collier's pulse again, hoping his heart was still thumping. The pulse was slight, and Collier was barely breathing. Blood was gurgling out of his mouth.

Another cruiser screeched to the scene forty-five seconds after Henniger's arrival. It had felt like forty-five minutes to him. West, momentarily stunned, froze in place, and Henniger looked at him: "Let's get him out."

West grabbed Collier's shoulders, Henniger his legs, and the two men gently tried to lift their friend out of the car. The blood was everywhere, making it hard for the two to get a grip on Collier.

"You'll be okay," West repeated to Collier over and over. "Just hang in there. Hang in there. You'll be okay." But everyone knew Collier would not be okay. He had been shot at such close range that there were muzzle burns on his head, including one from a bullet that had been fired directly between his eyes. Collier never had a chance to pull the 0.45-caliber Smith and Wesson locked in the gun holster of his duty belt. There was a bullet still in the service weapon's chamber, and its magazine was loaded with ten more. His killer or killers had tried to yank the weapon out of his gun belt, leaving fingerprints behind, but service weapons for police officers are holstered in specially made retention systems so that they cannot simply be pulled out.

Another magazine was attached to Collier's duty belt, which was bloody and—investigators would later discover—covered with his killer's fingerprints. There were spent rounds from a 9-millimeter Sig Sauer everywhere in and around Collier's cruiser: rounds were recovered behind the vehicle, one from the front passenger's seat, and another from the blood-soaked driver's seat. Projectiles and fragments were scattered all over the car from the close-range shots.

Angrily, West asked his friend, "Who did this to you?"

There was no response. A medical examiner, Renee Robinson, would later explain that Collier "just died. Essentially rather quickly."[7] He had been shot six times. The fatal blast had been fired into his forehead, right between the eyes.

When DiFava had been appointed to head the MIT police force two years earlier, he had seen the position as a retirement job, a way to stay in the law enforcement game without the constant violent chaos and political maneuvering he had experienced as colonel of the MSP, where 2,300 troopers worked. In contrast the MIT police force consisted of 62 officers—though the life of their commander was by no means sleepier than that of the state troopers' colonel. For one thing, there were roughly eleven thousand students at any given time on MIT's Cambridge campus. Though the student population boasted more than its fair share of geniuses, many of the students had a staggering lack of common sense or street savvy, making them targets for all kinds of shenanigans. For another, the politics of dealing with the governor and state lawmakers as a colonel in the state police was easy in comparison with the ever-shifting landscape of an elite university whose primary goal is to ensure that the school's reputation for safety remained intact—especially among the parents and students who had to shell out or borrow more than $60,000 a year for tuition and housing.

In the days after the Boston Marathon bombing, more than a few of those parents writing big checks had grown concerned. DiFava was, too. One of the three people slain on Boylston Street was Lingzi Lu, a Boston University student who, like so many students at MIT, had come to Boston from China to pursue higher education. Parents all over the world were looking for answers. The phones rang nonstop.

The Boston Marathon attack was at the forefront of everyone's minds and was the focus of dozens of federal agents who flew in from all over the country to assist agents in the FBI's Boston field office, as well as every rank-and-file cop in the state and DiFava. In the months before the marathon bombings, MIT had its own set of problems that did not, at first glance, appear to have anything to do with the bloodbath on Boylston Street.

Those problems came from a group of anarchist hackers who belonged to an underground network known as Anonymous. One of the group's heroes, Aaron Swartz—a technology visionary, political activist, and cofounder of the website Reddit, which he helped launch in 2005 out of an apartment in Somerville—had been found hanged months earlier, a tragic end to a two-year saga that began when the millionaire was arrested on charges of violating the Computer Fraud and Abuse Act. The Secret Service, which was among the multiple federal agencies prosecuting Swartz, had noted his suicide with a memo to federal prosecutors, now part of the public court filing, that read: "On 1/11/13 Aaron Swartz was found dead in his apartment in Brooklyn, New York—an apparent suicide." It continued: "A suppression hearing in this had been scheduled for 1/25/13 with a trial date of 4/1/13, in U.S. District Court of the District of Massachusetts." A suppression hearing meant that the charges would be dropped—in this case, because the target of the criminal charges was dead.

However, a trial of a very different sort—in the court of public opinion—was about to rock the Massachusetts US Attorney's Office.

Swartz had first attracted the interest of investigators in 2008, when he and other Internet activists published the now infamous "Guerilla [sic] Open Access Manifesto" that began: "Information is power. But like all power, there are people who want to keep it for themselves."[8] It was a public lament about how expensive it was to be an academic these days. Swartz had a solution: he would steal the books that students historically had to pay for, not with a heist but with a computer.

All it took was a cheap Acer laptop, one that was registered in the name Gary Host (a clever word play on the term "computer server host" and an indication that Swartz thought of himself as a ghost, according to prosecutors[9]), an encrypted e-mail address, and a break in at an MIT closet. Then Swartz began downloading thousands of articles from a pay-for-use site used by the university, JSTOR, using the MIT's own network. It worked, at least temporarily. When officials at MIT caught on, they blocked Gary Host from MIT's network, but that move that did little to stop the technological genius.

On January 4, 2011, he snuck into the basement of MIT's Building 16, hid an electronic notebook connected to a hard drive under a box in a dusty wiring closet, and began to download material. Two days later he went back for the hard drive, hiding his identity hacker style. "As Swartz entered the wiring closet he held his bicycle helmet like a mask to shield his face, looking through ventilation holes in the helmet," federal prosecutors said in a court document. Swartz, who was not affiliated with MIT, was arrested on federal charges. On January 19, 2011, he pleaded not guilty and posted a $100,000 bond. Swartz's arrogance was obvious even when he was arrested. Secret Service agents noted that he demanded, "What took you so long?" when they showed up at his apartment with an arrest warrant. This arrogance was one of the reasons that his suicide came as such a shock to the technology community, and even to the law enforcement officials who were prosecuting him.

US Attorney Carmen Ortiz announced that her office would drop the case against Swartz on January 14, 2011, three days after his suicide, and released a statement reading:

> As a parent and a sister, I can only imagine the pain felt by the family
> and friends of Aaron Swartz, and I want to extend my heartfelt
> sympathy to everyone who knew and loved this young man. I know
> that there is little I can say to abate the anger felt by those who
> believe that this office's prosecution of Mr. Swartz was unwarranted
> and somehow led to the tragic result of him taking his own life.
> I must, however, make clear that this office's conduct was appropriate
> in bringing and handling this case. The career prosecutors handling
> this matter took on the difficult task of enforcing a law they had
> taken an oath to uphold, and did so reasonably. The prosecutors
> recognized that there was no evidence against Mr. Swartz indicat-
> ing that he committed his acts for personal financial gain, and they
> recognized that his conduct—while a violation of the law—did not
> warrant the severe punishments authorized by Congress and called

for by the Sentencing Guidelines in appropriate cases. That is why in the discussions with his counsel about a resolution of the case this office sought an appropriate sentence that matched the alleged conduct—a sentence that we would recommend to the judge of six months in a low security setting. While at the same time, his defense counsel would have been free to recommend a sentence of probation. Ultimately, any sentence imposed would have been up to the judge. At no time did this office ever seek—or ever tell Mr. Swartz's attorneys that it intended to seek—maximum penalties under the law.

As federal prosecutors, our mission includes protecting the use of computers and the Internet by enforcing the law as fairly and responsibly as possible. We strive to do our best to fulfill this mission every day.[10]

Her apology did little to appease the twenty-four-year-old hacker-activist's supporters. In the days after the bombing on Boylston Street in April 2013, even as the mayhem resulting from that attack made international headlines and the hunt for the bombers continued, Ortiz was still receiving death threats from Swartz supporters who blamed her office and what they called "overzealous prosecution" for his suicide. The threats were part of an ongoing battle against the government and MIT that had begun three days after his death, when Anonymous hacked the university's website and posted a memorial to Swartz followed by a list of demands.[11]

On January 26, weeks after hacking into the MIT network, Anonymous defaced and dismantled the website of the US Sentencing Commission, disrupting for days the work of that government agency—one that ironically had nothing to do with the sentences meted out to hackers. Anonymous members dubbed that action "Operation Last Resort." Anonymous hackers announced in a YouTube video that the attack on the government website was part of what would become a prolonged protest of unfair prosecution against technology programmers like Swartz, intended to "engage the United States Department of Justice and its associated executive branches in a game of a similar nature."[12]

The hackers carried out their threat. On February 23, 2013, an e-mail was sent to Cambridge Police Department reporting that a "male with a large firearm and wearing body armor" was on the MIT campus, a threat that caused immediate panic and sent university police, Cambridge cops, and state troopers to the campus. As the manhunt for the gunman was under way another e-mail was sent and a phone call was made, both of which warned that the gunman on campus was "retaliating against the people involved in the suicide of Aaron Swartz" and named an MIT employee as a possible target. But there was no gunman. It was a hoax, and a dangerous one at that, as MIT Executive Vice President Israel Ruiz exploded in a campus-wide e-mail: "As we all know by now, there was never a gunman on campus."[13] Anonymous, it seemed, wanted to point the finger at an MIT employee who they felt had been complicit in the investigation of Swartz. Ruiz's e-mail continued: "This hoax also involved a malicious allegation against a member of our community and direct threats of physical harm to MIT staff. We should all understand that this is not a game."

Anonymous's orchestrated stunts would only get worse. In March a group of people wearing the trademark Guy Fawkes masks adopted by Anonymous members showed up at Ortiz's tony suburban home carrying wanted posters showing her face along with the word "Murderer." The guests left a cake on her stoop decorated in frosting that read "Justice for Aaron."[14] Her neighbors were horrified and called police. The cake was shipped to the FBI for investigation.

Ortiz was furious. In a terse written statement, she said: "I respect the rights of individuals to express their views, [but] when they came into my neighborhood wearing masks, my neighbors and young children were frightened. Some of those neighbors called the local police, who responded and handled the situation. I think it would have been more appropriate for them [the protesters] to have expressed their views at the courthouse."[15]

Anonymous would express its views over and over again. There were written threats to federal prosecutors. The home address of Stephen Heymann, the lead prosecutor in the case against Swartz, was published online, along with the names of his family members. E-mail threats and taunts became commonplace. "Just saw you were totally dox'd [referring to having one's real personal identity publicly revealed] over the weekend by Anonymous," read one e-mail sent to Heymann. "FYI, you might want to move out of the country and change your name."[16] Then a postcard was mailed to his house that depicted his father's head decapitated by a guillotine. The assaults were relentless.

It got so bad that the US attorney's office complained to a federal judge about the "various harassing and potentially threatening emails directed at United States Attorney Ortiz and the United States Attorney's Office following Mr. Swartz's suicide."[17]

The harassment continued even after the jihadists bombed the finish line of the Boston Marathon. In fact, four separate unfounded bomb threats were made in Cambridge on the day of the marathon bombing, including on one of MIT's campuses—threats that officials have since blamed on hoaxers like the members of Anonymous.

Not only was every cop on high alert looking for the bombers, but there was also chatter from Cambridge cops about federal agents inexplicably setting up surveillance teams all around MIT's campus. As the former head of the state police, DiFava was likely all too familiar with the FBI being uncooperative—even abrasively evasive—with local police. He thought his biggest problem would be dealing with a turf war between the feds and the Cambridge locals, both university cops across the city and the city's police. He had no idea that Collier's murder would be connected to the Boston Marathon attack four days earlier when bullets began to ring out in Watertown.

That gunfire began not long after a young businessman named Dun Meng was carjacked in Cambridge at 11:20 P.M.—fifty minutes after Collier was killed. The two assailants kidnapped the young businessman at gunpoint and made him drive them around.

"Do you know about the Boston Marathon explosion?" the larger of the two men asked.

Meng answered, nervously, "Yes, I know."

"Do you know who did it?" the carjacker then asked. He was a hulking man, roughly six feet tall and weighing more than 200 pounds. He was the guy with the gun.

"No, I don't," Meng answered.

"I did it," the gunman said and then pointed a 9-millimeter gun at Meng's temple. "And I just killed a policeman in Cambridge."[18]

That same night another incident sent Cambridge police officers racing to the area around MIT. Around 10:20 P.M., at the same time Collier was murdered, a bearded man in a floppy hat pulled a gun on a clerk at a 7-Eleven—while talking on his cell phone. The robber held up the convenience store while calmly chatting with someone.

Today multiple law enforcement officials say—but only privately, for fear of reprisals because there have been no charges—that they believe the robber was a man named Daniel Morley, an anarchist who was photographed by the New York Police Department (NYPD) as he led an Occupy Wall Street march through lower Manhattan. His activities that day led to his arrest in New York, though the charges were later dropped. His rabid anti-establishment politics led him to join groups like the Free Staters, and he had links to Anonymous.

3

GOOD JOB, BOY. GOOD JOB

Dun Meng loved his Mercedes Benz SUV 350, black and chrome with top-of-the-line features. He leased it for $652 a month and had no problem paying the bills. After a long day working as a transportation engineer in Kendall Square, he liked to drive along the Charles River, see the lights, and pull over and just think for a while or answer a few text messages. That's what he was doing on April 18, 2013, just after 11:00 P.M., when he heard a car screech up to the curb behind him. He looked in his rearview mirror and saw a green Honda Civic sedan behind him. A tall man emerged from the car and approached Meng's passenger's side window, motioning for Meng to open it. When Meng hesitated, the man knocked—insistently.

"I thought he was trying to ask for directions," Meng later recalled.[1] He rolled the window down just enough for a hand to reach inside and snap open the door. Then the man was inside the car, and there was a gun in Meng's face. A 9-millimeter Sig Sauer was pushed against his temple.

"Where's the cash?"

Flustered, Meng rooted around in the car, grabbed his wallet out of the side pocket in the door, and threw a couple of twenties and a five at the gunman. Then he just handed over the wallet, which was empty. The gunman flung it into the side pocket in the passenger's door.

"First after I give him the cash, he said, 'You only have that amount of cash? That's not enough.' He asked me, 'Where's your wallet?' So I give him my wallet too. And there's no cash in the wallet," Meng said.

Meng heard the metal sound of a magazine being pulled out of the gun. He didn't want to look, but he turned and saw the bullets lined up in a deadly row in the clip that had been slid out of the gun.

The gunman didn't need to tell Meng he was serious. Meng was terrified. He was being carjacked by a man who confessed that he was at least one subject of the around-the-clock manhunt for those responsible for detonating two deadly blasts near the finish line of the Boston Marathon. Meng knew the man who had a gun to his head had no problem killing a police officer. He was in deep shit, and he had to be very careful with his words and actions.

"Drive!" the gunman yelled. "Pull out."

Shaking, Meng drove. His kidnapper started making small talk.

"What's your name?"

Meng answered with his American nickname, Manny.

"He said, 'Money?,'" Meng recalled. "So he laughed about it. 'Money? You must got a lot of money.' So I said, 'No, not Money.' I said, 'My name is Manny, M-A-N-N-Y.'"

"Where are you from, Money?"

"China. I'm Chinese," Meng answered.

"Okay, you are Chinese. I'm Muslim. Muslims hate Americans."

Meng thought for a second and answered. "I'm Chinese. Chinese are very friendly to Muslims."

"Okay. I love you are Chinese. Just be relaxed and keep driving."

_____

The gunman directed Meng to drive down dark streets, turning left, then right, then left again. Some of the streets were familiar, like Commonwealth Avenue and Market Street in Brighton. But then Meng found himself in a cluster of small dead-end streets not far from Watertown's Arsenal Mall. The gunman wanted to talk. "How long have you been in the United States? What do you do?"

"I came here for study," Meng answered. "I went to Northeastern University. My English is not very good."

"Who do you live with?"

Meng told his carjacker about the roommates he shared a Cambridge apartment with.

"Is there anyone you care about?"

Meng hesitated, and his hesitation bought him just enough time to avoid having to reply. As he pulled up in front of a house on Dexter Avenue in Watertown, the gunman became distracted and did not press him for an answer. The number on the house said 89. It was a two-family house that looked similar to the other homes on the labyrinthine blocks that surrounded it. Then a smaller man came out of the right-side door of 89 Dexter Avenue, Dun Meng told police. According to law enforcement officers, the building housed English-language students from all over the world, including Saudi Arabia, Pakistan, and Chechnya.[2] The house would give investigators another clue about whether there was a larger network of people who might have helped the bombers.

The gunman climbed out of the car and began chatting with the smaller man. The hatchback of the BMW SUV was opened, and Meng felt the weight of heavy items being loaded into the back. He thought about running, but he looked around at the deserted street and thought better of the idea. Apparently the smaller man had driven the green Honda that had pulled up behind Meng originally—the one that the gunman had gotten out of—to Watertown and parked it on Dexter Avenue. Now the smaller man slid wordlessly into the backseat of Meng's car.

"I'll drive," the man with the gun said, motioning for Meng to move over. The six-foot-two, 205-pound man with a boxer's build climbed into the SUV behind the driver's side. Within minutes they had pulled in front of a Bank of America ATM in Watertown. The smaller man got out and rapped on Meng's window. He noted that the smaller man was wearing a hooded sweatshirt with neon lettering that spelled out the brand: Adidas. A cream-colored scally cap covered his curls. Unshaven, he appeared to be younger than the other man, and probably only in his twenties.

"What's your PIN?"

Meng told him the four-digit code, his girlfriend's birthday. It ended with 86—the same year he was born. The driver started to chat again.

"Do you—do you think all the white people look the same?"

"What?" Meng remembered asking. "What was the question? I'm sorry."

"Do you think all white persons looks like same, like do you think the black person looks the same? And so you won't remember my face, right?"

"I don't remember anything," Meng answered. And then the smaller, younger man was back. The door slammed, and the Mercedes headed back toward Dexter Avenue. As they drove, there was a tense moment when one of Meng's roommates called him, the number showing up on the SUV's GPS panel. No one moved, and Meng let the call go to voice mail. Then his iPhone text-message tone pinged. The text was written in Mandarin. The driver demanded a translation. Meng told him that the roommate had written: "Where are you? It's dangerous outside."

The driver, who would later be identified as Tamerlan Tsarnaev, asked him how to say "no" in Mandarin, and Meng told him. Tamerlan was suspicious and asked Meng for an English-Mandarin dictionary, which was available as an app on his phone. Meng gave him the phone, and Tamerlan responded to the roommate's text.

That prompted a phone call from another roommate, the first roommate's boyfriend. Tamerlan got rattled. He pulled his gun from the driver's side pocket, and for a second time that night pointed it at Meng's head, telling him: "You have to answer the phone right now. If you say any single word in Chinese, I will kill you right now."

Meng later told investigators, "I pick up the phone, answer in English, 'How you doing?' Which is very weird because my roommates are Chinese too. . . . I say, 'I feel sick. I am going to stay at friend's house.'"

"What?" Meng's roommate answered in Chinese. "Why are you speaking English?"

Meng said, using English again: "I'm staying at a friend's house. I have to go right now." He hung up, and Tamerlan's face softened.

"Good job, boy. Good job."

Meng knew he had to find a way to escape. Tamerlan's demeanor went from friendly and understanding to angry and volatile during the course of the drive. Eventually, Meng asked: "Are you going to kill me tonight?"

Tamerlan laughed. "I'm not going to kill you. Just relax, man. Maybe we will drop you off at someplace very far away from any person and you will have to walk about five or six miles to find any person."

Then they pulled into a Shell gas station near Memorial Drive in Cambridge. Throughout the ride the smaller man never spoke, except when he asked Meng to pop in a CD he had brought with him from the green sedan. It was a disc of jihadi *nasheed*, eerie "religious" music, Meng remembered. It sounded like nerve-wracking wails to him. The smaller guy slipped out of the SUV to go into the convenience store and made his way back to the door weighed down with packages of Doritos and cans of Red Bull. Tamerlan was preoccupied with his portable Garmin GPS device, which had been retrieved from the Honda Civic. Meng decided it was now or never. He quietly unbuckled his seat belt.

In his head he began a countdown: One. Two. Three. Four. Then he yanked open the door and ran faster than he had ever run in his life across Cambridge Street and into an adjacent gas station. He felt the breeze from the gunman's hand brush his left hand and heard him yell "*Fuck!*" as he dashed across the street. The half-block sprint felt like a mile.

He ran into the Mobil station and held the door shut behind him, sliding down toward the floor in case shots came in through the windows. The tension of the night overwhelmed him and he begged the confused clerk to call 911. He put his hands together in prayer and began to sob: "Please, please, please call 911." As the clerk picked up the phone, Meng ducked into the storage room and hid.

"I have a man who says he was carjacked," the clerk explained to the dispatcher.[3] Meng grabbed the phone and screamed at the dispatcher that the men who had his car "did the marathon explosion!" The dispatcher was stunned: "What? What did they say when they took your car?"

Meng answered: "They have guns."

The dispatcher kept Meng on the phone with mundane questions as Cambridge detectives raced to the gas station, some who had been nearby at the MIT crime scene. Meng explained that his carjackers might be Middle Eastern. "They are Muslims," he told the dispatcher. "One guy is pretty skinny." And he said: "They have guns. They want to shoot at me."

Meng told the dispatcher that he had left his iPhone, which had a GPS tracking device, in the Mercedes and said that he wanted investigators to "find them quickly" so they didn't come back for him.

Then he waited for the police to come.

4

BOLO

Late on the night of April 18 the murder of Sean Collier became a cautionary tale at police roll calls all over Massachusetts, including in Watertown, a blue-collar city adjacent to Cambridge. In Watertown, when the shift change began just before 11:00 P.M., the ongoing investigation at the crime scene of Collier's murder was just three miles away. Extra vigilance, especially for officers in one-man cruisers, was urged by duty sergeants at roll calls all over the Commonwealth, police officers would remember. They took it to heart. At that time, it appeared that Collier's murder could be connected to a robbery at gunpoint of a 7-Eleven in Central Square, Cambridge. Two armed and dangerous men were still at large.

Officer Joe Reynolds had watched the FBI's press conference that afternoon, as he got ready for work as a patrolman in Watertown. He was the epitome of a townie, and most of the cops in the Watertown Police Department were just like him. They had gone to Watertown High School, taken the civil service test, and then joined the police force in their hometown. Reynolds was working the midnight shift on April 19, 2013. He was on patrol in the east end of Watertown, a residential neighborhood abutting upscale Belmont, Brighton, and Cambridge, when a BOLO warning was dispatched over the radio by his sergeant, John MacLellan. It was 12:28 A.M.

"Suspect One is five-seven, the second with darker skin, both suspects armed with firearms, driving a Black Mercedes SUV registration 1-3-7-N-Z-1. Carjacked at 816 Memorial Drive at the gas station in Cambridge. Suspects are two Middle Eastern males, one with darker skin, no description on clothing yet, both are armed with firearms," said the dispatcher. "They fled in the vehicle towards Harvard Square. Victim said one of the suspects went into the Shell station and paid cash for gas, put gas in the car, before they fled and that was when the victim was able to get out of the vehicle."[1]

Now the radio traffic started to get intense, with police officers in neighboring towns on the frequency weighing in with questions, as Reynolds listened in Watertown and MSP Trooper Chris Dumont listened from Logan Airport, where he had been working on a detail to oversee President Barack Obama's arrival and departure the day before.

"They went into that gas station, paid cash for gas and then fled towards Harvard Square!" announced the dispatcher.

By then BPD officers and Cambridge Police Department detectives were at the scene of both gas stations, the Shell station where the younger suspect had gone on the junk food buying spree, and the Mobil station—where a terrified Meng was "trembling" as he was interviewed by BPD Officer Michael Nickerson about his ordeal, the cop would later remember.[2] Nickerson responded "I believe they have video in that Shell station, I am with the victim and believe they have video in the station."

"Does the victim report the operator, that was operating the vehicle, was armed with a firearm but he was unsure about the passenger?" the dispatcher asked.

"He said the operator of the vehicle displayed a firearm."

As more information became available from Dun Meng, the dispatcher continued to advise cops that the carjacking could be connected to Collier's murder and that the perpetrators could be headed to New York City.

"The victim is stating 137-NZ1 Mercedes 350, possibly heading to New York and involving that shooting at MIT," the dispatcher repeated over the channel that every cop in the vicinity was tuned into.

There was no such thing as days off or down time for any law enforcement officer in the Commonwealth. Everyone was tired, anxious, and working mandatory overtime—and until the bombers were caught, most of the officers didn't mind a bit. Dumont had watched the FBI press conference at his barracks at Logan Airport, and given the quality of the pictures of Suspects Black Hat and White Hat, he'd thought that they would have been caught by the time he heard the 10:36 P.M. report of Collier's murder. But they hadn't been. And when he arrived at Main and Vassar Streets to assist in the perimeter search for the cop killers, he couldn't help but wonder if the bombers had anything to do with Collier's murder.

Meanwhile, Joe Reynolds, the Watertown cop, had headed to Mount Auburn Street, the main drag that connected Cambridge to Watertown and was waiting there. He was thinking the same thing as Dumont when the radio crackled again.

Den Meng's GPS locator in the Mercedes had pinged in the area of 61 Dexter Avenue and then again at 89 Dexter Avenue. It was on the move, and the narrow street was just a hundred yards from Reynolds's location. He made his way slowly toward the address. It had been twenty minutes since the original BOLO warning had been issued.

Reynolds picked up his radio to report: "I'm headed in that direction."

MacLellan heard his transmission and issued an immediate caution over the radio: "I believe there is a gun in that vehicle. Please wait for backup before you take any action or pull it over."

MacLellan had heard the BOLO warning and written the license plate number on his hand with a black Sharpie. He looked at the number again and memorized it as he drove toward Reynolds's location. Two male suspects in their twenties who carjacked a young businessman, claiming to be the Marathon bombers and bragging about murdering a cop—it sounded like the at least one of those men was in the Mercedes, the terrorist whom everyone in the country had been looking for since Monday. In front of the Mercedes was a battered green Honda Civic with a black hood that was traveling at the same speed as the Mercedes.

"Affirmative," Reynolds acknowledged as he made his way to Dexter Avenue.

And there it was—the black Mercedes with license plate 137-NZ1, following the Honda. Both vehicles were driving at a snail's pace. "It was very suspicious," Reynolds would remember. They were going only "five to ten miles an hour."[3]

First the Honda drove past, and Reynolds barely paid attention. But when the Mercedes drove by his marked Watertown Police Department cruiser, the driver stared at the cop. "We locked eyes at each other," Reynolds remembered

The Honda turned onto Laurel Street, followed by the Mercedes. Reynolds made a three-point-turn in his cruiser and started to pursue the vehicles. "As I was following them, they both sped up for a bit. I thought they were going to take off, it might be a car chase." He radioed his dispatcher and reported that he had spotted the vehicle everyone was looking for. MacLellan, his sergeant, immediately got on the radio and reiterated that Reynolds should wait for the backup that was just minutes away. MacLellan knew the driver had bragged that he had just killed a policeman in Cambridge not long before and was likely to do it again if he had the chance.

Suddenly both cars stopped in the middle of Laurel Street. Reynolds was two car lengths behind the vehicles when a hulking man opened the driver's side door of the Mercedes and stepped out, his right arm outstretched and holding a gun. He walked fearlessly toward the cruiser and began firing. Reynolds ducked down behind the dashboard and threw the cruiser into reverse, while grabbing his shoulder radio. "Shots fired! Shots fired!" He yelled into the mic. It was dark and chaotic. Shards of glass showered him, and the metallic sound of bullets ripping into metal was disorienting. All he could see were muzzle flashes, over and over again. The bullets came non-stop. He stopped the cruiser and dove behind the driver's side door, taking cover to return fire.

MacLellan could hear the unrelenting explosion of bullets even before he rounded the corner and pulled up to the left side of Reynolds on Laurel Street. Bullets had pocked Reynolds's cruiser door and continued to rip through metal and glass—too many rounds to count. MacLellan also yelled into his radio: "Shots fired! Shots fired! Shots fired!" It was unusual to hear multiple 10-13 radio calls (the code for a police officer in trouble) at the same time. The cries for help heard by surrounding departments brought a cavalry of uniforms racing toward Watertown.

As MacLellan pulled alongside Reynold's cruiser a bullet smashed through his own windshield, spraying him with broken glass. The bullets kept coming, and the gunman was making no move to retreat. He stood right in the middle of the street like a cowboy in a black-and-white movie standing firm. That's when MacLellan had an idea: to put his own cruiser into drive and let it roll toward the gunman.

"Maybe I could gain some time," MacLellan remembered thinking. "Try to figure out how many suspects we had. I let the vehicle go, and I stepped to the side of it and used it as cover as it was rolling and I tried to throw some rounds down range."[4]

Reynolds dashed out from behind his cruiser door and crouched behind the sergeant's slow-moving cruiser. Both men emptied their guns at the suspect, who didn't go down but instead ran behind the Mercedes for cover. That's when it became clear to both cops that there were two men firing at them. One was taller than the other and both fit the description in the BOLO warning: Middle Eastern men with dark hair and scraggly beards. "I could see muzzle flashes," Reynolds would say later. "And at that time I saw Sergeant MacLellan run into the side yard, so I followed him over there to communicate what he wanted."

It was mayhem. Residents on the leafy block peered out windows and live Tweeted about the two suspects crouched behind the stolen Mercedes for cover, with bags and backpacks—similar to the ones used to conceal the bombs on Boylston Street—at their feet. They came in and out of cover as they retrieved ammunition and other bags from the nearby green Honda. MacLellan and Reynolds took cover behind a small tree. They emptied the magazines of their 0.40 caliber Glocks, reloaded, and emptied their magazines again. "I had two spare mags on my belt as well as the one in my gun, and I used all my bullets," Reynolds would say later.

The gun battle lasted eight or nine minutes, but it felt like hours. And the situation was about to get worse.

MacLellan and Reynolds saw the smaller of the two men light something and fling it their way. It was a pipe bomb, and it landed next to MacLellan's cruiser. Then came a boom.

"I think they are throwing M-80s at us," MacLellan reported over his radio. "They keep coming."

He moved from behind the tree to look at what the suspects were doing and saw that they were both grabbing materials from the back of the Mercedes. Then came another flash of light and an explosion. Then a third and a fourth. The bigger man was throwing the bombs like baseballs, while the smaller one used a hook shot. The explosions shook the street but didn't affect the officers. By this time more cops were arriving on the scene.

Sergeant Jeffrey Pugliese was off duty and had been driving home in the family minivan when he heard the beginning of the firefight transmitted over the radio and drove eighty miles per hour until he was in the cluster of narrow streets exploding with bullets and bombs. Like Reynolds, he was a Watertown native, and knew the backyards and side streets of the neighborhood very well. He slid open the door of his minivan, grabbed his bulletproof vest, and began pulling it on as he started jogging toward the gunshots.

In one of the driveways he saw Reynolds and another Watertown police officer, Miguel Colon, who turned and yelled: "Sarge. Sarge! Get down. They're shooting at us."[5]

At that point MacLellan was behind a tree returning fire and shouting at the suspects, "Give it up! Give it up! You're not going to win this! You're surrounded!"

The cops scuttled behind cars in the driveways of Laurel Street. The residents were terrified. Bullets were hitting houses, searing the bark of trees, and ripping through street signs. One family had the surreal experience of seeing a round pierce their television set as it was broadcasting news of the insanity going on outside their house, watching live coverage of reporters who were either corralled outside the neighborhood or outside satellite trucks parked in a nearby mall (I was one of them). Residents forced their family members to the floor, hands covering their heads, or squeezed into bathtubs or rooms where bullets couldn't reach. The usually sleepy area of Watertown had become a war zone. Exploding pipe bombs shook the houses, and bullets pierced clapboard or vinyl siding. Then came an unimaginable blast.

Reynolds saw it first. There was a cylinder flying through the air, a big cooking pot. It was a pressure cooker bomb like the ones detonated along the Boston Marathon's finish line five days earlier. A Laurel Street resident named James Floyd put his three-month-old son down in a crib at the back of his house to protect the baby from the bullets flying outside the front door and peered through a blossoming plum tree to watch the mayhem. He saw lit fuses and heard pipe bombs hitting the ground, like metallic baseball bats connecting with a ball: clink, clink, clink. Two clattered but didn't explode. Two others did, rattling the house's windows. Floyd watched the gunmen continue firing at police and then saw the smaller gunman grab a book bag from the rear of the Mercedes. "That looks heavy," Floyd said to his wife. "This isn't good." The smaller man grabbed the bag by its strap and launched it as far as he could.

"Run, Sarge! Run! Run! Run!" Reynolds yelled.

Looking toward MacLellan, he knew his sergeant hadn't seen the size of the bomb. Reynolds grabbed MacLellan's shoulder and pulled him along. The blast knocked both policemen and Floyd to their knees and terrified everyone in the neighborhood.

Reynolds's ears were ringing so loudly that he couldn't hear the car alarms that had begun to blare. A black cloud of smoke covered the two policemen as debris from the blast zone rained on their heads. MacLellan was so shaken that he holstered his weapon. "It was incredible. It was horrendous. Very loud. I had to reholster my weapon to be able to straighten my head to be able to see," MacLellan would later say. He could feel "debris raining down. For some reason I thought shingles were coming off houses, but it was just stuff landing all around us, smoke, car alarms going off, people screaming."

And the bullets kept coming, he remembered. "To me there were simultaneous flashes coming toward us. There were two handguns being shot." That recollection would prove interesting, as only one gun and a BB pellet rifle were recovered at the scene, which raised questions about possible accomplices.

Neighbors peered out of windows and watched as the taller gunman walked straight toward the cops. He was not firing or hurrying—just walking with the gun at his side. By then Pugliese had flanked the Mercedes from a side yard. He climbed over a chain-link fence and a picket fence and then reached the rear of 89 Dexter Avenue. The sight of a white male in a white T-shirt sitting outside the house briefly delayed his progress toward the gunfight.

"Stop right there," Pugliese yelled.[6] This man was not showing any weapons but was clearly up to no good, since he was just sitting calmly in a shootout, and Pugliese was concerned he could be connected to the suspects somehow. That suspicion was heightened when, on seeing the cop, the man hopped over a fence and sprinted away. He was the least of Pugliese's worries at that moment, but the man's presence would eventually raise questions when investigators began to look into the actions of anyone who might have helped the Boston Marathon bombers.

"There is an individual fleeing the area," Pugliese radioed the dispatcher and then he quickly put the unidentified man out of his mind. So did the rest of the police in the area. They had more pressing concerns, such as running out of ammunition. Each magazine only held thirteen bullets, and there was one in the chamber. Two magazines and the single bullet meant twenty-seven shots for each of the officers on the scene.

Pugliese approached the yard where MacLellan and Reynolds had taken cover. He heard MacLellan yelling at the suspects: "Give it up! Give it up! You don't have a chance!"[7] MacLellan was yelling partly because he was out of bullets. But the gunmen didn't know that. They kept firing. Reynolds knelt on one knee, trying to get off a good shot just as Pugliese flanked the gunmen from a side yard. "I drew my service pistol, I took aim at the one individual," said Pugliese. "I took careful aim, and I fired three or four shots at the individual. I thought I was hitting him but I didn't know whether or not I did. I just—you know, I wasn't rushing my shots so I thought I was probably, you know, hitting my target, but it didn't seem to be having any effect."

The suspect just wouldn't go down. Pugliese had been a firearms instructor for more than three decades and decided that he would squeeze off a few "skip shots," aiming at the ground in front of the man and hoping that the bullets would bounce back up six to eight inches to hit the gunman. He later explained that he was thinking "maybe I could take their ankles out and get them to, you know, stop with the aggressive behavior they were doing."

But the larger man turned and stared directly at Pugliese. He charged toward him, weapon extended, and fired off six rounds. Pugliese returned fire until he'd used all fourteen rounds in his gun (one in the chamber and thirteen in the clip). He dropped the empty magazine at his feet, quickly reloaded, and continued to fire. Then a miracle happened: the suspect's gun either jammed or ran out of bullets. In a fit of fury, he hurled the useless weapon at Pugliese, hitting him in the left bicep, and ran. Pugliese holstered his gun and chased the suspect down the street. He took a running leap and tackled him. The suspect was bleeding and slippery. He was also strong. Mac-Lellan arrived and flipped the suspect over face down. The suspect continued to struggle with the cops, flailing wildly as they tried to pull his muscled arms behind his back to put the handcuffs on. Reynolds raced over to help and smashed his gun, which had been emptied, into the man on the ground. Colon joined his colleagues and tried to wrestle the suspect's left wrist from beneath his body behind his back. No one noticed that the smaller man had gotten behind the wheel of the Mercedes SUV and had pressed the gas pedal to the floor until Reynolds looked and saw the vehicle's headlights as it spun into a U-turn and then pointed straight at the huddle of police officers and the suspect on the ground.

"Sarge, Sarge, look out! The other guy's in the car. He's coming at us," Reynolds yelled.

By then other officers had arrived. There were four Boston cops standing on the northeast corner of Laurel Street and three others across the street, and Watertown and Cambridge cops had taken positions along Dexter Avenue and Laurel Street. To this day it remains unclear how many of those officers opened fire on the vehicle as it sped toward the Watertown policemen on the ground wrangling with the suspect. At least one bullet splintered the windshield, and—investigators would later learn—smashed into the driver's jaw. Still he kept advancing at full speed. The car was only thirty yards away, then twenty.

Pugliese tried to pick the suspect up by his belt to drag him out of the way. But the suspect jerked himself out of Pugliese's grasp and directly into the path of the oncoming SUV. The three Watertown cops leaped out of the way just in time. Pugliese felt the breeze of the racing car on his face. Then he heard a thud. The Mercedes rocked as it rolled over the larger gunman, smashed into a Watertown cruiser, and took off. The larger suspect had been caught in the undercarriage of the SUV and was being dragged along. The Mercedes slammed into MacLellan's bullet-riddled police cruiser, dislodging the body under it, and kept moving rapidly, with one cop chasing behind it on foot. The scene was bedlam.

As other officers continued to fire at the now-fleeing SUV, Reynolds asked the stunned Pugliese, "Are you all right?" Pugliese answered, "I'm okay."

The Mercedes crossed Dexter Avenue, kept going down Laurel Street, and was soon out of sight. By then the cavalry had arrived. Two BPD officers assigned to the gang squad, Sean McCarthy and Scott Pulchansing, were ordered to pursue the Mercedes, which had managed to get away despite the fact that up to a thousand cops from at least twelve different jurisdictions had responded to the firefight.

The bomb blast left BPD Officer Dennis Simmonds stunned with what would later be called a "severe head trauma"[8]—and which would later be cited by his family as the ultimate cause of the aneurysm that took the twenty-eight-year-old cop's life a year later. His name is now etched alongside the names of other fallen heroes killed in the line of duty at the department's headquarters, the fifth victim of the Boston Marathon bombings.

Two officers assigned to the JTTF, BPD Detective Ken Conley and Massachusetts State Trooper Dan Wells, had arrived in Watertown driving an unmarked black State Police pickup truck that, inexplicably, had mistakenly been reported stolen. As noted in a previous chapter, their vehicle was fired upon when a state trooper spotted it and thought they were suspects. One of the rounds pierced the detective's headrest but missed him. Detectives recovered twenty-one spent casings around the vehicle. An MBTA transit police officer was grazed in the buttocks by a bullet. They were lucky.

MBTA cop Richard "Dic" Donohue was not. Donohue felt himself staggering and then his partner, Luke Kitto, lowered him gently to the ground as other cops began to radio for help. "Officer down! Officer down!" was heard over the radio channels of multiple police departments. One of the bullets fired at the suspect's getaway car had ricocheted off the vehicle and into Donohue's groin. It was bad. The color was quickly draining from his skin. His eyes were open, lifeless.

That's the first thing State Trooper Dumont noted. A medic and combat veteran, like many of the cops on the scene, he knew Donohue didn't have much time. The ambulance was forty-five seconds away, which could be an eternity given the blood loss Donohue had suffered in such a short time.

"Pick him up," Dumont directed.[9] "We'll carry him to the ambulance." Kitto had his partner by the shoulder, and BPD Officer John Moynihan and two others grabbed his torso. A Cambridge cop and Harvard University officers helped hoist Donohue, and together the men hustled toward the back of the ambulance operated by Watertown firefighters and EMTs Patrick Menton and Jimmy Caruso. Caruso applied pressure to the wound, which had stopped bleeding. "He lost most of his blood," Dumont whispered, more to himself than anyone, as he and Menton performed CPR on Donohue. Because both EMTs were in the back of the ambulance, Menton's brother Tim, a Watertown cop, drove it—with the emergency brake still on. Kitto was in the passenger seat, saying: "You're going to be okay, Dic. Hang on. Hang on."

It took just under three minutes to arrive at Mount Auburn Hospital. By the time he arrived "he had bled out almost his entire blood volume on the street in Watertown, and . . . because his heart wasn't beating, there's no blood forward flow to cause any bleeding there," Heather Studley, a physician in the emergency room, would later recall.[10] "He looked dead."

By then cops from all over the state had already started showing up to donate blood. And every bit of it was needed. Studley was working the overnight shift in the emergency room. When Donohue was brought in, he was unresponsive: he was not breathing, and his heart had stopped. He was dead and had been for roughly fifteen minutes. The only chance he had at life came from the constant breaths of his police brethren who had performed CPR nonstop.

Studley inserted a breathing tube and a large IV into Donohue to start pumping in blood. She gave him a shot of epinephrine to help his heart start beating again. When it did, the blood began to shoot out of the wound. Studley climbed on top of the stretcher and dug her knee into Donohue's groin to stop the bleeding as they raced toward an operating room. "There's no other way," she told the shocked cops. She was right. After hours of surgery and receiving twenty-eight pints of blood, eleven pints of fresh frozen plasma, and six pints of platelets, Donohue had a pulse. Donohue's wife and police brethren would consider what the team at Mount Auburn Hospital had done for Dic to be a miracle.

Donohue had been technically dead for forty-five minutes, Studley would say, explaining that "in the emergency department," his heart had stopped beating for "approximately thirty minutes, I would say, and then add on the prehospital time, anywhere—you know, like I said, ten to fifteen minutes." But he lived.

The same would not be the case with the gunman who was treated at Beth Israel Deaconess Medical Center in Boston, a Jewish hospital that would later seem an ironic choice.

The burly gunman had been shot seven times and hit and dragged by a speeding SUV, but he was still combative, even as he was lifted into the back of a Boston EMS ambulance. Cops wanted to keep him alive, talking. Paramedic Michael Sullivan rode in the back with the wounded man, who had "multiple trauma and road rash," and began to treat "the top"—in paramedic parlance, the upper body—as his partner, Sean Murphy, worked on "the bottom," near the patient's legs.

Sullivan remembered how bad the patient looked. "He was pale. He was sweaty."[11] Sullivan asked the cops what had happened, and they explained that the patient was believed to be one of the Boston Marathon bombers. "All we knew is that he was the suspect. We didn't have a name," Sullivan recalled. "When I asked about the road rash, they [the officers] said, 'No, no, no. It was a blast-type injury from an errant explosive device.'" The man believed to be the bomber also had been shot multiple times, Sullivan noted, and had been hit with shrapnel. He was alive—but barely.

"We were making eye contact. He was awake. We suspected he was in shock," Sullivan remembered. The patient thrashed violently, though he was handcuffed and secured with seatbelts to the ambulance's gurney. "He would lift himself off the stretcher, he would yell and scream and resist us touching him," Sullivan said. "We couldn't get an IV into his arms because he was handcuffed, and he resisted any attempts to put a line into his legs. He was yelling loud. It seemed like he was trying to get out of the seatbelts holding him on." Sullivan attempted to dress the patient's head wound and tend to the evisceration across his stomach. All of that would be pointless.

Using its lights and sirens, the ambulance took about five minutes to reach Beth Israel from the bloodstained spot where the gunman's body had been dislodged from the undercarriage of the Mercedes SUV. As the paramedics lifted the dying man out of the ambulance and began rolling him toward the emergency room doors, Sullivan recalled, the patient uttered one last echoing groan while thrashing around. "He was literally yelling GRRRRR-RRRRR," Sullivan said—like a bear.

Hospital staffers tried to keep the gunman alive. But at 1:35 A.M.—roughly an hour after the wild bomb and bullet fight had begun just miles away—the suspect was pronounced dead. The cause was listed as "gunshot wounds to the torso and extremities" along with "blunt trauma to the head and torso."[12] An autopsy photo taken by a Boston police officer (who then texted it to another law enforcement officer, who forwarded it in turn, until it was posted on social media) that night showed him on the autopsy table, his body ripped open by the impact of the SUV, and his head crushed and bruised. At that point no one at Beth Israel had any idea who he was other than a suspect in a bloody attack on civilians at an iconic Boston event, a terrorist bombing that had killed two women and a beloved little boy. At that point, hours after the FBI had released the clear photos of the suspects' faces, not a single phone call had come into the FBI regarding the identity of the shooters, officials now say.[13] They had set up extra phone banks. Agents from all over the Northeast were in Boston to help handle the expected deluge of tips. But the phones didn't ring. The silence was so obvious that Kieran Ramsey—the FBI assistant special agent in charge of the FBI's Boston field office and a military veteran who spoke fluent Arabic—had the phone lines checked to make sure they were working before he went to Watertown to investigate the scene of the firefight there.

That firefight had lasted twenty minutes. A total of 210 rounds had been fired, littering the neighborhood with shell casings.[14] Dozens of bomb technicians had arrived in Dexter Avenue by 1:00 A.M. to "render safe" the unexploded pipe bombs. Dexter Avenue, Laurel Street, and nearby Cyprus Street were shut down as a crime scene.

The 9-millimenter gun used by the larger gunman and thrown at the Watertown sergeant was recovered. An Airsoft pellet gun that fired .177 BBs was found in a front yard, not far from where the pressure-cooker bomb thrown at cops had been embedded in the side of a car. But the second firearm that Watertown police—including Pugliese, the firearms expert—swear was being fired at them by the suspects was never found, leaving lingering questions in the minds of law enforcement officials about possible accomplices who were never found.

People in Watertown were terrified, especially after the Watertown Police Department sent an emergency alert message at 1:57 A.M. to the city's residents urging them to "stay in their homes because of an active incident and report any suspicious activity."[15] Meanwhile the FBI enhanced the photos released earlier with clearer shots of the suspects' faces. And 911 calls began to come in: roughly 500 would be made to Watertown Police Department by the end of the day.

By 4:15 A.M. Massachusetts National Guard military police began to roll into Watertown on 21 armored Humvees. The MBTA suspended service at 5:15, around the time when Governor Deval Patrick issued a mandatory shelter-in-place order for the more than one million people who lived in the greater Boston area. Stores were closed and shuttered. The streets were eerily quiet. The only traffic came from law enforcement officials and the military. Black Hawk helicopters flew overhead as SWAT teams went door to door throughout Watertown looking for the missing suspect.

"Suspect One is dead. Suspect Two is on the run. We have a MBTA officer who was seriously wounded and is in surgery right now. We have a MIT security officer who has been killed," Patrick announced at a 5:45 A.M. press conference. "There is a massive manhunt underway. A lot of law enforcement involved in that. To assist in that we have suspended all service on the MBTA. That will continue until we think it's safe to open all or some of that. We are asking people to shelter in place, in other words to stay inside, with the doors locked and not to open the doors for anyone other than a properly identified police officer. That applies here in Watertown, Cambridge, Newton, Belmont, and that includes all of Boston. All of Boston. This is a serious situation. We are taking it seriously. We are asking the public to take it seriously as well. We have every asset we can possibly muster on the ground right now. They are doing a terrific job coordinating with each other. We need the public to help us help them stay safe."[16]

FBI agents then congregated at a two-family house at 89 Dexter Avenue in Watertown that would soon become a focus of the Boston Marathon bombings investigation, one that would be conducted in top secrecy by the FBI. This was the two-family house that the carjacking victim Dun Meng told investigators the smaller carjacker emerged from when Meng pulled up with the larger man. Agents went into the house multiple times on the night that Meng reported its address to police.

The Marathon bombers did not come to live in that tightknit Watertown neighborhood by accident. They had friends in the area, fellow Muslims who were in the United States to study English. One eighteen-year-old resident of 89 Dexter Avenue—Ahmed Al-Ruwaili, from Saudi Arabia—looked so much like the smaller suspect at large that he was handcuffed, spirited out of Watertown, and questioned for hours and later moved from Watertown altogether. He told a Saudi Arabian newspaper that the "officers were armed to the teeth. Everything you can imagine, guns, machine guns, electronic devices, etc."[17] Al-Ruwaili was in a common kitchen on the students' side of the two-family house when the officers broke into the house. The first thing they asked all the students to do was to get on the floor and put their hands behind their backs. Then they took off the students' shoes, handcuffed them, and led them outside the house for individual interrogations. Half an hour later, they freed all the students and let them go inside—except for Al-Ruwaili. "They pulled out a picture and flashed it in front of my eyes and asked me if it was my photo," he told the Saudi Arabian newspaper.

The photo was the one released just hours earlier by the FBI of the man known as Suspect White Hat. The same man had gotten away from the firefight in Watertown, likely killing his associate in the process.

Another resident of the house became known as "Naked Guy," because he was videotaped by a CNN news crew sprawled face down on the ground after he had been ordered to strip in case he was strapped with explosives. He bore a striking resemblance to the older suspect, muscular and with dark skin, thick dark hair, and a scraggly beard. BPD Deputy Superintendent Dan Linskey was the one who ordered the man to remove his clothes, fearing that he was the man wearing the suicide vest that corresponded with a dead man's switch (a device used to detonate such a vest found in the bushes on Laurel Street after the shootout ended). The man was questioned but released that night.

However, the FBI would be back. There was no explanation for the smaller man's emergence from 89 Dexter Avenue that the carjacking victim had reported. When I visited the house in the days after the gun battle, the landlord, an electrical engineer who collected toy car parts like the ones used to build the detonator found on Boylston Street after the bomb blasts, pressed a finger to his lips and warned me, "Be careful what you say. This place is bugged by the FBI." To this day no one from the house has been publicly identified as a possible codefendant—although some cops suspect that members of a larger cell working with the Marathon bombers had been living there.

Tom Pasquarello was in law enforcement for thirty-five years, first as a special agent with the US Department of Justice assigned to both the DEA and FBI on cases all over the world, and then appointed to head the Somerville Police Department, where Sean Collier had been slated to become a sworn officer three weeks after he was assassinated on the campus of MIT. Retired from law enforcement and now working for an international homeland security company, Pasquarello is now one of the officers willing to raise an eyebrow about many of the missing details connected to the two-day crime spree of the Boston Marathon bombers: "Suffice it to say there are a lot of unanswered questions about exactly what happened that night and who might have been involved."[18]

5
FACES BUT NO NAMES

In the days after the Boston Marathon bombings the FBI set up a command center on the eighth floor of One Center Plaza, the nondescript office building across from Boston's City Hall that serves as the bureau's Boston headquarters. That's where the call center was located, the place where the phones didn't ring with any substantial tips at first. As noted above, the command post for the twenty other agencies—including the BPD and the MSP—involved in the investigation and ensuing manhunt was at the Westin Copley Place hotel, and still other investigators worked in the Black Falcon Cruise Terminal. It was hard to hide the movements in and out of the hanger-sized warehouse that the FBI took over to process evidence. The warehouse was the size of two football fields, and it contained two forensic evidence intake areas as well as ten viewing stations. No piece of evidence was too small to be investigated. Pieces of the bombs had been recovered from rooftops, ledges, and on the ground all around Copley Square, mixed with the blood of victims. There were problems after a rookie FBI agent spray-painted evidence numbers around the debris on the ground, since when the wind blew, the paint contaminated the evidence.

Each bomb, FBI agents believed, contained "thousands of pieces of tiny shrapnel" meant to "shred flesh, shatter bone, set people on fire, and cause its victims to die painful, bloody deaths."[1] The bombs had been packed with BB pellets, sealant, and pieces of cardboard—intentionally placed inside to set the flesh of victims ablaze, experts would later say. And that is exactly what happened.

Every fragment of evidence needed to be processed and catalogued. In the first twenty-four hours after the dual blasts were detonated, the FBI computer forensics teams had amassed an astonishing ten terabytes of data, enough to fill the hard drives of ten high-end laptop computers. Every shred of material had been painstakingly collected during three straight days of work at the Boylston Street crime scene by agents from the FBI and the Bureau of Alcohol, Tobacco, Firearms and Explosives (ATF), working with BPD crime scene technicians and even firefighters from Ladder 15/Engine 33, who used ladders to retrieve shrapnel from rooftops.

One BPD technician, Terrence "Shane" Burke, was a former US Marine who had barely survived a similar attack fighting in Fallujah, Iraq, in 2006. He could not help but be reminded of the horror he witnessed overseas—fatal IED attacks similar to the blood-splattered street in Boston where he collected evidence after the attack.

BB pellets were put in evidence containers that resembled paint cans. As noted above, a pressure-cooker lid had also been recovered on a rooftop—with the help of the Boston Fire Department's Ladder Company 15. Other evidence was recovered from hospitals all over Boston—such as a zipper from one of the two backpacks that had concealed the bombs embedded in a woman's leg, molten nylon removed from burned flesh, and BB pellets and shrapnel removed from wounds. Hospital staffers had been told by administrators that the FBI had asked for anything removed from patients' flesh to be set aside for evidence collection by specialized teams of agents. As part of routine annual training for mass catastrophes—like the Boston Marathon attack—every hospital in Boston had undergone training alongside local law enforcement for exactly this type of response. Doctors and nurses had trained for disaster, but nothing could have emotionally prepared them for the bloodletting that had taken place in the Back Bay of Boston.

By Friday, April 19, the FBI had collected 655 videos from tourists, restaurants, department stores, and news crews. All of the footage had been reviewed over and over to try and trace the bombers' paths. Then investigators caught a break. The manager of Whiskey's, a bar on Boylston Street a block and a half west of the second bomb blast, called BPD Lieutenant Detective Mike McCarthy and said, "I have something you need to take a look at."[2] The surveillance video from Whiskey's showed a man in the white hat with a black backpack walking with a bigger man who wore a black hat and sunglasses and carried a similar backpack. They were headed in the direction of the first blast site. The footage had been taken twelve seconds before the first explosion. It was the only video that showed them together.

Another video came from inside the Forum restaurant. It showed in graphic detail the carnage and destruction left after the second bomb was detonated: Martin Richard's last breaths, Lingzi Lu's face twisted in anguish, the victims whose flesh had caught on fire, the limbs scattered on the sidewalk next to blood-splattered baby carriages. The Forum video showed something else that would become a key piece of evidence in the case. Behind Martin Richard's family was the same man whose face was on the most wanted poster released by the FBI the day before.

But it was a photo turned into the FBI that a tourist had taken on his iPhone at 2:37 P.M. on Monday that would prove to be the most critical piece of evidence identifying the bombers. The photo showed Suspect White Hat. Standing behind Roseann Sdoia and the Richard family on Boylston Street, the man was smirking. He lowered his right shoulder and dropped his backpack right behind a row of children. Three minutes later he made a phone call. The first blast came at 2:48 P.M., and he didn't even turn his head at the explosion.

"Look at this," remarked Kieran Ramsey, the FBI assistant special agent in charge of the FBI's Boston field office.[3] "He stood behind that family for five full minutes knowing he was going to bomb that family." As a father, Ramsey was horrified. As an agent, he was apoplectic that terrorists would target children, a tactic he was familiar with in the Middle East but not on the East Coast.

Then there was another video recovered from a surveillance camera inside the Forum restaurant, which would prove horrifying. The video showed the reactions of spectators enjoying drinks and lunch and cheering on the runners as they were jolted by the first explosion, which sounded like a cannon blast. Everyone turned left, many of them screaming—except White Hat, who turned right, smirked a little, and hustled away up the street. Then came the second explosion, twelve seconds after the first explosion and roughly 328 feet away, and the ensuing scenes resembled a horror movie, with body parts lying all over the street like gruesome puzzle pieces, blood-splattered store windows, and shattered glass. It had been four hours and forty-eight minutes since the marathon had begun that morning, and there were still hundreds of runners making their way toward the finish line.

Roseann Sdoia was blown over the metal barricade between spectators and the race course. She looked down at the blood she felt flowing out of her and saw a foot. She didn't know it was hers until she realized that her strappy sandal was still attached to it.[4] Not far from her was Jessica Kensky and her new husband, Patrick Downes. "I remember being happy. I remember feeling sunlight on my face. I remember feeling really free. I remember holding each other," Jessica said. Then came the boom: "There's smoke, there's blood." She saw her husband with one leg and foot missing. She had no idea that her own legs had also been mangled.[5] They would never be able to return to their first apartment because they could no longer climb the stairs.

Further evidence was captured in a video shot by Colum Kilgore, a tourist who remembered taking a last video before he was in the air, then tumbling to the ground in a tangle of bodies and faces. His camera fell on the ground and kept recording. It captured the screams and chaos and the actions of Frank Chiola, a BPD cop who had been a Marine and served during Operation Iraqi Freedom. Boston was worse than Baghdad, he remembered. In Boston, "you couldn't tell who was alive, who was dead," he said.[6] He raced to a woman who he remembered was wearing blue eye shadow and tried to administer CPR. "She had a friend near her calling out her name. As I applied compression smoke was coming out of her mouth . . . I helped her best I can," he said, choking up. "She was suffering. She was in pain. She was in shock. From the waist down it's really tough to describe, complete mutilation. That's as far as I want to say." He later learned her name was Krystle Marie Campbell. Not far away was Rebekah Gregory, who would lose her leg. Her son, Noah, was playing at her feet when the street suddenly shook. "I looked down and I couldn't see my legs. My bones were literally on the sidewalk next to me. I thought that was that day I would die," Rebekah said. "I could hear Noah. I don't know how. I could hear my little boy. 'Mommy! Mommy! Mommy!' Over and over again." Her eardrums were perforated. She barely felt the skin on her arms being ripped apart by shards of glass on the sidewalk as she tried to crawl to her bleeding son.

Sydney Corcoran, a nineteen-year-old psychology student at Merrimac College, had gone to watch the marathon with her parents. Then she was hurled to the ground, her skin on fire, her leg gone. She couldn't find her mother or father: "I remember thinking, this is it. I'm going to die. I'm not going to make it. I remember feeling like I was just going to sleep."[7] Not dying was a relief, but her parents were still missing. She was convinced that they were dead until a doctor told her that her mother, Celeste, had survived but lost both her legs. Doctors wheeled Celeste into Sydney's room and they held hands and cried, "just appreciating that we were still alive."

The carnage was too familiar for many of the first responders and investigators on the scene, like BPD Officer Burke, who came back to the force despite his critical injuries; and Lynn, Massachusetts, firefighter Matt Patterson, who had served several tours of combat duty before he jumped over a metal barricade to help Jane Richard in Boston. Combat veterans made so many comparisons between the war zones where they had served and Boylston Street that Dzhokhar Tsarnaev's defense attorneys would successfully argue that all references to Iraq should be stricken from first responders' testimony.

Jeff Bauman was also captured on Kilgore's film and provided one of the more compelling images from the bombings. He was standing near the Corcoran family, waiting for his wife to cross the finish line, when the first bomb went off. He looked down and almost laughed at his macabre predicament, his legs gone, his body mangled, and blood gushing from his lower body. "This is how it's going to end. This is it," he told himself, and then comforted himself with the thought that he had enjoyed a great life.[8] Then along came a man in a cowboy hat who held Bauman's femoral artery pinched between his fingers as frantic first responders hoisted Bauman into a wheelchair from the tent set up to treat exhausted or injured runners near the finish line. The man in the cowboy hat was peace activist Carlos Arredondo whose eldest son, Lance Corporal Alexander Arredondo, had been killed during Operation Iraqi Freedom in 2004, on his father's forty-fourth birthday. In 2011, his youngest son Brian, who had battled drug addiction and depression since Alexander died, took his own life. Those deaths, Arredondo would later say, motivated him to keep Bauman alive. And he did.[9]

Bauman woke up in the hospital the next day. His best friend, John Sullivan, was in the room with him. "I knew I wasn't in heaven because Sully was standing there," Bauman remembered. "I knew my legs were gone. I knew my legs were gone instantly."

That was his first thought. His second was that a suspicious man had abruptly bumped into him before the explosion and then turned and scowled when Bauman protested with a mild "hey." The rude man was just over six feet tall, wearing a black baseball cap and aviator sunglasses, and sporting what Bauman called "a five o'clock shadow": "This guy, he was about my age, he came up and he was trying to make his way through the crowd, he kind of nudged me, I looked back at him. He was alone, he wasn't watching the race, he didn't look like he was having fun like everyone else. I just thought it was odd." It was odd enough for him to mention the man to the FBI, especially when he recalled the backpack. He had noticed the man first and then seen an unattended backpack on the sidewalk, but he didn't really put the two together before the explosion. "I looked back and I saw a bag there unattended. It looked like a regular school backpack." He had paused then shaken the event off, thinking, "You're in Boston. Stuff like this doesn't happen."

But in the hospital Bauman realized that the man who had bumped him was probably connected to the backpack. Bauman was intubated and made a scribbling gesture to Sully, who handed him a pen and paper. The first thing Bauman wrote was "Lieutenant Dan?" a reference to the character in the movie *Forrest Gump* who lost his legs. Sully nodded. The second thing he wrote was more serious: "Sull, I know what happened. I saw the kid. I know what happened."

The man Bauman saw would be identified by FBI Special Agent Jeffrey Rowland, who had been summoned to a secured examining room in the emergency area at Beth Israel Deaconess Medical Center, where Tamerlan Tsarnaev's body lay uncovered. The area around him was still slick with blood. "His body was very badly damaged. He had been shot nine times. He had been scalped," Rowland said.[10]

Rowland saw how big the dead man was and knew this wasn't Suspect White Hat. Like most law enforcement officials, he had studied the videos. He was looking at Suspect Black Hat. "We had two suspects. We had two faces, faces but no names," he later recalled. But there was one thing that he and others in the FBI were certain of—the explosives thrown at police officers in Watertown were identical to the ones detonated on Boylston Street. This was not just a cop killer or a carjacker who wanted to commit suicide by cop. Rowland was looking at a terrorist, one of two most wanted men in America.

In a small suitcase Rowland carried a device called Quick Capture Platform, technology that was purchased by the US government in 2003 during the George W. Bush Administration and initially used by the military in the war zones of Iraq and Afghanistan. The device allowed intelligence officials to analyze fingerprints of possible terror suspects. For instance, one Iraqi applied to become a US-trained police officer in Baghdad, but when he was fingerprinted as part of the application process, his prints were linked to latent prints recovered on a bomb that had targeted coalition soldiers. The device worked quickly, and well, in combination with a laptop, a fingerprint scanner, and a satellite unit.

The examining room was tiny and narrow, and the way it was shaped made it awkward work to get the large man's fingerprints on the pad of the Quick Capture device. Rowland put the device on an office chair and rolled it from one side of the table where the dead man lay to the other, getting prints from both his right and left hands. Rowland connected the device to the Integrated Automated Fingerprint Identification System—a database containing sixty-two million records, including 77,000 records of known or suspected terrorists—and the Department of Defense's Automated Biometric Identification System. In ten seconds he had identified the dead man. "The world was waiting to hear this name," Rowland later said. "And we had it in ten seconds."

That name was Tamerlan Tsarnaev. The twenty-six-year-old had a Massachusetts driver's license that listed his address as 410 Norfolk Street in Cambridge. He also had an arrest record with the Cambridge Police Department: four years earlier, he had been arrested for slapping a former girlfriend in the face because she dressed lasciviously. There were other people associated with the Norfolk Street address: Tamerlan's mother, Zubeidat; father, Anzor; sisters Bella and Ailina; and little brother, Dzhokhar—the man on the run.

6

SLIP AWAY II

Dzhokhar Tsarnaev was wounded—badly. One bullet had come in through the driver's side window, hit his left cheek, and exited through his right. His head hurt badly, his entire skull feeling like it was on fire. His left wrist was useless, its bones shattered with gunshots after he raised his arm in an attempt to shield himself from the oncoming barrage of bullets. Shattered glass had rained into his eyes, which were swollen and bloody. He was a mess. The carjacked Mercedes SUV was smashed and riddled with bullets, hardly inconspicuous. He pulled the SUV over at the corner of Lincoln and Spruce Streets, about a half mile from Dexter Avenue, and left it there. There was a spray of blood on the driver's side door and a small amount of blood on the floor mat. He was bleeding, but not profusely. That would come later.

BPD homicide investigators were at the scene of the firefight in Watertown, along with an MSP trooper with a trained dog, but they were ordered to keep beyond the perimeter by the FBI, two investigators there would later say, on the condition of anonymity. No one knew why, since the suspect could not have been far away.

Evidence would later show that Dzhokhar staggered up Franklin Street, leaving droplets of blood on the street. Investigators later found a bloody palm print on the hood of a car at 73 Franklin Street and another on a garage door at 71 Franklin Street. Down the street broken glass was found in the rear of a shed, and on the floor of the shed—in a slick of blood—were two smashed iPhones and an ATM debit card in the name of the carjacking victim Dun Meng. The phones would eventually connect the bombing suspects to other Muslim men, one of whom would vanish entirely. There were nearly two thousand cops in Watertown at the time, but none of them noticed the blood trail that led to the backyard of David Henneberry at 67 Franklin Street—where his 1981 Seabird, the *Slip Away II*, was dry-docked under a tarp.

Dzhokhar used the last of his strength to hoist himself up onto the swimming platform at the stern of the boat, peel back the plastic tarp and climb into the boat. His blood-streaked fingers stained the covering as he pulled it back over himself and then curled up in the fetal position on the floor of the boat. He was sure he was going to die, but he had some things to say first. In a toolbox on the floor he found a pencil emblazoned with the name of Henneberry's son-in-law's business, Duffy Plumbing. He gripped the pencil in his right hand, the one that wasn't mangled, and began to write on the boat's fiberglass walls. What he produced was a neatly written anti-American missive that would be discovered streaked with blood and pocked with gunshot holes some fifteen hours later:

I'm jealous of my brother who has received the reward of jannutul Firdaus heaven inshallah before me. I do not mourn because his soul is very much alive. God has a plan for each person. Mine was to hide in this boat and shed some light on our actions. I ask Allah to make me a shahied, to allow me to return to him and be among all the righteous people in the highest levels of heaven.

He who Allah guides no one can misguide!

I bear witness that there is no God but Allah and that Muhammad is his messenger [hole] r actions came with [hole] a [hole] ssage and that is [hole] ha Illalah. The U.S. Government is killing our innocent civilians but most of you already know that. As a M [hole] I can't stand to see such evil go unpunished, we Muslims are one body, you hurt one you hurt us all, well at least that's how Muhammad (pbuh) wanted it to be [hole] ever, the ummah [community of Muslims] is beginning to rise/awa [hole] has awoken the mujahideen [*sic*; holy warriors], know you are fighting men who look into the barrel of your gun and see heaven, now how can you compete with that. We are promised victory and we will surely get it. Now I don't like killing innocent people it is forbidden in Islam but due to said [hole] it is allowed.

Dzhokhar also scratched a message into the portside wooden slats under the railing of the boat. Ingeniously, he then sprayed a fire extinguisher onto his messages so that they would be highlighted by the extinguisher's white powdery discharge.

As the wounded man wrote, SWAT teams were hunting him. Police in protective gear raided a house in Chelsea that was home to a Chechen family close to the Tsarnaevs. The youngest son had posted photos of him shooting off fireworks with Dzhokhar in the months before the blasts. The son wasn't at home, and Tsarnaev was not hiding there. Pot dealers in Watertown who lived on the street where Dzhokhar had received a parking ticket for leaving the green Honda on the street overnight during a snow emergency were dragged out of their apartment in handcuffs. The dealers were the sons of prominent Boston restaurateurs and had smoked weed with both Tsarnaev brothers. Members of the FBI's elite Hostage Rescue Team (HRT) were outside an off-campus housing apartment used by many University of Massachusetts at Dartmouth students, training red laser sights on the occupants inside after a cellphone connected to Tsarnaev "pinged" off of a nearby cell phone tower, an indicator that he could have been nearby. The blood trail—which included a bloody handprint on a car parked on Franklin Street—had ended. The suspect was nowhere to be found.

At the same time, evidence teams were counting the bullet and bomb remnants that were sprayed across Laurel Street and Dexter Avenue, placing as many as three hundred small yellow evidence cones in front yards, near children's swing sets. Members of the teams marked the fifty-six 9-millimeter bullets fired by the suspects from a Ruger P95 during the twelve-minute gun battle and the rounds fired by multiple police agencies. Markers were put near the remnants of the exploded pressure-cooker bomb, including the spot next to a sedan in which the pot had become embedded. One of the transmitters that investigators believed had triggered at least one of the bombs on Boylston Street—a modified Flysky transmitter ordinarily used for a remote control toy truck, but altered as a way to detonate a device from a distance—was also found. Alarmingly, a dead man's switch (a mechanism used to set off the charge from a suicide vest) was also found in the bushes, sparking concerns that Dzhokhar was wearing one.

Because bomb technicians were afraid that the Tsarnaevs had left unexploded devices at the scene, they decided not to use x-rays to determine whether abandoned bags or packages were explosive. Instead they used what is known as a general detonation, a technique using a water cannon to determine what might have been hidden in any unattended box or bag—as Bobby McCarthy, a trooper with the MSP Hazardous Devices Unit, would later explain.[1] The pipe bombs that the bombers hurled at police in Watertown—the two that exploded and the two that didn't—needed to be "rendered safe," a procedure that used specialized robots to blast the devices with water cannons. And that's when the cops at the scene, including McCarthy, heard someone yell, "There's a bomb!"

McCarthy was among the bomb scene technicians who made their way to the stolen Mercedes. The SUV's doors were open, and on the floorboard in the backseat on the driver's side was a plastic container with a long piece of green hobby wire (part of an explosive's chain that acts to ignite items like fireworks or toy rockets, hobby wire burns down and then hits an explosive charge to spark a blast).

The device was referred to by investigators, and eventually by federal prosecutors, as a Tupperware bomb because of the container it was kept in. (Tupperware released a statement in 2015 pointing out that the description was inaccurate because the device was actually constructed in a Rubbermaid plastic container, but the name Tupperware bomb stuck.) The bomb was clearly created to take out emergency responders or bomb squad technicians who came to search the vehicle, and it was not an item that anyone wanted to handle. It was too heavy for a bomb robot to disarm, so the specialists on scene put on their bomb suits and attached a heavy clamp to the device. McCarthy attached the clamp to a rope, wrapped the rope around a tree limb, went behind a house to take cover, and pulled the rope. The Tupperware container flew out of the vehicle and into the street, where the specialists examined it. Three pieces of hobby wire were snaked into three pounds of explosive powder. The long piece of green hobby wire appeared to be have been designed specifically to allow the bomb to be detonated from a distance.

Strangely, though the FBI and MSP bomb experts would later describe the Tupperware device—which possessed "all the components, the non-electrical fusing system, the main charge and the container," including three pounds of explosive powder, needed to create an extremely powerful IED[2]—no one would ever be charged with possessing it. Tsarnaev would be charged with possession of the four pipe bombs, two of which had been detonated two of which were duds, and the four-quart Fagor pressure-cooker bomb detonated in Watertown, as well as the weapons of mass destruction that exploded on Boylston Street—but not with possessing the Tupperware device.

Henneberry was a retired phone company employee who had the patience to stay in his house and wait for the shelter-in-place order to be lifted. He was content to watch the chaos outside his window. At one point he noticed that two of the chafing guards had fallen from his boat and the plastic tarp looked a little loose, but he let that discovery go until the shelter-in-place order was lifted, around 6:00 P.M.

"I'm going to go out and see what's going on," Henneberry told his wife. Besides, it would give him a chance to enjoy his first cigarette of the day. He remembered that he wanted to "put the pads back up. Simple." He thought it must have been the wind and made his way to the tarp, which was looser than it should have been with a strong gust.

He grabbed a stepladder, and as he climbed it he noticed the loosened strap. "Oh my God. Is that blood?" he said aloud to no one in particular.[3] Blood was smeared all over the boat's interior, and in some spots dripping streaks of it had dried. His eyes followed the trail of blood, and that's when he saw the body—a man in black shoes, khaki pants, and a hooded sweatshirt lying on his side. Henneberry scrambled down the ladder and rushed into the house. Wordlessly his wife handed him the phone, and he called 911. BPD Deputy Superintendent Bill Evans was six blocks away in Watertown when he heard about the 911 call placed from 67 Franklin Street. He grabbed a Watertown cop. "Take me to this address," he ordered.[4] In the car with him was BPD Commander Bobby Merner, a hard-charging cop who led the city's homicide unit.

"I'm at the boat," Evans transmitted to the dispatcher less than a minute later. "We have it secure. All we need is a tactical team. Send the tac team."

Dzhokhar Tsarnaev was poking at the plastic tarp from underneath with what looked like a gun. Evans had been all over the Watertown crime scene. He knew that there had been two muzzle flashes but only one gun recovered, so he had to assume the suspect in the boat was armed. Then there was the dead man's switch that had been found in the bushes near the scene of the shootout. Cops had been so paranoid during the daylong manhunt that an old Armenian man with a Walkman had been stopped and frisked by a Watertown cop so young that he didn't recognize the device and thought it might be an arming mechanism.

Overhead troopers from the MSP Air Wing hovered overhead and pointed a forward-looking infrared camera into the boat. Ordinarily one of these cameras, which can detect a heat source, picks up just a blob. But the image the pilot saw made it clear that there was someone inside that boat. The troopers needed to be the eyes for the tactical team on the ground, although thirty-knot winds were bouncing them mercilessly. "No movement," A dispatcher transmitted, "no movement from the boat on the last pass from the air wing."[5]

Police on the ground began evacuating the residents of surrounding homes. There were cops everywhere. Everyone was on edge. Commanders from different departments tried to take control at the scene.

"Any vehicle in front of 67 Franklin with lights on. Shut down your lights. You are backlighting the crime scene," a dispatcher transmitted. Then came a call for radio silence.

Revere Police Department Chief Robert Cafarelli, a former US Marine, was the commander of the North Metro SWAT team that on this day consisted of roughly a dozen officers from the Everett, Malden, and Revere Police Departments who had already been outfitted with what those officers referred to as their "call-out gear": helmets, M4 rifles, bullet-proof vests, protective eyewear, extra magazines for pistols and rifles, and plastic cuffs. The North Metro SWAT team worked with officers from the transit police who were also geared up, and some team members moved to the right side of the Henneberry house. BPD SWAT officers took up positions at the left side of the small white house. Everett Police Department Officer Matt Cunningham—a trained sniper who had served in the US Marine Corps during Operation Iraqi Freedom and in the US Army in Sarajevo, Bosnia, during NATO's intervention during that country's bloody internecine war—took up a position with his fellow SWAT team member Revere Police Department Officer Joe Turner at a window on the second floor of the Henneberry house—they had been invited in by the owners—and trained their rifles' red laser sights on the boat below.

All of the cops on the scene had been working for at least fourteen hours, since responding to the scene of MIT Police Officer Sean Collier's murder. The North Metro SWAT team had sprinted, loaded with heavy equipment, roughly a quarter-mile to the Franklin Street address. It had been a long, long night.

"We ran to the yard and took position on the left side of the house. Boston Police were on the right side of the house," Cafarelli remembered.[6]

SWAT team commanders decided to lure the suspect out with flash-bang and stun grenades, both nonlethal devices designed to disorient a suspect with bursts of light and noise. "All units do not return fire," an FBI supervisory agent broadcast over his radio. "There might be a flash bang from the FBI. Do not return fire."

There was a blast and then a flame in the stern of the boat. "The suspect is sitting up in the boat. Repeat. The suspect is sitting up in the boat inside the stern," a dispatcher broadcast over the police radios.[7] He was trying to set what he thought was a can of gasoline ablaze, raising a new concern: fire and a forty-gallon tank of gas on the boat made a bad combination. It was now dark. A floodlight from the Lenco BearCat—a small armored tactical vehicle that provides cover for police officers in an urban environment much like a tank would in warfare—that was situated beside the *Slip Away II* illuminated the boat. On the vehicle was Cafarelli's brother John, also a Revere Police Department officer assigned to the North Metro SWAT team.

Then the suspect stopped moving. "Air Wing reporting no movement in the back of the boat," a dispatcher transmitted. Evans listened to every word and asked once again for radio silence from officers so that the commanders in charge of the scene could communicate with each other. The FBI was about to throw flash-bang and stun grenades into the boat to disorient the suspect. "There is movement on top of the stairs. Beware of booby traps," a dispatcher transmitted over the radio.

That movement sparked chaos, and at 6:54 P.M. all control was lost. A police officer saw something shifting in the boat, thought the suspect was armed, and opened fire. That prompted more gunshots—all fired by cops, and none by the suspect, who turned out to be unarmed. To this day no one knows who fired that first round. The gunfire went on for ten to fifteen seconds, and when it was over, 126 bullets had been fired into the boat.

"Shots fired! Shots fired," Evans screamed into his radio. Bullets kept ringing out. He couldn't believe it. A cop was more likely to be hit than the suspect inside the boat. Furious, Evans jumped out of his car with a megaphone in his hand: "Hold your fire! Hold your fire! There are friendlies all around this boat."[8]

When the bullets stopped, an FBI supervisor named Derek Bailey approached Evans and told him, "From now on every decision at this scene will be made by you." Evans nodded. By 8:30 P.M. the BearCat had been sent in to rip back the plastic tarp. From inside the bullet-riddled boat came a voice. It was heavily accented and weak, but Cunningham could hear it from his perch at the second-floor window. So could the FBI negotiator from the HRT who was standing next to him.

"They're going to kill me! I don't want to die. They're going to kill me," the teenager yelled, Cunningham remembered. "I need help. They're going to kill me."[9]

The HRT negotiator responded over his bullhorn: "Come out! No one is going to hurt you. Keep your hands visible. You have to climb out. No one is coming in."

Dzhokhar Tsarnaev's leg came out first. He slung it over the side of the boat and slowly hoisted himself to the deck, blood dripping from his wounds, his face smeared with blood and highlighted with red laser sights from multiple rifles, including Cunningham's. The negotiator ordered him to lift his shirt. He did, weakly.

"He lost so much blood he started wavering. He was bleeding from everywhere. No one wanted him to fall back into the boat. No one had any idea what was inside it," Cunningham remembered.

Cafarelli's team was ready to act and got into what SWAT teams referred to as a "stick formation," officers in a line. This line consisted of Cafarelli, Malden Police Department Sergeant Rich Correale, and Revere Police Department Officer Mike Trovato (another combat veteran, he had served in the US Army during Operation Iraqi Freedom). Then, on three, they swarmed the boat.

"I grabbed a leg," Cafarelli remembered. "Everyone had a limb and we pulled him to the ground and he landed on his back."

Trovato ripped open the suspect's shirt looking for a suicide vest or IEDs and patted him down for weapons. Nothing was found. The teenager was then held down by a North Metro SWAT officer as he was handcuffed by a transit officer, and tactical EMTs and medics from the FBI and ATF swarmed in to treat the bomber's wounds.

Then came the radio dispatch that sent up a roar from the cops who had massed along the streets and in the backyards of the homes surrounding 67 Franklin Street: "North Metro SWAT has one in custody."

Dzhokhar was handcuffed by a transit police officer—a sign of respect for Dic Donohue, who was still fighting for his life—and then two Boston EMS paramedics were called to transport the suspected marathon bomber and transport him to Beth Israel Deaconess Medical Center, the same hospital where his brother had been pronounced dead early that morning.

Laura Lee was one of the paramedics. She took a position at Dzhokhar's head and "grabbed a pulse," she remembered.[10] He was still breathing but bleeding. Lee and her partner grabbed a "scoop board" and rolled Dzhokhar onto it to hustle him into the back of the ambulance. So many cops tried to crowd inside "the bus," to protect the handcuffed suspect that the paramedics had to push all but a few out. "Everybody wanted to get in. But, you know, there was only room for that many," Lee recalled. Besides, the paramedics needed room to work. But investigators wanted to keep the suspect alive and talking.

Lee assessed his wounds: "His hair was all matted, so we didn't really sort of examine it very, very closely or it might have started to bleed again. He had a wound along the jaw here that was open. It looked like one of the fragments had probably gone off. His cheek looked a little deformed." At some point, Lee remembered, his eyes rolled up into the back of his head. But she and her partner kept him alert by asking him a series of questions, intentionally using a loud voice. Among those questions was asking the bleeding teenager—a man suspected of an imaginably evil act—if he had any allergies.

"He said he was allergic to cats," Lee recalled. That was odd, given that the Tsarnaev brothers' friend Khairullozhon Matanov, the cab driver who had dinner with the marathon bombers on the night of April 15, 2013, said that in the hours after detonating the second deadly bomb on Boylston Street, Dzhokhar spent a portion of the night watching footage of the carnage on television while stroking the family's cat.[11]

As Dzhokhar was raced to the hospital, the BPD posted a Tweet: "CAP-TURED!!! The hunt is over. The search is done. The terror is over. And justice has won. Suspect in custody."[12]

Governor Patrick, Mayor Menino (still in his wheelchair), and public safety officials from all over the state met a massive swarm of reporters to announce that the manhunt was over. "We have a victory," announced MSP Colonel Tim Alben. "We got him," said BPD Commissioner Davis.[13] The mood was jubilant but chaotic at the Watertown mall's makeshift command center, where by then reporters and cops had been for more than twenty-four hours straight, with political big shots and police brass jockeying for position in front of the cameras.

Evans wanted no part of it. He turned to Merner and said, "Let's go get a beer."[14] They had earned it. And when they arrived at Doyle's—a bar in Jamaica Plain that was popular with civil servants—no one would let them pay for a single drink.

Dzhokhar Tsarnaev arrived at the hospital in critical condition just after 9:00 P.M. He had suffered gunshot wounds to the side of his head, face, throat, jaw, left hand, and both legs. He was intubated and rushed into surgery. The next morning he woke up in the Surgical Intensive Care Unit heavily medicated, his jaw wired shut, deaf in his left ear, and handcuffed to his bed. In the room with him were FBI agents from the High-Value Detainee Interrogation Group (HIG), a cooperative effort between the FBI, the CIA, the Department of Defense, and other government agencies. They handed him a notebook and paper.

He wrote his address, incorrectly, on the first page. The agents asked him if there were any more bombs. He wrote "NO!" Then he wrote "lawyer"—ten times.[15]

"Is it me or do you hear some noise," he wrote.

At another point he scribbled, "I am tired. Leave me alone," and his pen trailed off the page. For hours, the terrorist wrote short notes complaining of his pain or exhaustion. He also asked questions about his brother, whose death he had caused by dragging him under the wheel-well of a stolen Mercedes. The agents wouldn't tell him if Tamerlan was alive or dead until he answered some questions about "danger from other individuals, devices, or otherwise."

"Is my brother alive? I know you know. Is he living? Is he alive?" Dzhokhar wrote on his second day in the hospital. "Is he alive? One person can tell you that."

The next day he wrote, "Is he alive? Show me the news. What's today? Where is he? Can I sleep? Can you not handcuff my right arm? Where is my bro????"

PART TWO

TIMELINE OF TERROR

*Who Are
the Marathon
Bombers?*

7

GROWING UP TSARNAEV

Raisat Suleimanova remembered the last time she saw her aunt Zubeidat Tsarnaeva, which was in 2010. Zubeidat was wearing a black hijab and a burka that covered her body. It was unnerving for Raisat: "It was a shock for me. Knowing what kind of person Zubeidat used to be, it was very strange to see that. She used to be such a fashionable person. She loved to wear bright clothing; and now to see her wearing a hijab it was a shock, and not just for me, but for my mother and everyone else."[1]

Raisat said that Zubeidat used to be known as a flamboyant dresser, with her fur coats, leopard-print bags, big sunglasses, and magenta lipstick. Zubeidat even put highlights in her hair, a rarity in the Republic of Dagestan. She "had this bright personality," Raisat remembered. "She's a strong person. She's a very determined person. She always wanted everything excellent, to be ideal in her life, to be beautiful."

Her niece remembered Zubeidat's garrulous nature, saying that she was "very social, very loud" and drove her husband, Anzor Tsarnaev, batty. He was a quiet man, hardly the life of the party, and what little personality he possessed seemed to drain out of him when his wife was around. Still, he followed her like a puppy, Raisat explained, not exactly a trait that Russian men are known for. "Anzor was crazy in love with Zubeidat, crazy, crazy in love. He was worshipping her. He wouldn't go anywhere without her. He was very jealous of her." But she could not be tamed, not even as a little girl.

Zubeidat Khiramagomedovna was born on May 8, 1967, in Chokh, a village in the Guibskii District of Dagestan, in the mountains along the Caspian Sea. Her native village is now a hotbed of an ultra-conservative strain of

Islam known as Salafism, which declares that Salafi Muslims are the only true interpreters of the Quran and that moderate Muslims are nothing more than kaffirs—nonbelievers or infidels. The most visible proponents of Salafism right now are the barbarous Islamic State of Iraq and Syria (ISIS) militants.

Zubeidat was seven years old when her mother died of breast cancer. After that, she was then shuffled from brother to brother, and from region to region. She was living with one brother in a little town on the border of Chechnya when she finished the tenth grade, and before that she had lived in a town outside of Dagestan. Later she moved to Novosibirsk, Siberia, where she met Anzor, who was serving his mandatory military term in the early 1980s. They married in 1986—exactly one day before their eldest child, Tamerlan, was born. A photograph of the baby and his parents shows Zubeidat's wild, Western style: her raven hair is piled haphazardly atop her head, and streaks of bright color highlight her face. Other family photos from that era show her in low-cut dresses and wearing red lipstick. The couple settled in Kyrgyzstan, where other children were born: Bella in 1988, Ailina in 1990, and Dzhokhar in 1993. The region was ravaged by a bloody, internecine war, and the Tsarnaev family moved to Chechnya, another cauldron of ethnic violence, and then back to Kyrgyzstan before finally following Anzor's brothers to the United States.

By then, though, the tensions between the husband's and wife's families were already palpable. Zubeidat's family felt that Anzor was weak and under-employed, chasing odd jobs all over Russia to the detriment of his children. "Unfortunately they moved around a lot, and the children had to switch schools a lot. So the children didn't have time to adapt to the new school when it was time to move again," Raisat recalled. "So they always lived out of suitcases, so to speak. We would even say: 'You're like gypsies. You always move around. You never stay in one place for a long time.'"

Besides Anzor wasn't an Anvar, like Zubeidat; he was Chechen. And everyone knew that Chechens were troublemakers who were not very observant Muslims—a stereotype of Russians from the Northern Caucasus who prayed at mosques only when convenient, practicing a looser form of Islam which seeped into the Tsarnaev household. In one family photo Zubeidat erected a Christmas tree filled with lights and ornaments and served wine, all considered by her family a sign that she was falling away from Islam.

"They would celebrate the major Muslim holidays, but they wouldn't pray five times a day," Raisat remembered.

In 2002 the odd jobs dried up for Anzor, and he had some trouble with local government officials. Anzor and Zubeidat successfully applied for a ninety-day tourist visa to visit family members in the Boston area.[2] Even though it was one of nearly a dozen moves the family had made, this time they were leaving the country. Zubeidat met her family for a last goodbye before she left. The mood was subdued. For once, Zubeidat was quiet and acting like a dutiful wife to Anzor. For one thing, would be his family they would be relying on for help in the United States—in particular, his younger brother Ruslan Tsarni (he had changed his surname). A lawyer, Ruslan had moved to the United States in 1995 and had become an American citizen after marrying the daughter of a Russian-speaking CIA official, a Harvard University graduate who had served as the vice chair of the National Intelligence Council, a prestigious post reserved for the most revered spooks.

Ruslan having to take care of his older brother and Anzor's family was not the way things usually went in Chechen families. Historically the eldest son would take care of his younger siblings, as Zubeidat's older brothers had taken care of her after their mother died. Anzor was ashamed that he needed Ruslan's help, and not just in the United States when they arrived there. He also needed Ruslan to take care of Tamerlan, Bella, and Ailina in Kazakhstan, where Ruslan had temporarily settled as an American working abroad.

Anzor and Zubeidat would travel with Dzhokhar, the baby of the family. At that point, according to the testimony of multiple family members, he was an unusually happy eight-year-old who could melt the hearts of even the harshest relatives. Dzhokhar's presence could prove helpful when his parents applied for political asylum as refugees from the war-torn region of their country that had long been mired in bloody internecine conflicts between Islamic insurgents and Russian forces.

Zubeidat's family was devastated. Everyone loved the baby, whom they called Jahar. "He was a very sunny child," Raisat said. "Very kind, very warm." One of the last memories of her cousin that she cherished was watching him cry when he watched the Disney classic, *The Lion King*, and Mustafa died. He was a sensitive child who adored his big brother and was his sisters' favorite playmate.

It was Ruslan who found Dzhokhar and his parents a place to live in the United States. One of the benefits for political refugees was eligibility for housing whose cost was subsidized by the Department of Housing and Urban Development's Housing Choice Voucher Program Section 8.[3] The Tsarnaevs moved into a cramped top-floor apartment at 410 Norfolk Street in Cambridge, owned by a friend of Ruslan's, a Russian émigré named Alexander Lipson who taught Russian and Slavic linguistics at Harvard University. One of Lipson's brightest students was a longtime CIA operative named Graham Fuller, whose biography states that he "first became smitten with the Middle East at age 16 while reading *National Geographic* magazines and being enticed by the exotic landscapes, the culture, and the crazy shapes of the Arabic language that I decided I had to learn. I studied a lot about the Middle East, and Russia, when I was in university. I always expected to become an academic, but my draft board deemed otherwise; I was drafted and sent into intelligence work. I had an extraordinary chance to learn about the Middle East first hand while serving as a CIA operations officer all over—Turkey, Lebanon, Saudi Arabia, Yemen, Afghanistan and Hong Kong for two decades. It was an education in itself, and a chance to travel and learn a lot of languages, which I loved. I then 'came in from the cold' and was appointed a top analyst at CIA for global forecasting."[4] He retired from the CIA in 1987 but continues to write about the Middle East for various think tanks.

According to some of Fuller's writings, he advised the administrations of both President Ronald Reagan and President Bill Clinton to use Muslim extremists to fight the former Soviet Union. Fuller knew that the Northern Caucasus was full of angry young Muslim Salafists who could be recruited, along with jihadists from Saudi Arabia, Pakistan, and other Middle Eastern countries whose people were angry at the Russians. All of these recruits could be trained in techniques of guerilla insurgency and sent to fight against the Soviets in occupied Afghanistan. These soldiers were called mujahedin. CIA-trained mujahedin operated later in Chechnya, Dagestan, and other Muslim-occupied areas of the former Soviet Union and Afghanistan. In fact, one of them was a Saudi named Osama bin Laden.

It remains unclear how Ruslan and Fuller met, but there is no question that they became close. Fuller now says that his daughter was married to Ruslan for about five years and spent a year living with him in Bishkek—one of the cities where the Tsarnaev family had lived before immigrating to the United States.[5]

Immigration officials believed Anzor's story that his life was in danger because of his Chechen heritage and granted the family refugee status within weeks of their arrival in 2002. That meant that Tamerlan, Bella, and Ailina—then sixteen, fourteen, and twelve, respectively—would also be invited into the United States as refugees. Inexplicably, the siblings traveled to Turkey to make the trip to the United States, rather than fly out of Moscow; they arrived in the United States on July 19, 2003.[6] It is worth noting that Fuller had lived in Turkey extensively and wrote a book about the region, *The New Turkish Republic: Turkey as a Pivotal State in the Muslim World*, that was published five years later.

A strange question would emerge in 2016 when Tamerlan's immigration records were released after a Freedom of Information Act Request was granted, nearly three years after a similar request made by members of Congress was denied by Department of Homeland Security (DHS) Secretary Janet Napolitano. In the records, which included dozens of pages of entirely redacted material, were two "Medical Examination for Immigrant or Refugee Applicant" forms for Tamerlan. Both listed the same name (Tamerlan Tsarnaev) and date of birth (October 21, 1986). Both had been filled out at the US embassy in Ankara, Turkey. Both noted that Tamerlan did not have an "apparent defect, disease, or disability" or HIV 1 or HIV 2.[7] However, he did test positive for tuberculosis in Cambridge and received medicine for the condition, which is often cited as a reason not to admit an immigrant seeking asylum into the country, immigration experts say.

Both were dated July 10, 2003. But the photo attached to one form showed a blue-eyed man who did not resemble Tamerlan at all. The photo stapled to the other form showed the sixteen-year-old Tamerlan. Both men were photographed wearing identical patterned shirts with black collars, something the State Department—which perhaps not coincidentally oversees the CIA—has yet to explain.

Shortly after the older three Tsarnaev children left for the United States, Ruslan moved to the Washington, D.C., area with his second wife, Zalina. He still interacted with his nieces and nephews and continued to despise his brother's wife and to blame her as his brother began to spiral into a dark depression. "I helped that family. I raised that family. I tried to save those children. But they are all like their mother. Evil spawn from an evil woman," Ruslan said.[8]

By 2006, everyone in the Tsarnaev family had obtained legal permanent alien status and green cards, which made them all eligible for employment. But not a single member of the family has held a job in the United States, including Anzor. The rent was paid with the federal subsidy, their food was paid for with benefits from the Supplemental Nutrition Assistance Program (SNAP), their clothing was bought with cash withdrawn through Electronic Benefit Transfer (EBT) cards. The only work performed by a member of the family was off the record, work that produced income on which they never paid taxes. Zubeidat did facials in the cramped apartment for cash. Tamerlan delivered pizzas, his immigration paperwork said. Dzhokhar sold drugs, according to court testimony.

Sam Lipson, Alexander's son, would remember Anzor as a reserved, strong man—a former boxer in Russia who pushed his eldest son into the ring, too. But then he seemed to wither, especially in the presence of Zubeidat. Her English was better than his, and she was "loquacious," Sam remembered, while Anzor "was a person of few words, is kind of the way I imagined, you know, sort of a cowboy. He made good eye contact, was very warm, but didn't speak much. She spoke a fair amount. Her English was fairly good."

When Alexander died, his wife, Joanna Herlihy, grew closer to the Tsarnaev children and tried to watch out for them, her son said—especially the girls. Ruslan, too, was worried about the corrupting influence of their mother on Bella and Ailina.

No one could stop the girls from following their mother into a world of welfare dependency and unmarried pregnancies. The older daughter, Bella, had attended Cambridge Rindge and Latin School but dropped out after getting pregnant at sixteen. She had been briefly married to a Chechen Muslim named Mamakev Rizvan—a marriage her father had arranged for her after she became pregnant. After that she had a series of boyfriends, including one who helped her get arrested on drug charges just months before her brothers dropped the bombs on Boylston Street.

On December 11, 2012, police were called to the home in Fairview, New Jersey, that Bella was sharing with her then-boyfriend Ahmad Khalid, after she allegedly scratched him. The police smelled pot and raided the house, finding drugs and $537 in cash. Both Bella and Ahmad were arrested at the scene. She pleaded not guilty to drug charges a month after the Boston Marathon bombings, and a judge allowed her to enter a rehabilitation program that would wipe her record clean if she stayed out of trouble. So far, she has. Still, the FBI raided that New Jersey house again, during the manhunt for her brother Dzhokhar.

Ruslan became a national figure four days after the marathon attacks, when he held a press conference on the lawn of his home in Montgomery Village, Maryland, to denounce his nephews as "losers" and added, "we are ashamed." He also had harsh words for Dzhokhar and urged him to turn himself in: "He put a shame on this family. He put a shame on the entire Chechnyan ethnicity."[9]

By then Tamerlan was dead, shot by police and then run over by Dzhokhar, who was in a hospital with multiple gunshot wounds, being relentlessly grilled by the FBI. However, Ruslan did not call the FBI when photos of his nephews—then identified only as Suspects Black Hat and White Hat—were released, according to FBI investigators who did not want to acknowledge that publicly.

Ruslan may not have recognized them. He claimed he had not seen his brother's family for years. "I wanted my family away from his family," he said, but he declined to explain why. But documents in a case in a Massachusetts state criminal court pertaining to a shoplifting charge for Ailina give details about what caused the initial rift between Ruslan and his brother's family in 2010. The conflict centered on Ruslan's favorite niece, Ailina, who he said was a "sweet, sweet girl, growing up."

Ruslan wanted to get her away from Zubeidat so badly that he arranged a marriage for Ailina in 2007. She was only sixteen, as Bella had been when she became pregnant. Bella waited until she was legally able to get married at seventeen. Ailina was too young to get married unless she petitioned the Commonwealth of Massachusetts Probate and Family Court to approve her marriage, and she signed the form requesting that a judge allow her to become an underage bride on September 12, 2006. That same day her marriage request was granted and signed by a district court justice.[10] Her husband, Elmirza Khozhugov, was close to Ruslan. "She threw that marriage away," Ruslan said later. Police records tell a different story. After the wedding Ailina moved with her husband to the West Coast. Months later, she called the police and reported that her new husband had tried to strangle her. Khozhugov pleaded guilty to assault charges, and the couple divorced. But Ailina's troubles with the law didn't end with her marriage.

On April 6, 2010, Ailina, now twenty-three, was among a group of diners at an Applebee's restaurant in Boston who paid the bill with counterfeit money. Their server knew something was awry, ran outside, and jotted down the driver's license plate number. Boston police found that the car was registered to Zalina Tsarni of 410 Norfolk Street, in Cambridge. Zalina, of course, didn't live there and hadn't even been to Boston since 2003, information that was not shared with the Secret Service agent and two BPD detectives who showed up at the Tsarnaevs' home. Zubeidat was there, and she was fully aware that Zalina's identity had been stolen and then used to register the family car and obtain an alternative driver's license, thereby qualifying the family for additional EBT funds in Zalina's name. But none of that was mentioned to investigators. Zubeidat told them Zalina wasn't home, and police went on their way.

Subpoenas were then mailed to Zalina Tsarni at the Tsarnaevs' address, but of course they were ignored. In September 2010, an arrest warrant was issued for Zalina Tsarnaeva, the woman cops believed had been driving the car used in a counterfeit money crime. An arrest warrant was issued for Ruslan's wife, and he was livid. He faxed paperwork proving that his wife lived in Maryland with him to the BPD detectives, who paid Zubeidat another visit. This time she had a different story. Her daughter Ailina had used her aunt's information, perhaps accidentally, but detectives couldn't ask Ailina about it because she had moved out. "Zubeidat Tsarnaeva stated that her daughter Ailina had moved about three months ago into a shelter with her son and sister Bella," BPD Detective Robert Kenney wrote in a police report. "Mrs. Tsarnaeva stated the reason was that her daughters felt that she was too strict."[11]

Kenney then recalled the arrest warrant for Zalina, and her legal troubles were over. So was Ruslan's relationship with his brother's family: "I officially disowned them from my soul in 2010 after they caused my wife and me so many problems. I did so much for them. Helped them in Russia, helped them here. Took the kids into my home. Gave them money. They disgraced me."

At the time of the bombings, Ailina Tsarnaeva had moved on to a new man, and with him came more legal problems. The father of her baby had three children with another woman, and she was giving him a hard time in a custody battle, according to the NYPD. Ailina took matters into her own hands, allegedly calling the woman and making this threat: "Leave my man alone. Stop looking for him. I have people. I know people who can put a bomb where you live."[12] Considering the charges that Ailina's brother was facing then, the woman took the threat very seriously. So did the NYPD. Ailina turned herself in at the 30th Precinct, but the charges were later dropped. She still had some loose legal ends to contend with in Boston, and she drove from her New Jersey home in July 2014 to appear in a South Boston court. When asked about the charges against her brother Ailina screeched, "Everyone knows he was framed. Accept it!"[13]

———————

Tamerlan Tsarnaev had his own problems with relationships, court records show. In 2009 he was dating two women. One was a pretty petite brunette named Katherine Russell, who had grown up in the posh Rhode Island town of North Kingston under the watchful eyes of her father, an emergency room physician, and her mother, a nurse. At the time Katherine was attending classes at Suffolk University and working at a *gelateria*—or Italian ice cream shop—in the North End, Boston's Little Italy. The other woman was a neighborhood girl, Nadine Ascenscao, who would tell reporters that she had lost her virginity to the muscular boxer and had been in love with him for three years, starting when he was a fun-loving party boy who loved to dress colorfully in metallic shoes and designer jackets. But then things started to change. He started watching jihadi videos and told her she had to convert to Islam. Matters would quickly get worse.

On August 12, 2009, Nadine was leaving to go to a family barbeque when Tamerlan told her she was dressed too provocatively and slapped her face. Nadine called 911 from her cell phone, crying hysterically that her boyfriend had "just beat her up."[14] When a Cambridge police cruiser showed up, Tamerlan arrogantly confessed. "Yeah, I slapped her," he said, according to the Cambridge Police Department report of the incident, adding that the two had been arguing about his other girlfriend. The police arrested Tamerlan for domestic violence. But Nadine refused medical attention and declined to file charges, so the case was eventually dismissed.

By then Tamerlan's relationship with Katherine had begun to heat up.

———

Katherine was an unlikely Muslim convert. She had grown up in a sprawling home in an upscale suburb, and her parents were respected medical professionals. She was attending a prestigious college and was living with a roommate in an apartment above the gelateria where she worked. Life was good. Then she met Tamerlan, an overbearing and abusive man who was accused of hitting her more than once.[15]

Katherine's mother, Judy, was horrified when at some point in 2010 her daughter began to wear a hijab and study the Quran. Her grades at Suffolk University began to suffer, and she eventually dropped out. Gina Crawford, Katherine's best friend from fifth grade on, saw the changes in her best friend and reached out to Judy. Katherine's roommate, Amanda Ransom, was so afraid of Tamerlan's explosive temper that she moved out.

Judy knew it was time for her to talk to both Katherine and Tamerlan about where their relationship was headed, and she invited them for dinner in North Kingston. The evening didn't go well, she remembered later. Katherine and Tamerlan were nearly two hours late and had only a poor excuse for their tardiness. "It really irritated me. It wasn't a good way to start off," Judy recalled. Besides, "it was hard to get to know him, and he didn't really seem interested in getting to know us, so it didn't start off on a really good footing."[16]

Tamerlan was not just verbally and physically abusive; he was also a womanizer who cheated on Katherine repeatedly. The cheating came as a relief to Judy, she said: "I didn't really want her to be with him. I didn't think they were a good match. He didn't seem to have any—[pause]. The only thing he had passion about, what really was driving him was boxing at that point. So he didn't really have a job."

Judy's concerns only increased as her daughter and Tamerlan tried to push their Islamic views onto her and the rest of the Russell family, who had never been very religious. All of a sudden her daughter—her little Katie, who loved ballet and jazz and who had worked hard to get into Suffolk University—was quitting college in her junior year, converting to Islam, and talking about marrying the unemployed boxer, Judy said: "He became much more religious and talked about it much more frequently. Like anytime I saw him, he would talk about it and try to, you know, show me books and get me to learn about it."

The close relationship she had had with Katherine began to grow more distant, especially when her daughter told Judy on the same day both that she was pregnant and that she was going to start not just covering her head but wearing a burka. Her mother tried to talk her out of marrying Tamerlan, telling her that he was no good. Katherine responded to her mother's criticism by not inviting anyone from her family to her wedding. "No one went," Judy said. The memory made her voice shake with hurt even six years later.

The family didn't miss much. The June 21, 2010, nuptials exchanged in the Masjid al-Qur'aan mosque in Boston were anything but romantic. Katherine called the imam at the mosque in the hardscrabble neighborhood of Dorchester and said, "We want to get married," Taalib Mahdee later recalled.[17] He was quick to agree, because Muslim teachings say it is good to be married. He had never met the couple until they showed up on a ninety-degree day, Katherine sweaty and heavy under the burka, Tamerlan in a button-down shirt and dress pants. In the cluttered and carpeted second-floor mosque, they exchanged promises to be good to Allah and each other. Mahdee never saw them again. It was bizarre that they hadn't gotten married in Tamerlan's own mosque, the Islamic Society of Boston's mosque on Prospect Street in Cambridge, just a few blocks from their Norfolk Street home.

In October Katherine gave birth to a little girl. By then she had adopted the Muslim name Karima Tsarnaeva, and she and Tamerlan named their daughter Zahira. But there was no room for the new mother and a wailing baby in the Tsarnaevs' cramped Cambridge apartment, so she moved home with Judy, who welcomed her daughter and granddaughter with open arms. Sometimes Tamerlan would visit his wife and new baby on the weekend, Judy said, but what was supposed to be a temporary visit so Zahira could get acquainted with her grandparents stretched into a ten-month stay, with no financial support whatsoever from Tamerlan Tsarnaev. The Russells were paying for diapers and baby food. Enough was enough, Judy told her daughter. "I thought it was time that he supported his—you know, his wife and daughter," Judy recalled.

That's when her relationship with her daughter really grew distant, especially as she learned more about the Tsarnaev clan. Katherine had told her parents that Tamerlan's father was a lawyer, but that was a lie. Anzor, Judy discovered after she did some checking, had "bought his law degree," which, she was told, "is typical in Chechnya." Tamerlan's sisters—divorced teenagers—had babies of their own. Tamerlan's mother was terrifying, stern and completely covered with a black headscarf and burka. And all of them were living in that tiny apartment on Norfolk Street in Cambridge, decorated with multiple black Islamic flags often associated with jihad, as evidence photos would come to show.

Tamerlan may have started a new life with Katherine—growing a five-inch beard and beginning to abstain from drugs and alcohol like a good Muslim—but his arrest for domestic violence against Nadine continued to haunt him. In fact, the arrest made him ineligible for US citizenship for five years, under the morals clause condition contained in the naturalization process that political refugees like the Tsarnaevs were eligible for: he had committed an act of "moral turpitude."

That was a devastating blow for someone who dreamed of fighting in the Olympic games as a member of the US boxing team. Tamerlan had been granted a green card in 2006, but legal permanent residents are not eligible for any US team that competes in the Olympics. Nor could they compete in the National Tournament of Champions. Tamerlan was a two-time heavyweight Golden Gloves Champion, a laudable accomplishment, but he was barred from participating in the national tournament because of his immigration status. He was so desperate to change his status that in 2009 he participated in an online photo essay by the photographer Johannes Hirn called "Will Box for Passport." It was shot at Wai Kru, a mixed martial arts gym in Brighton that was like Tamerlan's second home. In fact, mixed martial arts, or MMA, would become the only other thing besides Islam that Tamerlan was dedicated to.

Tamerlan started keeping a journal with entries on Islam and his life. In one he wrote: "Now I live because I'm a warrior . . . and someday I want to stand before the One. The mujahedeen spent a long time living in a dream. And is slowly waking up."[18] He wanted to wake up his brother, Dzhokhar, who was living too much like an infidel, dealing marijuana at his college (the University of Massachusetts at Dartmouth) and partying unrelentingly, sometimes with Tamerlan's old friends.

Investigators believe that Tamerlan woke his inner mujahedin with his participation in a grisly triple homicide that took place on the ten-year anniversary of 9/11 terrorist attacks.[19]

8

IT LOOKS LIKE AN AL QAEDA TRAINING VIDEO IN HERE

The ten-year anniversary of the deadliest terror attack on American soil was significant all over the country but especially in Massachusetts, because two of the hijacked planes took off from Boston's Logan Airport. The grisly details of the terrifying minutes on those flights were contained in *The 9/11 Commission Report*.[1] The bloodshed began at 8:13 that morning, when Mohamed Atta took control of American Airlines Flight 11 one minute after the Boeing 767 carrying ninety-two people took off.

Atta used a box cutter to take out the pilots, as fellow hijackers Waleed al-Shehri and his brother, Wali al-Shehri, fatally stabbed two female flight attendants. The murderers were Pakistani, but they had received terrorist training "in the forests" of Chechnya before they joined the 9/11 hijackers. Their victims' screams that morning were heard by American Airlines ground workers after flight attendant Betty Ong managed to call a gate attendant from an air phone, before she was killed.

"The cockpit is not answering, somebody's stabbed in business class—and I think there's Mace—that we can't breathe—I don't know, I think we're getting hijacked," Ong screeched into the phone.[2] It was one of the last communications from the plane before it hurtled into the World Trade Center towers, beginning what would become the darkest day in American history.

The ten-year anniversary of the 9/11 attacks was the last thing on Erik Weissman's mind. He was in a lot of trouble. Nine months earlier his landlord, concerned when he couldn't reach the tenant of his one-bedroom apartment in the Rosindale section of Boston, let himself into the apartment at 10 Brownson Terrace. Then he saw the drugs. They were everywhere: twenty-three five-pound bags of marijuana, pot bagged up everywhere, cocaine hidden in a suitcase, hashish in hermetically sealed bags, and a shoebox full of pills. Two digital scales and a currency counter were found, along with $21,504 in cash. Weissman even kept a ledger in which he jotted down drug transactions. The landlord, Paul Thurston, drove straight to the Boston police station in Brighton, which prompted detectives to apply for a search warrant for Weissman's apartment, using Thurston's information. Upon execution of that warrant, according to court records, narcotics detectives noted the same drugs stashed everywhere in the apartment and issued a warrant for Erik's arrest. He had been arrested three years earlier and would plead guilty to possession of marijuana with intent to distribute. In 2011 the police were waiting to arrest him when he got home, and now he was facing some serious charges. He wanted to avoid his place and spent most of his time at the apartment of a buddy, Brendan Mess, on a quiet dead-end street in Waltham. The apartment was on the second floor of a Victorian house at 12 Harding Avenue.

On the night of September 11, he had a quick meal with his sister and then parked his Mercedes SUV in front of Brendan's apartment around 7:30 P.M. It had been quiet there ever since Brendan's girlfriend had moved out. That woman, Hibatalla Eltilib, was definitely hot—tall and long-legged, with skin the color of warm caramel and stunning green eyes. But Hiba, as they called her, was also a real psycho, the type of girlfriend who would get mad and throw knives. It didn't take a lot to get her mad, either. She was a Sudanese immigrant who in recent months had become increasingly radical in her Islamic faith. She would argue with Brendan's friends about the wars in Iraq and Afghanistan or complain about the friends, calling them a bunch of lazy, pot-smoking lowlifes. Recently she had been trying to get Brendan to convert to Islam, so he could pray with her at the Cambridge mosque. He refused. She tried to bring some of her Muslim friends to the house to convince him to be more pious, but he just laughed. Friends remembered that that had prompted an outburst so irrational that Hiba hurled knives and beer bottles at Brendan. It had been a fiasco. Brendan had kicked her out, and a few days earlier she had gone to stay with friends in Florida.

Erik was excited when he got to Brendan's. It was going to be their first boys' night in a while. Brendan and Erik had been friends for a long time, even though Brendan was twenty-five and Erik thirty-one. Both men were from Cambridge and had graduated from Cambridge Rindge and Latin. Raphael "Rafi" Teken—at thirty-seven, the oldest of the group of friends—was a rich kid who had gone to private school, but he enjoyed the company of Erik and Brendan. All three were regulars at Wai Kru, the mixed martial arts gym in nearby Brighton that Tamerlan Tsarnaev also frequented. Tonight the boys planned to smoke weed and stay in. Rafi had never been a fan of Hiba either, so when Erik walked in, they high-fived each other that the crazy bitch was gone and they could go back to the lifestyle they liked. They also liked to record that lifestyle in cell phone videos, like the one that showed Brendan at a pool party taking a deep drag on a fat blunt and then blowing it out, smiling, and declaring it "extra funky."[3] Brendan had no room in his life for drama—even if it came from a smoking hot woman, and especially when she started to say what his friends would remember as "a lot of controversial shit."[4]

It was a nice night—warm, without a cloud in the sky. Neighbors on the leafy block left their windows open to let in the fresh air. So did Brendan. But the pot smoke from the second-floor apartment wafted upward and didn't bother anyone below.

All three men were unlikely bad boys. Brendan had graduated from Vermont's Champlain College with a degree in professional writing and was a talented mixed martial arts fighter who made a living training other cage warrior wannabes. Rafi had grown up in a sprawling estate in tony Brookline and graduated from prestigious Brandeis University. His father was an assistant rabbi, a spiritual leader of a Jewish synagogue in Newton, and his brother was an extremely popular jazz musician. Even Erik, despite his penchant for getting in trouble with the law, was a devout Jew who took care of his ailing elderly father in his spare time. MMA brought them together—and weed. All three had police records.

Erik, a body builder, owed a lot of people money for the drugs that he was supposed to sell, narcotics that had been seized by the police in the January raid. One of his suppliers was a dangerous Armenian named Safwan Madarati. He had a lot of connections to the dirty Watertown cops who had been arrested on May 25, months after Weissman's stash had been discovered by his landlord and then the drug unit of the BPD. One of those dirty cops had even been captured telling Madarati in a wiretapped phone call: "You need to lie low. Someone is making you out to be the biggest mule in Massachusetts. The rats were talking."[5] That cop, Robert Velasquez-Johnson, was right. The rats were talking. In May the US Attorney's office unsealed an indictment after the arrests of Madarati and eighteen others involved in his distribution network, whose activities included drug dealing, money laundering, and extortion across the country—in California, Florida, Maine, New York, and Nevada—and into Canada. Madarati mainly worked locally, though. He controlled sales of steroids and hydroponic marijuana in Bedford, Burlington, Newton, Waltham, and Watertown, where he kept an apartment in which to manufacture and distribute marijuana and Ecstasy, prosecutors announced after his arrest.[6]

Madarati's arrest had international implications. The dirty Watertown cop had warned him that his case involved agents from the DHS's US Immigration and Customs Enforcement drug unit, an elite squad designed to investigate narcotics trafficking that funded overseas terrorism—which clearly included Madarati's ties to an Eritrean crew of narcotics traffickers in Portland, Maine. Agents assigned to Immigration and Customs Enforcement were concerned that the Portland dealers might be sending proceeds back to relatives connected to Al Qaeda's Somalia-based outfit Al Shabab.[7]

Erik was all too aware that Madarati probably thought he was one of those rats, which was why he and his drug dealing associates in nearby Waltham were lying low and hiding out. He might have been held without bail, but he had reach all over the area. To make matters worse, the high-end bong company he had invested in was going belly up. Unfilled orders meant angry customers. Erik had trouble sleeping these days and was happy to be surrounded by his friends, none of them pussies themselves.

Rafi—who worked as a personal trainer—had been arrested for assault on a girlfriend, while Brendan was still facing charges that he had beaten up a group of people without provocation in Cambridge. When the cops showed up to question him, he threatened one, saying, "I can knock you out if I wanted to."[8] Three additional officers soon arrived, and Brendan was hit with a chemical spray, wrestled to the ground, and handcuffed. That case was still wending its way through the legal system.

Erik, Brendan, and Rafi shared more than just a propensity for violence and pot. They were prolific marijuana dealers, and some of their best customers hung out at Wai Kru. That was where they would meet up with one of Brendan's closest friends, Tamerlan Tsarnaev, who usually traveled with another Chechen named Ibragim Todashev. Brendan and Tamerlan were close: Brendan was a respected cage fighter, and Tamerlan was a prizefighter. Both had attended Cambridge Rindge and Latin. After graduation they had even briefly shared an apartment, back when Tamerlan was a party boy dating more than a few women at the same time and rhyming with a Boston hip-hop crew called The FlyRydaz.

Tamerlan was married now, living in his parents' home, and he had been trying to talk Brendan into marrying a Muslim woman too, someone like Hiba. In fact, Brendan had met Hiba through Tamerlan. But Brendan began to fight with both his girl and his best friend over adherence to Islam. Tamerlan and Hiba were obsessed with 9/11 conspiracies and the wars in the Middle East, blaming the United States for killing Muslims without provocation. Both Tamerlan and Ibragim made spectacles of themselves at Wai Kru these days, every time they rolled out their prayer rugs to praise Allah. Being with Hiba and Tamerlan had become a nightmare, every night spent listening to them espouse anti-American views a teeth-grinding experience. They were both a pain in the ass, lecturing everyone about how living a life of depravity was like spitting in the eye of Allah. Tamerlan had even told Brendan that "the FBI is watching me, they think I'm a terrorist"—a story Brendan told his other friends later, giggling.[9]

But Tamerlan was a boxing hero with two Golden Glove heavyweight championships behind him, and Brendan wanted to get better with his fists, so he tolerated some of Tamerlan's rants. And Tamerlan was known to throw his arm around Brendan's shoulders at Wai Kru and declare, "This is my only American friend"—especially when there were other Russian Muslims around, which was most of the time these days. On June 11, 2012, Brendan introduced Tamerlan to his old jujitsu trainer, Scott Wood, an army ranger who owned Vermont Brazilian Jiu-Jitsu, near Champlain's campus. They were all at the Shriner's Auditorium in Wilmington, Massachusetts, to catch World Championship Fighting 11. As Tamerlan walked around the stadium, people stopped him to take selfies with him and shake his hand, calling him

"Champ." He was an idol, a giant who towered in over Micky Ward, a professional boxer, in one famous photograph that hung in a Lowell boxing gym.

"This guy is the man," Brendan said as he introduced Wood to Tamerlan. Wood shook his hand, noting Tamerlan's height, girth, and honed muscles. "Big dude," Wood said to Brendan. They all laughed.

That was the last time Wood saw Brendan alive.

"I didn't hear a thing until the girl was screaming," a Harding Avenue resident would tell reporters and police on the evening of September 12, 2011, as police lights lit up the narrow dead-end street with blue and white strobes. "She was in the street yelling, 'they're all dead. There's so much blood.'"[10]

The girl was Hiba Eltilib, and she had run crying out of her estranged boyfriend's apartment, her feet splattered with blood. She had flown back from Florida that morning, hoping to make things right with Brendan. When she landed she called his cell phone. No answer. She rang the house phone— again, nothing. She jumped in a cab to 12 Harding Avenue and walked into the scene of a massacre.

Brendan's body was face down on the floor near a door in the kitchen. It looked like someone had grabbed his hair as he ran toward the exit and raked a machete or sharp knife against his throat with enough force to nearly cut his head off. Erik's throat had been slashed the same way. Then his penis had been cut off and tossed onto his face. Rafi had been killed in a similar ritualistic fashion, gruesomely sexually mutilated and nearly decapitated by what prosecutors would call a "blunt object."[11] It was likely a machete, multiple police sources said. All of the bodies were sprinkled with marijuana, and on a table was five thousand dollars in cash.

"Oh my God," exclaimed a uniformed Waltham policeman who was one of the first officers to arrive on the scene. "It looks like an Al Qaeda training video in here."[12] The date was not lost on the officer either: the tenth anniversary of the bloodiest jihadi attack on the United States. None of the weed was gone, and the cash had not been taken. Clearly the massacre in the suburban apartment was meant as a message, albeit an indecipherable one at that point. Investigators believed that the murders had happened sometime between 9:00 P.M. and midnight. The last call placed from the apartment had been made from Erik's cell phone at 8:54 P.M. Erik had called a neighborhood restaurant, Gerry's Italian Kitchen, to order three chicken parmigiana dinners, three meatballs, and three sausages. When the deliverywoman rang the doorbell twenty minutes later, no one responded. Calls placed to Erik's cell phone went unanswered. Hiba discovered the bodies the next morning.

The bloodbath at 12 Harding Avenue could not be written off as the killings of three drug dealers who had pissed off the wrong machete-wielding thugs. It was clearly much more than that—especially given the sexual mutilation of the two Jewish victims, sources said.[13]

On the afternoon of September 12, Middlesex County District Attorney Gerard Leone held a press conference about the murders on Harding Avenue and described the crime scene as "graphic." He also said detectives had information that there had been other people in the apartment earlier but declined to elaborate: "We know there were at least two people who are not in that apartment now who were there earlier."[14]

He went on to describe the slayings. The men were found in separate rooms, all "killed by sharp wounds to their neck area." Leone said. "We don't know how many people were actually at the crime scene when they were killed. But there were many factors that led us to believe there was more than one person at the scene when the decedents were killed."

Waltham politicians showed up at the scene to calm fearful residents, all of whom said that they hadn't heard a thing—not a shout or a scream despite their wide-open windows in the balmy weather. When homicides happen in small, tightly knit neighborhoods, people often say in disbelief, "not in my neighborhood." City Councilor Gary Marchese told reporters: "What's sure is the neighborhood will never be the same. It'll take some time to heal."[15]

The murders quickly faded from the headlines. Hardly anyone was clamoring for justice for the three dead drug dealers. Brendan came from a fractured family, and his brother Dylan was not exactly cooperative with police. Erik was out on bail for dealing drugs—again. And Rafi was his wealthy family's black sheep.

On September 19 Brendan's family held a memorial service for him at Ryles Jazz Club in Cambridge. His divorced parents, Derek and Susan, were there, together and distraught. The service was well attended by friends and former teachers. But Tamerlan was conspicuously absent from the service and the funeral. "It's no coincidence that the last time I saw my friend Brendan alive he was walking out of that fight with that kid Tam," said Wood. "I really thought I would have been coaching that kid [Brendan] in the Ultimate Fighting Championship. Brendan's no saint, he liked to party. But nothing that he was into should have taken him to his end."[16]

Wood was not the only one who found Tamerlan's failure to pay his respects strange. Brendan's only brother was extremely concerned and passed the information about Tamerlan along to investigators. He also noticed that his brother's girlfriend had left town after the murders, which fueled suspicions about her hair-trigger temper and close association with Tamerlan. "She's shady and she's lying," Dylan said shortly after the murders. "So is her friend Tam."[17]

Furthermore, cops and many customers who used the Gerry's Italian Kitchen's delivery service remembered that Tamerlan was one of the many drivers who worked for the restaurant under the table. Managers of Gerry's denied that, but there were scores of people—including Waltham police officers—who swore that Tamerlan had delivered the restaurant's food to their offices and homes. But for some inexplicable reason, despite his name's having been mentioned to the state troopers assigned to the Middlesex County District Attorney and to a Waltham detective working on the murders, Tamerlan was never a suspect.

That reason, some seasoned investigators said (on background, because the unsolved triple homicides are an open investigation) is because he was too valuable as an asset working for the federal government on a drug case with ties to overseas terrorism, and as an informant who had infiltrated a mosque right around the corner from his house that had ties to radical Islam and convicted terrorists. The murder victims were players who had played too hard, and their deaths were soon forgotten.

Tamerlan was a handsome multilingual US resident desperate for American citizenship. Federal investigators had been assigned to take down a crew of Muslim multinational immigrants who were selling crack cocaine all over New England and sending the proceeds overseas. The men bought the drugs from Madarati and others in Boston, according to court records, and brought them to Portland, Maine. Confidential informants became part of the case, dubbed by the FBI and DHS Operation Run This Town.

One of the operation's targets was a former Cambridge resident named Hamadi Hassan, who had moved to Portland. Like Tamerlan, Hassan was in his twenties, and he had lived around the corner from the Tsarnaevs until he moved to Maine in 2010. Federal records filed in Hassan's case show phone calls between him and an informant that included references to Wai Kru, the place that connected the three murdered men, Tamerlan, and Ibragim Todashev. It would take eighteen months for the public to learn the identities of the two men that Leone had talked about at the press conference: the ones that walked out alive, leaving three dead men behind. Ibragim confessed to the murders in May 2013, but he would not get a chance to take the stand in the case.

Ibragim's involvement should have been obvious. He had fled Boston the night of the murders and headed to Florida "real fast," as his roommate would later tell the FBI. Tamerlan left the country four months later, in January 2012, for his motherland—the very place that the Federal Security Service of Russia (FSB), the modern equivalent of the old Soviet KGB, had warned the FBI and the CIA he would head to in a series of communications that began in March 2011.

9

MUAZ IN THE MOTHERLAND

The Russians were very worried about Tamerlan Tsarnaev and his crazy mother, Zubeidat, and, in an unusual move, they shared their concerns with their counterterrorism counterparts in the United States. There had long been tensions between the American FBI and the Russian FSB. FSB agents had been known to break into apartments of American agents and defecate on their pillows. The relationship between the two countries—both of which were trying to eradicate Islamic terrorism—was based more on need than trust, to say the least.

Still, on March 4, 2011, the FSB sent its first message about Tamerlan and Zubeidat to the FBI's legal attaché (LEGAT) in Moscow, and later it sent the same letter to the CIA. The letter, which to this day the FBI refuses to release, was read by FSB officials to a Congressional delegation that included Representative William Keating, a Democrat from Massachusetts and a former prosecutor. "I asked them for a copy and they said, 'Well, can't you get it from your own people?' They read to me that document . . . and it was amazing in its detail dealing with Tamerlan Tsarnaev," Keating said.[1]

The letter described intercepted text messages between Tamerlan; his mother; and Magomed Kartashov, her second cousin—a former Dagestan police officer who had become a prominent Islamist and leader of a group called Union of the Just (a Muslim advocacy group that has been banned in Russia because of its affiliations with Muslim militants) in their homeland that sympathized with radical Islamic insurgents who had declared war against Vladimir Putin's Russian forces, Keating said. Zubeidat and Tamerlan, the letter said, "were becoming adherents of radical Islam."

The FSB also provided full names, addresses, and phone numbers for many of the members of the Tsarnaev family, including Tamerlan and his mother. It warned that Tamerlan "had changed drastically since 2010" and was preparing to travel to a part of Russia "to join unspecified underground groups" namely, violent radical Islamists in the Caucasus who formed their own "bandit groups," which were essentially ragtag gangster insurgency groups.[2] The FBI's legal attaché in Moscow sent a translated copy of the FSB's warning about the Tsarnaev mother, son, and cousin to the Counterterrorism Division of the FBI's Boston Field Division, telling them "to take any investigative steps deemed appropriate and provide Moscow with any information derived," with the promise that the information would be forwarded to the Russians.

Around the same time the FSB picked up and interrogated a suspected Chechen terrorist named William Plotnikov. Plotnikov gave up some of his fellow English-speaking jihadis under questioning. One of them was Tamerlan Tsarnaev.

Five days after the FSB sent its letter, the legal attaché in Moscow sent a letter to the FSB acknowledging receipt of the information and requesting that the FBI be kept in the loop, according to a report released in April 2014 by the Office of the Inspector General for the Intelligence Community. "According to available information," the report stated, "the LEGAT did not coordinate with or notify the CIA in March 2011 after receiving the lead information concerning the Tsarnaevs."[3] According to a declassified summary of the report (which has not been fully released as of September 2016), "In September 2011, the FSB provided the Central Intelligence Agency (CIA) information on Tamerlan Tsarnaev that was substantively identical to the information the FSB had provided to the FBI in March 2011. In October 2011, the CIA provided information obtained from the FSB to the National Counterterrorism Center (NCTC) for watchlisting purposes, and to the FBI, Department of Homeland Security (DHS), and the Department of State for their information. Upon NCTC's receipt of the information, Tamerlan Tsarnaev was added to the terrorist watchlist."

Months later, with both the CIA and the FBI notified about his increasingly dangerous and radical views, Tamerlan was headed to Russia, where he would meet the very men the FSB had warned the American counterterrorism officials about: Plotnikov, the extremist, and Tamerlan's mother's cousin, Magomed.

Strangely, evidence would later show that Tamerlan somehow clandestinely recorded many of the conversations he had with that cousin, without his cousin's knowledge—recordings that would eventually be played by defense attorneys for jurors in the trial of his brother, Dzhokhar, to bolster the defense's assertion that the teenager had come under the corrupting influence of his older sibling, just as Tamerlan had been turned into a jihadi by his mother.

Tamerlan departed from Boston's Logan Airport and connected at John F. Kennedy International Airport (JFK) for a flight to Russia. He landed at Moscow's Sheremetyevo Airport on January 21, 2012. By then he was on two different terrorist watch lists. The first was Terrorist Identities Datamart Environment (TIDE) database, which is the repository of all international terrorist identifier information shared by the FBI, CIA, Defense Intelligence Agency, and National Security Agency (NSA) and maintained by the National Counterterrorism Center (NCTC). The NCTC maintains TIDE by adding biographical or biometric identifiers. The second was TECS, which is not an acronym but takes its name from an outdated system of identification checks formerly run by the now-defunct federal agency Treasury Enforcement Communication System. TECS is another way of flagging potential terror suspects as they cross borders. DHS describes the program as a way for customs agents at entry points to file reports about any "encounter with a traveler, a memorable event, or noteworthy item of information particularly when they observe behavior that may be indicative of intelligence gathering or preoperational planning related to terrorism, criminal, or other illicit intention."[4] Despite Tamerlan's being on both of those lists, he still left Boston's Logan Airport without a hitch.

Then there was the odd list of aliases Tsarnaev has used over the years. For example, among the names found in Tamerlan's declassified DHS US Citizenship and Immigration Services (USCIS) file were Anzorvich Tsarnaev, Tamerlan Tsarnaev, and Tamerlan Tsarnaeu (each of which had both of the birthdates above).

Finally, there was the name he used in Russia, the one he introduced himself by there: Muaz Tsarnaev (in tribute to a celebrated Dagestani rebel named

Emir Muaz)—which also appeared with both birthdates in his USCIS paper-work. After getting the FSB's letter, David Cedarleaf, the special agent in the counterterrorism unit of the FBI's Boston field office, had been assigned to conduct what the FBI called a "threat assessment" based on the information that FSB had shared with both the bureau and the agency regarding Tamerlan's and his mother's increasing extremism. Cedarleaf insisted that Tamerlan did not pose a threat and closed the case in June 2011, the FBI now says.

In the months before Tamerlan left Boston for Russia, Cedarleaf inter-viewed Tamerlan and his parents (Zubeidat and Anzor) and reported his findings, the Office of the Inspector General noted. He also reported that Cedarleaf did not contact Tamerlan's wife (Katherine Russell, also known as Karima Tsarnaeva)—at least, notes about any contact with her never became part of any official file. Nor did Cedarleaf visit the controversial Prospect Street mosque in Cambridge where Tamerlan prayed, despite its connections to radical Islamists—including its founder, Abdurahman M. Alamoudi, who would later be sentenced to twenty-three years in prison for, among other crimes, giving money to Al Qaeda leaders.

Still, none of Cedarleaf's findings from the March 2011 investigation into the Tsarnaevs, which the FBI would later say had been closed three months later, were shared—not with the police in Cambridge, where the Tsarnaevs lived, and not with the police in Boston, who ran the Boston Regional Intel-ligence Center. Cedarleaf didn't even share the information with his JTTF counterparts from the DHS or his local police partners. The FBI's Coun-terterrorism Division isn't called the "spook squad" for nothing. The agents in it operated in total autonomy, sometimes away from the prying eyes of their own bosses. Cedarleaf was part of an even more secretive unit nick-named "the red brigade," a tightknit crew with military backgrounds whose members worked and socialized together outside of the circles that most law enforcement officials worked in. They all happened to have reddish hair.

The Boston FBI field office sent a letter to the FSB dated August 28, 2011, through its legal attaché in Russia that its agents found "nothing deroga-tory" about the Tsarnaevs.[5] Still, inexplicably, despite any lack of derogatory information, Tamerlan Tsarnaev's name was added to TECS on May 22, 2011, by the customs agent from Boston assigned to the Joint Terrorism Task Force, Jim Bailey. Tamerlan's name was added with his correct date of birth: October 26, 1986. Russian counterterrorism officials added his name, and the multiple aliases that Russian law enforcement agencies had dug up for him, to the TIDE database in October 2011. A USCIS Form I-912, which would waive fees connected to processing an immigrant's naturalization, showed up in Tamerlan Tsarnaev's A-file. On the form, signed by Tamerlan Tsarnaev on August 28, 2012—just weeks after his return from Russia—there is a column "name of agency awarding benefit." Inexplicably, the name of that agency is redacted on the form. The "date benefit was awarded," however, was not. It reads: "APPX. 10/2011"—a month after the Waltham triple murders.

When Tamerlan left the United States for Russia just months later, his presence on those lists should have raised alarm bells. Somehow it didn't. Defense attorneys for Dzhokhar would soon make an accusation in a court filing, writing that "the FBI made more than one visit to talk with Anzor, Zubeidat and Tamerlan, questioned Tamerlan about his internet searches, and asked him to be an informant,"[6] a claim the FBI would quickly deny: "The FBI checked U.S. government databases and other resources to look for such things as derogatory telephone communications, possible use of online sites associated with the promotion of radical activity, associations with other persons of interest, travel history and plans, and education history. The FBI also interviewed Tamerlan Tsarnaev and family members. The FBI did not find any terrorism activity, domestic or foreign, and those results were provided to the foreign government in the summer of 2011."[7]

All of this was suspicious. No one would dismiss such detailed information about a man that seemed to be exactly the sort of dangerous person that FBI Director James Comey warned about, who posed the greatest threat to the US homeland: an American jihadi. The multiple names and dates of birth and Tamerlan's ability to travel to a hotbed of terrorism without an American passport while simultaneously being on two terror watch lists are extraordinary, especially since the FSB had specifically warned the FBI about him. Law enforcement officials in Massachusetts began to say that Tamerlan was an informant for the feds, a spy sent to Russia to help track and kill the men he was in contact with. They believed that he was working for the US government, motivated by the promise of citizenship.

These suspicions soon seemed to be corroborated. Plotnikov was tracked to a terrorist compound in Dagestan and killed. So was another militant with ties to radical Islam. And another man on counterterrorism officials' radar, Magomed Kartashov, the leader of an Islamic organization in Dagestan called Union of the Just, and his mother's second cousin—the man that Tamerlan had recorded his conversations with—would be prosecuted.

Shortly after the bombings, that cousin was jailed in a Russian penal colony, which is where the FBI tracked him down to interview him in the weeks after the Boston Marathon bombings.

———————

Muslim informants have become a controversial topic since 9/11. It is no secret that the same techniques the FBI used to flip informants in the drug wars were redirected toward finding so-called mosque crawlers to inform on radical Muslims after 9/11. The practice had led to multiple lawsuits filed by Muslims who said that police had infiltrated dozens of mosques and student groups, which was tantamount to unconstitutional profiling. When former NYPD Commissioner Ray Kelly was appointed under Mayor Rudolph Giuliani, he even created a secretive unit that operated alongside the Zone Assessment Unit, Intelligence Analysis Unit, and Cyber Intelligence Unit. It was called the Terrorist Interdiction Unit, and its purpose was to recruit Muslims who took the civil service test to become cops, pull them from the police academy, and turn them into undercover operatives.

These operatives, trained in espionage and surveillance with the help of the CIA, were nicknamed "rakers." They got their name because of their ability to scrape up information while blending into a mosque or Muslim community to observe anyone who might be espousing radical Islamic beliefs or plotting to commit an act of Islamic extremism. But the most useful tool used by counterterrorism investigators came to be dubbed "catch and capture," a practice in which an informant, the mosque crawler, was sent into a community under suspicion to "create" conversations about jihad or terrorism, and then that informant would "capture" the responses from investigative targets to report to the informant's handlers. The practice was effective. The vaunted NYPD Intelligence Division—working alongside intelligence officers in the NSA, caseworkers in the CIA, and agents in the FBI, with the help of Muslim patriots—uncovered jihadi-inspired plots and led to multiple criminal prosecutions.

Several of those types of plots involved the mosque where Tamerlan Tsarnaev underwent a transformation from a womanizing Euro trash party boy to a pious Muslim, albeit one who first picked up the Quran only in 2010, when he was twenty-four years old.

Tamerlan was a perfect candidate for recruitment by the US government. Broke, desperate for citizenship, and with a new wife and baby girl to take care of, he spoke fluent English, Russian, and a dialect of Chechen. And his mosque had long been a target for investigators because of its ties to the Muslim Brotherhood, along with convicted terrorists like Lady Al Qaeda Aafia Siddiqui, the MIT-trained neuroscientist who is currently serving an eighty-six-year federal sentence for trying to kill Americans in Afghanistan;[8] and Tarek Mehanna, a pharmaceutical student convicted in 2010 of an Al Qaeda–inspired plot to shoot up a Massachusetts mall.[9] Mehanna's codefendant, Ahmad Abousamra, fled to Syria after his indictment and remained on the FBI's list of ten most wanted terrorists until a drone strike targeting ISIS leaders killed him.

The Islamic Society of Boston was started in 1982 by a loose association of Muslim student organizations at Harvard University, Boston University, MIT, Northeastern University, Wentworth Institute, Suffolk University, and Tufts University. One of the students involved was Abdurahman Alamoudi, who would become the founder of the society's first mosque, at a building on Prospect Street that had been a Knights of Columbus hall. Alamoudi is currently serving twenty-three years for terrorism after being arrested in 2003 in London on US federal charges that he had funneled money to Al Qaeda. He eventually pleaded guilty to three charges of illegal financial transactions with the Libyan government, unlawful procurement of citizenship, impeding administration of the Internal Revenue Service, and receiving more than $500,000 in cash from Libyan officials as part of a bizarre plot to assassinate a Saudi prince.

Libyan leader Muammar Gaddafi wanted Prince Abdullah killed after a 2003 Arab League summit at which Gadhafi felt he had been insulted. At one point during the summit, Abdullah wagged a finger at Gadhafi and said, "Your lies precede you, while the grave is ahead of you."[10] Gadhafi determined that the prince had to die, and Alamoudi was convicted of helping plan his assassination. That conviction came as an embarrassment to Pentagon officials and two US administrations: as the founder of the American Muslim Council,

Alamoudi visited the White House during the administration of President Bill Clinton to promote a program that brought imams into the US military. He also participated in 2000 in a group discussion with Muslim activists in Texas and George W. Bush in 2000, during Bush's presidential campaign. He posed for selfies with both former US presidents.

Tamerlan was just the man to infiltrate a mosque that had long been in the crosshairs of federal counterterrorism investigators, law enforcement officials in Massachusetts say privately. And he was just the guy to help the fight against terrorism overseas in one of the most dangerous regions for Islamic extremists: his Mother Russia.

When Tamerlan flew to Russia in 2012, his name should have been flagged at Logan Airport. After all, he was on TIDE and TECS terrorist watch lists. His travel documents were an American permanent resident alien card that had been issued to him in 2007 and a passport issued in Kyrgyzstan in 2001 when he was fourteen, which would expire in August 2012.

He wasn't stopped at JFK for additional screening, and he wasn't stopped when he arrived in Moscow as a suspected terrorist. Before long the men at the mosque he attended and his Dagestani relatives gave him a different moniker—"the American"—and connected him with his mother's second cousin, the leader of the Union of the Just and the very man the FSB had warned both the CIA and the FBI about: Magomed Kartashov.

The Union of the Just did not outwardly preach the use of violence, but neither did its members condemn it. Magomed was outspoken about the United States and its involvement in the Middle East. And the Union of the Just shared the goals of mujahedin fighters in every hotbed of international terrorism: to impose Islamic law (*sharia*) worldwide and politically unify all Muslims in a caliphate.

Magomed had grown up across the street from Zubeidat Tsarnaev's grandmother and had known the Tsarnaev family when Tamerlan and Dzhokhar were small children. Since then he hadn't seen either boy, until Tamerlan showed up in the Kizylar region to visit with relatives and Magomed came over to say hello.

"I didn't recognize you, cousin," Magomed said, pulling Tamerlan into an embrace. Tamerlan was dressed "like an American," Magomed later recalled, wearing a long raincoat and eyeglasses, spectacles that he didn't need for reading. He slicked his hair back with olive oil and wore too much cologne for the pious Muslims who surrounded Magomed. "I haven't seen you since you were about ten. Wow. Big guy."[11]

All of those memories were gleaned from interviews conducted by the FBI in June 2013 at the Russian penal colony where Magomed was jailed for supporting terrorism, according to court records.

Tamerlan knew a lot about Magomed from his mother, who had been texting with him. He didn't wait long to ask Magomed to help him achieve the goal that had brought him to Russia. He told Magomed: "I want to go into the forests. I want to train. I want to go to Syria. I came here to get involved in jihad."

It sounded at first like boasting from a spoiled American. But Tamerlan was puffed up as if he had already been a mujahedin, and he told Magomed that he had followed one segment of the Quran that urged Muslims to follow orders like "cut off their heads and make them kneel in front of you." That is exactly what investigators believe happened to the three men in Waltham months earlier.

Magomed was stunned. To preach radical Islamic viewpoints that openly could get you killed in that part of Russia. This talk of Syria, where brutal young mujahedin were gaining a stronghold, was babble from someone who spent way too much time on the Internet being wooed by the slick propaganda and speeches from men like slain American Al Qaeda leader Anwar al-Awlaki.

"Brother, there is not jihad in the streets," Magomed told the FBI he had explained to his relative.

"How well do you even know Islam?" he asked, knowing that Tamerlan had hardly grown up in a pious family. After all, his mother had left Russia with a reputation of being a flighty overdressed woman with a big mouth. And his father Anzor had never been a devout Muslim, and was a bit whipped by his wife. He had been laughed at behind his back for letting Zubeidat run the show.

Besides, the family had always been "holiday only" Muslims, as Nadia Suleimanovak would tell the court that decided the fate of her cousin, Dzhokhar. "What I mean is they would celebrate the major holidays, Kurban Bayram, Uraza Bayram, but they wouldn't pray five times a day."[12]

Magomed was suspicious of Tamerlan's newfound devotion to Islam, asking him, "How many times a day do you pray?" They talked about the proper way to praise Allah five times a day and about nonviolent jihad, fighting against the Russian aggressors without bullets or bombs.

"I cannot argue with you," Tamerlan answered. He had seen the lectures Magomed had posted on YouTube, the ones disseminated by the Union of the Just. "I am not on your level."

Magomed then lectured him about Muhammad, who had been beaten mercilessly but never responded with violence: "You have to stop or you won't make it to the next tree."

The lectures Magomed gave Tamerlan in Russia were similar to the ones he posted online, where he pushed for the establishment of Islamic law inside of Russia and said that he desired the reestablishment of the Caliphate. A defense witness, Princeton University associate professor Michael Reynolds, who is an expert on the Middle East, would explain the goal of Magomed's Union of the Just this way: "the Caliphate was the political union of all Muslims. . . . And the Union of the Just seeks to recreate this political union of all Muslims throughout the world."[13] The Union of the Just, he explained, is affiliated with Hizb ut-Tahrir al-Islami (Islamic Party of Liberation), another group that espouses anti-Semitism and hatred for the west that also seeks the establishment of an international caliphate. Hizb ut-Tahrir al-Islami was classified by the Russian FSB as a terrorist organization in 2003. However, as of 2016 the US State Department had not yet declared Hizb ut-Tahrir al-Islami to be a terrorist organization.

Magomed was not a bomber or a beheader of infidels. But he certainly didn't condemn his Muslim brethren who used violence as a tool. Those men included Mamakaev Rizvan, the former husband of Tamerlan's sister Bella—another person whom the FSB had found was exchanging frightening text messages with his former mother-in-law supporting jihad. The FSB warned the FBI that Mamakaev was considered an extremist, a warning that the FBI would dismiss as questionable intelligence because the text messages had been obtained illegally.

Mamakaev was among the men who attended the Kotrova Street mosque, where Salafism was preached and a black flag now associated with ISIS hung over the door. It was known as a hotbed of terrorism and was constantly under surveillance by Russian antiterrorism agents. That's where Tamerlan had met Mamakaev for the drive into the rural area where Magomed lived. Tamerlan's mother had another former son-in-law who traveled with Tamerlan and Mamakaev on those visits—Elmirza Khozhugov, Ailina's former husband, to whom she had been introduced by her Uncle Ruslan.

Elmirza had stayed in touch with the Tsarnaev family because Ailina was raising his son, Ziyaudi (called Zia). In fact, he later recalled that the last time he had seen Zubeidat—at the airport where she dropped off his son in 2011—he had almost laughed in her face because she was wearing a hijab: "It made me laugh. I know that wearing these clothes isn't going to change her, the way she is actually. So I just saw it as an attempt to cover up what she had on her mind as if it could help."[14] Elmirza wanted his son to live with him, and he met with Tamerlan in Dagestan to see if his former brother-in-law could help make that happen. Together they drank coffee, gossiped about the family, and discussed Islam.

Neither of Tamerlan's former brothers-in-law nor his mother's cousin traveled with him to Georgia to attend an event run by the Jamestown Foundation, a think tank in Washington, D.C., that was created in 1984 by a former head of the CIA. Graham Fuller, the CIA agent with ties to Ruslan, contributed to the foundation as an analyst. So did Brian Glyn Williams, a former CIA agent who was then an associate professor of Islamic history at UMass/Dartmouth, the school Dzhokhar had enrolled in a year before, in September 2011.

Investigative reporters in Russia obtained a document—drafted by Colonel Grigory Chanturia of the main security service of the Georgian Ministry of Internal Affairs—that said Tamerlan had been spotted at the Jamestown event, run in conjunction with the Kavkaz. The Jamestown Foundation categorically rejected the Russian investigative reports, calling them "entirely false and groundless," and added: "Our organization has never had any contact with the Tsarnaev brothers, and we have no record or knowledge of either of them ever attending any Jamestown event in Washington, DC, or elsewhere."[15]

Nonetheless, when it came to the CIA and the Tsarnaev family there seemed to be a lot of coincidental overlaps. Glyn Williams even posted photos of his trip to Georgia that summer on the website,[16] where he boasted of his CIA past as a field operative in Afghanistan, Uzbekistan, and elsewhere in Central Asia in the early 2000s, calling himself an expert on suicide bombers. He told *South Coast Today*, a small Massachusetts newspaper, that he had been in touch with Dzhokhar Tsarnaev, who had e-mailed him to begin a discussion about Chechnya when he was still a high school student at Cambridge Rindge and Latin, saying: "That kid and his brother identified with the Chechen struggle."[17]

Like Fuller, Glyn Williams often sympathized with the struggles of Muslims in Russia's unrelenting fight against Islamic extremists—which, some argued, under Vladimir Putin was violent and overzealous. Those struggles would become common laments of Tamerlan that, before long, were echoed by his little brother, Dzhokhar.

————

With Tamerlan gone in Russia (Katherine had moved back in with her husband after living at home in Rhode Island for a short time), Katherine was alone with their baby, Anzor, and Zubeidat. Anzor was unraveling. His doctor, Alexander Niss, would later describe him as a "very sick man"[18] who suffered from panic attacks, anxiety, and post-traumatic stress disorder from his days growing up under the watchful eye of parents who had lived through the regime of Joseph Stalin. Zubeidat had claimed her husband had been tortured in a Soviet prison camp, and as a result he often hallucinated that KGB agents were following him, the same story that the couple had told US immigration officials in 2002 to get political asylum. In fact, they had then gone so far as to say that they would be killed if they ever returned to Russia.

Anzor was seeing a psychiatrist and taking a handful of pills every day: Trazodone to help him sleep; Zoloft, an antidepressant; Klonopin for panic attacks; and Zyprexa, an antipsychotic medication to treat his paranoia. On top of that, there was Provigil to counteract the zombie-like state the other medications put him in, a drug to provide "alertness," Niss explained. Some of the medications worked to counteract the injuries that Anzor said he had suffered during a brutal beating outside a Russian social club in 2009.

Anzor had been sipping Cognac at Arbat, a Russian deli not far from Wai Kru, Tamerlan's gym. One night a week Arbat operated as a clandestine illegal (because it didn't have a permit to sell alcohol) social club for Russian expatriates. Anzor was drinking alone when a Russian came up to him and demanded that he apologize for bumping a woman's chair. Anzor told Tamerlan the story from his bed at Massachusetts General Hospital, and his son then went to the Boston police to report his father's assault. "My father said, 'I'm not apologizing. I didn't do it,'" Tamerlan reported.[19] The unknown man then took the fight outside. Anzor was "punched in the back of the head, and then attacked by the large group including a couple of females," Tamerlan told BPD detectives. Anzor spent a week in the hospital and was never the same afterward.

The beating left Anzor broken, and Zubeidat became bossier than ever. A short time later she underwent a complete metamorphosis, eschewing the fashion she loved for shapeless long clothes and a black head scarf. Anzor couldn't take it. The couple divorced in August 2011, according to family court records in Middlesex County, but continued to live together.

Zubeidat always had some plan to make money on the side, while simultaneously collecting government assistance—whether it was a home health care job under the table or giving facials in her apartment, without a license. One of her clients remembered her as funny, swearing at an appointment in 2011. She always had a jar of quarters near her aesthetician chair so clients could feed the parking meters. A month later, "she was saying that her son taught her the government attacked the World Trade Center towers and she was wearing a burka," the client said.[20]

Despite their claims that a return to Russia would be a death sentence, Anzor went back to Dagestan in June 2012, and has since stayed there. A month later, back in Massachusetts, Zubeidat ran into some legal trouble. She was arrested for shoplifting $1,600 in expensive clothing from the Lord and Taylor's department store at the upscale Natick Mall. It seemed a good time for her to leave town, so she went to Dagestan in July—"covered," to use the Islamic term. When her former son-in-law Elmirza saw her, he had to stifle a laugh at her new look and Islamist attitude. "She didn't even know how to cover properly," he would remember. "Her daughters don't know anything about Islam."[21] It was a joke. Still, Zubeidat was his elder, and he showed her the proper respect. Everyone did, even Magomed Kartashov, the respected leader of the Union of the Just.

Sometime in July Tamerlan and Magomed were chatting on their cells when Zubeidat took Tamerlan's phone. She had a request for her cousin: "Take care of my son."[22]

With Tamerlan, Anzor, and Zubeidat gone, Katherine Russell and her daughter were alone in the apartment. Bella and Ailina were living with new boyfriends or in homeless shelters, depending on the day. Dzhokhar was living in a dorm at UMass/Dartmouth, selling weed on campus with two Russian buddies, Dias Kadyrbayev and Azamat Tazhayakov—both sons of rich parents who had sent their sons to the United States for a better education than they could get in Russia. Azamat even drove a brand-new BMW 330xi with a UMass bookstore vanity plate affixed to the front that read "Terrorista." They also smoked weed with two Eritrean brothers who had graduated from Cambridge Rindge and Latin with Dzhokhar, the twins Stephen and Steven Silva, and an Ethiopian American named Robel Phillipos. (The Silvas' mother would explain why she gave her sons the same name with different spellings by haughtily remarking to a Cambridge police officer that Stephen was pronounced Steff-an, two law enforcement sources recalled.) The Silva twins and Phillipos lived in the same Cambridge high-rise building, ironically over the gas station to which the carjacking victim Dun Meng would escape on the morning of April 19, 2013, before the wild Watertown shootout. On July 4, 2012—just before Zubeidat left Cambridge for good—Dzhokhar celebrated his independence outside a house party in Arlington with Stephen and a man from the Bronx. They sat in Dzhokhar's green Honda, talking and throwing beer cans out the window, until an Arlington police officer showed up. The cop took their names and wrote Dzhokhar a citation for having an open container of alcohol in his vehicle. Of course, the officer had no idea that Dzhokhar was asking Stephen to get him a gun, along with "food for the dog"—bullets.[23] Dzhokhar wanted to rob some rival drug dealers who went to a Rhode Island college, he told Silva. Silva knew some Eritrean drug dealers in Portland, Maine, who were connected to his friend "Icy"—the same narcotics traffickers who were targeted in Operation Run This Town—who could get Dzhokhar a gun. When the Arlington cop showed up, the conversation stopped temporarily. They were spooked.

Through it all Dzhokhar stayed in touch with his brother in Russia, at least via e-mail. Tamerlan sent him online links and materials about the jihad in Chechnya and Dagestan and the mujahedin's interpretation of Islam.

Tamerlan was mired in extremist rhetoric and patriotism for his homeland. His screensaver was a picture of Makhachkala, the capital of Dagestan. The password for the files he kept encrypted, away from prying eyes or government spies, was AllahAkbar. Tamerlan e-mailed his brother about going "into the forests." Dzhokhar kept his replies short, too stoned to really care. "Sounds interesting," he wrote in one.[24]

Katherine Russell stayed busy, too. Tamerlan had told her that he was only going to be in Russia for a few weeks, but then he called her and said that his passport had been stolen and he had to stay in Dagestan to fill out the new paperwork. She spent much of her time, courtroom testimony would later show, searching the Internet using phrases like "can women become shaheed," "nasheed jihad," "wife of mujahedeen," and "what are the rewards for wives of mujahedeen?" She was trying to find out what kind of rewards she had coming as the wife of a martyred jihadi.

Magomed Kartashov was in a Russian penal colony when the Boston Marathon was bombed, having been arrested for fighting with police not long after his third cousin had recorded their conversations and left the country. As he watched the footage of the attack, he immediately thought of Tamerlan, he would tell the FBI in the weeks after the deadly blasts, during an interview that took place at the penal colony. One of the last things Tamerlan had said to him, Magomed told the FBI, was: "You have convinced my head but my heart still wants to do something."

After Tamerlan returned to the United States in July 2012, he stayed in touch with Magomed using the Russian social networking site VK (that country's version of Facebook), on which he opened an account using Muaz, the name he used in Russia and the one he would try to legally make his American name on January 23, 2013, according to his USCIS file. The last time Magomed spoke to Tamerlan was via Skype sometime in early March 2013. In that call, Tamerlan complained that he had become a stay-at-home dad while his wife worked full time, under the table, while simultaneously collecting taxpayer subsidies including free rent, food stamps, and EBT cash from an ATM card. "I'm home all day watching the kid, or I'm training at the gym," Tamerlan said.[25]

He then complained about two public arguments he had had with an imam at his Cambridge mosque. In November the imam talked about American holidays being celebrated by Muslims, and Tamerlan lost his cool, stood up, and shouted: "That is not allowed in the faith!" The second time Tamerlan was escorted out of the mosque after the imam lectured about Martin Luther King and compared him to the Prophet Muhammad. "You're a kuffar! You are contaminating peoples' minds! Hypocrite! Hypocrite!" The congregation had tired of Tamerlan's antics and drowned out his words with shouts of "leave now!" Leaders of the mosque told him that one more such incident would ban him from the mosque for life.

"Why do you need to do that?" Magomed asked, shaking his head in the Skype call. "Why do you keep getting into that kind of trouble?" Tamerlan didn't answer him. That was their last call. Magomed had no idea that all those conversations in Russia were being recorded on Tamerlan's laptop, recordings that would later be discovered by investigators.

In a legal brief the government called the recordings "extremely difficult to understand even in translation. They appear to consist of several men talking about religious issues, including the proper form in which to do jihad, which can be violent or non-violent depending on one's religious philosophy."[26] But no one ever explained why Tamerlan was recording his conversations with Magomed in the first place.

Then came the bombings on Boylston Street.

"I saw everything on Russian television," Magomed told the two FBI special agents who visited the penal colony where he was being held on June 5, 2013. The FSB had already been there to interview him weeks earlier.

"I had a thought," Magomed said to the FBI agents. "It could have been Tamerlan. When Tamerlan arrived in Russia he was already thinking about jihad and looking to do something."

He explained to the FBI agents that the videos of the American Al Qaeda cleric Anwar al-Awlaki and the posts on the Kavkaz Center had inspired Tamerlan long before he traveled to Dagestan. Then Magomed mentioned Tamerlan's going to visit a friend in Utamysh, Dagestan, "in the forests." That visit did not end well for Tamerlan's friend Plotnikov.

10

INTO THE FORESTS

In July 2012, Tamerlan Tsarnaev likely traveled to Utamysh, a small village in the Kayakent District of Dagestan, Russia, not far from the Caspian Sea. He wanted to see his longtime Internet friend, a man whom he had exchanged ideas with online as part of a group called World Association of Muslim Youth, someone whom he had texted repeatedly—so often that the text messages had raised alarms within Russian anti-insurgency circles. A one-time champion boxer and student at Seneca University in Toronto, the Russian-born man had been reported missing by his parents in Canada. But the man, William Plotnikov, wasn't missing at all. He was training to be a terrorist in the Caucasus Emirate, alongside a militant group in a mountainous region of southern Russia that the US State Department had added to its list of foreign terrorist organizations in 2011 because of its allegiance to Al Qaeda. All of the group's militant jihadis shared the goal of expelling non-Muslim Russians from the region and establishing an Islamic state.

Tamerlan and Plotnikov had a lot in common. In Dagestan Plotnikov was called "the Canadian," and many people had taken to calling Tamerlan "the American." Both were obsessed with mixed martial arts fighting. Both had earned championship titles in boxing. Both spoke English and Russian fluently. And both had developed a Westerner's fascination with online Islamic extremism through lectures from Anwar al-Awlaki and Tamerlan's relative Magomed Kartashov.

Like Tamerlan, Plotnikov had once been just another Euro trash teenager in a big city, clad in designer clothing, well spoken and traveled—a man who dated local women and ate at posh restaurants. Plotnikov's first name alone, unusual for parents giving birth to a boy in 1989 at a Siberian hospital in the former Soviet Union, hinted at the Western life that his parents envisioned for their only son. Calling him William was an indication of the Plotnikovs' determination to flee the burgeoning violence in their homeland for better opportunities in North America. Still, his parents did the best they could with him until they could leave. By the time Plotnikov was fifteen, he had twice been a Russian youth champion fighter. That made his parents proud, of course, but it also made him a target for underworld gangs. So in 2005, William's father, Vitaly Plotnikov, quit his job as an oil industry executive and moved the family to Toronto. He was willing to stock supermarket shelves to keep his son away from the criminal element in his homeland, he would tell reporters in Canada and the United States. Young, strong athletes were perfect recruits for criminal crews.[1]

Nevertheless, while his parents were vacationing in Florida in 2010, Plotnikov slipped out of Canada and into Chechnya, his father later told the *National Post* of Canada.[2] Plotnikov would later tell his parents that he had finally found something outside the boxing ring to fight for: radical Islam. He and Tamerlan were among the hundreds of Westerners recruited on jihadi Internet sites, where they became so inspired that they joined the jihad. FBI Director James Comey has since said ISIS has managed to recruit 250 Americans who were willing to travel overseas to work for the caliphate.[3] Comey has also said that there are aspiring jihadis under twenty-four-hour surveillance in all fifty states.[4]

In three short years Plotnikov had become a dangerous man, a trained killer who had earned the admiration of the men that he now lived and trained with in Dagestan. Now twenty-three, he was wiry and strong, his sinewy muscles honed in the boxing ring and by the rugged life of the camps. His training in mixed martial arts skills had given him keen instincts. Any man on watch outside the Utamysh compound ordinarily had a machine gun slung over his shoulder. They considered themselves soldiers of the Caliphate and trained like any other military. They were always at the ready.

Since he had run away from his parents in Canada three years earlier, Plotnikov had become the type of man his family had tried to protect him from:

a fanatic, a thug, a Muslim mujahedin who burned with such a white-hot hatred for strangers that it led to inexplicable bloodshed all over the world.

———

Like in Utamysh, Plotnikov was known as the Canadian in the online chat rooms where he had found Allah and converted to Islam, and on jihadi online portals where he began to post videos that showed the once clean-shaven and reserved young man with a scraggly beard and a sinister smile. In one of the videos, narrated by Plotnikov and shot in what appeared to be a well-stocked bunker, he offered up a prayer that he would have the opportunity to kill infidels, nonbelievers like his own parents.[5]

In one scene Plotnikov turns the camera on himself and in Russian espoused alarmingly violent views.

> We are not suffering, we are not in need. We need only Allah's
> help and he does not leave us, his servants. We have food, we have
> someone to make that food and there are other brothers who
> perform their duties and this will be rewarded.
>
> And therefore non-believers you will never see what you would
> like to see. We have food. Allah is with us, we have our guardian,
> Allah, but you do not have one. We will kill you, We are not
> superheroes, we are also in need of Allah's help and he is helping us
> and I am asking Allah that by next spring he gives us an opportunity
> to kill more non-believers, so the military trucks blow into pieces, fly
> around like rags. Allah is almighty and he will assist.[6]

He could have just as easily said those words in English or French. He still had traces of the middle-class young man he had been with a Western education, a closet crammed with designer ensembles, a quick wit, and the nickname "Willy." In high school he had talked about joining the Canadian army. Now he was living in the woods undergoing terrorism training. Chechen rebels have been found fighting alongside Al Qaeda insurgents all over the world. In fact, one such terrorist trained in Chechnya was Nawaf Alhazmi, who boarded American Airlines Flight 11 on the morning of September 11, 2001, and with his younger brother, Salem Alhazmi, slit the throats of two flight attendants as the plane left Logan Airport and hurtled toward the World Trade Center towers with Muhammad Atta at the controls, according to the *9/11 Commission Report.*[7]

Plotnikov, and the others training in the woods, had been trained that nonbelievers, infidels, were all those who did not embrace radical Islam or sharia. Even moderate Muslims were the enemy. Certainly Plotnikov had not been raised Muslim. His father had been born an Armenian Christian. His mother, a Ukrainian Tatar, practiced Russian Orthodox Christianity, unlike many of her fellow Tartars, who were Sunni Muslim. The couple had baptized their son as a Christian. When Plotnikov was nineteen, his parents became members of the Jehovah's Witnesses. Kaffirs, in the mind of their son.

Back in Canada, a friend of his had alerted Plotnikov's parents to the videos, and they were alarmed. His father would later describe the difficult decision he was forced to make. His son was clearly headed down a dangerous and disturbing path, and Vitaly Plotnikov knew that some members of the FSB were notoriously brutal to Muslim insurgents. Tracking down his son could put him in even more danger with the Russian antiterrorism forces, but it was a choice he felt he had to make. Investigators from the Royal Canadian Mounted Police took their missing person's report and shared it with the FSB in early 2011.

"The Canadian" would not be hard for the FSB to locate. Even after he shed his expensive clothing for camouflage, he stuck out among the Chechens in Dagestan. Plotnikov was picked up and interrogated after his father called the Royal Canadian Mounted Police, who contacted their counterterrorism counterparts in Russia. But there was not a lot Russian investigators could do. Plotnikov had every right to be in the country. He was Russian by birth, and the missing person's report filed his parents would not be enough to compel him to go home. Certainly, his Internet activity was a concern, but not a crime. The FSB demanded that Plotnikov give its agents the names of all of his contacts in Canada and the United States who were English-speaking Russian natives and who, like him, identified with the beliefs of the Caucasus Emirate. Some of those contacts came from the online network World Association of Muslim Youth, whose website was riddled with propaganda from Al Qaeda sympathizers.

One of the people Plotnikov named was Tamerlan Tsarnaev.

Instead of being scared into coming home after the FSB interrogation as his parents had hoped, Plotnikov slipped back "in the forests." The last time his family had heard from him, his father told a Canadian reporter, was an exchange of messages on VK.[8] A year before his death and after he had been questioned by the FSB, he contacted his parents to ask for money. According to a transcript of the conversation posted by the *Wall Street Journal*, he then chastised them for posting photos of his mother "half-naked on the beach" and added, "Praise to Allah, Lord of the Worlds."

"It has turned out that our understanding of life has diverged. We have to accept this and that we don't understand each other. I understand you already. I hope that you understand me someday and accept me. Forgive me for disappointing you," Plotnikov wrote. "My life changed so accept me as I am."

His father responded with gratitude: "Thank you for writing Willy." Then he added: "There's no need for fanaticism. . . . If you want to devote your life to your faith, then join a religious school or preach in a mosque. . . . Mom removed the photos. . . . We miss you."

"Dad, my life isn't compatible with the people who live in sinful America," Plotnikov wrote.

The elder Plotnikov logged onto the site repeatedly to message his son, with his last message reading, "Are you coming home?"

There was no answer, but he learned his son's fate from the site when some of "Willy's" friends sent condolence messages in the hours after he died.

———————

As darkness descended over the Utamysh compound on a night in mid-July 2012, Plotnikov was likely exhausted. Camps like the one he lived in were comparable to Marine training sites like Combat Town at Camp Lejeune, in North Carolina. Only at the terrorist training camps in Dagestan and Chechnya, the focus was on building bombs and hitting civilian targets. On this night, Plotnikov's fingertips likely ached from the tedious task of rewiring tiny toy car parts and remote controls until they became ignitions for pressure-cooker bombs, and his shoulders probably ached from the weight of machine guns even after he put them down. His feet were sure to have throbbed from long runs. He had slimmed down since leaving Canada—hearty food in the forests was scarce.

Maybe if he hadn't been so tired, Plotnikov would have heard the counterterrorism forces approach. The international soldiers and Russian intelligence agents and police officers made their way to the carefully hidden compound in a convoy of five-ton troop carriers. They even brought a small light armored tank, knowing the men inside were heavily armed. The raid had been well planned, and those in charge wanted to ensure it was well executed.

Plotnikov's hide-out, a small farmhouse, was home to seven other mujahedin, guerrilla fighters who had all vowed to bring sharia back to Russia's Northern Caucasus. They flew their own nationalist flag and consistently referred to Russian authorities as "invaders." Two of the men that Plotnikov had been training with, Islam and Arsen Magomedov, were not just guerrilla insurgents. The men were notorious terrorists, commanders of the region's most brutal criminal gangs, and suspected in orchestrating dozens of murders and deadly bombings of police checkpoints, civilian-filled trains, and Russian Federation television stations.

Along with the Magomedovs were five other men who ranged in age from twenty-five to thirty-five, budding jihadists who had had very few other prospects when they left their families than to go "into the forests." In comparison, Plotnikov had led a privileged life.

After a long day, the other seven men went to bed and left the Canadian standing guard, completely unaware that just outside the tiny village, under the cover of darkness, a raid was being prepared that would level their camp.

Russian Interior Ministry counterterrorism forces wanted to move in without being seen by the prying eyes of Utamysh villagers, so they had evacuated some women and children living near the camp. Not everyone in the Muslim village supported the continuing carnage in their region, but most completely distrusted Russian Federation law enforcement officials. As in most military operations, the men moved as silently as possible as they carefully checked their guns and grenades, switched the safeties off automatic weapons, and even loaded a small rocket-propelled grenade. They wore combat gear, and not for aesthetic reasons. Inside the hide-out were some of the most violent men in the Northern Caucasus, an area that has long been one of the most volatile and lawless places in the world. At that time, it was not unusual for a Russian police officer to be assassinated every week. The insurgents inside the Utamysh compound had been trained to believe that the Russians were aggressors, invaders who—like pigs—deserved nothing less than slaughter, and they had been taught that there was no greater honor than to die taking a Russian out.

Plotnikov had already dealt with the FSB and had been given a chance to return to his comfortable life to Canada. He had refused. The Russian Federation forces outside the farmhouse were not going to give him a second chance and knew it was unlikely that the Canadian would surrender. Nor would any of his comrades inside, not even when they heard dried dirt and rocks being crushed under the tracks of the tank and the wheels of the troop carriers that brought the enemy from the command post in a valley outside of Utamysh to their front door, according to a video that was later released by the Russian Interior Ministry. When the first bullets were fired, the mujahedin grabbed their own guns, prayed that Allah would give them strength in battle, and fired.

The village was lit up with tracer rounds and bombs for hours, the video would show.

When the sun rose over the mountains on July 14, 2012, all seven of the Islamic militants were dead. The Russians photographed their slain bodies lying in the scrubby grass as proof of their deaths.

The camp was a smoldering shell. Cars belonging to the insurgents were still burning. The walls of the farmhouse were pitted with gunfire, and its windows had all been blown out. Russian Federation counterterrorism coalition forces also lost a man: an officer with the Russian Interior Ministry. Three other Russian agents had been wounded.

Overall, however, the mission was a considered a success.

The Russian Interior Ministry's National Anti-Extremism Center (NAC) released a statement that praised the Utamysh killings and hinted at how the terrorist enclave had been discovered. "We received information about their possible movements from an informant," the statement, posted on the now-defunct Kavkaz.org, read. Kavkaz.org—a news portal for the Caucasus Emirate which at the time was run by the late Doku Umarov, the man known internationally as Russia's Osama bin Laden—also released an online statement about the dead, but it celebrated their martyrdom: "May Allah reward all the brothers, who sincerely believed in the promise of their Creator, with gardens of Firdaws, and exchange this transitory world to the eternal Paradise."[9] These gardens, the mujahedin believed, were the highest form of paradise for the martyred.

Interestingly, the statement also mentioned the informant who had led the Russian Federation "invaders" to the remote hide-out: "Invaders have announced that they identified the personalities of Mujahedeen killed near the village of Utamysh. According to the Russian aggressors, mujahedeen got into an ambush because of a tip from an informant."

As the farmhouse smoldered, the militants mourned, and the Russian Interior Ministry prepared to bury its dead agent, one man left the region, paying 2,050 euros for a one-way Aeroflot ticket from Sheremetyevo International Airport in Moscow to JFK, and then to Logan Airport on July 17, 2012. Investigators found a receipt for the ticket in Tamerlan Tsarnaev's bedroom on Norfolk Street and photographed it as evidence. It remains unclear how the unemployed twenty-six-year-old on welfare paid for the flight.

11

THE INFORMANTS

High-level generals in the Pentagon and CIA agents likely exchanged classified intelligence regarding the successful Russian raid in the Northern Caucasus. The region had become an international problem not just because of persistent internecine war between Chechens and the Russian Federation, but also because of its geography. It is located at Europe's doorway into Asia and contains critical oil and gas pipelines. World leaders were interested in Russian oil, and many of them paid attention when seven armed militants with a history of targeting civilians in Chechnya and Dagestan were killed in the troubled Caucasus. Any reduction in the number of Islamic insurgents there was indeed something to crow about.

If the informant who had been partly responsible for the deaths was tied to the United States, as many people believed—flipped into cooperating by foreign counterintelligence agents from the CIA, DHS, Immigration and Customs Enforcement (ICE), NSA, or FBI—some officials could be catapulted to higher-level jobs at the Department of Justice or the Pentagon, or maybe even into higher-paying private-sector ones in the lucrative defense industry, as a result.

Ironically, it may have very well been Plotnikov himself who helped to turn the informant, when he gave the FBS a list of names of the men he had exchanged jihadist ideals with online. One of those men was Tamerlan Tsarnaev—as noted above, a celebrated bilingual boxer born in Russia, just like Plotnikov. Another was a notorious nineteen-year-old jihadist recruiter named Mahmud Mansour Nidal.[1]

Nidal had been under surveillance by the United States for months.[2] And he had been marked as one of Russia's most wanted men after being accused of recruiting a brother and sister to serve as suicide bombers in one of the bloodiest attacks attributed to his ragtag group of insurgents. The bombers drove vehicles packed with explosives into a police checkpoint in Dagestan. The brother detonated the first blast. His sister followed, but only after emergency responders had arrived. Fourteen people were killed and dozens more wounded, according to Russia's National Antiterrorism Committee. After the blasts, Nidal went underground. So Russian counterterrorism officials building the case against him were surprised when he showed up in May at the Al-Nadiriya Mosque on Kotrova Street in Makhachkala—the main Salafi mosque in Dagestan's capital—and chatted with Tamerlan, the man they had identified as "the American." The mosque was so brazen about its affiliation with extremist terrorism that its imam allowed the black flag of jihad to be hung just inside its doors. Multiple reports citing Russian sources say that Tamerlan was put under surveillance during his trip by counterterrorism officials after he was spotted meeting with Nidal multiple times near the mosque. And on May 19, 2012, Nidal died. He had been tracked to his hideout and cut down in a blaze of gunfire after he launched a grenade at the counterterrorism forces that were trying to arrest him. A video of the standoff posted on YouTube shows that a crowd of Nidal's supporters surrounded the counterterrorism forces and shouted "Allah Akbar" (God is great) at the masked commandos, urging them to repent of their sins.[3]

At a Congressional hearing after the Boston Marathon bombing, Congressman William Keating referred to Tamerlan's meeting with Nidal and the fact that one of the most wanted men in Russia surprisingly emerged from hiding to meet with the American at the mosque several times in May: "He [Tamerlan] was meeting with a known terrorist insurgent Mahmoud Nidal; someone already on their radar screen in Russia. . . . Now he came back to the US after the person he met with reportedly was killed, and the other person who was known to him was killed. So he sort of beat feet [made tracks] and went home."[4]

The purpose of the FBI's and CIA's placing Tamerlan on two terror watch lists—and TIDE—was to create an alert any time he traveled. But inexplicably, that did not happen when he landed in the United States after spending six months overseas in a terrorist hotspot. Then there was the question of his passport, which he had reported stolen—or at least that's what he told Katherine Russell. "He told Katherine that he had been robbed, his papers had been robbed, and he needed a new passport," her landlord, Joanna Herlihy, said.[5]

Tamerlan's father, Anzor, would tell the *New York Times* an entirely different story. "His passport was about to expire in June or in July [actually, in August] and that is why I said, 'You have to get a Russian passport.' Because we left Kyrgyzstan for the States to seek political asylum in the States and Kyrgyzstan refused us citizenship," Anzor explained to a reporter from his home in Dagestan, where he was living with his divorced wife after the Boston Marathon bombings.[6] The last valid passport that Tamerlan possessed came from the Kyrgyz Republic, where he had been born, and was slated to expire on August 11, 2012.

Tamerlan applied for a Russian passport to replace the one issued in Kyrgyzstan that he had used to gain entry into the United States as political refugee in 2002. But, as Congressional investigators would find, he left Russia without picking the new passport up.

"I was here at that time and went there [to an office to apply for the passport] together with him," Anzor said. "We gathered documents and he had to wait. It's not done instantly, some time passes, up to six months, maybe three or four months. He left Russia on a Kyrgyz passport because we came from Kyrgyzstan; we have Kyrgyz passport. We were in Kyrgyzstan. His Kyrgyz passport was about to expire, and he did not have time to get a Russian passport."

The *New York Times* reporter then asked Anzor why Tamerlan needed a Russian passport when he had a US green card. "He did not have American citizenship," Anzor said. "The Kyrgyz passport was about to expire, and if it expired then the man finds himself without citizenship, without anything. He would not be able to go anywhere, neither in Russia nor anywhere."

But when Tamerlan landed at Boston's Logan Airport on July 17, 2012, he had no problem whatsoever. A customs agent "scanned Tsarnaev's Alien

Registration Card [green card] into the computer system . . . and admitted him into the country based on his LPR [legal permanent resident] status," according to the Office of the Inspector General for the Intelligence Community. This was the very loophole in immigration laws that the 9/11 Commission had said needed to be closed. Even more alarmingly, the report states, the customs agent, Jim Bailey, told investigators "he cannot recall" if he alerted the FBI regarding Tamerlan's return to the United States without a passport: CBP [Customs and Border Protection] officers, he explained to the inspectors, communicate with the FBI about potential terrorist watch list suspects' travel with "email, orally or via 'sticky note.'"[7]

Surely to stop Tamerlan at the airport for additional screening based on his physical profile alone—he was a Muslim male with a long beard—or because he was leaving a terrorist hotbed would have been insensitive racial profiling. But the idea that a man whose name was on two terrorist watch lists somehow managed to clear customs because, government officials claimed, his name was misspelled on those lists is inconceivable. This is especially true given the multimillion-dollar computer program the DHS had purchased to prevent that very sort of thing from occurring. Even after the Russians had inexplicably notified the United States in writing about the American's radicalization, he was able to travel to a terrorist hotspot and return without being questioned.

Certainly if he was the informant who helped arrest high-level terror targets or provoke deadly encounters between them and counterterrorism forces in Russia, then only a small handful of intelligence agents and DHS officials would know his identity, or even his code number as a human source. Of course, none of them would ever discuss it publicly. They would not earn the front-page headlines like those awarded to informants at the center of Mafia takedowns, nor would any federal agent involved with Tamerlan be publicly lauded at a press conference. But they would have earned prestige and recognition at the highest level of the Department of Justice and the DHS.

Additionally, history shows that Tamerlan was not the first federal informant to go rogue.

The DHS secretary at the time of the Boston Marathon blasts, Janet Napolitano, was grilled about lapses at a Senate Judiciary Committee Hearing on immigration in April 2013. Napolitano said that even though Tsarnaev's name had been misspelled, redundancies in the DHS computer system allowed US authorities to be aware of his departure from the country in January 2012. But she said that by the time he came back six months later, an FBI alert on him had expired, so his reentry was not noted. "The system pinged when he was leaving the United States. By the time he returned all investigations had been closed," Napolitano testified.[8]

Senator Richard Blumenthal, a Democrat from Connecticut, pushed her for more answers and got this reply: "There's a lot of misinformation out there as to the two brothers. And of course this is an ongoing criminal investigation, so all threads are being followed." Napolitano mentioned a classified briefing scheduled for that very week and added, "Let's have that briefing and then see what, if any, questions arise at that point that may have any relevance at all to immigration legislation." Senator Charles Grassley asked Napolitano how a misspelling could have caused problems with Tamerlan's return to the United States in 2012 when the Implementing Recommendations of the 9/11 Commission Act of 2007 had amended certain sections of the Immigration and Naturalization Act pertaining to the control of foreign nationals' travel. The 2007 law reiterated the need for exit data and required that such data be collected on all foreign nationals who entered the United States under the visa waiver program with the provision that air carriers are required to "collect and electronically transmit" passenger "arrival and departure" data to "the automated entry and exit control system" developed by the federal government. Clearly, according to Napolitano's testimony, that didn't happen. Inexplicably, once again she was willing to answer only in a classified setting. "It would be better," Napolitano told Grassley at the hearing, "if we could discuss those with you in a classified setting."

Whatever information was in Tamerlan's immigration records, the DHS secretary was not at liberty to talk about it. That was a staggering admission, especially after the DHS had been forced to release Tamerlan's Alien File pursuant to a Freedom of Information Act request filed by multiple news organizations, including the *Boston Globe,* in February 2016. The request was made three years earlier and was steadfastly stalled by DHS until after

Tamerlan's younger brother had been sentenced to death. Even with dozens of pages completely redacted, along with redaction of the names of federal agencies that requested Tamerlan Tsarnaev receive citizenship (and waive any fees for the application process) the immigration file still contained troubling information.[9]

First, there were multiple names and dates of birth (mentioned above) that Tamerlan had used. Then there were the two State Department Medical Examination for Immigration or Refugee Applicant forms, which had startling discrepancies. In one, as discussed above, the attached picture was of a blue-eyed man wearing a black-collared polo shirt and contained a passport number. In the second, the picture was of a teenage Tamerlan wearing an identical shirt, and in that case the passport number had been redacted. The other troubling form seems innocuous at first glance. It was Tamerlan's notification of the time and place for his taking the oath of citizenship. He was told to report to 170 Portland Street in Boston on October 16, 2012, so he could finally become an American citizen, even though he was ineligible for US citizenship.

It remains unclear if Tamerlan showed up at 170 Portland Street and what happened if he did show up. But the document certainly suggested that someone was pulling strings to help him obtain the very thing he had been craving so desperately since 2009.

But Janet Napolitano could no longer be compelled to answer questions about this information. She quit her job at the DHS months after the Boston Marathon bombings, and at the time of this writing is the president of the University of California. In May 2016 her official portrait was hung in the DHS's headquarters.[10]

Representative Michael McCaul noted the inconsistencies repeatedly as federal lawmakers tried to make sense of the Boston Marathon attack. That event would be the deadliest on American soil since 9/11 until another American, Syed Farook, and his wife, Tashfeen Malik, murdered fourteen people at a Christmas party in San Bernardino, California, in 2015. And then in June 2016, an ISIS devotee, Omar Mateen, murdered forty-nine people at a gay nightclub in Orlando, Florida. In one of his 911 calls to authorities, Mateen "gave a shoutout to the Tsarnaev brothers," the FBI said. In fact, Mateen told an Orlando police hostage negotiator that the mass murder was sparked by the US bombing of an ISIS leader in Syria and that the "US is collaborating with Russia and they are killing innocent women and children," according to a transcript of that phone call, one of many Mateen had with the negotiator during the bloodbath. "My homeboy Tamerlan Tsarnaev did his thing on the Boston Marathon . . . okay, so now it's my turn."[11]

It remains unclear what Mateen's connections to the Chechens were, or whether he knew Ibragim Todashev, who told investigators that he and Tamerlan had murdered three men in Waltham, Massachusetts, on September 11, 2011—the same day that Ibragim packed up and moved to Orlando. Like Tamerlan, the FBI had multiple interactions with Omar Mateen, and like Tamerlan, the FBI would have closed the threat assessment investigation into Mateen—despite a call from the owner of a gun shop just weeks before the Orlando massacre alerting the FBI that Mateen had attempted unsuccessfully to buy body armor but had succeeded in purchasing a large number of bullets.

Tamerlan Tsarnaev clearly did not become a citizen on that October day when he was summoned by USCIS to attend his oath ceremony. To this day the DHS will not explain whether he attended that October oath ceremony or if something happened to disrupt the promise of citizenship. What is clear, however, is that in the weeks after that scheduled appearance, the FBI continued to email immigration officials prodding them to approve Tamerlan's citizenship application, according to the Office of the Inspector General's report. And although Tamerlan's 2009 arrest for domestic violence made him ineligible for US citizenship for five years, as noted above—because he had committed an act of "moral turpitude"—inexplicably his naturalization application was reopened on August 28, 2012.[12]

Also in the USCIS file was a form sent to Tamerlan telling him he was scheduled to take the oath of citizenship on October 16, 2012, which would have meant an impossibly short turnaround for a naturalization application opened just months earlier. Clearly something went wrong, and many would say that the gaffe would expose how far the FBI was willing to go to help Tamerlan.

On October 22, 2012—days after the initial oath ceremony for Tamerlan was somehow scuttled—a USCIS officer emailed David Cedearleaf, the FBI's special agent in the Boston field office's counterterrorism unit, saying that

Tamerlan's name had popped up on the terrorist watch lists and asking if he "represented a national security concern." The next day, on October 23, 2012, Cedarleaf, who was also the special agent in Boston assigned to investigate Tamerlan after the FSB warning in 2011, assured USCIS officials in writing that Tamerlan was deserving of full citizenship: "There is no national security concern related to [Tamerlan Tsarnaev] and nothing that I know of that should preclude issuance of whatever is being applied for." Cedarleaf would tell officials that he did not remember whether he searched Tamerlan Tsarnaev's file or public sources before he replied to the USCIS official.[13]

To this day, the FBI insists that Tamerlan's case file was closed after Cedarleaf's initial investigation in 2011, and was only reopened after the Boston Marathon attack.

On January 23, 2013, Tamerlan made a second attempt to become a US citizen. That was the day he had an interview to discuss the documentation related to his arrest for domestic violence. He fully expected to walk away from the interview with a USCIS officer with his citizenship. Instead, the officer wrote: "The paperwork relating [to] the dismissal of charges in his domestic violence arrest did not arrive and his status was delayed."[14]

Again.

Two weeks later, on February 6, 2013, an angry Tamerlan walked into Phantom Fireworks in Seabrook, New Hampshire, and asked for the "biggest and loudest" pyrotechnics in the store.[15]

12

RATS

The US Department of Justice began its relationship with cooperating informants on March 14, 1961, the day Attorney General Robert F. Kennedy instructed FBI Director J. Edgar Hoover to order every agent in every field office throughout the country to infiltrate organized crime groups. Of course, the FBI would need to reach to the bottom of the underworld to bring its targets to the surface, and the way to do that was to tempt bottom feeders up into the light.

Hoover was crafty enough to know that crime did indeed pay, and that most criminals would do almost anything for money. With that premise in mind, the FBI began its Top Echelon Criminal Informant Program.

Piling criminals from the bottom of the heap on top of one another with their courtroom testimony and wiretaps and tip-offs paid off, as the FBI began to topple the highest levels of the sophisticated underworld outfits, loosen the Mafia's stranglehold on the garbage industry, and level entire construction unions. The tactic worked against the Bonanno crime family in New York City when, in 2004, Joseph Massino became the first mob boss in history to flip on his underlings. And Sammy "the Bull" Gravano helped put his former boss, John Gotti of the Gambino crime family, in jail. The FBI had informants in the KKK and biker gangs all over the country. And after 9/11 most of its informants were Muslims, the mosque crawlers and rakers identified by counterterrorism officials.

With the resulting arrests came power for case agents in the FBI, and that power brought unfettered authority for federal investigators to offer sweetheart deals to turncoats, no matter how treacherous the cooperating informant was. More than fifty years since the inception of the Top Echelon Criminal Informant Program, what had been once the biggest tool the federal government could use against organized criminal outfits had become a scam used by murderous criminals to become government employees protected by the FBI. The damage done to law and order by these unlovely marriages between rats and their sometime rogue agents can be found all over the country.

The FBI tracks the productivity of its confidential informants, or CIs (also known as cooperating witnesses, or CWs) by aggregating their "statistical accomplishments"—that is, the number of indictments, convictions, search warrants, and other contributions to investigative objectives for which the CI gets credit. But what the FBI does not track are its agents who let CIs run amok.

Some rogue agents are seduced by sex—like James "JJ" Smith, the disgraced former Los Angeles–based special agent who admitted in court that he had an affair for nearly twenty years with Katrina Leung, an asset he had recruited as an informant on Asian gangs. He thought Leung was a Chinese American businesswoman. In fact, she was a high-level spy for the Chinese government who gathered classified information about the United States during pillow talk with her FBI handler.

Others are motivated by money, like Dante Jackson, the special agent in the FBI's Atlanta field office accused of accepting the use of luxury cars and taking fancy handmade Italian shoes, tickets to sporting events, and cash from a Russian gangster named Mani Chulpayev who became an FBI informant. Prosecutors in Fulton County, Georgia, alleged that Chulpayev—who says he has worked with the FBI since the 1990s—worked with four other men to arrange the murder of a well-known rapper named Lil Phat. A grand jury indictment charged the five with murder, felony murder, street gang criminal activity, and weapons counts. However, after Chulpayev was indicted, he told officials that his FBI handler had taken a number of high-end gifts to help him cover up the crime, and Jackson is now part of an ongoing federal probe.

Entire FBI field offices have been tainted, as in the case with infamous Boston mobster James "Whitey" Bulger. Bulger's FBI handler was John Connolly, who had admired the rough-and-tumble mobster while growing up in the same South Boston housing development. Connolly's boss was John Morris. Both men took bribes, and Connolly is now serving time in a Florida prison for allowing Bulger to set up mob-style hits on innocent people, while the agents made a name for themselves arresting Italian and Italian American mobsters whom Bulger was trying to put out of business. Connolly went so far as to alert Bulger to an indictment pending against him. As a result of that tip, the mobster was on the lam with his companion, Catherine Greig, for sixteen years, until he was captured in a rent-controlled hide-out in Santa Monica, California. Morris testified against Connolly, leading to the latter's conviction in the 1982 murder of a Florida businessman named Roger Wheeler, whom Bulger had ordered to be killed. Connolly is serving a forty-year sentence in a Florida prison.

Another dirty agent, H. Paul Rico, was also indicted in that case. Once a bureau favorite, legend had it that he could flip an informant as easily as a short-order cook could flip a pancake. Rico made a career out of using cooperating witnesses to take down high-ranking underworld crime figures, even when they were innocent. In the 1980s he framed four Italian men—Joseph Salvati, Peter Limone, Henry Tameleo, and Louis Greco—in a trumped-up murder case on the word of one witness, the longtime FBI informant and prolific murderer Joseph "the Animal" Barboza. Greco, who had won two Bronze Stars for his heroism at Bataan in World War II—even had an alibi. At the time of the murder, he had been partying in Florida, in front of a slew of witnesses. Rico was forced to testify before the US House Judiciary Committee when it was looking into the corrupt past of the FBI's Boston field office, a contentious hearing that contained jaw-dropping allegations of FBI misconduct.

At one point, Connecticut Congressman Christopher Shays asked Rico, then 78, if he was sorry that innocent men died or were falsely imprisoned for life—including Greco, a war hero—based on his malfeasance. Rico famously responded from the witness table, "Would you like tears or something?"

Incredulous, Shays asked, "Pardon me?"

Rico rephrased his cold remark. "What do you want, tears?"[1] He died a short time later in federal prison.

During the height of Hoover's COINTELPRO operations in the 1960s and 1970s, the FBI had roughly 1,500 informants. In the 1990s the drug wars brought that number up to about 6,000. Then, after 9/11, the FBI recruited so many new informants—including derelicts looking for leniency in their own legal problems or upcoming jail sentences, liars looking for immigration favors, Muslims looking for revenge on the members of competing Islamic sects, and narcissistic egomaniacs who wanted to be revered as a Jason Bourne–type figure—that it had to hire an outside software company to help agents track their secret spies. Today, there are anywhere from 15,000 to 20,000 snitches on the FBI's payroll, and many of them are "mosque crawling" to inform on fellow Muslims in the United States and overseas, as part of a preemptive counterterrorism initiative that former NYPD Commissioner Ray Kelly helped create by recruiting Muslims who took the civil service test to become police officers. He would send appropriate applicants a letter that they had been accepted into the police academy. Meanwhile they were trailed, evaluated, and—if selected by commanders of the NYPD initiative, trained like CIA operatives before being placed in undercover operations all over the country.

At the start of 2015, the House Homeland Security Committee unanimously voted to approve the Countering Violent Extremism Act of 2015 written by Republican Congressman Michael McCaul that created an agency in the DHS dubbed Countering Violent Extremism (CVE). Congress earmarked $10 million in additional funding to counter what McCaul called "the long reach of international terrorists into our communities or the homegrown hate spread by domestic extremist groups."[2] To counter that long reach, CVE would need to develop informants, and that would take funding.

There is a valid argument for using informants to prevent terrorist attacks from occurring. For example, BPD Captain Robert Ciccolo, a vaunted veteran commander who had been in Kenmore Square working the Red Sox game detail on April 15, 2013, when the bombs exploded blocks away, later received a disturbing text message from his son Alexander. The text was sent to him on September 11, 2013, and indicated that Alexander sympathized with the jihad. Captain Ciccolo called the FBI, which initiated an investigation that used an informant. The informant "befriended" Alexander and furnished the FBI with secretly wiretapped conversations that he had with the informant. Because of this evidence, an act of horrible bloodletting was prevented.

Alexander Ciccolo was giving his new "friend" insight into his admiration for the Tsarnaev brothers. His plan, he explained in a wiretapped conversation according to court records, was to "take a pressure cooker . . . Uhm [*sic*] fill it up with, ah, black powder . . . ball bearings, nails, glass, rocks . . . you know."[3] The pressure cookers would have built-in timers, he said, and he boasted that the "brothers in Boston paid four hundred dollars for the amount of fireworks they used." Ciccolo wanted his attack to be bigger than what the Tsarnaev brothers pulled off. He wanted to plant a bomb at a school and then shoot the students as they ran from the carnage. He told the informant he would be wearing a Go-Pro camera (just like the one the San Bernardino attackers Syed Farook and Tashfeen Malik would wear when they killed fourteen people at a California office party nearly three years later).

On July 4, 2015, Ciccolo purchased a 0.223 Colt, an AR-15 rifle, a 556 Sig Arms SG550 rifle and two powerful Glock handguns. Members of the JTTF arrested him minutes after he illegally bought the weapons—from the informant. Prosecutors said in an indictment that Ciccolo had planned to "kill innocent people in support of ISIL [ISIS]."[4] A day before his arrest, Ciccolo's mother, Shelley Reardon, had driven him to Walmart in Adams, Massachusetts, where he bought a pressure cooker. He went home and typed a message on Facebook to the informant, a member of a jihadist sympathizer closed group. "Allah Akbar!" Ciccolo wrote. "I got the pressure cookers today. Alhamdulillah."

Ciccolo also mentioned that he had built ten firebombs, Molotov cocktails made from Styrofoam soaked in motor oil. The bombs were meant to be evil. The Styrofoam "would cause the fire from the exploded devices to stick to people's skin and make it harder to put the fire out," Ciccolo explained to the informant. Investigators also recovered two machetes and a long curved knife from his western Massachusetts apartment, the same weapons he had seen used in the ISIS videos he had downloaded on his computer.

As of 2016, Ciccolo was being held without bail on charges of being a felon in possession of a firearm and of assaulting a nurse with a pen during his intake at a federal prison. Those charges will likely be superseded with an indictment for more serious crimes. Ciccolo's father has been lauded as a hero by BPD Commissioner William Evans, who called him a commander who made "the incredibly hard decision to turn in his own blood to save him from shedding the blood of innocent people."[5]

———

In February 2016, the DHS alerted twenty-nine "high target" cities, including Boston and New York, that their DHS funding would be slashed by 1.3 percent. Boston, which had received $18 million from the federal government earmarked for homeland security initiatives in fiscal year 2015, received $17.7 million in fiscal year 2016.[6] Rene Fielding, chief of Boston's Office of Emergency Management, explained that the cuts collected from the cities would be used to fund "nonprofits"—primarily to provide security to mosques and synagogues.[7]

Privately police officials complained it was a way for DHS officials to pay imams at mosques like the Islamic Society of Boston, which ran the Prospect Street mosque the Tsarnaev brothers prayed at, for good will. The feds need to make nice with angry activists who are part of the Council on American Islamic Relations (CAIR), the reasoning went, and grant money goes a long way with nonprofits.

Then federal judges started to take a look at the use of Muslim informants after the case of the so-called Newburgh Four, four Muslim men who were arrested in 2009 for allegedly planning to shoot down military airplanes flying out of the Air National Guard base in Newburgh, New York, and allegedly participating in another plot to blow up two Bronx synagogues. There were allegations that the FBI had actually organized both plots and encouraged the four men to carry them out by plying them with food and money. In fact, a report issued by the Human Rights Institute at Columbia University Law School stated that roughly half of the federal prosecutions of Islamic terrorism cases relied on informants: "Indeed, in some cases the Federal Bureau of Investigation may have created terrorists out of law-abiding individuals by conducting sting operations that facilitated or invented the target's willingness to act. According to multiple studies, nearly 50 percent of the more than 500 federal counterterrorism convictions resulted from informant-based cases; almost 30 percent of those cases were sting operations in which the informant played an active role in the underlying plot."[8]

The American Civil Liberties Union (ACLU) was also concerned that

Muslims were being targeted and coerced into informing on their neighbors, especially given the NYPD Terrorist Interdiction Program started by NYPD Commissioner Ray Kelly and continued under his successor, Commissioner William Bratton. Both Kelly, a Harvard University graduate, and Bratton, a longtime commissioner of the BPD and the MBTA Transit Police, had ties to Boston and New York and saw those cities attacked by extremists. The ACLU said that sending Muslim spies into mosques and hookah bars was illegal and the NYPD's "purported rationale for this unconstitutional surveillance" was nonsense.[9] The NYPD disagreed and released its own report in 2009, titled "Radicalization in the West: The Homegrown Threat." The report stated that some of the warning signs that someone was becoming radicalized were changes in appearance and behavior, and cited "wearing traditional Islamic clothing [and] growing a beard," abstaining from alcohol, and "becoming involved in social activism."[10]

Those warning signs had certainly been observed in Tamerlan Tsarnaev. He had stopped drinking and doing drugs. He had traded his designer clothes for traditional Muslim robes, wearing them to the pizza parlors and Starbucks stores in his Cambridge neighborhood. In addition, he was bilingual and hulking. A perfect recruit, according to Dzhokhar Tsarnaev's defense attorneys. In a court filing they would write, "The FBI made more than one visit to talk with Anzor, Zubeidat and Tamerlan, questioned Tamerlan about his Internet searches, and asked him to be an informant."[11]

The US Attorney's office and the FBI responded in a letter sent to the defense on March 14, 2014, writing that "the government has no evidence that Tamerlan Tsarnaev was solicited by the government to be an informant. As for information about any contacts between the government and other Tsarnaev family members, it appears from your letter [cited in defense legal brief] that this information is already available to you through the family members themselves."[12]

To be fair, the government couldn't disprove the defense's claims that Tamerlan had been recruited as an asset in those FBI proffer reports, family interviews, and information they received from their client, Dzhokhar. But the defense team still wanted answers. They wanted details about Tamerlan's trip to Dagestan, for example. The defense wanted to know why the government refused to hand over any of the immigration records for any member of the Tsarnaev clan other than their client, writing, "While Dzhokhar's own A-file contains his father's claim that he had been arbitrarily arrested and tortured in the family's home country of Kyrgyzstan, and that he had a well-founded fear of further persecution justifying political asylum in the United States, the documents in Dzhokhar's file do not include any of the reasons why the United States government concluded that the father's asylum claim was valid." Certainly it would be interesting to know whether Anzor's brother Ruslan's ties to a CIA official were relevant at the time.

More important, however, was the mystery swirling around the FBI's involvement with Tamerlan Tsarnaev and whether or not the pressure he felt to be an informant led to the attack on the Boston Marathon, questions Dzhokhar's attorneys asked in the filed defense brief. "The FBI made more than one visit to talk with Anzor, Zubeidat and Tamerlan, questioned Tamerlan about his internet searches, and asked him to be an informant, reporting on the Chechen and Muslim community. We further have reason to believe that Tamerlan misinterpreted the visits and discussions with the FBI as pressure and that they amounted to a stressor that increased his paranoia and distress. We do not suggest that these contacts are to be blamed and have no evidence to suggest that they were improper, but rather view them as an important part of the story of Tamerlan's decline. Since Tamerlan is dead, the government is the source of corroboration that these visits did in fact occur and of what was said during them."[13]

To this day, that question has not been answered. And more questions have been raised with a separate investigation into a drug trafficking crew of Eritrean immigrants, a group that would eventually be tied to the gun used to assassinate MIT Police Officer Sean Collier.

Tamerlan had been desperate to become a citizen, as shown by his participation in the 2009 photo essay, "Will Box for Passport." He wanted to box in the Olympic games on the US team, which only citizens were eligible to do. He also had connections in the drug world, as the murders on Harding Avenue in Waltham certainly suggest.

The FBI was hoping to arrest a multinational crew of Muslim immigrants in Portland, Maine, who were selling crack cocaine and sending the proceeds overseas. Confidential informants were at the center of the investigation, called Operation Run This Town. And ATF agents would trace the Ruger P95 Tamerlan used to murder Sean Collier, the MIT police officer—the same gun that was later fired at police during the Watertown shootout—to that same crack crew in Portland, Maine. It had been given to Dzhokhar by a childhood friend from Cambridge, Stephen Silva, an Eritrean immigrant with ties to the leader of the crack crew.

There were those unanswered questions, such as how Tamerlan was allowed to travel to a terrorist hotbed; why he recorded his conversations with his mother's second cousin, a leader in an Islamist organization in the Caucasus; and why his application for citizenship—for which he wasn't eligible because of his arrest for domestic violence, as explained above—was reopened after his return from Russia.

The Office of the Inspector General for the Intelligence Community examined those issues and the questions of whether Tamerlan was an asset (and if he wasn't, why not) in its report on information sharing among the intelligence agencies:

1. Why did the CT [the Counterterrorism Unit of the FBI] agent not visit Tamerlan's mosque [in Cambridge]?
2. Why did the CT agent not interview the woman Tamerlan was accused of assaulting?
3. Why did the CT agent not interview Tamerlan's wife, Katherine Russell aka Krina [*sic*] Tsarnaeva?
4. Why was Tamerlan not asked about if he sympathized with Chechen rebels?[14]

The report also lamented that the FBI had been less than cooperative with the inspector general's review, a complaint that Senator Charles Grassley would repeat: "The FBI has a pretty dismal record of responding to my questions. I wish I could say that all of those unanswered issues have been fully dealt with, but they have not. Ignoring my questions does not make them go away. They need to be answered fully and completely, and in good faith."[15]

Former Somerville Police Chief Tom Pasquarello heard Grassley's remarks. Pasquarello was a longtime DEA agent who had run his own informants, and he noticed the similarities between Tamerlan's case and his own use of confidential informants, or CIs, in multiple takedowns all over the world. As a longtime law enforcement official the seeming coincidences could not be ignored. Not Tamerlan's trip to Russia, not his return without a passport while on terror watchlists. For Pasquarello it was personal. He had been very close to Collier and had issued him a Somerville police badge to honor him after his death. He muttered angrily to another Somerville police official before his November 2013 retirement announcement, that cop would recall, "Good luck, Chuck."

PART THREE

HEAVEN DOWN
THE BARREL
OF A GUN

Countdown
to Detonation

13
MAYBE, MAYBE NOT

Khairullozhon Matanov couldn't keep quiet any longer. The Quincy cab driver turned to his passenger, a businesswoman named Ann Munson whom he picked up most mornings to drive to the MBTA's station in Braintree so she could take the Red Line into town. "Those guys on TV," he said. "The bombers. I know them. I was just at their house. I was at their house that night. They are from Chechnya."[1]

Matanov would later describe that visit to the Tsarnaev's messy third-floor apartment at 410 Norfolk Street in Cambridge in a series of interviews with the FBI. On April 15, 2013, he knocked on the door and heard his friend, Tamerlan Tsarnaev, yell, "Open." The twenty-six-year-old Tamerlan was in the living room with his nineteen-year-old brother, Dzhokhar, watching the news on TV. Nearly every channel was running nonstop coverage of the chaos and carnage on Boylston Street: the smoke, the screaming, the severed limbs scattered in the street, and blood everywhere. In the apartment, a laptop streaming CNN also aired endless loops of the chaos and heroic rescue efforts: spectators using their belts, shirts, and shoelaces as tourniquets to tie off the mangled limbs of strangers; doctors who ran the marathon sprinting to operating rooms; and former New England Patriots offensive lineman Joe Andruzzi carrying an injured woman to safety.

Khairullozhon was twenty-three, a Russian-speaking immigrant with a scrawny frame and floppy black hair. He and Tamerlan had met years earlier at the mosque on Prospect Street in Cambridge, part of the Islamic Society of Boston, which came under the leadership of the Islamic Society of Boston Cultural Center, and became friends. They attended Friday prayers together and went to the mosque on holidays such as Eid al-Fitr, the highest of Muslim holy days. Tamerlan, a New England Golden Gloves champion, gave Khairullozhon boxing lessons, and they played weekly pickup soccer games together in Cohasset. Khairullozhon had even met the Tsarnaev clan's matriarch, Zubeidat, who cooked chicken and salad for him at their home. After Eid al-Fitr the year before, the two friends had climbed Mount Monadnock in New Hampshire. That was the first time Tamerlan talked about the mujahedin to Khairullozhon. "We didn't have secrets," Khairullozhon would tell the FBI.

He claimed to have never suspected the Tsarnaevs were the bombers. How could he? Tamerlan had called him less than an hour after the blasts, at 3:31 P.M.—a call that cell phone records confirm. Tamerlan said that he was at the store buying milk. "During this conversation they discussed the bombings in Boston," an FBI report states. "Matanov suggested that maybe something blew up in a kitchen near the finish line, to which Tamerlan responded: 'Maybe, maybe not.'"[2]

The two made plans to have dinner together that night.

It was sundown by the time Khairullozhon walked into the Norfolk Street apartment. The Tamerlan who greeted him that day was more like the old Tam he had known when he first arrived in the country. Tamerlan's face was freshly shaved. Wearing sweatpants and boxing shoes, his appearance reminded Khairullozhon of the old days when Tam was the handsome party boy who had frequented Boston nightclubs and smoked pot with his friends. Neither Tamerlan's wife, Karima (neé Katherine Russell), nor their toddler daughter, Zahira, was home.

After greeting the brothers, Khairullozhon commented that the bombing was very bad and voiced his concerns that the public might direct its outrage at Muslims. He plopped down on the couch next to Dzhokhar, who was stroking the family cat. Khairullozhon also expressed sympathy for eight-year-old Martin Richard, who had died in the second blast. Tamerlan turned on him and snapped: "Do you think the US drones that dropped bombs in Pakistan and Afghanistan did not kill any children?" Then he softened his tone: "So what if a kid dies. God will take care of him."[3]

As Tamerlan watched the coverage on TV, he smiled. There was one image that every newscast replayed over and over: the seventy-eight-year-old marathoner, Bill Iffrig, being hurled to the ground after the first bomb exploded, his bright orange tank top juxtaposed against the gray billowing smoke behind him. He lay prone on the ground, stunned, just yards from the finish line. Half a dozen Boston police officers sprang toward Iffrig and stood around him in a protective huddle, as chaos erupted behind them. A blue-and-yellow clad volunteer helped Iffrig to his feet.

There was something about that old man on the ground—Tamerlan loved it. When he saw the shot of Iffrig falling as the smoke rose in the background, Tamerlan laughed.

The image of Iffrig crumpled on the ground became emblematic of the pandemonium and bloodshed near the finish line of the Boston Marathon. A child was dead, along with two young women. In all, the bombs injured more than 260 people, 17 of whom lost limbs. Four lost two limbs. And at that time no one knew why.

Except for Tamerlan and Dzhokhar Tsarnaev.

Tamerlan disappeared into his brother's room, and Khairullozhon tried to engage Dzhokhar in conversation about what had happened. Khairullozhon said that the bombings were going to be a big problem for Muslims because innocent people had been killed. For the first time that night, Dzhokhar responded by saying that for some people the bombing was a good thing, for others it was a bad thing.

Dzhokhar was always a quiet kid, Khairullozhon told the FBI, but that night his demeanor was particularly aloof. Maybe he was concentrating on the tweet he transmitted from his account @J_Tsar at 5:04 P.M. that day: "Ain't no love in the heart of the city. stay safe people." Dzhokhar also marked another tweet, from an account called "Death," @GMCoderGoddi. It read: "The ultimate sacrifice is within you, the battle within is defined by the word jihad."[4]

When they were finally ready for dinner, Khairullozhon told the his passenger later, he and the Tsarnaev brothers had climbed into his cab and gone out for kabobs at a storefront eatery in Somerville called Man-O-Salwa, a little more than a mile away. He saw Tamerlan again Wednesday night, along with his wife and baby. Nothing seemed out of the ordinary, he said to his passenger. "I didn't think they would do anything like this."[5]

When Khairullozhon had told all this to his passenger, she insisted that they go to the police and told Khairullozhon that she would go with him. They drove directly to the Braintree police station and sat down with Detective Matt Heslam, who started the interview by saying, "Crazy set of events, huh?"

"I can't believe it. I can't believe that happened with them, like they—they were nice people, like the way they talk," Khairullozhon responded.

The detective continued, according to a transcript of the interview: "Everybody is kind of in shock. Everything that's going on. Do you guys mind if I record it? Just so I don't miss anything."

"Yeah, you can record it."

"Okay, awesome," Heslam answered. "You guys came here to share information, whatever you have with us, so we appreciate that, and uh, just fire away whatever you guys have. We'll probably pass it on to the feds and they'll take it from there."

"My name is Khairullozhon Matanov."

"Do you want to write that down for me? What's your nationality?"

"I am Uzbek."

The detective nodded. "Okay."

"So, I know this guy uh Tamerlan. Tamerlan Tsarnaev."

"He's the older brother, right?"

"Yeah," Khairullozhon answered. "The thing is, uh two years ago I met him in the mosque, Cambridge mosque . . . I pray, and just like, you know."

Khairullozhon's phone rang in his pocket, and he answered it in Russian, telling the detective that it was his mother calling. Heslam looked at Ann Munson as Khairullozhon chatted on the phone. "Umm. Can you do me a favor? Can you just open up your purse for me real quick?"

She did, saying: "It's fine. Bless your heart. My father was a policeman. And I came in to verify that I know him. I call him Mike because I can't pronounce his name."

Heslam asked the woman if she knew the Tsarnaev brothers, which she did not. "Nope," she said. "Just him."

Khairullozhon hung up the phone and said: "My mom is like worried. So I know him since that time and we used to play sometimes soccer. I have their, like, you know the phone number and they call me sometimes."

"Okay," the detective answered. And waited.

"So then like I heard today in the morning that like it was him and actually I didn't see their photos last night and then they said like he got shot and he's dead and I can't imagine that he did it, that kind of stuff, and if anything, I can help, like to do, I am open to that."

The detective waited again.

"But only think I know that I used to call them and just like for the soccer reason, like you guys, you guys gonna come play with us today. We spoke in the Russian language."

Heslam asked for the younger brother's phone number. It was Friday morning, and the only trace of Dzhokhar was the abandoned stolen SUV and bloody handprints on the hoods of cars on backstreets in Watertown. Khairullozhon had been calling Dzhokhar's phone all morning, he said: "It says it was blocked or something happened with it."

"Anything happen in their lives in the last year or so that you saw a change?" Heslam asked.

"No, they were like so, so nice people," Khairullozhon answered, stammering. "We talked about football. That's all. I don't know what they shared about family life. He told me about his life, he was a boxer, he won like the championship in the New England a couple of times I think."

"Older brother?"

"Yeah," Khairullozhon answered. "The only thing I know about the younger is he used to study. That's why I don't see him too many time, ya know, couple times I just saw him and like I took his phone number."

Heslam asked about the other Tsarnaevs: "Maybe something happened to their mother or their father or family member or anything?"

"Their father and mother were also nice people. I think they left this country."

"Have you ever met them?"

"Yeah. I met the father."

"And they left and went back to Russia?"

"I don't know, Russia or Kyrgyzstan or somewhere like that."

Heslam continued to press for more information: "Do you know if they left willingly or if the government had anything to do with it?"

"No, I think they like just wanted to like go there, see their relatives there, down there."

"Do you know if the younger brother has a girlfriend or anything somewhere?" Heslam asked.

"No. As I told you, I don't know the younger brother too much. But I know the older brother has a wife and a very sweetheart daughter. And I don't think they live together, but I'm not sure where they live right now."

"Anything else?"

Khairullozhon stammered again: "That's only I know, you know, like I was just like you know life is someone sees me, like anyways, like and I have a call to them so they will like definitely probably say like, hey, you call them, what you doing?" He explained that it had been Munson's idea to tell the police what he knew, and that he hadn't called the FBI because he had really limited his friendship with Tamerlan to the mosque.

"Every Friday, we, we as a Muslim, we go at noontime to pray over there," he said. "We exchanged the contacts, like this and that. We went to play soccer. If you want to become the boxer, I can take you, like I know some coach that can train you to the boxing. And then there was like, this event we went together to the box last year I don't remember a lot. He took me there. He was a gold something. He said everyone knows me here because I, I become champion."

"Golden Gloves?" the detective interjected.

"Yeah. I think. In Lowell somewhere."

The detective asked for Khairullozhon's address and phone number and then rose to say goodbye.

"Should I contact the FBI?" Nervously, Khairullozhon added, "I don't think it's like really big, my information because like I've studied the law, that's not gonna have anything cause I just saw him, like ya know?"

"It's what?"

"I studied the law. I didn't really graduate, but I almost am done there back home."

Heslam explained that any information could be helpful, especially as the younger brother still had not been captured. Khairullozhon agreed to cooperate as long as it was before the noontime prayer.

"I feel better already," Matanov told the detective as he stood up. He had not mentioned the visit to the Norfolk Street home, or the sweets he had brought for Tamerlan's little girl. He didn't mention that he had seen Tamerlan on Wednesday night, a day before Sean Collier, the MIT Police Officer, was murdered. The repeated phone calls to Dzhokhar's cell phone—while he was on the run and despite Matanov insisting earlier the number had come up as blocked (which investigators say it did not)—didn't come up either. Nor did he tell Heslam that he had posed in front of a black flag of jihad with Tamerlan on a high Muslim holiday, a photo of which was still on his laptop.

All of that information would be revealed later, after Khairullozhon was trailed by a low-flying plane, followed around the clock, and eventually arrested by the FBI.

Maybe, Maybe Not

14

VASELINE, FIREWORKS, BACKPACK

The first thing Dias Kadyrbayev noticed was the red laser lights. They were concentrated on the forehead of his girlfriend, Bayan, but they were all over her body. He looked down and saw that he was covered with the same red laser dots. Then came a voice over a bullhorn outside.

"Jahar! Come outside! Come outside now! Come out with your hands up!"[1]

Dias pulled back the plastic shade. It was still daylight but raining. Outside his building were three unmarked cars and six FBI agents from the elite military-like HRT team wearing full SWAT gear, with night vision goggles on their helmets, and holding long guns with their scopes focused steadily on Dias and his girlfriend. In the middle of the men was FBI Special Agent John Walker, a tall, well-built man who wore a jacket emblazoned with his agency's initials. He held the bullhorn and was clearly giving the orders. It was five P.M. and Dzhokhar Tsarnaev was still missing. By then investigators had learned that two days after the bombings he had nonchalantly gone back to the campus of UMass/Dartmouth. On Wednesday, he had gone to the gym with Azamat Tazhayakov, and he had partied with his boys in New Bedford that night. Then on Thursday afternoon Dzhokhar went back to his Pine Dale dorm room and Skyped with his brother Tamerlan sometime before 4:02 P.M., which is the time his swipe card registered that he left the UMass/Dartmouth dormitory. He climbed into his battered green Honda Civic with its black replacement hood and drove back to Cambridge: home. Hours later, one cop would be dead, another would be clinging to life, a young businessman would be traumatized, and a suburban neighborhood would be littered with bomb parts and bullet casings.

The next day, Friday, the campus had been evacuated. Agents were searching Dzhokhar's room in Pine Dale and interviewing his shy, nervous roommate Andrew Dwinells.

Dzhokhar had not only been in New Bedford on the previous day. On Friday morning, the FBI got a hit on an iPhone registered to him, which pinged from a cell tower roughly 984 yards away from his buddies' off-campus apartment at 69A Carriage Drive. The cell phone ping made investigators believe they had found Dzhokhar in New Bedford, while the hunt for him was still under way in Watertown.

The call was made at 10:06 A.M. to Zubeidat in Russia, whose phone was being monitored by counterterrorism officials as her younger son continued to elude authorities. What the FBI didn't know was that a group of friends had shared a cell phone plan to save money. All of their calls were billed to Dzhokhar, the only American (through naturalization) among them. It was Dias who had called Zubeidat, but the call convinced FBI agents that they had found their fugitive.

Not only did Walker firmly believe that Dzhokhar was hiding inside, but he also thought that the entire apartment might have been booby-trapped with bombs.

"Come out with your hands up!" Walker shouted.[2]

Dias and Bayan put their hands in the air. She was crying and saying: "They're going to shoot us. They're going to shoot us." Azamat came out of his bedroom to join them, his own arms aloft. Shaking, he exclaimed, "What the fuck!"

Together they walked outside. Azamat went first and began walking toward the man in the FBI windbreaker.

"Stop right there!" Walker ordered. "Take off your shirt."

He turned to Dias and said, "You too." He ordered a female ICE agent to search Bayan.

"Do you have any bombs? Weapons?" Walker demanded. They all shook their heads, and Azamat yelled "No!"

Dias threw his T-shirt on the ground and let his basketball shorts fall to his ankles. He stepped out of them and walked toward the FBI agent. He was forced to his knees, his hands bound by plastic handcuffs behind him. Then Azamat was told to get on his knees.

"Where the fuck is Jahar?" Walker demanded, using Dzhokhar's nickname. "Who's in the house?"

"Nobody!" Dias answered. He had his keys in his hand, and he threw them to Walker. An agent in SWAT gear escorted Dias to an unmarked sedan, bare-chested and wearing basketball shorts. His T-shirt was still on the ground. He couldn't see Azamat or Bayan. Then Walker climbed into the front seat of the car, reclined his seat, and turned around. He was a frightening man.

"He didn't look at me. He looked through me," Dias would later say.

"Listen to me. Where the fuck is Jahar? Don't fuck with me. Tell me where he is," Walker said.

Dias fought back tears. "I don't know. I don't know."

"This is the biggest thing to ever happen in Massachusetts. Jahar Tsarnaev is dead," Walker told Dias. "Whether he is still living or going away, his life is over. LOOK AT ME!" Dias did. "Repeat back what I said!"

"Jahar is dead."

There was another reason why Walker thought Dias knew exactly where the fugitive was. The night before (Thursday), after photographs of Suspect White Hat and Suspect Black Hat were released, Dias had exchanged text messages with Dzhokhar.

"Yo, bro. You saw the news?" Dias texted him at 8:43 P.M.[3]

Shockingly, Dzhokhar answered. He and his brother were getting ready to kill a cop and go on the run, but he had time for his college pals, fellow Russian immigrants.

"Yeah, bro. I did."

"For real?"

"I saw the news," Dzhokhar answered. "Better not text me, my friend. LOL."

"You saw yourself in there? ahahaha . . . hahahaha," Dias responded.

"If you want," Tsarnaev texted, "you can go to my room and take what's there ☺ but ight [sic] bro Salam aliekum."

"what's wrong with u?" Dias texted, ending the conversation, "hahah ☺"

The FBI was searching the apartment and Dias was still cuffed in the car when he heard the dispatcher say on the radio that the suspect had been found in Watertown: "Captured. . . . The suspect is in custody." Still, Dias and his roommate were hardly in the clear. At that point the media had begun to swarm into the area. Interviews of the suspects in the car were no longer tenable. Walker repeated what he had told Dias about Dzhokhar's life.

"His life is over. He's dead. One way or the other he's dead. Your life does not have to be. You have to tell me the truth right now. Don't make a mistake," Walker told them. Dias simply nodded, agreeing to cooperate.

Walker ordered a uniformed New Bedford police officer to transport Dias to the nearby Dartmouth State Police barracks for questioning. They didn't have an arrest warrant, and the occupants of 69A Carriage Drive were not in custody. But Dias was all too happy to get away from the TV and still cameras that were outside his home. So was Azamat. When Walker's decision to detain the men without an arrest warrant was later questioned, he snapped: "This was a sophisticated crime, a sophisticated act of terrorism. The suspects were able to flee the scene. It was likely . . . [part of] a larger conspiracy."[4]

Azamat and Dias were questioned in separate rooms, both still shirtless. It was freezing. They were shivering and all too willing to talk.

Dias told agents he had sent Azamat a text: "Dzhokhar is on the news as the marathon bomber."[5] It had been just hours since the FBI's 5 P.M. release of photos of Suspect White Hat and Suspect Black Hat, the two men in baseball caps accused of detonating two deadly blasts near the finish line of the Boston Marathon. Dias didn't call the FBI. Neither did Azamat. Instead, they met in Dzhokhar's dorm room.

"He [Dzhokhar] told me to take whatever I want,"[6] Dias later testified that he told Azamat and a third friend, Robel Phillipos, who met them there. The three were stunned. They had seen Dzhokhar nearly every day that week. They had gone to the gym, played video games, and watched news coverage of the carnage left on Boylston Street. All three had exchanged texts with Dzhokhar on the day of the attack and had talked about martyrdom in the weeks before the bombs exploded. Azamat had even discussed opening a Starbucks in Kyrgyzstan with Dzhokhar after graduation.

Then they started to recall other conversations, ones that had seemed like harmless rants about Islam at the time but in the context of the bombings were alarming. Weeks earlier they had been setting off fireworks along the banks of the Charles River in Boston when Dzhokhar began to brag: "I know how to build a bomb. I know all the ingredients to build a bomb."[7]

Another time he had confessed to Azamat that he thought "martyrdom would be a peaceful death."

This is what they talked about as they moved around Dzhokhar's side of the dorm room just after 10:00 P.M. on Thursday. Azamat pointed out a backpack like the one used to conceal the pressure-cooker explosive devices used days earlier, but he didn't want to touch it. Dias picked it up, pulled out a jar of Vaseline, and exclaimed, "He used this to make the bombs!" Then he pulled out firework casings, with the black gunpowder emptied out. "Take it," Azamat said.

Robel sat at the edge of Dzhokhar's bed, watching, Dias told the agents. Then they grabbed Dzhokhar's laptop and got ready to leave. It was 10:30 P.M.

Roughly fifteen minutes earlier the Tsarnaev brothers parked Dzhokhar's battered green Honda on Ames Street in Cambridge, near the MIT campus. They walked through a courtyard and down the median in front of MIT's Stata Center until they came up behind Sean Collier's cruiser, which was parked on campus facing Main Street at the corner of Vassar Street. Tamerlan ripped the car door open and opened fire. The first shot destroyed Collier's hand. Then Tamerlan fired two rounds at his head and two bullets into his chest. "If they had contacted law enforcement with the identity of the marathon suspects it would have expedited their arrest," former Somerville Police Chief and longtime DEA agent Tom Pasquarello said. "MIT police officer Sean Collier would still be alive today living his dream as a Somerville Police officer."[8]

That fact didn't seem to bother Azamat or Dias as they were grilled at the Dartmouth State Police Barracks until roughly 3:00 in the morning of Saturday, April 20. By then anyone with a smartphone, including the students, knew Sean Collier was dead. Still, they had dumped the backpack in the apartment building's Dumpster, the contents of which had been picked up and brought to the massive Crapo landfill of the Greater New Bedford Regional Refuse District. Under questioning they joked about smoking weed. Dias asked about his girlfriend, Bayan, who had also been arrested. Dias and Azmat complained about the cold and asked for T-shirts, which the troopers gave them.

They were driven back to their apartment around 4:00 A.M., still free men and not charged with any crime—if only briefly. The next morning they were arrested by federal agents on immigration violations. The charges would be upgraded to obstruction of a federal terrorism investigation in the coming months. Robel was arrested at his mother's Cambridge apartment and charged with lying to federal investigators. It took twenty-five federal investigators five days to find the discarded backpack at the Crapo landfill. By then, the "condition of the backpack and its contents had been altered," federal prosecutors would come to say repeatedly during the trials of Dias Kadyrbayev and Robel Phillipos.

Dzhokhar's laptop hadn't been used much. He was well known for dealing weed, but he was hardly a good student. At the time of his arrest he had a cumulative GPA of 1.094. His grades were abysmal the entire time he attended UMass/Dartmouth, as his transcript would show. He earned seven Fs over three semesters: two in the fall of 2011 for chemistry, two in the spring of 2012 for critical writing and reading and a math course, and three in the fall of 2012 for chemistry, American politics, and psychology. Those poor grades were going to lead to the loss of his financial aid, which would mean he would be kicked out of school. Around the same time, spring 2012, Dzhokhar began to express jihadi-inspired views online, using an identity that he mostly kept secret from his UMass classmates and weed customers.

FBI Special Agent Stephen Kimball would uncover a secret Twitter account @Al_Firdausi, a profile Dzhokhar created in early 2012 that was full of tweets praising an American Islamic militant, Anwar al-Awlaki, and hoping for "victory over kfur [kaffirs]."

"Dua [calling out to God] is truly the weapon of the believer, pray for the oppressed it is your duty," read one tweet. Another read: "It's our responsibility my brothers & sisters to Allah to ease the hardships of the oppressed and give us victory over kufr [kaffirs]."[9]

Investigators were especially concerned about a tweet sent from that account on April 16, 2012, which the FBI later said could be interpreted as a threat against the Boston Marathon runners. It read: "They will spend their money and they will regret it and then they will be defeated."

There was a second Twitter account under the name @Ghuraba—which can be loosely translated as the Arabic word for strangers—that showed a picture of Mecca.

Even if Dzhokhar was beginning to show more interest in Islamic extremism than in obtaining an American education, getting kicked out of school would cut into his drug dealing proceeds, as students, many of whom would come to testify about buying weed from him, were his best customers. So he told a sob story about his homeland to university administrators and asked for help, Mark Prebel, vice chancellor of administration and finance and the chief financial officer at UMass/Dartmouth, would tell investigators. Dzhokhar filled out a Satisfactory Academic Progress Report, which, strangely, allowed students to plead for forgiveness citing hardship. It was a last-ditch plea to remain a student and keep his financial aid. It was signed January 24, 2013—the day after his brother met with immigration officials in Boston—and in it Dzhokhar blamed "terrorist accusations" made against relatives in Chechnya (a country he had never set foot in, as prosecutors would show) for his failing marks: "This year I lost too many of my loved relatives. I was unable to cope with the stress and maintain schoolwork. My relatives live in Chechnya, Russia, a republic that is occupied by Russian soldiers that falsely accuse and abduct innocent men under false pretenses and terrorist accusations. I am at a point where I can finally focus on my schoolwork. I wish to do well so one day I can help out those in need in my country, especially my family members."[10]

Dzhokhar's interest in Chechnya became apparent in 2011, when—as a seventeen-year-old high-school student—he wrote to an expert on Chechnya who just happened to be an associate professor of Islamic history at UMass/Dartmouth, Brian Glyn Williams. As noted above, the professor was a former CIA agent who wrote material for the Jamestown Foundation. Dzhokhar wrote him looking for information on Chechnya, which led to a brief correspondence, the professor later told *South Coast Today*, a small newspaper published near his campus: "I hope I didn't contribute to it [the brothers' radicalization, which led to the marathon attack]. That kid and his brother identified with the Chechen struggle." There was no mention in the article of

Tamerlan's participation in the Jamestown-sponsored event in the country of Georgia, which Russian intelligence officials later told investigative reporters that he attended in the summer of 2012.

————

One thing prosecutors and the FBI know for sure is that not a single one of Dzhokhar's pot customers or classmates called 911 when they saw their friend "Jahar" on the news on Thursday, April 19, 2013. Elizabeth Zamparelli, who had been a friend of Dzhokhar since childhood, would later explain it this way in a Boston federal courtroom, with her friend at the defendant's table in front of her. "Just none of us thought it could be. It was like a joke."[11]

That prompted Assistant United States Attorney Nadine Pellegrini, who was on the government's prosecutorial team, to explode: "You thought the marathon bombing was a joke?" Zamparelli giggled nervously and then answered, "No, not at all. Because it just was very much not who I knew my friend to be."

15

BETTER TO BE A DOG THAN
THE YOUNGEST SON

Seven days after the deadly blasts on Boylston Street, Carmen Ortiz, the United States Attorney General for Massachusetts, drafted a sealed criminal complaint against Dzhokhar Tsarnaev, who was still hospitalized in critical condition, and filed it in South Boston US District Court, known in Boston as the Moakley courthouse, its name a nod to the late Congressman John Joseph Moakley, who served Massachusetts in the US House of Representatives from 1973 until his death in 2001. The charges contained in the thirty-count indictment were long and complicated. They included use of a weapon of mass destruction and conspiracy, bombing of a place of public use and conspiracy, malicious destruction of property and conspiracy, use of a firearm during and in relation to a crime of violence, use of a firearm during and in relation to a crime of violence causing death, carjacking resulting in serious bodily injury, interference with commerce by threats or violence, and aiding and abetting others in criminal acts.

Dzhokhar had already confessed to being involved in the Boston Marathon attack via his note written in Number 2 pencil on the side panels of the *Slip Away II* and the carvings he had made in the wood and highlighted with fire extinguisher concentrate:

"The US Government is killing our innocent civilians."

"I can't stand to see such evil go unpunished."

"We Muslims are one body, you hurt one, you hurt us all."

"Now I don't like killing innocent people it is forbidden in Islam."

"Stop killing our innocent people and we will stop."[1]

When he was brought to Beth Israel Deaconess Medical Center, he was questioned without having been read his Miranda rights, after someone in the office of US Attorney Carmen Ortiz cited what has been dubbed the public safety exception. He was questioned for sixteen hours by FBI agents Gregory Hughes and Matthew Dowd, without a lawyer—largely because the government feared that the sophistication of the bombs recovered in Watertown and at the finish line of the Boston Marathon was a frightening indication that there were more suspects on the loose, a larger cell responsible for the deadly attack on Boylston Street. Counterterrorism officials wanted to grill Dzhokhar immediately to see if any more bloodletting was in the works.

FBI Special Agent John Walker would describe it this way: "Immediately we had apprehension that a coordinated attack of this nature was a sophisticated crime, a sophisticated act of terrorism. They were able to flee the scene. It was likely not one person, likely two or more people or a larger conspiracy."[2]

Dzhokhar cooperated, more or less. He told the agents that he had driven his battered green Honda, with its black hood, to Boston with Tamerlan around 2:30 P.M. on Monday and that the brothers each had a "backpack containing an explosive device," as the agents would write in a proffer report. (Proffer reports are essentially FBI agents' interview notes filed in written form.) Dzhokhar's backpack was brown; his brother's was black. Together they cost $99.98.[3] Tamerlan had bought them a day earlier at a Target department store in Watertown, just blocks from the scene of the firefight that would leave Transit Police Officer Dic Donohue clinging to life. Investigators now believe that the brothers parked the green Honda somewhere near Boylston Street, at a spot from which it would have been easy to walk toward the finish line. Prosecutors said the bombers picked their own blast sites, stating in court records that "each of them decided on their own where they would stop near the finish line."[4] They picked their targets intentionally. Tamerlan stood behind a swarm of people not far from an area for dignitaries—including survivors of the Sandy Hook massacre in Newtown, Connecticut—who sat in metal stands near a media riser and dropped his backpack bomb on the sidewalk. Dzhokhar dipped his right shoulder down and slid his concealed explosive to the ground behind a row of children standing on a metal grate closer to the marathon route.

"Jahar could not remember whether he or his brother was closer to the finish line," the agents wrote. "Just before detonating the device, Jahar placed a call to his brother with the other device to try and synchronize the two detonations. He used a trigger mechanism built according to the instructions in the *Inspire* magazine article.

"Jahar stated that there were no other attacks planned, there were no unaccounted devices, and the only two individuals involved in the attack planning and execution were Jahar and Tamerlan," the report, filed as part of the indictment, states.

Even as investigators prepared to watch Dzhokhar's bedside arraignment, no one was buying the claim that the Tsarnaev brothers acted alone. When the agents' proffer reports regarding multiple visits to Tsarnaev's bedside were finally released, most of the interviews were redacted. Only a few paragraphs would be legible.

It was at this hearing on April 22 inside Dzhokhar's heavily guarded room at Beth Israel that he would meet his death penalty defense team for the first time. Two FBI agents had grilled him again that morning before federal public defenders Miriam Conrad, William Fick, and Timothy Watkins came to his room to protect their client's rights. It was only then that he was read his Miranda rights. Assistant US Attorneys William Weinreb and Aloke Chakravarty represented the government in the crowded room. Judge Marianne B. Bowler, a US magistrate, oversaw the proceedings.

She started by reciting the date for the court clerk: "Today is Monday, April 22, 2013. The case of U.S. v. Tsarnaev will now be heard. Will counsel please identify themselves for the record?"[5]

"Good morning, your Honor. William Weinreb and Al Chakravarty for the United States."

"Miriam Conrad with Tim Watkins and Bill Fick from the Federal Public Defender's Office."

"Thank you very much," answered Bowler.

An attorney who introduced himself to the court as Jamie Katz, general counsel for Beth Israel Deaconess Medical Center, represented the hospital.

"For the benefit of counsel and for the physician, I have called this conference because I want to establish before we conduct the initial appearance the mental state of the defendant," Bowler said. Then she turned to Stephen Odom, one of Dzhokhar's surgeons. "So, Doctor, I am going to have a few questions for you.

"Please take your time and be relaxed about this."

"Yes, your Honor," Odom said.

"I will ask you to state your name, spelling your last name for the record."

"Stephen Ray Odom, O-D-O-M."

"And what is your occupation?"

"I'm a trauma surgeon."

"Can you give me a brief summary of your professional education, training, and credentials?"

"I went to medical school at Texas Tech University in Lubbock, Texas. I did a general surgery residency at Stamford, Connecticut. And I did a trauma/critical care fellowship at Beth Israel Deaconess Medical Center in Boston."

"Are you Board Certified, Doctor?"

"I am, in general surgery and critical care."

"Thank you. Do you have any publications? Can you give us a summary of the area you have published in?"

"Mostly in emergency general surgery and traumatic illness."

"And you are currently an attending physician here at Beth Israel?"

"I am."

"What has your role been in the care of the defendant, Mr. Tsarnaev?"

"I was the attending trauma surgeon on call when he presented to the hospital, and I have subsequently been his attending during the duration of his stay."

"What is his medical state at the present time?"

"Guarded."

"Can you define what you mean by that?"

"He has multiple serious injuries that require ongoing inpatient medical care at this time. He is currently in an intensive care unit, though his status is not critical."

"Can you give me a brief summary of his injuries?"

"He has multiple gunshot wounds, the most severe of which appears to have entered through the left side inside of his mouth and exited the left face, lower face. This was a high-powered injury that has resulted in skull-base fracture, with injuries to the middle ear, the skull base, the lateral portion of his C1 vertebrae, with a significant soft-tissue injury, as well as injury to the pharynx, the mouth, and a small vascular injury that's been treated. He has, in addition to this, some ophthalmologic injuries that have been treated. He has multiple gunshots wounds to the extremities that have been treated with dressings to the lower extremities; and in the case of his left hand, he had multiple bony injuries as well that were treated with fixation and soft-tissue coverage, as well as tendon repair and vascular ligation."

The judge interrupted with a question: "Internal or external fixation?"

"The pins are internal, but the wound is still open."

"When did he last receive sedation or pain medication?"

"He received Dilaudid at around ten o'clock."

"What was the dose?"

Odom reviewed Tsarnaev's thick medical chart before answering. There was a pause, for which he apologized. Then he answered: "Point-25 milligrams."

"And that is the only pain medication or sedation that he has had recently?"

"Yes."

"Does he know where he is, and does he know what has happened since arriving at the hospital in terms of procedures?"

"He definitely knows where he is. He knows that he has had multiple procedures, but I'm not sure how aware he is of the specifics. He knows that he has an injury to the neck and to the hand."

"In your professional opinion, based on your training and experience, is he lucid enough to understand and respond to basic questions, if not vocally, using hand signals?"

"He is able to respond vocally," Odom answered.

The judge then summed up: "All right. At this time, I find Dr. Odom to be a very credible witness and fully informed about the medical and mental state of the defendant, and on this information I will proceed with an initial appearance forthwith. Doctor, thank you very much for your time. We stand in recess."

The public was already clamoring for information about the surviving

Boston Marathon bomber, so William Fick, one Dzhokhar's lawyers, made a request: "Your Honor, may I ask that the record be sealed?"

"It will be sealed."

Weinreb immediately objected. Police had worked around the clock since 2:49 P.M. on the 15th to bring Dzhokhar to justice. The public had a right to know exactly what charges he would face and what kind of shape he was in.

"In conjunction with the initial appearance, we will make an oral motion to unseal the complaint," he told the court.

"That will be granted once we commence the initial appearance," answered the judge. The arraignment was short and sweet. Dzhokhar at that point was likely thinking about an old Chechen saying, one that he had joked about with his former brother-in-law multiple times in the past: "It is better 167 to be a dog than the younger son."

He had followed Tamerlan down Boylston Street, and now his older brother was with Allah and he was handcuffed to a hospital bed with a shattered jaw and broken bones, facing the death penalty. It would have been easier to die on the boat in Watertown. Nonetheless, Dzhokhar didn't feel any remorse. He would soon have another message to deliver to America: a one-finger salute aimed at a security camera.

16
DEAD MEN TELL NO TALES

On September 11, 2011, Khairullozhon Matanov, the cab driver who had dinner with the bomber brothers on the night of the Boston Marathon attack a year and a half later, came home just after 10:30 P.M. to find the door to his Brighton apartment open and unlocked. He was perplexed, but not panicked. He was letting his friend Ibragim Todashev crash at his place, and Ibragim had already proven irresponsible about things, like locking the door behind him. He dialed his roommate's phone and heard it ring in the bathroom. The shower was running. Khairullozhon went into his garage where he could steal his neighbor's wireless signal and download some videos on his laptop. Ibragim came in a few minutes later and said, "I'm leaving town." He had three duffel bags packed in his room, and his laptop under his arm. A car was waiting outside. Khairullozhon helped him carry the bags out. As they hugged goodbye, Ibragim gave his EBT card to Khairullozhon, scribbling the PIN on the top so his friend could withdraw the cash still available on it, and returned the spare key to the apartment. Khairullozhon went back inside and threw away the towel that Ibragim had used after his shower.

Khairullozhon didn't remember later whether or not the towel was bloody. He couldn't explain why he had thrown it away. He wouldn't talk to Ibragim again until April 16, 2013, the day after the bombings in Boston. Then he called Ibragim on his cell phone at home in Orlando, Florida, and they talked for twenty-two minutes. Khairullozhon insists that the subject of their friends the Tsarnaev brothers never came up, and neither did the bombing. The date of the call was just a coincidence.

"I got my green card," Ibragim told Khairullozhon. "I'm going back to Russia."

———————

This was the first of the many inconsistent stories that Khairullozhon would tell the FBI. He thought that his cooperation with the Braintree police on that Friday morning when the manhunt was underway for Dzhokhar would leave him in the clear. He was wrong. The FBI would not only interview him more than a dozen times, but they would overtly track him using what Special Agent Tim McElroy would describe as "bumper lock surveillance," explaining that the surveillance was meant to be noticed and the FBI wanted Matanov to be "certainly aware of people following him, cars following him, things of that nature. It was not covert in any manner."[1]

He was under around-the-clock surveillance from the time he left the Braintree police station on April 19, 2013, until he was arrested on May 26, 2014, on charges that he had destroyed evidence connecting him to Dzhokhar and Tamerlan Tsarnaev, and that he had lied to the FBI about contacts he had with the brothers after the marathon bombing, including the dinner they had shared on the night of the attack. In fact, McElroy said, Matanov tried to lose his tail several times by using "evasive driving styles. He was making sharp turns, traveling in an erratic manner on the expressway, going through different lanes of traffic quickly, things that were obviously a sign of concern to the surveillance personnel at the time for public safety and other reasons." Twice he even confronted FBI agents demanding to know why he was being followed. The FBI even used a drone to follow the Tsarnaev brothers' pal, officials confirmed during Matanov's arraignment, prompting 911 calls to the Quincy Police Department more than once.[2]

There was a reason the FBI was keen on Khairullozhon Matanov in connection with the bombing. That night he and the Tsarnaev brothers seemingly celebrated the Patriots' Day murders with dinner at a Somerville kabob restaurant. It was Matanov's treat. And then there was the issue of an unsolved triple murder in Waltham, a gruesome slaying that Tamerlan Tsarnaev would be connected to in the days after the attack.[3]

Investigators assigned to the Middlesex County District Attorney's Office were under pressure to explain the unsolved ritualistic murders of three young men in Waltham, Massachusetts, a triple slaying that had all the earmarks of Islamic terrorism and that had taken place on the tenth anniversary of the 9/11 attacks.

It was a night that Khairullozhon was reluctant to discuss. "I am worried about the date. I don't want to make a problem for myself or something else,"[4] he explained to the FBI agents, according to proffer reports. That problem, Khairullozhon knew all too well, would likely lead investigators to his old roommate's new apartment in Orlando.

Ibragim had fled Boston on September 11, 2011, and headed south in a hurry, Khairullozhon told the FBI agents. Tamerlan left the country four months later for his motherland—the very place that the Russian FSB had warned the FBI and the CIA in March 2011 that he would go to join the jihad.

After the marathon attacks, friends of the three victims in Waltham—Brendan Mess, Rafi Teken, and Erik Weissman—began to tell investigators about Tamerlan's connection to the dead men. The case was reopened with a vengeance. Especially after relatives publicly complained that they had told investigators in 2011 that Tamerlan Tsarnaev was the most likely killer, but for some reason that was inexplicable—at least to the dead men's loved ones—he was never questioned. A clandestine federal investigation being conducted in Maine could very well be the reason why.

That investigation centered on a dirty cop in Watertown who had warned Safwan Madarati about a pending indictment. Madarati, of course, was tied to the Eritrean drug crew in Portland, Maine, that the DEA and DHS investigators had targeted. The case had Cambridge connections and cooperating witnesses in Massachusetts.

A review of court records related to Operation Run This Town suggests that Tamerlan very well could be the CW cited repeatedly by prosecutors. Remember that one of the targets was Tamerlan's old friend and former Cambridge Rindge and Latin classmate, Hamadi Hassan. In wiretapped conversations one CW makes plans to meet up with Hamadi in Boston-area locations, locations that Tamerlan had connections to—such as a parking lot near Wai Kru and a 7-Eleven near the Cambridge mosque.

That connection to the larger investigation could explain why the triple homicide had not been solved, despite the tips to detectives and reporters from relatives including Dylan Mess, Brendan's brother—who said that they should investigate his brother's "shady girlfriend" and "her friend Tam."[5]

It is plausible that the killings of three drug dealers in a Boston suburb—most of whose relatives had disowned them—was not a big enough case to lose a CW in Operation Run This Town, especially if the Eritrean dealers were funding overseas terrorism. Any media interest in the unsolved murders had died down, and the families were not demanding updates from detectives, which is usually the case with so-called innocent victims.

Strangely, Gerry Leone, the Middlesex district attorney who first mentioned the "two men" who left the Waltham apartment alive on September 11, 2011, quit his job four days after the Boston Marathon attack, on the same day that the world learned the bombers had killed a police officer, carjacked a young businessman in Cambridge, and engaged investigators in a wild firefight that had left another police officer in critical condition and one of the Tsarnaev brothers dead. As the governor of Massachusetts issued a "shelter in place" order for a large swath of the Commonwealth, Leone quietly resigned and announced that he would be joining Nixon Peabody, a prestigious 150-year-old law firm that counted many former federal prosecutors, judges, and political advisors among its attorneys. Nixon Peabody boasted of its new hire by describing Leone this way: "As the Department of Justice's first ever Anti-Terrorism Task Force Coordinator for Massachusetts, Leone initiated nationally recognized and unprecedented cooperation among federal, state and local authorities to protect the Commonwealth from terrorist threats following September 11."[6]

It was a stunning announcement in law enforcement circles. Leone was not only a storied prosecutor respected by rank-and-file police officers and the young district attorneys who worked for him; he was also viewed as a political star with a bright future. No one could imagine him taking a quiet desk job in the private sector, no matter how much that move increased his income. His resignation came in the midst of the largest case in Middlesex County—Sean Collier's murder—and while the office was also embroiled in a controversial shaken-baby murder case that had wrongly imprisoned an Irish nanny. It was a very odd time to bow out, especially considering Leone's ties to terror cases.

It remains unclear whether or not Leone ever alerted the FBI about the bizarrely savage triple murder on Harding Avenue in Waltham on September 11, 2011, or about the connection of Tamerlan, who once lived with Brendan Mess as roommates, to the victims. He did, however, call the scene graphic at the time of the slayings.[7] Then there was the odd coincidence of Tamerlan Tsarnaev's title fight wins for Team New England in the National Golden Gloves in 2009 and 2010, which coincided with Gerry Leone's second job as a Golden Gloves referee at Lowell Stadium, the very same place where Tsarnaev was crowned champion.[8]

When the men were murdered on Harding Avenue, Leone was an executive board member of the Massachusetts Anti-Terrorism Advisory Council, a perfect fit for the former federal prosecutor who had successfully sent failed shoe bomber Richard Reid to Administrative Maximum Facility (ADX) Supermax (which has solitary cells for 490 male prisoners), in Florence Colorado, for life. He was also familiar with the FBI's Joint Terrorism Task Force, for which he still acted as a consultant. Certainly Leone knew that the date of the murders and the manner in which the men had been nearly beheaded and the two Jewish victims sexually mutilated were indications that Islamic terrorists should have been suspected as the perpetrators. Leone was a very sharp investigator, which led to questions being asked among his peers about whether he had been pressured to put the Harding Avenue investigation on the back burner so some federal agency could continue to run Tamerlan as an asset. Of course, no one would ask those questions publicly.

And in any case Leone was gone in May 2013, when detectives who used to work under him flew to Orlando to talk to Ibragim.

There is a gag order in place on the entire triple homicide both in the trial of Dzhokhar Tsarnaev and in the Middlesex district attorney's office even at the time of this writing, in 2016. All testimony and evidence in Tsarnaev's trial pertaining to the Waltham triple murders would be filed under seal, and remain under seal as late as December 2016.

———

Khairullozhon told the FBI he met both Ibragim and the Tsarnaev brothers at the Prospect Street mosque in Cambridge. All of them were Russian Muslims. Each of them had distinctive personalities. Khairullozhon was the floppy haired goofball who liked fedora hats and American women. Ibragim was the fighter, all cauliflower ears and sinewy muscles and with a nose smashed flat as if he had fallen on his face too many times. Dzhokhar was the quiet one, garrulous with his own friends but painfully shy in the presence of his older brother. Tamerlan was the most devout Muslim among them. The one-time party boy had given up drinking, drugs, and all other forms of debauchery. Instead he liked to lecture endlessly about Islam, Anwar al-Awlaki videos, and US government conspiracies. Ibragim hated the change in his one-time hard-partying friend.

"This guy, Tamerlan, he smoked more marijuana than anybody. Anybody," Ibragim complained to his roommate, Matanov would later recall in interviews with the FBI. "We were always at the clubs. He changed."[9]

That change was even more noticeable when Tamerlan came back from Russia. Now even his appearance was different. He had a six-inch beard and was wearing a long white robe rather than designer jeans and button-down shirts. For Ramadan, Tamerlan wanted Khairullozhon to hike up Mount Monadnock with him because "Islam teaches people to be brothers." All the way up the mountain Tamerlan talked about his plans to join the jihad, Ibragim told the FBI.

In August 2012, a few weeks after his return from Russia, Tamerlan met Khairullozhon at the Prospect Street Mosque for a service on Eid al-Adha (the festival of sacrifice). Celebrated at the end of the Hajj, the annual pilgrimage to Mecca, Eid al-Adha is one of the highest of Muslim holidays. Although only pilgrims in Mecca fully participate in the Hajj, Muslims around the world join in spirit with those who travel to Saudi Arabia to celebrate. The FBI would note in its reports that sometime during the day someone snapped a photo of Tamerlan and Khairullozhon "seated in front of a black flag with a sword and a shahada phrase," referring to the statement of faith in Islam, adding that the photo was taken "at the mosque."[10] That flag is ordinarily dubbed the black flag of jihad, and it is flown by members of ISIS and other extremist groups linked to Al Qaeda. The picture was appropriate because all Tamerlan wanted to talk about, Khairullozhon later told the FBI, was jihad. He showed his friends videos of insurgent attacks on Americans in Afghanistan and ranted about Syria: "Everybody there is dying and no one cares in this country."[11] He boasted that he was going to be a mujahedin.

"Did you see the bombing in Chechnya?" Khairullozhon asked at one point. "Government people died."

"I hope it was Ramzan Kadyrov," Tamerlan answered. Khairullozhon knew that was the Chechen president. Another Muslim friend overheard the remark and defended Kadyrov. Tamerlan quickly grew heated. Khairullozhon stepped in: "*Brats* [brothers], it is Eid, a time for celebration. Let's go to the beach."

That was the second time Khairullozhon would have to intervene between Tamerlan and a friend. Tamerlan had also been fighting with their Russian pal Ibragim.

Tamerlan, who was unemployed, drove a white Mercedes at the time. He used it to drive to the beach, while Khairullozhon got in his taxi. They posed for more pictures, which were among the photos Khairullozhon deleted from his laptop after leaving the Braintree police station. That night Khairullozhon went to Norfolk Street for Eid dinner with Tamerlan's family. Zubeidat was there, covered, making chicken and salad for the family. Then they sat down in front of the TV and watched a jihadist video, Khairullozhon remembered, and Tamerlan asked him about Ibragim.

"He's in Florida with his wife," Khairullozhon answered. Tamerlan nodded. He hadn't seen Ibragim in a while, not since September 2011. Ibragim had been lying low, and Tamerlan had been busy planning a terrorist attack.

On April 21, 2013, Ibragim got a call on his cell phone from the FBI. Agents wanted to talk about Tamerlan, the Prospect Street mosque, and the calls and texts Ibragim had exchanged with Tamerlan on September 11, 2011, evidence that put them both in Waltham at the time of the triple killings.

Ibragim had lived in Orlando since moving out of Boston the same night as the Harding Avenue murders, and he wasn't willing to go back. When the agents called in 2013 he made it clear that he would cooperate, but only if he would be allowed to go back to Russia right afterward. The FBI told Ibragim it would probably be difficult for him to leave the country as he had been put on a no-fly list, and his only way off it was to sit down with investigators. Ibragim agreed.

The meeting came on May 22, 2013, at his Florida apartment. In attendance were the detectives assigned to the case of the unsolved murders of the three men in Waltham, Massachusetts state troopers Kurt Cinelli and Joel Gagne from the specialized CPAC unit within the Middlesex County District Attorney's Office, and FBI Special Agent Aaron McFarlane, assigned to the bureau's Boston field office. They knew time was of the essence. Ibragim had purchased a ticket on a flight to Russia scheduled to leave on May 24, telling his family back home that he was sick and tired of what he called "the harassment of Chechens in America."[12]

It was 7:30 P.M. when the investigators showed up Ibragim's apartment at 6022 Peregrine Avenue in Orlando. It would have been preferable to conduct the interview at the police station, but Ibragim refused: "If you want to meet you come to me."[13]

Caution was also of the essence. Ibragim was a violent man with a long rap sheet and a rapid-fire punch that had knocked out more than a few mixed martial arts fighters in the cage. In fact, he often sparred with Brendan Mess, one of the men who had nearly been decapitated in Waltham. The investigators had studied some of Ibragim's fights on YouTube and familiarized themselves with his criminal record, which was full of minor brawls and fights that escalated to bloodsheds within minutes. He wasn't a big guy—only five feet six and wiry—but he had a short fuse. "On a scale of one to ten, I believe Todashev was an eight as far as his inclination and ability for physical violence," McFarlane told investigators from both the Department of Justice Civil Rights Division and the Florida Attorney General. Both agencies conducted separate investigations into what happened in Todashev's Orlando apartment that night.

Once Ibragim had gotten into a fender bender in downtown Boston that had turned ugly fast. At 3:21 P.M. on February 11, 2010, BPD officers arrived on the scene to find Ibragim red-faced and screaming: "You say something about my mother? I will kill you!"[14] He might have been short, but he was strong. It took three officers to pin him to the ground and handcuff him. Cinelli had talked to one of the arresting officers. "He was an animal," the cop told the trooper. "It was like fighting a refrigerator."

And on May 4, just weeks before the Massachusetts investigators' arrival in Florida, FBI agents from the Tampa field office had been surveilling Ibragim's movements with low-flying surveillance planes and around-the-clock teams when they saw him get into an argument over a parking spot with a father and his son. It was vicious. Ibragim tried to pull his white Mercedes into the spot at an outlet mall that the other two men had been waiting for. The father yelled: "No way, I was here first. My blinker was on."[15] All hell broke loose. The argument turned into a fistfight. The son was knocked unconscious and lost several teeth. His father was badly bloodied. The FBI watched the entire event but could not intervene. It was their job to watch a possible terrorist, not stop a felonious assault. Off-duty Orange County Deputy Sheriff Larry Clifton responded to a 911 call placed by a passerby and arrested Ibragim for aggravated battery. Clifton wrote in his report: "I immediately recognized the marks on his ears as [those of] a cage fighter/jujitsu fighter. I know from training, experience, and watching a lot of sanctioned fights how dangerous these men can be. I told this suspect that if he tried to fight with us I would shoot him."[16] With that warning Ibragim quieted down and was taken into custody.

These incidents were on the minds of the three Massachusetts investigators as they knocked on Ibragim's door in Orlando.

"You can't come into my house with your shoes on," was the greeting they got from Ibragim. "I'm Muslim." The investigators slipped off their shoes and entered the sweltering apartment through a door emblazoned with the image of an AK47. The floor was sticky under their socks and the room was dark, but McFarlane noticed a samurai sword hanging on the wall in the living room, exactly the type of sharp weapon that could have delivered the fatal blows to the Waltham victims. He kept an eye on it as Ibragim sat on the edge of a mattress on the floor. Cinelli sat on a folding chair across from the suspect and quietly switched on a small tape recorder concealed in his the pocket of his suit jacket. McFarlane sat on a step in a nearby staircase, and Gagne stood next to him.

The conversation started off friendly enough. The investigators tried to make Ibragim comfortable by paying him compliments about his accomplishments in the cage and commented on some of the bouts they had watched. They told him they were going to audio- and videotape the conversation, and Ibragim nodded. But when the conversation turned to the night of September 11, 2011, Ibragim became agitated. He twitched and stammered and denied knowing anything about the murders, despite the cell phone calls that put him in Waltham with Tamerlan that night. McFarlane also described what the investigators knew about the phone calls that the two had exchanged.

"I didn't kill nobody and I need your help," Ibragim told them. He repeatedly changed his story. The investigators waited. They gave him water and watched him smoke one cigarette after another. After about four hours of idle chitchat combined with repeated questions about his whereabouts on the night of the murders, Ibragim broke. First he asked them to turn off the video camera. They did.

"If I tell you my involvement is there any chance . . . you need me to testify?"[17]

McFarlane didn't respond immediately, and Ibragim then blurted out a confession: "Okay. I was involved in it, okay. I, I had no idea Tam was gonna kill anyone. Will you guys help me?"

Cinelli immediately read him his Miranda rights and prepared a document from the FBI called an Advice of Rights form. Ibragim became more anxious: "After I tell you, are you going to take me to jail right away?"

He then dropped his chin to his chest and mumbled, "How much time will I get?" Cinelli recited his Miranda rights again and had him sign the form. It was 10:25 P.M. The investigators had been there for just under four hours. "I need more butts," Ibrahim said.

Gagne volunteered to go get more cigarettes and took the opportunity to step outside and text the prosecutor who was overseeing the Waltham investigation about their progress: "He signed Miranda. He's about to tell us his involvement. Standby."[18]

"Amazing," the prosecutor texted back.

"He will be in custody after interviews."

"Don't put him in custody until we get warrant," the prosecutor texted both troopers (the arrest warrant was still being sworn out back in Massachusetts). Cinelli—who was eager to put cuffs on Ibragim after his confession of nearly beheading three men, and sexually mutilating two of them, or at least being in the room when it happened—showed the text to McFarlane. The order to wait had come from the top.

With Middlesex District Attorney Gerry Leone gone, the Democratic governor had put a political appointee in his place. Her name was Marian Ryan, and she was not exactly known as a risk taker before she got the promotion. This was a big case, and it involved international radical Islamic terrorism. She told her office to direct the troopers to wait until they had hard evidence or a confession in writing before taking Ibragim into custody.

"Okay he's writing a statement now in his apartment," Gagne texted the prosecutor, excited that the unsolved triple murders could be closer to a conclusion. He added, "Who's your daddy?"

Cinelli handed Ibragim a white legal pad and a pen. He sat on the mattress, pulled over a small white coffee table to use as a desk, and started to write:

My name is IBRAGIM TODASHEV
I wanna tell the story about the robbery
me and Tam did in Waltham in September
of 2011. That was [illegible] by Tamerlan.
He offered me to rob
the drug dealers. We went to their
house we got in there and Tam had
a gun he pointed it with the guy that
opened the door for us [illegible]
we went upstairs into the house
with 3 guys in there. [word crossed out] we put them
on the ground and then we [word crossed out]
taped their hands up.[19]

When Ibragim was almost finished, one trooper stepped outside to call a Middlesex County prosecutor. Then Ibragim asked to go to the bathroom, for the third or fourth time. Cinelli had a bad feeling. The energy in the room had changed. He whispered to McFarlane, "This is going to go bad." Then he grabbed the samurai sword that was hanging on the wall next to a black Islamic flag and stashed it behind a shoe rack in the kitchen, to be on the safe side. At 12:03 A.M. Cinelli sent a text to Gagne: "You better get back here." The suspect was jumpy.

"He is in vulnerable position to do something bad," Cinelli then began to text to McFarlane, not wanting to speak out loud in front of the visibly rattled suspect, who was still in the nearby bathroom. He couldn't finish the text. Ibragim came out of the bathroom and noticed the empty spot on the wall where his sword had hung, and his manner became noticeably strange. He sat back down on the mattress with the coffee table in front of him. Cinelli sat on a stair to continue his text. McFarlane moved the folding chair to sit in front of Ibragim as he picked up the pen to write. McFarlane was looking down at his own notes when he heard a loud noise and felt a blow to the back of his head that knocked him off the chair.

He had been hit with the white coffee table after it had been "propelled into the air," opening a gash in his head that would take nine staples to close. Ibragim raced past the stunned FBI agent into the kitchen and frantically rummaged through cabinets and drawers. Cinelli was right behind him. McFarlane drew his gun and followed.

"Show me your hands!" McFarlane shouted at Ibragim.

Ibragim had found what he was looking for: a red broom that he could use as a martial arts baton or karate stick. He raised it over his head and charged—"incredibly quickly," Cinelli remembered—back toward McFarlane, whose head was gushing blood.

"Stop right there! Stop right there!" McFarlane yelled. Ibragim kept coming. The agent fired. The bullets knocked Ibragim back for a matter of seconds, but he sprang up again and lunged headlong at the investigators. McFarlane fired again. "There was no doubt in my mind that Todashev intended to kill both of us," he would explain to other FBI officials. "In order to stop this threat I shot Todashev three to four times. Todashev fell backwards but did not go to the ground. He then reestablished his footing and suddenly lunged again toward us. I then shot him three or four more times in order to stop his continuing deadly threat. This time Todashev fell to the ground face first and I believed this threat has been eliminated."

Gagne drew his weapon and came through the front door with an agent from the FBI's Tampa field office.

Ibragim was indeed on the floor face down. The twenty-seven-year-old Chechen immigrant had been shot seven times in all during the two volleys of bullets, once in head and six times in the body, and was pronounced dead at the scene. McFarlane was "bleeding profusely," Gagne remembered. He called 911 from his cell phone.

Cinelli was grateful to be alive. "I am certain Agent McFarlane's actions saved me from serious physical injury or death," he told his superiors. He also turned over the recording device hidden in his pocket. It had captured most of the chaos inside the hot, crowded apartment.

The legal pad was spotted with Ibragim's blood. So was the rug. When he collapsed, he fell on Cinelli's feet, and the trooper had to wear hospital booties at the crime scene so the blood on his soaked socks could be preserved as evidence. His shoes were still at the door.

———

Ibragim's death became an international incident. His father, Abdul-Baki Todashev, held a press conference in Moscow where he called the FBI agents "bandits" who had tortured and executed his son. "I want justice and an investigation in accordance with American laws to punish those who are guilty," Abdul-Baki Todashev said. "They were not FBI employees, but bandits."[20] He held pictures of his dead son's bullet-riddled body over his head and described the carnage as a scene out of a movie. Of course, Ibragim was not a US citizen. He was instead, like Tamerlan, a lawful permanent resident holding a Russian passport. His brushes with the law should have led to deportation hearings, but that never happened. Tatiana Gruzdeva, his girlfriend, who had been arrested as leverage against him, would not be so lucky: she was deported.

Ibragim's father would not let up the pressure on US officials. With the help of his boss, the Chechen president whom Tamerlan had hoped was dead on Eid al-Adha, the senior Todashev wrote a letter to US President Barack Obama that he shared with the international press corps:

"Did my son know that he had the right to remain silent or did he have rights at all, including the right to live? Being a citizen of another country he might not be aware of the laws as he was only 27 years old and wanted to live so much. No, they left no chances for him inflicting 13 gunshot wounds and multiple hematomas on his body. After what FBI agents have done to him whatever excuses they come up with nobody would believe them because my son is dead and cannot talk for himself. They did it deliberately so that he can never speak and never take part in court hearings. They put pressure on my son's friends to prevent them from coming to the court and speaking the truth. I rely on you, Mr. President, and hope that the prosecutor's office and the court do not let the agencies conducting internal investigation on this case prevent the truth from coming to light so that at least some part of our grief, caused by the murder of our son, is relieved, and that the murderers stand trial instead of sit in their desk chairs."[21]

The FBI imposed a gag order on its agents about the case, and Ibragim's death certificate was sealed. But the less the FBI said, the more suspicious his death looked. To make matters worse, the *Boston Globe* uncovered Mc-Farlane's shady past as an Oakland, California, police officer. By the time he was thirty-one, he had been investigated by Oakland Police Department's internal affairs staff multiple times and retired under a cloud of suspicion with a disability pension, saying that he had been hurt on the job (but apparently not hurt enough to pursue a career in the FBI, which he managed to do without giving up his $52,000 annual disability pension).[22]

CAIR immediately got involved, providing legal advice and a driver for Ibragim's father when he obtained a tourist visa to travel to the United States. CAIR said that the FBI had been trying to bully Ibragim into becoming an informant and had used similar tactics to intimidate his Muslim friends. "FBI agents have threatened to wrongfully arrest them [the Muslim friends] unless they became informants and spied on local mosques, Muslim restaurants and hookah lounges. The DOJ [Department of Justice] must rein in the atrocious abuse of ethics and the rule of law by overzealous agents who have apparently disregarded the protections enshrined in our Constitution, which are essential to maintaining liberty and justice in our legal system. We also urge community members never to be intimidated by abusive law enforcement tactics and to maintain their right to remain silent and their right to an attorney when approached by FBI agents,"[23] Hassan Shibly, the executive director for CAIR in Tampa, said in a press release after Ibragim's death.

The FBI would not confirm or deny the allegations.

As the chorus of critics grew louder, Florida Attorney General Jeff Ashton ordered an independent investigation into Ibragim's shooting. Ashton met with CAIR representatives and Ibragim's father to try to assuage their anger. In the end Ashton's office released a 161-page report that exonerated the three Massachusetts investigators of any wrongdoing.

"Mr. Todashev, a trained Mixed Martial Arts fighter, struck the FBI agent in the head with a coffee table and then armed himself near the front door of the address. As he then re-engaged [McFarlane] and [Cinelli] they both perceived Mr. Todashev's movements towards them as being potentially life threatening," according to the report, written by the attorney general's chief of investigations, Eric Edwards. "The use of deadly force by [McFarlane] on May 22, 2013, was reasonable and justified, and therefore, lawful."[24]

The cops were cleared, and to this day the Waltham triple homicide case remains open. Dead men tell no tales. But their friends do.

Roseann Sdoia in the arms of a stranger, Northeastern University college student Shores Salter, who helped her after the blast. They remain friends to this day. Photo courtesy of US Attorney's Office. Trial exhibit.

Leo Woolfenden in the arms of BPD Officer Tommy Barrett. Leo's dad Steve lost his leg in the attack. Photo courtesy of US Attorney's Office. Trial exhibit.

Detonation, from a surveillance photo inside the Forum restaurant.
Photo courtesy of US Attorney's Office. Trial Exhibit.

BPD Unified Command Center during the hunt for the Boston Marathon bombers.
Photo courtesy of Boston Police Department.

FBI Special Agent Vincent Lisi, then the agent in charge of the bureau's Boston field office (left), revisits the scene of the Boston Marathon attacks with ABC News Chief Investigative Correspondent Brian Ross, March 2016. Photo courtesy of the FBI's Boston field office.

FBI Special Agent Kieran Ramsey, then assistant agent in charge of the bureau's Boston field office and now the FBI's legal attaché in Rome, talks about the victims of the blasts in March 2016. Photo courtesy of the FBI's Boston field office.

BPD Commissioner William Evans on Boylston Street with ATF Agent and a BPD captain, April 2013. Photo courtesy of Boston Police Department.

Dzhokhar Tsarnaev tweet in the hours after he detonated a weapon of mass destruction on Boylston Street, April 15, 2013. Photo courtesy of US Attorney's Office. Trial exhibit.

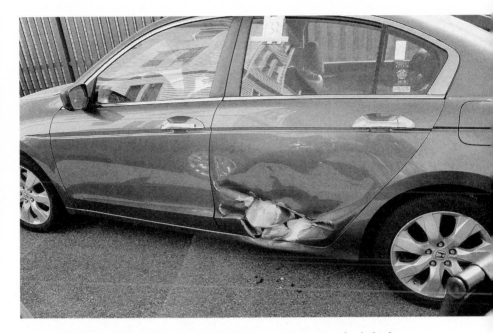

Aftermath of the gunfight in Watertown on April 19, 2013: a pressure cooker lodged in the side of a car. Photo courtesy of US Attorney's Office. Trial exhibit.

Note written by Dzhokhar Tsarnaev on the inside of the dry-docked boat *Slip Away II*, April 19, 2013. Photo courtesy of US Attorney's Office. Trial exhibit.

MIT Police Officer Sean Collier. Photo courtesy
of US Attorney's Office. Trial exhibit.

Inside the cruiser of MIT Police Officer Sean Collier, April 18, 2013.
Photo courtesy of US Attorney's Office. Trial exhibit.

USA (*bottom of the photo*) written by Watertown residents in the hours after Dzhokhar Tsarnaev was pulled out of the *Slip Away II* at the spot where Tamerlan Tsarnaev had lain bleeding. Photo by Michele McPhee, April 20, 2013.

From left to right: Watertown Police Department Sergeant John C. MacLellan, Sergeant Jeffrey J. Pugliese, Officer Miguel A. Colon Jr., Officer Timothy B. Menton, and Officer Joseph B. Reynolds. Photo courtesy of Watertown Police Department.

Tamerlan (*right*) and Dzhokhar Tsarnaev outside of their Cambridge home. Photo courtesy of Dzhokhar Tsarnaev's defense team. Trial exhibit.

Tamerlan in front of an Islamic flag often associated with jihad that investigators discovered in executing a search warrant at his Norfolk Street home after the blasts. Photo courtesy of US Attorney's Office. Trial exhibit.

Zubeidat and Tamerlan Tsarnaev. Photo courtesy of Dzhokhar Tsarnaev's defense team. Trial exhibit.

Tamerlan in his American boxing helmet. Photo courtesy of Dzhokhar Tsarnaev's defense team. Trial exhibit.

The Tsarnaev family arrives in the United States (*left to right*): Dzhokhar, Tamerlan, Anzor, Ailina, and Bella. Photo courtesy of Dzhokhar Tsarnaev's defense team. Trial exhibit.

Tamerlan Tsarnaev and Katherine Russell at the start of their romance. Photo courtesy of Dzhokhar Tsarnaev's defense team. Trial exhibit.

Documents found in Tamerlan Tsarnaev's US Customs and Immigration "A-file," with a photograph of him. State Department documents obtained through a Freedom of Information Act request to USCIS.

U. S. Department of State
MEDICAL EXAMINATION FOR
IMMIGRANT OR REFUGEE APPLICANT

EXPIRATION DATE: 1/31/2004
(ESTIMATED BURDEN: 40 minutes)
(See Page 2 - Back of Form)

Name (Last, First, MI) **TSARNAEV TAMERLAN**
Birth Date (mm-dd-yyyy) **10.21.1986** SEX: ☐ M ☒ F
Birthplace (City/County) **RUSSIA**
Present Country of Residence ____ Prior Country ____
U. S. Consul (City/Country) **ANKARA / TURKEY**
Passport Number ____ Alien (Case) Number ____
Date Exam Expires (6 months from examination date, if Class A or TB condition exists, otherwise 12 months) (mm-dd-yyyy) **10 JUL 20**
Exam Place (City/Country) **ANKARA / TURKEY** Panel Physician **Dr.** ____
Radiology Services (name) ____ Screening Site (name) ____
Lab (name for HIV/syphilis/TB) **DÜZEN** **DÜZEN** **DUZEN**

(1) Classification (check all boxes that apply):
☑ No apparent defect, disease, or disability (see Worksheets DS-3024, DS-3025 and DS-3026)
☐ Class A Conditions (From Past Medical History and Physical Examination Worksheets)

☐ TB, active, infectious (Class A, from Chest X-Ray Worksheet)
☐ Syphilis, untreated
☐ Chancroid, untreated
☐ Gonorrhea, untreated
☐ Granuloma inguinale, untreated
☐ Lymphogranuloma venereum, untreated

☐ Human immunodeficiency virus (HIV)
☐ Hansen's disease, lepromatous or multibacillary
☐ Addiction or abuse of specific* substance without harmful behavior
☐ Any physical or mental disorder (including other substance-related disorder) with harmful behavior or history of such behavior likely to recur
*amphetamines, cannabis, cocaine, hallucinogens, inhalan opioids, phencyclidines, sedative-hypnotics, and anxiolyti

☐ Class B Conditions (From Past Medical History and Physical Examination Worksheets)

☐ TB, active, noninfectious (Class B1, from Chest X-Ray Worksheet)
   Treatment: ☐ None ☐ Partial ☐ Completed
☐ TB, inactive (Class B2, from Chest X-Ray Worksheet)
   Treatment: ☐ None ☐ Partial ☐ Completed
☐ Syphilis, treated within last year
☐ Other sexually transmitted infections, treated within last year
☐ Current pregnancy, number of weeks pregnant ____
☐ Other (specify or give details on checked conditions from worksheets)

☐ Hansen's disease, prior treatment
☐ Hansen's disease, tuberculoid, borderline, or paucibacillary
☐ Sustained, full remission of addiction or abuse of specific substances
☐ Any physical or mental disorder (excluding addiction or abuse of specific* substance but including other substance-related disorder) without harmful behavior or history of such behavior unlikely to recur
*amphetamines, cannabis, cocaine, hallucinogens, inhalan opioids, phencyclidines, sedative-hypnotics, and anxiolyti

(2) Laboratory Findings (check all boxes that apply):

Syphilis: ☐ Not done

	Test name	Date(s) run (mm-dd-yyyy)	Negative	Positive	Titer 1	Notes
Screening	VDRL	10 JUL 2003	☑	☐		
Confirmatory			☐	☐		

Treated	If treated, therapy:			Date(s) treatment given (3 doses for penici)
☐ Yes	☐ Benzathine penicillin, 2.4 MU IM			
☐ No	☐ Other (therapy, dose):			

HIV: ☐ Not done

	Test name	Date(s) run (mm-dd-yyyy)	Negative	Positive	Indeterminate	Notes
Screening	HIV 1 / HIV 2	10 JUL 2003	☑	☐	☐	
Secondary			☐	☐	☐	
Confirmatory			☐	☐	☐	

DS-2063 (formerly OF 157)
01-2001

Page 1 o

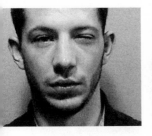  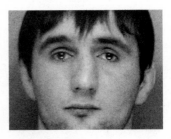

Left Brendan Mess, one of the three men killed in Waltham on September 11, 2011, after a 2012 arrest in Cambridge on assault charges. Photo courtesy of Cambridge Police Department. *Middle* Tamerlan Tsarnaev after being arrested for slapping his girlfriend in the face on July 10, 2009. Photo courtesy of Cambridge Police Department. *Right* Ibragim Todashev after being arrested in connection with a violent road rage incident in Boston, February 11, 2010. Photo courtesy of Boston Police Department.

U. S. Department of State
MEDICAL EXAMINATION FOR
IMMIGRANT OR REFUGEE APPLICANT

OMB No. 1405-0113
EXPIRATION DATE: 1/31/2004
ESTIMATED BURDEN: 40 minutes
(See Page 2 - Back of Form)

Name (Last, First, MI) TSARNAEV TAMERLAN
Birth Date (mm-dd-yyyy) 10.21.1986 SEX: ☐ M ☒ F
Birthplace (City/Country) RUSSIA
Present Country of Residence Prior Country
U. S. Consul (City/Country) ANKARA / TURKEY
Passport Number A2517957 Alien (Case) Number
te Exam Expires (6 months from examination date, if Class A or TB condition exists, otherwise 12 months) (mm-dd-yyyy) 1 0 JUL 2003
m Place (City/Country) ANKARA / TURKEY Panel Physician (name) Dr.
iology Services (name) DR. Screening Site (name) DR.
 iname for HIV/syphilis/TB) DÜZEN DÜZEN DÜZEN

Classification (check all boxes that apply):
☐ No apparent defect, disease, or disability (see Worksheets DS-3024, DS-3025 and DS-3026)

Class A Conditions (From Past Medical History and Physical Examination Worksheets)
☐ TB, active, infectious (Class A, from Chest X-Ray Worksheet) ☐ Human immunodeficiency virus (HIV)
☐ Syphilis, untreated ☐ Hansen's disease, lepromatous or multibacillary
☐ Chancroid, untreated ☐ Addiction or abuse of specific* substance without harmful behavior
☐ Gonorrhea, untreated
☐ Granuloma inguinale, untreated ☐ Any physical or mental disorder (including other substance-related disorder) with harmful behavior or history of such behavior likely to recur
☐ Lymphogranuloma venereum, untreated
  *amphetamines, cannabis, cocaine, hallucinogens, inhalants, opioids, phencyclidine, sedative-hypnotics, and anxiolytics

Class B Conditions (From Past Medical History and Physical Examination Worksheets)
☐ TB, active, noninfectious (Class B1, from Chest X-Ray Worksheet) ☐ Hansen's disease, prior treatment
  Treatment: ☐ None ☐ Partial ☐ Completed ☐ Hansen's disease, tuberculoid, borderline, or paucibacillary
☐ TB, inactive (Class B2, from Chest X-Ray Worksheet) ☐ Sustained, full remission of addiction or abuse of specific* substances
  Treatment: ☐ None ☐ Partial ☐ Completed
☐ Syphilis, treated within last year ☐ Any physical or mental disorder (excluding addiction or abuse of specific* substance but including other substance-related disorder) without harmful behavior or history of such behavior unlikely to recur
☐ Other sexually transmitted infections, treated within last year
☐ Current pregnancy, number of weeks pregnant _____
☐ Other (specify or give details on checked conditions from worksheets) *amphetamines, cannabis, cocaine, hallucinogens, inhalants, opioids, phencyclidine, sedative-hypnotics, and anxiolytics

) Laboratory Findings (check all boxes that apply):
Syphilis: ☐ Not done

Test name	Date(s) run (mm-dd-yyyy)	Negative	Positive	Titer 1	Notes
Screening VDRL	1 0 JUL 2003	☒	☐		
Confirmatory		☐	☐		

Treated If treated, therapy: Date(s) treatment given (3 doses for penicillin)
☐ Yes ☐ Benzathine penicillin, 2.4 MU IM
☐ No ☐ Other (therapy, dose):

HIV: ☐ Not done

Test name	Date(s) run (mm-dd-yyyy)	Negative	Positive	Indeterminate	Notes
Screening HIV 1 / HIV 2	1 0 JUL 2003	☒	☐	☐	
Secondary		☐	☐	☐	
Confirmatory		☐	☐	☐	

-2053 (Formerly OF 157)
-2001 Page 1 of 2

Nearly identical documents found in Tamerlan Tsarnaev's US Customs and Immigration "A-file," with a photograph of a different man in an identical shirt. State Department documents through a Freedom of Information Act request to USCIS.

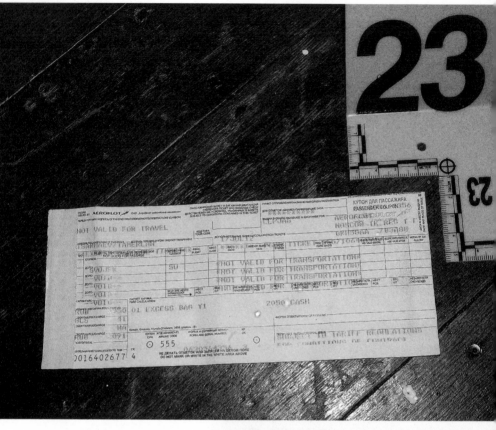

Airline ticket for Tamerlan Tsarnaev's return to the United States two days after a deadly raid in Russia that left seven Islamic militants dead. Photo courtesy of Dzhokhar Tsarnaev's defense team. Trial exhibit.

Tupperware bomb—for the possession of which no one was charged—recovered from the back of the Mercedes carjacked by Tamerlan and Dzhokhar Tsarnaev. Photo courtesy of US Attorney's Office. Trial exhibit.

Daniel Morley after being arrested for threatening to kill his mother, June 9, 2013. Photo courtesy of Topsfield Police Department.

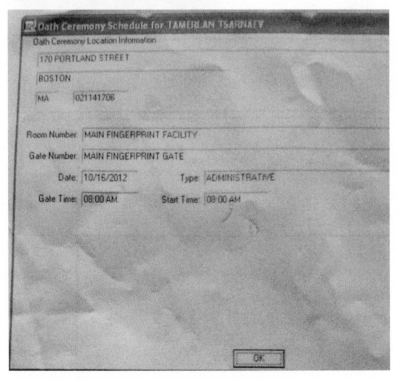

Copy of Tamerlan Tsarnaev's invitation to take the oath of US citizenship—citizenship for which he was not eligible. State Department documents through a Freedom of Information Act request to USCIS.

****

Dzhokhar Tsarnaev in front of a black flag associated with jihad in his bedroom.
Photo courtesy of US Attorney's Office. Trial exhibit.

Blood-splattered bottom of the *Slip Away II* after Dzhokhar Tsarnaev was captured on April 19, 2013. Photo courtesy of Dzhokhar Tsarnaev's defense team. Trial exhibit.

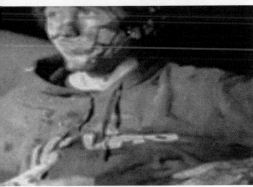

Dzhokhar Tsarnaev pulled from the *Slip Away II* in Watertown, April 19, 2013. Photo courtesy of Massachusetts State Police. Trial exhibit.

Dzhokhar Tsarnaev's one-finger salute to the camera as he awaited arraignment at the John Joseph Moakley Courthouse in South Boston, July 10, 2103. Photo courtesy of US Attorney's Office. Trial exhibit.

Ailina Tsarnaeva and her attorneys at South Boston Municipal Court, just miles away from the federal court where her brother would be tried, after an appearance in connection with a shoplifting charge, October 2013. Photo by Michele McPhee.

17

ALLAH SENT HIM MONEY

One of the questions that died with Ibragim Todashev was about a gun that was stashed "for protection" at 12 Harding Avenue in Waltham, a gun that went missing after the murders. The gun belonged to Brendan Mess, Hiba Eltilib, his girlfriend, told investigators in the hours after she saw the bodies of her boyfriend (with his throat slashed ear to ear) and his friends (sexually mutilated, with their necks sliced by a blade as well). Left in the apartment was $5,000 in cash and thousands of dollars' worth of hydroponic marijuana, but the gun was gone, she said. Ibragim had been in the process of confessing to the robbery that he committed with Tamerlan on September 11, 2011, when he died. He never got around to writing exactly what they had stolen.

The missing gun, investigators believed, could explain the two muzzle flashes observed by multiple witnesses during the Watertown firefight. Sergeant Jeffrey Pugliese, a firearms instructor and expert, insisted he saw two muzzle flashes. So did officers Joe Reynolds and Miguel Colon. Some of the residents of Laurel Street also thought there were two weapons, but only one gun, the Ruger P95 carried by Tamerlan Tsarnaev, was recovered—except for a BB gun that had been discarded on a resident's lawn. The muzzle flashes indicated that there could be another shooter on the scene, possibly a resident of the house at 89 Dexter Avenue that Dzhokhar Tsarnaev had emerged from, or even the man that Tamerlan had called right after the murder of MIT Police Officer Sean Collier: a native of the Caucasus named Viskhan Vakhabov. He and Tamerlan prayed together at the Cambridge mosque. Their brothers were friends and classmates at UMass/Dartmouth, and, prosecutors said, Viskhan was a liar who refused to testify in front of a grand jury on the ground that "he could incriminate himself in the Boston Marathon bombings," a statement that should have made him a person of interest in connection with the bombing plot. But for some inexplicable reason the federal government did not consider him a suspect and fought hard to keep his interviews with the FBI a secret, calling him an unreliable witness—albeit a witness who had spent a lot of time with both Tsarnaev brothers. The three had even been together in the days immediately before, and then again after, the Boston Marathon attack, going together to Wai Kru to work out.

There was immediate speculation among local law enforcement officials that the FBI was shielding Viskhan from scrutiny because he was another of the bureau's many Muslim informants—just like Tamerlan before he snapped. Considering the spy planes and around-the-clock JTTF teams of investigators used to monitor other friends of the Tsarnaev brothers like Ibragim and Khairullozhon Matanov, Viskhan's freedom seemed especially strange.

The theory that he was an informant gained momentum after a team from the FBI's own Cellular Analysis Survey Team, or CAST, studied the calls made on two prepaid T-Mobile "burner cells" purchased by Dzhokhar on April 14, 2013, the day before the Boston Marathon attack, using the name Jahar Tsarni. He gave Tamerlan one phone and kept the other. The next day Dzhokhar called Tamerlan at 2:49 P.M., the exact time the pressure-cooker bomb detonated in front of Marathon Sports. Twelve seconds later, Dzhokhar exploded the second bomb in front of the Forum restaurant. At 2:51 Tamerlan called Dzhokhar's phone, a call that lasted for thirty seconds. They connected somehow—to this day no one knows how they got out of Boylston Street in the mayhem—and made their way toward Dzhokhar's green Honda, which had been parked close enough for them to jog to. The burner phones gave investigators another lead: the brothers stopped at Whole Foods in Cambridge after the bombings. Dzhokhar ran into the store to buy milk, and Tamerlan called his friend Khairullozhon, the cab driver, at 3:15 P.M. Khairullozhon later discussed the call with the FBI. During the call, the FBI's report states, Khairullozhon and Tamerlan talked about the marathon, and Khairullozhon mused that maybe something had blown up in a nearby kitchen. Tamerlan responded, "Maybe. Maybe not."

With that call the burner phone's signal pinged off towers near the supermarket, leading investigators to request the surveillance video from the Whole Foods between the hours of 3:00 and 5:00 P.M. Bingo: the video showed Dzhokhar as he casually strolled into the Prospect Street store at 3:12. He lingered in front of the dairy section, picked up a half-gallon of milk, and then slowly walked to the register where he paid $3.49 for the milk and got change from a twenty-dollar bill. The video showed him as he left the store. Less than a minute later, he hustled back in to exchange the skim milk for regular. He left the store again and came back in seconds later to inexplicably exchange his second purchase for another half-gallon before he climbed into the passenger seat. With Tamerlan behind the wheel, the brothers headed home to Norfolk Street a few blocks away. Assistant US Attorney Aloke Chakravarty was astonished at the video, saying that the brothers "killed two young women that day. They killed a little boy. They maimed and permanently disfigured dozens of people. At least 17 amputees. At least 240 were injured. And after they did it, he coolly, not 20 minutes later, went to the Whole Foods to make sure he got the half-gallon of milk that he wanted." How could people be so "capable of such hate, such callousness that you could murder and maim nearly 20 people and then drive to Whole Foods and buy milk," he wondered.[1]

The phones were used again the next day, putting both brothers in Boston until that night, when Dzhokhar's phone was tracked to New Bedford and then shut off. At that point he partied with his boys. They smoked weed and went to the UMass/Dartmouth gym where they stayed, until his brother called him on another number to tell him to get his ass home: the FBI had released photos of them on the news, and their faces were everywhere. Dzhokhar turned the burner phone back on during the long ride from New Bedford to Cambridge. The phone put him back in Cambridge at 8:17 P.M., FBI special agent Chad Fitzgerald would testify.[2] Two hours later the brothers were on the campus of MIT, where they snuck up behind Sean Collier's cruiser and ambushed him with bullets. As they fled the crime scene in the Honda that had been parked on Ames Street, Tamerlan made another eighty-eight-second phone call from the burner phone. This call was to Viskhan.

"It's undisputed that Tamerlan Tsarnaev contacted him on April 18th, I believe, between the time that Officer Collier was murdered and the time that Dun Meng was carjacked," Assistant US Attorney William Weinreb said.[3] "He has given quite inconsistent statements about what that conversation was about and what Tamerlan Tsarnaev may have asked him or said to him."

The inconsistencies Weinreb referred to were in reference to the April 20, 2013, visit an FBI agent made to Viskhan's house in Allston, about a five-minute walk from the spot where Dun Meng was carjacked. The agent's interview of Viskhan didn't last long. Viskhan told the agent about his childhood in Russia and his family's move to the United States with the help of the United Nations in 2004. The Tsarnaev brothers were his first friends in the United States, and the two families were friendly with one another. In fact, Dzhokhar was so close to Viskhan's younger brother that they decided to attend the same college. When he first met Tamerlan, Viskhan told the agent, he and Tamerlan "would smoke, drink, and go to clubs."[4] According to the agent, Tamerlan even "introduced him to some of his weed smoking friends." Then in 2011, right around the time the FSB notified the FBI about Tamerlan's and his mother's radicalization, there was a dramatic change. He didn't want to go out anymore and even lectured Viskhan: "Just because you say you are a Muslim, it does not mean that you really are. A true Muslim would not go out and smoke and chill out." Viskhan refused to tell the agent what he and Tamerlan talked about in the phone call on the night of April 18, after Collier's murder and before Meng was carjacked—the night that ended with Tamerlan dead and a Watertown neighborhood pocked with bullet holes and bomb burns. All he would say was that Tamerlan was clearly inspired by the jihad during his trip to Russia and would repeatedly say that being a mujahedin was the only "proper path" for Muslims. Tamerlan had even called him from Russia during his six months in the motherland, talking about jihad and the like.

None of that was enough to lead the FBI to make Viskhan the subject of around-the-clock surveillance by two-man JTTF teams and spy planes overhead recording his every move—which had not been the case with Ibragim, the dead Chechen in Florida, or Khairullozhon.

Khairullozhon's first meeting with the FBI came on May 31, 2013—nine days after Ibragim had been killed. The agents told Khairullozhon they knew about the Waltham murders and they wanted him to start talking. Instead, he started lying, according to an FBI proffer report that recorded notes of the interview: "Matanov was untruthful in his answers because he was worried about the true date, 9/11/2011. Matanov did not want to either cause the death of someone or a problem for himself or someone else."[5] Khairullozhon was no dummy. He knew that the date itself—September 11—would be a red flag for the FBI and didn't want to be the rat who gave Ibragim up to the feds.

He told the FBI that Tamerlan didn't talk about Ibragim much other than to say that his move to Florida "was a good thing for him."[6] Khairullozhon, of course, had met Brendan Mess through Tamerlan but told the FBI he had no idea that Brendan had been murdered along with two other men: "I don't follow the news."

What Khairullozhon couldn't come up with an explanation for was the twenty-two-minute phone call he had with Ibragim on April 14, 2013—the day before the Boston Marathon bombings. That was the day that Ibragim told him he had finally gotten a green card and that he had purchased a ticket to Russia so he could go home. "They did not speak about Tamerlan or Dzhokhar," the FBI noted.

The FBI wasn't buying Khairullozhon's lies and assigned a team of agents to follow him around the clock. The bureau even dispatched a low-flying spy plane that hovered over Khairullozhon's neighborhood so often that his neighbors called the police multiple times to complain about "low flying planes" overhead.[7]

The day after his first FBI interview, Khairullozhon called Ibragim again, according to FBI reports. Both men were in a panic. Ibragim had canceled his trip to Russia after Khairullozhon told him that he had spoken to the FBI. Khairullozhon told the agents that Ibragim said, "I can't believe it was Tamerlan."

When asked by the FBI if the two discussed what had happened in Waltham, Khairullozhon said he didn't remember. The lies continued, the FBI would charge. Khairullozhon said when he picked the brothers up for dinner on the night of the bombings, he honked the horn of his taxi and stayed outside. He later admitted that he had gone upstairs but said he hadn't seen Tamerlan's wife, Karima. Then he recanted that statement too and admitted that Tamerlan's wife had been in the apartment that night and had also been home in the past when he and other Muslim men socialized and watched videos that glorified jihadi violence.

One of those men was Magomed Dolakov. And he fit the description of the mysterious man that Watertown Sergeant Pugliese had seen acting suspiciously during the firefight, hopping a fence and running away. A white male in his twenties, Magomed had a degree in physics from the National Nuclear Research University in Moscow. He had moved to Cambridge from Houston, Texas, in July 2012, a month before Tamerlan returned from his trip overseas. Magomed spent most of his time in the library at MIT, where he had been accepted into a master's program and was waiting for classes to begin, and that is where the FBI found him. They asked him to meet at a nearby Starbucks for a chat. Magomed complied.

The talk turned fairly quickly to politics in Russia, with Magomed claiming his family had been targeted by the FSB, whose agents "would go around and just kill people."[8] He told the FBI he had attended services at the mosque on Minskaya Street in Dagestan where the FSB had taken surveillance photographs of Tamerlan during his time in the area. "Yeah, I know Tamerlan," Magomed told the FBI agents. He met him at the mosque on Prospect Street in Cambridge during the celebration of Eid in 2012. He remembered that Tamerlan was wearing the traditional all-white robe worn by Muslims during holy days. "I could tell he was radical," Magomed said. "He was not open to any other beliefs." The next day Tamerlan picked him up so they could meet friends, including Khairullozhon, at the beach in Quincy and then invited him for dinner at his home. "Tamerlan's wife was there," the FBI noted in the proffer report. "They continued to talk about Islam, and Tamerlan continued to express his radical views on Islam." Karima did not seem to mind the conversation; in fact, she seemed to support it. She was there when Tamerlan began to describe the mujahedin as "brave" and say that was why he planned to become one.

"What about your wife, your daughter, your responsibilities?" Magomed said he asked. "Your daughter would grow up without a father."

Tamerlan scoffed. Karima said nothing. Magomed claimed he didn't see Tamerlan again for months, not until he started to attend services at the Prospect Street mosque.

"I asked him if he was working," Magomed recalled: "He said, Allah sent him money."

Of course that money was probably coming from the federal coffers that taxpayers filled—part of the money paid to assets who agreed to collaborate with the FBI against fellow Muslims in return for cash and favors, like the citizenship that Tamerlan craved so desperately. How else could an unemployed father drive a Mercedes and spend six months overseas?

The last time Magomed saw Tamerlan and Dzhokhar was on April 12, 2013. It was Friday, and he had gone to the mosque to pray around noon. The brothers were there together, praying. Dzhokhar had a runny nose and kept wiping at his face with a tissue, Magomed told the FBI.

"Are you still training?" Magomed reported asking Tamerlan. "I need to get into shape before the summer comes. Can I go with you one time and train?"

"How about right now?" Tamerlan answered.

Magomed hesitated. He hadn't meant that very minute. But Tamerlan wouldn't take no for an answer and insisted on going to Norfolk Street to pick up workout clothes for Magomed. As they climbed into a Honda CRV registered to the Tsarnaev family patriarch, Tamerlan grabbed a large box that was on the back seat and moved it to the rear of the SUV. A white sheet covered the contents. Tamerlan stared at Magomed and then said forcefully, "I am sending clothes to my mother in Russia." Then the three of them headed to Brighton to work out at Wai Kru, a two-hour workout that began at roughly 3:00 P.M. "Dzhokhar was doing his own thing. He was very quiet, as usual," Magomed said.

That interview was the last the FBI had with Magomed, who disappeared days later. Dzhokhar's defense attorneys were eager to talk to him about the radicalization of their client's older brother, but no one could find him. "We can't find him," defense attorney Miriam Conrad would tell the court, adding, "neither can the government."[9] The implication was that the government didn't want Magomed talking, so they may have let him flee.

The FBI, multiple sources told me, wanted to present evidence to a grand jury about what Katherine Russell knew about the plan to attack innocent civilians at the marathon. She lived in a house festooned with jihadi flags, knew Tamerlan was engaging in target practice with a BB gun that he fired at a target hung on the living room wall. The damage to the wall apparently didn't concern Tamerlan or Katherine, since they were leaving. After their eligibility for a housing subsidy from the Department of Housing and Urban Development's Section 8 ended in November 2012, they stopped paying rent to Joanna Herlihy, and she was forced to evict them from the home where the Tsarnaevs had lived for a decade thanks to US taxpayers. The FBI believed that Katherine knew more than she was saying and could be charged with obstruction of a federal terrorism investigation. The US Attorney's Office denied the FBI's recommendation that Tamerlan's wife should be charged, which subsequently caused tension between federal prosecutors and FBI agents. After all, she was googling "rewards for the wife of mujahedin."

No one believed that the Tsarnaev brothers had acted alone in bombing the Boston Marathon—what with the occupants of 89 Dexter Avenue who had mysteriously vanished from Watertown and the missing Chechens—but federal prosecutors were focused on the case against Dzhokhar. They had their man. To suggest others were involved might provoke panic about a larger network.

But then a man named Daniel Morley was arrested for attacking his mother, and with that arrest came the discovery of a massive cache of bomb-making materials, including a giant pressure cooker concealed in a duffel bag along with blue surgical gloves, a machete, Russian assault rifles, and an empty box that had contained the exact size and brand of pressure cooker—a six-quart Fagor—used in the bombs that had exploded at the Boston Marathon's finish line.

18

HAVE TO ANSWER TO GOD FOR

Glenda Duckworth was terrified. Her son Daniel Morley was a genius, but sometimes he just wasn't right in the head. Sunday, June 9, 2013, was one of those times. As soon as she returned to her Topsfield, Massachusetts, home after dinner with her live-in boyfriend she could feel Daniel's distress—even before she saw him. That's how long she had been dealing with his dramatic mood swings. She made him an egg salad sandwich and carried it into the living room where he was trying, without much success, to get an old VCR to play the antiquated videotape he had pulled out of storage. Though she could see that he was frustrated, she could never have anticipated what would happen next.

"He became madder and grabbed my glasses off my face and put them on the electric stove and switched the ring on high. He ripped [off my neck] a chain and heart pendant my son Matthew bought me for Mother's Day. He dragged me to the living room by the arm and pushed me into a chair and drew a cat face on me while yelling, 'Bitch burn in hell,'" Glenda explained to police, after she had flagged them down in the street, crying and in her bathrobe. She had escaped the rampage by crawling out of a bathroom window. Daniel had attacked her boyfriend, too, but he managed to climb out the bedroom window, leaving the twenty-seven-year-old inside. "My son is out of control!" she told officers, "He said he is going to burn down the house."[1]

Topsfield Police Detective Sergeant Gary Hayward had expected that he would be responding to another run-of-the-mill domestic call about some whacko off his meds who had barricaded himself in a bedroom. When he pulled up in front of the gate that surrounded the large suburban house on a picturesque street, there was chaos outside. The distraught woman and her boyfriend, David Bloss, were sitting on a bench across the street from their home near the Topsfield town library. Still crying, she said, "I've never seen him this bad; Daniel is very dark, unstable, but this is by far the worst I have ever seen him."

Hayward was quickly joined by other responding police officers, including the Massachusetts State Police STOP (Special Tactical and Operations) team, dressed in SWAT gear. They were ready to take Daniel out with force when he emerged with his hands up. Police bundled him into an ambulance to take him to Beverly Hospital for a psychological evaluation and then went inside the house with the shaken couple to take statements. Topsfield police officer Gary Wildes followed the ambulance in his cruiser.

The ambulance had pulled into the emergency room bay when behind it, Wildes lit up the ambulance with emergency lights, put the cruiser in park, got out and pulled the ambulance door open to stare directly at Daniel Morley. His colleagues had made an alarming discovery in the young man's bedroom closet: a twenty-four-quart pressure cooker had been found next to a brand-new duffel bag that was an exact fit for the pressure cooker. The pressure cooker was near a giant bag of fertilizer, the kind often used by bomb builders. Inside the duffel bag were bundles of blue surgical gloves.

"Is that pressure cooker bomb active?" Wildes asked.

"Yes, sir. I'm sorry sir. It is."

Wildes dispatched the answer over his radio: "It is an active bomb. Repeat. Suspect says it is an active bomb."

The discovery had been made during a standard search for weapons conducted after what is known as an "EDP (emotionally disturbed person) call." Bloss had signed a consent order for police to search the rest of the room, and what police found was terrifying.

The pressure cooker was bad enough. Then there was the fully loaded Mosin-Nagant M44 rifle, the standard rifle of Soviet troops during World War II, in an unlocked wooden box near his bed—which was a violation of Massachusetts gun laws. An unloaded 0.22 caliber handgun was found nearby, with two fully loaded clips in close proximity. There was an assortment of "plasticuffs" (plastic handcuffs) stored alongside hundreds of rounds of ammunition, including rounds created for the Russian military. Knives and swords, like the one Ibragim Todashev had on his wall in Orlando, were arranged in what the police described as a "makeshift temple" on a bookshelf. In the center of the swords was a painting of a man next to what appeared to be the Boston skyline as an airplane hovered over him. There were computer parts, wires, and ball bearings—ball bearings that were eerily similar to the projectiles that had been sprayed all over Boylston Street with the detonation of the two pressure-cooker bombs at the Boston Marathon. Dismantled phones were scattered in boxes all over the room, and there was a bucket with aluminum foil, along with brown rice flour and an Ignito-O fire starter log. There was a jug of the mineral calcium, and a coffee grinder with metal shavings was found next to commercial-grade aluminum and steel wool. What appeared to be emptied whipped cream containers that narcotics officers recognized instead as high-tech "hides" for paraphernalia such as explosives were found in a closet next to a T-shirt with an MSP emblem, the kind usually issued to troopers. A green stuffed animal had been set ablaze and left in a bucket in a screened-in porch. In the closet there was a shoebox with dead bird parts, air holes cut into the top of the box. It remained unclear how the bird had died.

Most alarmingly, police found a top for a box containing a six-quart Fagor pressure cooker, the exact size and brand that FBI bomb squad technicians said had been used at the finish line of the Boston Marathon. On the back of the box top was a chemical recipe for thermite—a combination of metal powder fuel and metal oxide that, when ignited by heat, can act as an accelerant and is often used for bomb fuses to create a more powerful explosion. The recipe was scribbled in pen like a laboratory formula, much like the ones Daniel used when he was employed as a veterinarian technician in MIT's Division of Comparative Medicine, a lab located inside the Stata building, outside of which MIT Police Officer Sean Collier had been killed. Daniel's employment with MIT had been terminated in July 2012. Morley told his mother he didn't want to conduct tests on animals any longer, but it was more likely that he had been fired.

The police knew what they were looking at in Daniel's cramped bedroom at his mother's house. They had all studied the pictures from the marathon bombing enough to know that they were looking at basically every component needed to build the kind of bombs that had been detonated at the marathon.

The houses around 18 Washington Street were quickly evacuated, and traffic was diverted away from Topsfield's town square. National Grid, the local utility, was called to turn the gas off in case there was an explosion. Law enforcement officials set up a command center at a nearby building, where cops, firefighters, paramedics, state police hostage negotiators, the bomb squad, and the STOP team strategized about how to proceed inside the house. The Boston Marathon attack had happened just two months earlier, and no one was taking any chances with this kid. Besides, the FBI had repeatedly indicated to its law enforcement officers that agents had not "definitively determined where the bombs were built," a statement that FBI special agent John Walker had even made on the stand in the trial of Azamat Tazhayakov. That statement was echoed by FBI supervisory agent David McCollum, a chemist forensic examiner in the bureau's Explosives Unit, who testified, "I do not, based on our analysis, think we can tell where these bombs were built."[2]

And then there was the government's own claim, made in a 2014 court filing—one filed under seal and only released in 2016—that there was a possibility of other bombers being out there, which is why they interrogated Dzhokhar Tsarnaev repeatedly in the hospital. The court filing read, in part, "The Tsarnaevs had access to a small arsenal of bombs. They used two of them at the Marathon and several days later used four more in Watertown. They also indicated to the man they carjacked that they planned to travel to New York to explode additional bombs. These facts suggested the existence of a larger plot to wage a multi-pronged attack on different cities, as well as the possible existence of yet more unused bombs and other bombers waiting to pick up where the Tsarnaevs had left off."[3]

In that same brief, the government made the startling assertion that the Tsarnaev brothers lacked the sophistication to build the bombs, raising the possibility that they had worked with accomplices. "The Marathon bombs were constructed using improvised fuses made from Christmas lights and improvised, remote-control detonators fashioned from model car parts. These relatively sophisticated devices would have been difficult for the Tsarnaevs to fabricate successfully without training or assistance from others."

And even the evidence, the government wrote, didn't bolster the belief that the brothers built the bombs. "The Tsarnaevs also appeared to have crushed and emptied hundreds of individual fireworks containing black powder in order to obtain explosive fuel for the bombs. The black powder used in fireworks is extremely fine; it was therefore reasonable to expect that if the Tsarnaevs had crushed the fireworks and built the bombs all by themselves, traces of black powder would be found wherever they had done the work. Yet searches of the Tsarnaevs' residences, three vehicles, and other locations associated with them yielded virtually no traces of black powder, again strongly suggesting that others had built, or at least helped the Tsarnaevs build, the bombs, and thus might have built more."[4]

———

So it was an odd coincidence that the bombs the Tsarnaev brothers used at the marathon had been made inside pressure cookers of the same brand and size that Morley kept a box top to in his house.

Before long, FBI agents from the Boston field office showed up, which struck the cops on the scene as strange. No one had called the FBI yet. One bomb squad technician would later say, "It was very surprising to us that the FBI responded immediately to a scene for a crackpot." The commanding officers from the MSP and the Topsfield Police Department looked at one another with raised eyebrows. *Did you call them?*, the questioning looks said. Both shook their heads. The FBI hadn't been notified, and it was unusual for them to respond without being summoned by a police official. No one knew if they had overheard the radio transmission to Topsfield PD, which was unlikely, or if they had gotten a call from someone inside the house.

The MSP bomb squad technicians geared up to go inside. They examined the pressure cooker. It was empty. But the room was not cleared. "The place is full of bomb components that could be used to build a device," the bomb squad sergeant told Topsfield police officers. "We need a further check."

A notebook on a table was opened to show bizarre drawings, such as a Star of David with a swastika scrawled inside. To make matters worse, Daniel's mother's boyfriend told police that on the day of the marathon attack he had looked at Glenda and demanded, "Where is your son?" That morning he had been doing yard work when Daniel had slipped away. Daniel came home two days later and told his mother he had gone fishing with his friend, Marc Pascuito. His mother's boyfriend didn't believe him and suspected Daniel had been involved in whatever happened on Boylston Street, a suspicion that only grew when Daniel's mother brought up the bombing with her son when he got back, telling him she had been worried.

"What's the big deal?" Daniel answered. "People are dying all over the place."

But the conversation that kept ringing in Glenda's head over and over again was the one that she had had with Daniel on June 12, the night before he attacked her. They were sitting at the kitchen table, and she asked about his friend Marc. She hadn't seen him in a while, and the two had been inseparable.

"I'm not hanging around with him anymore. Marc wanted me to do something really bad. I didn't want to do it. I need to get away from my friends, get a fresh start," Daniel answered. After a pause he continued in a shaky voice, near tears. "I'm sorry for what I've done with Marc and I will have to answer only to God."[5]

Glenda repeated the conversation to Hayward and urged him to investigate Marc, who had always struck her as a strange duck. Once he had looked out her living room's picture window and remarked: "This is great. You can see people coming and have time to grab your gun."[6]

"It was like he was looking around at the house as a fortress, not a home," David told Hayward. "Marc told us that he knew Tamerlan Tsarnaev. He said he had boxed with him, or against him or something. But the kid is not truthful all the time."

Police found rather disturbing letters that Marc, an Army washout who lived with his parents in Medford, had written Daniel. The letters were full of grandiose references to obscure gods and video games:

> What words capture the gravity of our friendship and its vast import
> to me? If such verbiage exists, it eludes me. I can only say that you
> are an individual whom I am glad to call my confidant, and that I
> am proud and honored that you may refer to me as the same. May
> Quetzalcoatl smile upon you.
>
> Yours in the glory of the Triumvirate, Marc Pascuito.

In another he wrote:

In the hopes that you never stop seeking the truth, never back down, and eternally remain skeptical of wizzids. Your homie, Marc Pascuito.

The Triumvirate, Glenda explained, referred to Daniel, Marc, and their friend Vladimir Zaitsev, a UMass/Amherst student who lived in western Massachusetts. All of them, Glenda reluctantly told police, had expressed some "anti-government and anti-Semitic views," Hayward wrote in a search warrant affidavit, "and was very unfavorable towards Israel."

Hayward also sent a report to the FBI and JTTF stating the following:

Daniel Morley had items consistent with bomb making materials.

Daniel Morley stated to his mother that he and his friend Marc Pascuito had done things that he could only answer to God for.

Daniel Morley stated to his mother that Marc Pascuito was trying to get Daniel to do something real bad.

Daniel Morley told both Mr. Bloss and Ms. Duckworth that Marc Pascuito stated he had boxed with or boxed against Tamerlan Tsarnaev, the suspect in the Boston Marathon bombing.

Daniel Morley had a Russian friend only known as "Vlad."

The pressure cooker and other items were purchased prior to the Boston Marathon bombing.

Daniel Morley had strong anti-government beliefs as well as anti-Semitic beliefs.

Dr. Breen, a terrorism expert, stated it was possibly containing a skyline in Boston and a plane that may be a potential target area, analyzed a painting located on a temple made by Daniel Morley.

An agent from the JTTF came to the Topsfield Police Department head-quarters to collect Morley's laptop, which was sent to Quantico where it could be analyzed and the findings listed in what is known as an FBI Forensic Toolkit report.

In the meantime Hayward started to dig into Daniel's past. His father, Peter, was an Englishman who moved to the United States to take a job at MIT. University officials say that he was employed there from October 1994 until December 2010 as a sponsored research technical supervisor in the Laboratory for Nuclear Science. After that he took over the MIT machine shop, from which the aluminum found in Daniel's room had allegedly been taken. Daniel also worked at MIT in various jobs between October 2005 until July 2012, when he was let go from his position as a veterinary technician in the Division of Comparative Medicine, a lab located in the Stata building, according to an MIT spokesperson.

Hayward also found other connections, all coincidental, that linked Daniel to Tamerlan Tsarnaev. For one thing, both men had taken classes at Bunker Hill Community College in 2008 and were involved in mixed martial arts and attended boxing gyms in the area, such as the Somerville Boxing Club, at that same time. Both were students of anarchist literature. Tamerlan subscribed to the *Sovereign* newspaper, which published stories exploring conspiracy theories such as those suggesting that 9/11 was an inside job. The examination of Daniel's laptop would show that he had a heavy interest in the group Anonymous (discussed in a previous chapter). His arrest record also raised some eyebrows.

The NYPD had arrested Daniel in 2011, as he led an Occupy Wall Street march in New York City. A photographer captured the moment when he was thrown to the ground and handcuffed by a captain. Also found in Daniel's belongings after a search warrant had been approved was a card naming him as a member of the New Hampshire Liberty Forum, a libertarian group based in Keene. The chief of the Keene Police Department was so worried about anarchist groups in the area that he applied for a grant from the federal government to obtain an armored BearClaw, exactly like the one used when Dzhokhar was pulled from the boat in Watertown, writing that "groups such as the Sovereign Citizens, Free Staters and Occupy New Hampshire are active and present daily challenges."[7] The chief also wrote that police were concerned about "several homegrown clusters that are anti-government and pose problems for law enforcement agencies." Groups like Liberty Forum—whose membership emblem reads "Free State Project. Liberty in Our Lifetime," which appears next to the slogan "Many Paths to

Liberty!"[8]—were not linked to any crimes but could rise up as anarchists against police, according to the chief.

At Beverly Hospital, Daniel was charged with two counts of assault and battery, possessing a hoax device (the pressure cooker that he had told the Topsfield officer was an active bomb), and making a bomb threat. His father had to post $20,000 in cash for Daniel's bail, an indication of how serious the charges were that his son was facing, and the state sent him to Bridgewater State Hospital for a psychological evaluation.

David had been worried that his girlfriend's son had been part of the plot to bomb the Boston Marathon, especially after flyers started to arrive at 18 Washington Street from Phantom Fireworks, the store in Seabrook, New Hampshire, where Tamerlan had purchased two "lock and load mortar kits"[9] that prosecutors said were likely used to build at least the pipe bombs hurled at police in Watertown. Before the marathon attack, David said, he had never gotten such a flyer, which was sent to his home without a name. Flyers are usually sent to repeat customers.

"I never purchased a firework in my life and I didn't know why I was suddenly getting these flyers," David explained.[10] He was puzzled that his girlfriend's son was not being looked at more closely, especially given the government's fears that a large network was involved in the marathon bombing plot. It was something that had been discussed by public officials and had been covered by the press after the US Attorney's office filed a motion for a search warrant at the Tsarnaevs' home.

"The Tsarnaevs had access to a small arsenal of bombs. They used two of them at the Marathon and several days later used four more in Watertown. They also indicated to the man they carjacked that they planned to travel to New York to explode additional bombs. These facts suggested the existence of a larger plot to wage a multi-pronged attack on different cities, as well as the possible existence of yet more unused bombs and other bombers waiting to pick up where the Tsarnaevs had left off.

"The Tsarnaevs also appeared to have crushed and emptied hundreds of individual fireworks containing black powder in order to obtain explosive fuel for the bombs. The black powder used in fireworks is extremely fine; it was therefore reasonable to expect that if the Tsarnaevs had crushed the fireworks and built the bombs all by themselves, traces of black powder would be found wherever they had done the work. Yet searches of the Tsarnaevs' residences, three vehicles, and other locations associated with them yielded virtually no traces of black powder, again strongly suggesting that others had built, or at least helped the Tsarnaevs build, the bombs, and thus might have built more.

"To determine if there were additional bombs, bombers, or bomb plots, the agents asked only those questions likely to reveal that information, namely: who constructed the bombs, and how, when, and where they were constructed; where any additional bombs were stored; who if anyone had assisted the brothers; who made the decision to target the Boston Marathon, murder an MIT policeman, kidnap a civilian, and attack additional policemen in Watertown; who Tsarnaev had contacted immediately before and after the bombings, and why; and how and when he and his brother had become radicalized.

"Tsarnaev is not an ordinary criminal; he is a terrorist who launched a coordinated bombing attack on an internationally-renowned sporting event, killing three people and maiming and wounding hundreds more. Nearly four days after the Marathon bombings, Tsarnaev was still deemed to pose such a grave threat to public safety that the Governor of Massachusetts asked nearly one million people to shelter in place for an entire day while law enforcement endeavored to find Tsarnaev and neutralize him. The possibility that other bombs existed and/or that others associated with Tsarnaev might engage in additional violence once he was captured posed a public safety threat of the highest order.

"The agents investigating the Marathon bombings were well aware of the danger of coordinated terrorist attacks, and they had an objectively reasonable belief that the Tsarnaev brothers might have been radicalized, trained, directed, and assisted by a terrorist group, the members of which might perpetrate other attacks."[11]

But for some inexplicable reason, the FBI insisted, and continues to insist to this day, that Daniel had nothing to do with the marathon bombings—despite the ball bearings in his bedroom alongside a giant pressure cooker, despite the top of a box for a six-quart Fagor pressure cooker, the same size and brand used in the marathon attacks, despite the fireworks flyers sent to his mother's house, and despite the connections to Tamerlan mentioned by his mother.

David asked the author in the driveway of his Topsfield home, "Can the FBI hide someone in a hospital?" He had dealt with Daniel's mental illness for more than a decade, and every previous hospitalization had lasted for five days. Never two years—which is how long Daniel would stay in the hospital this time.

————

Months after Daniel's arrest—when he was confined in a psychiatric ward at Tewksbury Hospital, where his mother visited weekly—Topsfield police officials were stunned to learn that he would not be indicted for possession of the explosive materials and weapons stashed in his room. He would not be held accountable for the chaos on his block or the massive police response after he attacked his mother. The office of Essex County Prosecutor Jonathon Blodgett referred all questions regarding Daniel's case to the FBI. And the FBI wasn't talking.

Carrie Kimball-Monahan, spokesperson for the Essex County District Attorney's Office, explained that all of the evidence in the case had been turned over to the FBI. "We *nolle prosequi*'ed the bomb threat charge," Kimball-Monahan said, meaning that the case against Morley would be dropped without even being heard in Superior Court, unusual for such serious charges. "Mr. Morley must comply with [the] Department of Mental Health, including medications, and not abuse his family. If he complies with these conditions and stays out of trouble, the case will be dismissed."[12]

Oddly, Kimball-Monahan then referred all questions about Daniel to the FBI with no real explanation as to why she did so. Not that it mattered, since the FBI would not answer them. In fact, to this day no one in the federal government has answered the question about whether Daniel may, however unwittingly, have been responsible for building the bombs used at the Boston Marathon. But a friend of Daniel's who asked not to be identified in these pages said he had told the FBI that Daniel had repeatedly boasted of building bombs that would target "corporate America" and be detonated under billboards for giant companies, like banks. Marc said much the same thing in interviews: "I don't think Danny bombed the marathon, but he had a lot of anger at corporate America."[13]

Then there were the similarities between the materials recovered in Daniel's home and the bombs used at the finish line. In an FBI affidavit filed on April 21, 2013, Special Agent Daniel R. Genck of the counterterrorism squad of the FBI's Boston field office wrote that "many of the BBs were contained within an adhesive material" and "contained green-colored hobby fuse."[14] Green-colored hobby wire was one of the items recovered in Morley's bedroom.

And there was the unrecovered machete that prosecutors mentioned in a superseding federal indictment against Dzhokhar Tsarnaev, a follow up indictment that was filed after the original with additional charges. The machete was not recovered at the crime scene on Boylston Street or near the Watertown firefight. No machete was found at 410 Norfolk Street or in Dzhokhar's green Honda. There was none in the stolen Mercedes SUV. It remains unclear why prosecutors would mention this machete, a weapon that was never entered into evidence and would never become part of the case against him at trial.

However, Tewksbury police recovered a machete at Daniel's house. A photo of it was entered into evidence and recorded on Hayward's report.

The new superseding indictment, filed June 27, 2013—just weeks after Daniel's arrest on June 9—stated: "DZHOKHAR A. TSARNAEV and Tamerlan Tsarnaev armed themselves with five IEDs, a Ruger P95 9mm semi-automatic handgun, ammunition for the Ruger, a machete, and a hunting knife, and drove in their Honda Civic to the Massachusetts Institute of Technology ('MIT') in Cambridge, Massachusetts."[15]

The machete is part of another mystery that continues to swirl around Daniel: the unsolved 7-Eleven robbery that took place at 10:20 P.M. on Thursday, April 18—at the same time Collier was murdered. A video of the robbery shows a man talking on a cell phone while he robbed the clerk of less than $29 in cash. Initially police officials, including MSP Colonel Tim Alben (now retired), blamed the bombers for the 7-Eleven robbery. The following day that statement was retracted, and police officials said the bombers were not responsible. But multiple sources—including David, his mother's boyfriend and the man he lived with—have said the robber was Daniel.

In 2014 I showed David a copy of the Cambridge Police Department screen shot of the tape of the robbery, and he gasped, saying, "Oh my God. That's Danny."[16]

The photo prompted David to open up about the fears he had harbored since April 15, 2013, the day "Danny disappeared" for two days. As noted above, when he came back he told his mother and stepfather he had been fishing with Marc. When Hayward asked Glenda where her son Daniel had been on Patriots' Day, she told him Daniel "was sleeping all day," clearly a lie to protect her son. The night he came back his mother talked with him about the marathon, and Davis was concerned at Daniel's response: "It was surprising. He was cold about it, used the term collateral damage."

To this day, no one has been charged with the 7-Eleven robbery that police initially announced the Tsarnaev brothers had been involved with. Friends of Daniel have also viewed the screen shot I showed David and have had the same reaction as he did. "No question," said one, who has been questioned by the FBI, "That's Danny." A Cambridge police official also referred questions about the still-unsolved 7-Eleven robbery to the FBI.

FBI officials claim Tamerlan and Dzhokhar Tsarnaev built the bombs they used at the marathon by following a recipe in *Inspire*, an Al Qaeda magazine.

But the FBI's analysis of the bombs debunked the bureau heads' insistence that the Tsarnaev brothers had constructed them. FBI technicians at the Terrorist Explosive Device Analytical Center in Quantico in late April 2013 found that the bombs in Boston had a much more sophisticated design than that shown in the online magazine, including differences in the initiators, power source, and switch or trigger, which used a toy car remote control. Those differences were contained in a list that compared the Boylston Street bombs to the result of the *Inspire* magazine instructions. For example, *Inspire*'s recipe did not contain instructions for that type of switch or trigger used to remotely set off the IEDs. Instead, the magazine had directions for a different type, using a motorcycle remote starter.

The FBI electronics forensics report also cited circumstantial evidence of Daniel's involvement. For example, on February 19, 2013, he searched the Internet for the term "learning Russian for beginners." Then on March 10 he searched for the address of a Manchester, New Hampshire, gun range called Firing Line. Exactly ten days later the Tsarnaev brothers visited that range, where they rented 9mm handguns and engaged in target practice for about an hour, prosecutors said. Daniel had posted pictures of himself on social media websites shooting guns at the Firing Line around the same time.

After spending nearly two years in a hospital, Daniel is a free man, as of this writing. All of the charges he faced in connection with abusing his mother, the bomb materials in his room, and even the guns (for which he had a license) were dismissed without prejudice.

In the days after he was released in June 2015, Daniel was asked if he had robbed the 7-Eleven to distract cops while the Tsarnaev brothers broke into the lab where he had previously been employed, the one where he could have been making thermite, the bomb accelerant for which a recipe had been scrawled on the back of the empty Fagor pressure cooker box. There has never been any explanation as to why the Tsarnaev brothers were on the campus of MIT, and the theory that they went to steal Collier's gun is debunked by video evidence played in Tsarnaev's trial. In the grainy video, Collier is shot and Dzhokhar and Tamerlan first flee the shooting, and then Dzhokhar goes back to get the gun as an afterthought, leaving his fingerprints in the cruiser and on the gun handle. (He was unsuccessful in taking it because of the holster lock.) Morley wasn't going to talk about the bombs, or the Tsarnaevs, or whether he helped them. He answered me with just two words. "Wasn't me." It was the same answer he gave me when I visited him at Tewksbury State Hospital months earlier. "Wasn't me."

PART FOUR

JUSTICE

SEEKERS

19

ONE-FINGER SALUTE

It was the second bomb blast that ripped Joseph "JP" Norden's right leg from his body. The thirty-three-year-old's body was burned and peppered with shrapnel. From that April day Boston firefighters wrapped a tourniquet tight around the severed leg and raced him to Brigham and Women's Hospital to July 10, 2013, JP had undergone dozens of surgeries and had nearly died a number of times. This was the day his mother, Liz, had been waiting for since the day of the carnage, the death of one terrorist, and the capture of another. She was determined to lock eyes with the man who maimed her sons.

JP had been through so much, but when doctors removed his breathing tube in the weeks before this July afternoon, his first question to his mother, asked with tear-filled eyes, was, "Where's Paul?"[1]

Liz remembered how she had fought back her own tears, gently squeezed her oldest son's raw, bruised hand and told him: "Paul's okay. He's worried about you."

Paul, JP's thirty-one-year-old brother, was alive but not at all okay. He had also lost his right leg and suffered serious burns. Flying ball bearings left his face swollen with bruises and seared scars into his skin. The brothers had been waiting near the finish line to cheer on their friend, Somerville firefighter Mike Jefferson, who was running in the marathon. After the first bomb—the one detonated by Dzhokhar Tsarnaev's dead brother, Tamerlan—exploded, the Norden brothers and their friend Marc Fucarile used their own bodies to shield Mike's mother, daughter, and aunt from harm just in case the attack wasn't over. They were right. The second blast came twelve seconds later, and the men took the brunt of the explosion. Marc lost both legs, his right leg gone from the hip down, his left from the knee down. Liz didn't know what had happened that bright Patriots' Day afternoon until she got a call from Paul, who was in the back of a van with other people who had lost limbs and were desperately fighting to stay alive.

"Mom, I'm hurt real bad and I can't find JP," he told her. Bleeding and burned, all he cared about was finding his brother.

"I was in shock," Liz remembered. "The ambulance driver told me he was in critical condition, and we had to get to the hospital right away. All he kept asking about is his brother. And we couldn't find him. I didn't know if I lost both my boys."

That day at Beth Israel Deaconess Medical Center, Paul reached for his mother's hand, though his knuckles were burned and raw. His eyes darted from one family member to another, searching for answers. His mother knew the question on Paul's mind and comforted him before he went into surgery.

"Don't worry," Liz told Paul. "JP's okay. Jackie's okay. I love you. I love you so much."

It didn't surprise anyone who knows the Norden family that the two brothers were so worried about one another, and that they had used their bodies as human shields to help protect the people around them. They are a close-knit clan, and Liz is a tough woman—a cancer survivor and a long-time single mom who raised her five children in Stoneham, Massachusetts, keeping a watchful eye on them. Everyone but JP still lived with her. She didn't know what would happen now that two of her sons had lost legs: "All my kids are real tight. This is absolutely devastating to everyone. I am glad they are alive but so sorry about what is happening to them. My poor boys. I want to see this cowardly piece of shit burn in hell."

The day finally came on July 10 when she could see the man who had maimed her sons. Dzhokhar would be transported from Fort Devens—where he was being treated for his injuries in a federal prison hospital—to the John Joseph Moakley United States Courthouse in South Boston to see him face the charges contained in the thirty-count indictment against him. He would be transported to the building under heavily armed guard and whisked into an underground garage to be held in a cell until the court proceedings.

Ailina and Bella Tsarnaeva were there for their brother's arraignment, cradling an infant—Ailina's baby with her new boyfriend. Court officials had designated two distinct sections for the spectators, almost like a wedding. Tsarnaev supporters sat in the rows to the right of the courtroom, behind the defense table. The victims and their families filled the rows on the left, behind the lawyers from the US Attorney's Office and the Department of Justice who would represent them and the entire country. Liz was in the front of this section. In the middle rows were the reporters who had been selected to be in the courtroom and the law enforcement personnel who had worked on the case, including MIT Police Chief John DiFava; BPD Commissioner Ed Davis; Watertown Police Chief Ed Deveau; and FBI Special Agent Vincent Lisi, the new agent in charge of the bureau's FBI field office, flanked by Kieran Ramsey, the assistant special agent in charge. Behind these top officials were first responders who were still traumatized by what they had seen on Patriots' Day.

As Dzhokhar's sisters sobbed and wiped tears from their faces with the ends of the hijabs wrapped around their heads, their brother was led into the courtroom in an orange jumpsuit, his legs shackled and chained to his hands, one of which was wrapped in a cast to set the bones shattered by gunfire in Watertown. His face was distorted and bruised from the bullet that had smashed through his face, his floppy black hair was disheveled, and a scraggly attempt at a beard hung on his chin. But he was smiling. He even swaggered a little.

"I would like to acknowledge and note for the record that there are 30 victims and family members here in the courtroom today, and they have the statutory right to be present at this proceeding pursuant to Title 18, United States Code, Section 3771," US District Court Magistrate Justice Marianne Bowler began. She would not be the judge at Dzhokhar's trial, but she was a well-respected court magistrate, known as a no-nonsense woman, and she was the same judge who had arraigned the accused bomber in the hospital in the days after his arrest.[2]

"We're here at this time for the purposes of arraignment. Ms. Clarke, Ms. Conrad, have you reviewed the indictment with your client?"

Judy Clarke put a comforting hand on Dzhokhar's shoulder as she answered. It was one of her signature moves, an attempt to make her client seem sympathetic, worthy of intimacy. She hoped it sent a message to jurors that the teenager in front of her was not just an evil barbarian. Dzhokhar's own mannerisms would make those attempts difficult. He looked around, yawned, and smiled crookedly. He almost appeared bored by the proceedings before they even began.

"We have."

"And have you explained the nature of it to him today?"

"We have."

"And does he understand it?"

"Yes," Clarke answered.

"And is he prepared to be arraigned here?"

"He is."

"And does he waive the reading of the indictment in its entirety?"

"He does."

"And what are the maximum penalties?"

Assistant US Attorney William Weinreb would take the lead on this day. It was a death penalty case. There had only been one capital punishment case tried in his time at the US Attorney's Office, and that defendant, Gary Lee Sampson, who had grown up in Massachusetts, had been sentenced to death in 2003 on federal carjacking and murder charges stemming from a week-long crime spree that had left three people dead. That trial had taken place in the same South Boston federal courthouse where Dzhokhar now stood. After his conviction, Sampson had become a serial killer celebrity of sorts, whose commissary account is filled with donations from strangers. Dzhokhar had already gained his own bizarre notoriety: A growing group of women and teenage girls saw him as dashing figure, a rock star, a folk hero who they insisted was the victim of an orchestrated government plot to frame an innocent man. Some of them had gathered outside the courthouse wearing T-shirts emblazoned with his face and the word "Innocent," or holding provocative signs like "Got Proof?" Some had even gotten tattoos of what had become his avatar, a roaring lion—a symbol adopted by many young jihadis who were radicalized primarily on the Internet—and they had even come up with a name for themselves: the Jaharians.

Weinreb had walked by them and others in the crowd on his way into court that morning. He had also shared the hallway with the wounded and the loved ones of the dead. It was an important day, a cathartic day for the city of Boston. He was ready.

"Your Honor, on Counts 1, 2, 4, 6, 7, 9, 13 and 15 of the indictment, the maximum penalty is up to life imprisonment or the death penalty, five years of supervised release, and a $250,000 fine. On Counts 3, 5, 8, 10, 12 and 14, there is a maximum penalty of life imprisonment or the death penalty, and a minimum mandatory term of imprisonment of life, except on Count 3, on which there is a minimum mandatory term of imprisonment of 30 years. The defendant would also be subject to a fine of up to $250,000 and five years of supervised release.

"On Count 11, the maximum term of imprisonment is life, followed by five years of supervised release and a $250,000 fine. On Counts 16, 17 and 18, there is a maximum term of life imprisonment or the death penalty, a minimum mandatory term of imprisonment of 25 years, up to five years of supervised release, and a $250,000 fine.

"On Count 19, a maximum term of imprisonment of 25 years followed by five years of supervised release and a $250,000 fine.

"On Count 21, a maximum term of imprisonment of up to 20 years, followed by three years of supervised release and a $250,000 fine.

"On Counts 23, 25, 27 and 29, a maximum term of imprisonment of life followed by five years of supervised release and a $250,000 fine. And finally, on Counts 24, 26, 28 and 30, there's a maximum term of life imprisonment, a minimum mandatory term of life imprisonment, a five-year term of supervised release, and up to a $250,000 fine."

Bowler turned toward the defense table. "Are you ready to proceed?"

Clarke answered, "Yes."

"Will the defendant please stand?"

Dzhokhar rose, and Bowler's clerk, Brendan Garvin, began to read.

"Mr. Tsarnaev, as to Counts 1, 2, 4, 23, 25, 27, 29 of the indictment, charging you with use of a weapon of mass destruction resulting in death and conspiracy to use a weapon of mass destruction resulting in death, a violation of Title 18, United States Code, Section 2332A, how do you plead, guilty or not guilty?"

Clarke interjected. "Your Honor, as to all counts we've advised Mr. Tsarnaev that today it's appropriate to enter not guilty pleas, and we would ask the Court to enter not guilty pleas."

That wasn't going to cut it for the judge. She wanted to hear the words from Dzhokhar, not his team of death penalty defense lawyers. "Well, I would ask him to answer."

"Thank you, your Honor," Clarke answered, patting Tsarnaev on the arm.

"Not guilty," he said, his voice heavily accented.

The clerk continued. "Counts 6, 7, and 9 of the indictment, charging you with bombing of a place of public use resulting in death and conspiracy to bomb a place of public use resulting in death in violation of Title 18, United States Code, Section 2332F, charging you with bombing of a place. How do you plead?"

"Not guilty."

"As to Counts 11, 12 and 14 charging you with malicious destruction of property resulting in death and conspiracy to malicious destruction of property resulting in death in violation of Title 18, United States Code, Section 844N. How do you plead?"

"Not guilty."

"As to Counts 3, 5, 8, 10, 13, 15, 16, 17 and 18, charging you with use and carrying of a firearm during and in relation to a crime of violence resulting in death in violation of Title 18, United States Code, Section 924J, how do you plead?"

"Not guilty."

"As to Count 19 of the indictment charging you with carjacking resulting in serious bodily injury in violation of Title 18, United States Code, Section 2119, how do you plead, guilty or not guilty?"

"Not guilty."

"As to Counts 20, 22, 24, 26, 28 and 30, charging you with use and carrying of a firearm during and in relation to a crime of violence in violation of Title 18, United States Code, Section 924C, how do you plead?"

"Not guilty.

"And as to Count 21 charging you with interference with commerce by threats and violence in violation of Title 18, United States Code, Section 1951, how do you plead?"

"Not guilty."

Bowler thanked Dzhokhar: "You may be seated."

Then she turned back to the prosecution: "How many witnesses does the government intend to call and what's the probable length of trial?"

"Your Honor, we anticipate the government would call 80 to 100 witnesses and that the trial would last approximately three to four months," Weinreb answered.

"And, Mr. Garvin, do we have a date for an initial status conference?"

"We do. It will be Monday, the 23rd of September, at 10 A.M."

"So noted by counsel?" Bowler asked the defense.

"That's a good date," Clarke answered. "Yes, thank you."

"Mindful of the potential cost of these proceedings, I direct counsel for the defendant at this time to consider sooner rather than later preparing a proposed litigation budget for the trial judge. And I note that the provisions of the Guide to Judiciary Policies and Procedure, Volume 7, Part A, Chapter 6, Section 640, encourages the budget to be filed as early as possible. Ms. Clarke, I know you have experience with this. So I would suggest, particularly in this time of sequester, the sooner you can get to this, the better."

The taxpayers were to pick up the tab for both the prosecution and the defense. Ironically, more often than not the US government paid more for the cost of the defense than for the cost of the prosecution, and the "proposed litigation budgets" did not factor in costs such as police overtime for security outside the courthouse—which in this case, was on an unprecedented scale. Taxpayers would also have to cover additional costs for the Coast Guard and BPD marine units that patrolled the South Boston waterfront, the federal agents from the DHS who ringed the courthouse, the US marshals who surrounded Dzhokhar, and the undercover BPD detectives who were nonetheless recognized by some in the crowd, monitoring the people who lined up at 6:00 each morning during the trial for a spot in the seats set aside for spectators. With victims, police, and media, and the public, the demand for seats was so overwhelming that two additional courtrooms had to be set up by the Office of Court Administration, where streaming video from the main courtroom could be viewed on televisions provided for the overflow of journalists from all over the world. And all this was at the taxpayers' expense.

"Thank you, your Honor." Clarke answered.

Bowler continued: "All right, I'd also like to remind counsel of the presumption of public access to judicial documents, and that this Court frowns upon the sealing of judicial documents unless it's absolutely necessary. To date, many of the filings in this case have been sealed, and the Court will look carefully in the future because the public has a right to know about the nature of the proceedings."

That was a request that would never be met. At least Bowler tried. But as the trial progressed, hundreds of files remained sealed. There was a shroud of secrecy around the entire prosecution that would continue long after the trial was over. (In fact, in January 2017, nearly two years after Tsarnaev was sentenced to death, hundreds of filings in the Tsarnaev case remained inexplicably sealed.)

"Are there other matters that counsel wish to bring to my attention at this time?"

Weinreb answered first. "None from the government, your Honor."

"No, your Honor. Thank you," Clarke then responded.

"All right." The judge got ready to stand up and concluded: "In which case the defendant is now in the custody of the United States marshals."

The hearing had lasted exactly eight minutes. Two US marshals flanked Dzhokhar, each taking an arm to guide him. Before reaching the door, he turned his face, still swollen and distorted by gunshot wounds, toward his sisters, smirked, and blew them a kiss. There was a gasp from the victims, who had seen how smug and arrogant the bomber looked.

Ed Fucarile, whose son Marc had been with the Norden brothers in front of the Forum restaurant, was aghast. "He came out and he smirked at the families," he told reporters who had set up a bank of microphones outside. He was visibly angry. "The lawyers put their hands on his shoulders like it was going to be all right. My son is not all right."[3]

Marc was still hospitalized. An X-ray showed his entire body was studded with BBs, and a nail was still lodged precariously close to his heart. He had lost a leg and nearly died.

DiFava didn't step up to the microphones but stormed away from the courthouse in a rage, saying, "I'm disgusted. I'd like to grab him by the throat. I didn't see a lot of remorse. That arrogant little piece of garbage didn't even look at the victims and was blowing kisses."[4] DiFava had come to court because he had to set eyes on the man who had robbed his officer, Sean Collier, of his future. "I wanted to see the person that so coldly and callously killed four people, one of whom being an officer of mine. He deserves to die."

One by one the victims expressed to reporters how astonished they were at the cold-blooded arrogance displayed by Dzhokhar in court. But they had no idea what he had done earlier in the day in the federal court's holding cell, a place he would become so familiar with that he would spend his time there playing "toilet roll basketball"—essentially he would use a toilet paper roll as a net and wad up pieces of paper to toss into the middle—and reading the Quran.

Kevin Roche was the US marshal assigned to monitor Dzhokhar's activities in the cell that day. He was a seventeen-year veteran of the federal force and had seen almost everything in the cellblock. There had been attempted suicides and inmate-on-inmate attacks. Some accused criminals flooded their own cell with toilet water and sat in the resulting rancid mess. Roche had been called names he hadn't known existed. He had seen feces thrown at marshals by inmates who had scooped it up with their bare hands. Nothing could surprise him. Roche was also familiar with Dzhokhar. He had stood guard over the Boston Marathon bomber after his arrest at Beth Israel Hospital, was there for his initial bedside appearance before a judge in April, and had seen him roughly six times before his arraignment that day working the detail at the hospital—one of six marshals assigned to the unit where Dzhokhar was being held until his transfer to Fort Devens. Roche had transported Dzhokhar to Fort Devens and to follow-up appointments at Beth Israel after the transfer. He had noted the prisoner's scowls, tears, and whining.

On the morning of July 10, 2013, it was business as usual for the marshals. Roche and others on his team transported Dzhokhar into the cellblock in the courthouse, which was monitored by a bank of cameras. A deputy assigned to the courthouse security detail had watched Dzhokhar, who was wearing an orange prison jumpsuit. He jumped up onto a bench in his holding cell and preened his hair in the reflection of the camera inside the small cell. And then, astonishingly, he raised his middle finger at the security camera, his face twisted into a sinister smile, and then flashed two fingers sideways into the camera, another international symbol that had the same meaning as the middle-finger salute: fuck you.

The deputy who was watching alerted Roche, who then went to Dzhokhar's cell.

"We saw what you did. That is not going to be tolerated in this house," Roche admonished Dzhokhar. "This behavior will be dealt with."[5]

The teen's bravado disappeared. He slumped and apologized: "Sorry."

"Are you going to be a problem for the rest of the day?" Roche demanded.

"No, I'm done. I'm sorry."

The one-finger salute was a hard thing to prove without a picture, but word of the obscene gesture spread including to the reporters at the courthouse. "This is Dzhokhar Tsarnaev," Assistant US Attorney Nadine Pellegrini told the jury, adding that the one-finger salute had been followed by another offensive hand signal more commonly used in Europe. But it meant the same thing. The prisoner was "unconcerned, unrepentant and unchanged."[6]

Dzhokhar's defense attorneys countered to the jury that the hand signals were in fact viewed as a "peace sign" in Russia.[7] Roche scoffed. "I'm purebred Irish, and all four of my grandparents emigrated here from Ireland so . . . I perceived it as defiance. The way that I understood it growing up around my family and circle of people, that was it. It was a disrespectful sign. To me," he added, the middle finger and the sideways two fingers into the camera "were one in [and] the same. They meant the same thing to me."[8]

A final fuck you. The jury got the message.

20
FOOD FOR THE DOG

Stephen Silva wanted to share a message with the world in the weeks after the man he considered his best friend, Dzhokhar Tsarnaev, was arrested for the murders of two young women and a little boy with a weapon of mass destruction designed to cause maximum harm (which, indeed it had) and the later murder of a police officer. The maximum harm inflicted was not limited to the victims and survivors but extended widely, affecting not only Boylston Street commerce, but Boston tourism and the very psyche of the region. Silva, as he said in a tweet on April 29, 2013, was "tryna live life feds free."

He would not be so lucky. The feds would be knocking at his door within a matter of months.

Stephen had grown up in Cambridge along with his twin brother, Steven. Steven was the good brother, the one who didn't get into trouble, at least not as often as Stephen, who spent most of his time dealing drugs and smoking weed with Dzhokhar and their other Cambridge Rindge and Latin classmates, including Robel Phillipos, who partied with Dzhokhar the week of the marathon attacks and would face trial, along with Azamat Tazhayakov and Dias Kadyrbayev, for obstructing the investigation into the Boston Marathon bombers.

Stephen's friends didn't invite him to Dzhokhar's dorm room on the night of April 18, 2013, to scrub it of evidence, like Robel, nor did Stephen try to delete any memory of his friendship with Dzhokhar from his life or laptop, like Khairullozhon Matanov, another pal of Dzhokhar. Quite the opposite. Stephen bragged about that friendship to reporters after Dzhokhar was arrested, in public tweets on his Twitter page, and even to the cops. In November 2013 he was caught selling bags of weed at the JFK stop on the MBTA's Red Line. As he was handcuffed he apologized to transit police officers, telling them that he did drugs himself to cope with his close link to the deadly Boston Marathon explosions. "I smoke a lot of weed every day because my best friend was the bomber," Stephen blurted out.

Stephen was already on federal investigators' radar before he called attention so publicly to his close association with Dzhokhar. For one thing, the two had been in a car together outside of that Arlington Fourth of July house party the summer before the bombings, tossing beer cans out the window of Dzhokhar's car. The FBI had that report. They had read Stephen's comments to reporters that Dzhokhar was one of "the realest and coolest kids" he knew—which, he acknowledged on the stand that he had said using his brother Steven's name.[1] Investigators knew Stephen had family ties to the Eritrean drug gang in Portland, Maine, the one that led to the Operation Run This Town investigation, so they set up a sting using an informant, just like the one used to take down the Eritreans in recent years. For months, both an undercover FBI agent and a CW captured Stephen on audio- and videotape selling drugs and boasting about how close he had been to Dzhokhar.

Stephen was not just a bigmouth. He was also stupid. It would not take much work for the FBI's undercover agent to follow Stephen around as he sold heroin. The sting was described this way in a federal court filing: "After Dzhokhar was charged in connection with the marathon bombing, the government identified Stephen and Steven Silva, two high school classmates of Dzhokhar who were well known Cambridge marijuana dealers, as individuals with potential information about the Ruger handgun that was used to kill MIT Police Officer Sean Collier. The Silva brothers refused to cooperate and both invoked their 5th Amendment rights. The government subsequently commenced this investigation of Stephen Silva with the goal of developing information about the gun that was used to kill Officer Collier."[2]

The undercover sting that would take Stephen down began in June 2014, according to court records, right around the time Dzhokhar's friends began to rat him out one by one. A month earlier Stephen had sent out yet another tweet: "I seen a lot a niggas tell on their man."

Before long he would be doing exactly that, testifying against Dzhokhar in federal court about the Ruger P95 he had lent him, the gun that the ATF had painstakingly identified despite its obliterated serial number and the convoluted route it had taken to reach the marathon bomber's hands.

In November 2011, Los Angeles native Danny Sun Jr. had purchased the 9mm Ruger P95 at a Cabela's hunting and fishing store in South Portland, Maine, as part of a multigun purchase. Sun later told police that at some point over the next year, he paid off a drug debt by giving the gun to his dealer, Biniam "Icy" Tsegai, the main target in the Operation Run This Town case. Sometime in 2012, Icy handed the gun off to twenty-one-year-old Merhawi "Howie" Berhe, a fellow Eritrean, who then gave it to Stephen. Stephen said he got the gun after Berhe's mother had cleaned his room, found it in her son's sock drawer, and ordered him to get rid of it.

"Howie was a friend of mine from my neighborhood. He asked me if I could do him a favor and hold down a firearm for him because he needed to get it out of his house," Stephen said. The gun, he said, was "black . . . looked a little rusty . . . the serial number was obliterated on a silver panel and it said 'P95' on the top slide and it also says Ruger on the side of the gun."[3]

Stephen made use of the gun himself when he ripped off buyers in a drug deal in Cambridge later that year. He also liked to show it off at parties, as he did on New Year's Eve in 2013, where Dzhokhar allegedly first saw it.

"Man, I need to borrow that gun," Dzhokhar told him. "I want to rip [off] some URI [University of Rhode Island] kids." Stephen agreed to lend it to him, and Dzhokhar picked it up roughly two months before the marathon bombings. Stephen gave it to him wrapped in a tube sock, along with bullets—which Dzhokhar had referred to as "food for the dog." Stephen then became annoyed with his friend, who kept "coming up with excuses" when he was supposed to return the gun. Howie wanted it back, and Stephen was now in a bad spot.

He told this story over and over as he dropped off drugs with the FBI undercover agent, the CW, or both starting in June 2014, according to federal prosecutors, who wrote in one court filing: "During the controlled buys, Silva repeatedly discussed, in detail, and on audio/video tape, with both the UC [undercover agent] and CW-1 [first CW], the fact that, in February 2013, he provided the Ruger handgun to Dzhokhar Tsarnaev that was subsequently used to kill MIT Police Officer Sean Collier on April 18, 2013. Silva told the UC that Dzhokhar wanted the gun to rob a drug dealer in Rhode Island,

and that Silva did not know anything about Dzhokhar's plans to bomb the Boston Marathon."[4]

Stephen's bragging would come to haunt him. In July 2014, as prosecutors continued to build their case against his best friend, Stephen would be arrested and charged with federal charges of drug dealing and firearms charges based on the evidence that he had "knowingly received and possessed a firearm, to wit, a Ruger model P95 9mm pistol, which had the importer's and manufacturer's serial number removed, obliterated, and altered and had previously been shipped and transported in interstate and foreign commerce."

The gun was a key piece of evidence in the case against Dzhokhar. Defense attorneys had repeatedly argued in court motions that he was a gullible teen who had come under the sway of his intimidating older brother. The gun proved that Dzhokhar was an integral part of the deadly plot to bomb the Boston Marathon, and Stephen would soon prove to be an important witness to substantiate that proof.

21
KILL TO BE AN AMERICAN

The trip to Russia was like part of the plot of a Steven Seagal movie.

Furious federal lawmakers, including Congressman William Keating, had demanded answers from the FBI about the Boston Marathon attack, but the bureau's top officials refused multiple requests to testify at Congressional hearings. So the lawmakers turned to Seagal—the swarthy action hero who has long been rumored to be a CIA operative and who counts Vladimir Putin among his pals and has connections to politicians in Chechnya—to lead them into a war-torn country full of suicide bombers and brutality, a region where there are roadblocks and cop killings and where people vanished without warning, never to be seen again. Yes, it sounded like a movie, but it was all too real.

Congressman Dana Rohrabacher had heard the stories about Seagal's connections to the highest levels of government in Russia and asked him if he could open some of the doors that a delegation of lawmakers would otherwise need to kick in to get any cooperation. The FBI had been stonewalling Congress for months—FBI Director Robert Mueller had even rebuffed an invitation to brief federal lawmakers on the Homeland Security Committee in a closed-door classified session—and by June 2013 lawmakers had decided to go to Russia in search of the answers that the FBI refused to give them. And Seagal was going to lead the group.

Before they left, Rohrabacher explained to reporters that he had known Seagal for a number of years and that the two had often discussed thwarting radical Islamic terrorism. He repeatedly praised the actor for going out of his way to set up meetings for the delegation in Russia. Rohrabacher had been a speechwriter for President Ronald Reagan and was all too familiar with the way things got done during the Cold War.

Seagal had offered to set up a meeting for the delegation with Chechen President Ramzan Kadyrov, a man who had been criticized in the State Department's latest annual human rights report for his heavy-handed antiterrorism tactics, which included abductions of suspected radicals. He was known for burning down the houses of the families of suspected terrorists. The six members of the Congressional delegation—four Republicans and two Democrats—thought that a photo op with Kadyrov might not play well with their constituents back home and declined that offer, so instead Seagal set up a meeting with Deputy Prime Minister Dmitry Rogozin, along with ranking members of the FSB, to go over the information that the Russian agency had sent to the FBI's Boston field office about Tamerlan Tsarnaev and his mother, Zubeidat, back in 2011—information that the FBI had refused to hand over to Congressional investigators. The delegation also wanted a detailed explanation about a communication between the FSB and the FBI on April 22, 2011, regarding another Russian native living in Massachusetts, Ibragim Todashev. Keating said that FSB letter had described Ibragim as among the "matters of significance"—another issue the FBI refused to explain, especially after an investigation had been opened into whether an FBI agent had been justified in shooting Ibragim seven times during an interview at the Russian's home in Florida (discussed in a previous chapter). "That letter was dated April 22," Keating said. "What information about Mr. Todashev did the FBI and CIA share with local law enforcement?"[1]

"The Russians challenged us about the FBI's claim that it requested more information about Tsarnaev, information that the Russians told us they never received. We asked the FBI for specific dates and who that request was sent to and we never got an answer," Keating said. "The Russians were more cooperative than the FBI." He found that worrisome.

There would be a mass exodus of federal investigators—including two appointees of President Barack Obama, the heads of the FBI and DHS—and agents, and even a state prosecutor, after the Boston Marathon attacks. Just months after her Congressional testimony on April 23, 2015, DHS Secretary Janet Napolitano resigned. Her testimony that a "spelling error" had allowed Tamerlan to pass through US Customs when he returned from Russia though he was on two terrorist watch lists, was laughable. But she didn't stick around to be scoffed at. She knew what was in the DHS USCIS file on Tamerlan: multiple spellings of his name, aliases, and two different dates of birth. There was also the letter that suggested he had been rewarded—telling him to show up to take the oath of citizenship when he wasn't eligible to become a citizen.

She announced her resignation on July 12, 2013. The very next day was the last day that Richard DesLauriers, the special agent in charge of the FBI's Boston field office, would spend with the bureau. DesLauriers announced that he was resigning—four years before he was eligible for full retirement benefits—just ten days before his boss, FBI Director Robert Mueller III, did the same thing. Mueller had always been viewed with skepticism by Massachusetts law enforcement officials. The crooked FBI agents who ran James "Whitey" Bulger (discussed in chapter 12) as an informant had reported to the criminal division of the US Attorney's Office in Boston, where for a time Mueller had been the acting US attorney. He had presided over the rogue agents during the time when Bulger committed crimes with seeming immunity as a top-echelon FBI informant. Every time local cops got close to making a move against Bulger, their case was blown. And they blamed Mueller and the FBI.

The fallout also affected a special agent whose name came up over and over, David Cedarleaf, a former captain in the US Marines and the agent who corresponded with USCIS to help Tamerlan get his citizenship. He was transferred out of the FBI's Boston field office. In 2016, US Attorney Carmen Ortiz celebrated the conviction of Dzhokhar Tsarnaev by awarding citations to everyone in that office who had worked on the case, with one exception—Cedarleaf.

By resigning, the FBI officials with direct knowledge of Tamerlan's relationships could not be compelled to testify in front of Congress. To this day no one in the FBI has.

The new director of the FBI was James Comey, appointed to the job in June 2013. Keating wasted no time in writing Comey to demand answers:

As a former District Attorney for twelve years, I share a great appreciation for the integrity of our judicial processes and understand the challenges faced by the Federal Bureau of Investigations (FBI). For this reason, I would like to start out by of course, congratulating you on your recent confirmation and thanking the men and women of the FBI for their exceptional work and commitment to protecting our country. I have been particularly engaged on the developments surrounding the Boston Marathon bombings in my home state and look forward to working with you on this matter further.

The dedication of the FBI's agents was made apparent in meetings I had in Boston (June 21, 2013) and Moscow (May 29, 2013). These official meetings were designed to investigate procedural and resource-related shortcomings leading up to and during the Boston Marathon bombings. The obvious intent of which is to help prevent future tragedies. Unfortunately, nearly all of these inquiries have gone unanswered. Further, the continued reluctance of the FBI to address Members of Congress on the Committee on Homeland Security (most recently on July 10, 2013) impairs Congress' responsibility to conduct proper oversight. It is not, as the FBI has described, an issue of who can provide testimony jurisdictionally, rather whether an agency that investigates homeland security issues is willing to share information critical to improving the security of our Nation. For example, we have no "jurisdictional" authority over the City of Boston, yet Boston's Police Commissioner has testified before Congress on improvements that can be made in our current homeland security processes and procedures.

Open questions remain, particularly in regard to inadequate information sharing, restrictive investigative guidelines/protocols, and an inability to follow up on suspicious activities/travel of individuals residing in the US. Finally, I would like to note that while in Moscow on May 30, 2013, I was able to obtain a readout of the March 4, 2011 and April 22, 2013 communications from the Federal Security Service of Russia (FSB) to the FBI and Central Intelligence Agency (CIA). Despite numerous requests to obtain a copy of and discuss this information, I have not heard anything back from the FBI.

For these reasons, I am detailing some of my unanswered inquiries in this letter in order to illustrate that I am not in fact asking for any "materials related to active, ongoing law enforcement investigations," but am rather seeking information that will help Congress better address the homeland security concerns of my constituents, particularly following the Boston bombings. Perhaps, when viewed on paper, the procedural nature of these questions will become apparent, and the FBI will agree to assist in closing loopholes that may hinder the future identification or capture of dangerous individuals before lives are lost.

1. As mentioned earlier, I was relayed the information contained in both warnings about Tamerlan Tsarnaev while I was in Moscow. The March 4, 2011 message, in particular, was quite detailed. The FBI has admitted to receiving communications from the Russians and has reportedly tried to follow up on the March warning twice. (According to former Director Mueller's recent testimony before the Senate, the FBI followed up in August and October of 2012.) When I asked the FSB why they didn't respond to the FBI's follow-up inquiries, the senior, deputy-level FSB officials in the room vehemently denied that any follow-up from the FBI occurred and asked me to provide them with concrete dates and names associated with such requests. I would ask that the FBI provide the exact dates of any follow-up communications stemming from the US and detail where they were sent. This information can aid in illustrating a lapse within the Russians' own internal communications and provide the opportunity to correct this in the future.

2. Your predecessor testified before the Senate Judiciary Committee on May 16, 2013 and stated that information in regard to Tsarnaev's travel to Russia was not adequately shared within the Joint Terrorism Task Force in Boston. He followed this statement by saying that the FBI has been doing better and improving its procedures since then. Please clarify what information in particular was not shared and how the system has been improved since the Boston Marathon bombings.

3. Further, Tamerlan Tsarnaev was flagged after his return from Russia and again when he applied for US citizenship. USCIS officials in Boston confirmed on June 21, 2013 that his name was flagged, but

when they contacted the FBI they were told that his case was closed and that they could move forward with his naturalization process. Tamerlan Tsarnaev was subsequently granted a citizenship interview. Is the FBI required to conduct a second background check on a previously investigated individual if this individual is applying for citizenship?

4. The March 2011 communication from the Russians also contained information pertaining to aliases that Tsarnaev may have used and indicated the possibility of him altering his name. Is there a mechanism that can override the algorithms in place that proved inadequate in flagging Tsarnaev's travel to Russia in January 2012? Is there any way to incorporate outside tips on name changes into the consolidated terror watch lists?

5. Two Homeland Security Committee witnesses, namely former Mayor Rudolph Giuliani and former Senator Joe Lieberman, cited existing "laws" and "guidelines" that constrained the Tsarnaev investigation early on. Even Russian security officials stated that the FBI had told them that "legislation" had obstructed their ability to investigate. Are there such constraints to FBI investigations? If so, how can Congress assist in easing them?

6. Police Commissioner Ed Davis of Boston has testified to the fact that information about Tamerlan Tsarnaev was not adequately shared with local officers until the aftermath of the tragedy in Boston. While the FBI has indicated that information about Tamerlan Tsarnaev was in a database that local members of the Joint Terrorism Task Force (JTTF) had access to, these local officials could not search the database for something that they did not know existed. Further, police chiefs throughout the country have expressed concern over the fact that officers assigned to JTTF cannot share critical information with other officials, including their superiors within the police department. Would you please explain why information about the Boston Marathon bombing suspects was not shared with the local police department in Boston? Further, would you detail current protocol in regard to information sharing between officers on the JTTF and their Department Heads?

7. The second communication from the Russian FSB on April 22, 2013 detailed Ibragim Todashev under "matters of significance." Did this communication initiate the FBI's investigation into Todashev? Since his name appeared in a mode of communication considered to be foreign intelligence, was it permitted to be shared with local authorities?

If need be, I would gladly discuss the sensitive nature of these requests in a secure environment. I thank you for your time and look forward to the FBI's response. Further, I look forward to working with you in your new position. My office remains open to your agency, and I hope that we can work together to facilitate greater communication between the FBI and Congress as we work together on matters of security and foreign emerging threats that affect homeland defense.

Lawmakers, including Keating, and law enforcement officials, including BPD Commissioner Ed Davis, were also confused about why Tamerlan's naturalization application—which had already been denied—was reopened after his return from Russia. During his trip, the Russian Interior Ministry—the country's version of the CIA—managed to track down and kill multiple high-level terrorists who had been spotted with Tamerlan, including the Canadian boxer William Plotnikov.

———

Dzhokhar was the only member of his family to become a US citizen. He swore an oath to his adopted country in a ceremony at the beloved TD Garden on September 11, 2012, just seven months before he would attack his countrymen in an act of terrorism on Boylston Street. Dzhokar's citizenship had to crush Tamerlan, who wanted nothing more in the world than to be considered an American, a US citizen who could box for his country in the Olympic games and compete in the National Tournament of Champions.

Federal prosecutors wanted to use Dzohkar's citizenship to level another aggravated charge against him in the thirty-count indictment, saying he had committed an act of treachery against his adopted country. They wrote that he "received asylum from the United States; obtained citizenship and enjoyed the freedoms of a United States citizen; and then betrayed his allegiance to the United States by killing and maiming people in the United States. By taking the oath of citizenship, Tsarnaev sought and received the trust of his fellow Americans. Among other things, he was granted the right to vote in American elections, run for public office, and thus to influence American foreign policy by peaceful means. Just seven months after swearing an oath to defend his adopted country and stand by his fellow Americans, Tsarnaev violated that oath by attacking America and terrorizing and murdering people on American soil. He did so, by his own account, to punish America for the actions of American soldiers who, in fulfilling their own oaths to protect and defend the Constitution, were waging a war against terrorism overseas."[2]

Defense attorneys were horrified by the motion to charge their client with treason and responded with their own legal filing protesting it: "The government's accusation, plainly expressed, is that the defendant received asylum (that he was eight years old at the time goes unmentioned), became a naturalized citizen, and then attacked the United States. The government has nevertheless already attempted to recast the 'betrayal' allegation, insisting that all it meant to allege is that the defendant betrayed his country by carrying out the Marathon attack only seven months after taking the oath of citizenship at the age of 19."[3] US District Court Justice George O'Toole sided with the defense, and the charge of treason was dropped.

Lawmakers were not the only ones with questions about Tamerlan's immigration status. The Office of the Inspector General for the Intelligence Community would examine Tamerlan's citizenship application as part of a sweeping probe into information sharing among federal agencies in a report released in April 2014. The report pointed out that Tamerlan had reported the passport that he had been issued as a teenager in Kyrgyzstan had been stolen, and that he had applied for a Russian passport during his trip. But he abruptly left Russia without it on July 17, 2012—two days after the raid that left Plotnikov and others dead in the forests of Utamysh. When Tamerlan landed at Boston's Logan Airport, he breezed through US customs with just his legal permanent resident identification. The *9/11 Commission Report* had recommended that the practice of allowing political refugees, like Tamerlan, to travel to terrorist hotbeds and return to the United States using such documents be stopped.[4] That loophole, however, is still open. The Office of the

Inspector General would report that the customs agent "scanned Tsarnaev's Alien Registration Card into the computer system . . . and admitted him into the country based on his LPR [legal permanent resident] status."[5] The agent, Jim Bailey, told the Office of the Inspector General that he could not remember if he alerted the FBI regarding Tamerlan's return to the United States, nor did he recall that Tamerlan had paid for his one-way airfare in cash. That was a stunning admission.

When pressed, Bailey told the Office of the Inspector General that communications with his JTTF colleagues in the FBI were usually "done orally or with a sticky note." It was only after Tamerlan had been admitted back into the United States that Bailey pulled up the TECS database in which Tamerlan had been identified as a potential terrorist, the report states.

The FBI pointed the finger back at Customs, telling the Office of the Inspector General that "there is a very good chance" that the FBI would have interviewed Tamerlan again upon his return from Russia had it known about the travel, but that this would have "depended on what was learned from the Russians and from any secondary inspection during Tsarnaev's travel."

Then there was the business of the Russian Interior Ministry's press release that stated it had "received information about the possible movements" of insurgents in Utamysh "from an informant." A similar story was reported on Kavkaz.org, the jihadist news portal then run by the late Doku Umarov. Kavkaz.org—a site bookmarked as a favorite on Tamerlan's laptop and one he referred to frequently in conversations with friends—reported: "Invaders have announced that they identified the personalities of Mujahedeen killed near the village of Utamysh of Kayakent district of Province of Dagestan. According to the Russian aggressors, Mujahedeen got into an ambush, because of a tip from an informer."[6]

Many police officials believe that Tamerlan was that informant. Of course, it is not an opinion that they will express on the record. Davis, then commissioner of the BPD, hinted at some federal malfeasance in his Congressional testimony after the blasts at the Boston Marathon. Grassley demanded answers, as did Keating and Republican Congressman Michael McCaul, and there was bipartisan outrage at the FBI's steadfast refusal to cooperate with Congress. The reopening of Tamerlan's naturalization application provided evidence for those who believe he was a federal asset.

Ironically, Tamerlan's lack of a passport would become an issue when his parents—who never returned to the United States, not even when their younger son was shot, arrested, and arraigned—requested that his body be shipped back to Russia for burial in his homeland. The funeral director said that would be impossible because Tamerlan did not possess a passport. The Tsarnaev family's spokeswoman in Dagestan told reporters that the Americans would not fly his body back to Russia for burial, citing passport problems. Tamerlan's father, Anzor, tried to explain those problems to a *New York Times* reporter: "His passport was about to expire in June or in July and that is why I said, 'You have to get a Russian passport.' Because we left Kyrgyzstan for the States to seek political asylum in the States and Kyrgyzstan refused us citizenship."[7]

In August 2012, weeks after his return from Russia, Tamerlan became more public about his radicalization. He opened a YouTube channel using the name Muaz, the name he had used when he introduced himself to people at the radical mosque in Dagestan. He and his Russian friends, including Khairullozhon Matanov, posed in front of the black flag of jihad at a Boston-area mosque, according to an FBI report.

"Immigration Services Officer asks FBI CT agent assigned to Tsarnaev case if he presents a national security threat," the FBI report states. That request was sent to Cedarleaf, the same FBI agent who had visited the Tsarnaevs in 2011 and claimed to have reported back to the FSB, a claim that Keating said Russian security officials denied.

On October 23, 2012, Cedarleaf responded to immigration officials, writing that "there is no derogatory information related to national security that would adversely affect the subject's eligibility for immigration benefit."[8] That statement was repeated in another e-mail sent on October 26, 2013.

The immigration services officer handling Tamerlan's application for citizenship was clearly concerned, and the e-mails went back and forth from October 2012 to January 2013, a period that coincided with Tamerlan's increased devotion to Islamic extremism. During those same months he began to post jihad-themed videos on his public YouTube channel.

Then there were the two incidents at the mosque he had complained about in Russia to his mother's cousin, Magomed Kartashov (as discussed in chapter 9). In November 2012 he had caused a commotion at the Cambridge mosque, arguing with the imam over a lecture on American holidays like Thanksgiving and shouting, "That is not allowed in the faith!" (That same week he had yelled at a Muslim shopkeeper in Cambridge for selling turkeys, calling him a kaffir.) And in January 2013 Tamerlan had been asked to leave the same Cambridge mosque after he disrupted Friday prayers again, an outburst caused by the imam's preaching that Martin Luther King was a good man like the Prophet Muhammad. Tamerlan stood up and shouted that the cleric was a "a non-believer" and accused him of "contaminating peoples' minds." People in the congregation shouted back at Tamerlan, telling him to "leave now," a member of the mosque told me, which would be repeated on the stand through Dzhokhar's trial. Khairullozhon told the FBI that he calmed Tamerlan down that day and escorted him outside.

But the real turning point for Tamerlan came on January 23, 2013. That was the day he fully expected to finally realize his dream of becoming a US citizen. Immigration Officer David McCormack sat him down and tested his English. Then came a battery of tests regarding his knowledge of US history and government, including some questions that might have stumped US-born citizens. He knew that Africans had been slaves, that there are twenty-seven constitutional amendments, and that the United States had bought Louisiana from the French in 1803. He also identified "Joe Biden" as the vice president and said that Congress makes federal laws and that the colonists in Massachusetts had fought the British over "high taxes." He read a question about voting and wrote the correct answer: "Citizens can vote."[9] He got only one question wrong, saying that the federal court—not the Supreme Court—is the highest court in the United States.

After all that, it would be a paperwork snafu that would delay the processing of his application—which, in Tamerlan's mind, he deserved to have approved. The only way that anyone would make a federal push for Tamerlan's citizenship would be to reward him for a job well done. He was an unemployed Muslim with a criminal history and ties to terrorists, a man who was currently on two terrorist watch lists via the CIA and the FBI, and officially ineligible for citizenship because of his arrest for domestic violence let alone someone likely to be fast-tracked for citizenship.

People like Tamerlan Tsarnaev, unemployed, with a criminal record, and a Muslim, were not exactly at the front of the line for citizenship. In fact, the lack of naturalization applications being processed by USCIS for much more qualified Muslims led the ACLU to study the denials of citizenship for employed, college-educated Islamic applicants in order to commission a report called "Muslims Need Not Apply," which argued that millions of Muslim applicants apply for asylum and citizenship every year and accused officials in the DHS's USCIS of secretly excluding "many . . . aspiring Americans from Arab, Middle Eastern, Muslim, and South Asian communities from the promises of citizenship, legal residency, asylum, and other benefits by delaying and denying their applications without legal authority. For years, and without notice to applicants, their lawyers, or the public at large, USCIS has been blacklisting law-abiding applicants as 'national security concerns' based on lawful religious activity, national origin, and innocuous associations. Once blacklisted, these aspiring Americans are barred from obtaining immigration benefits to which they are legally entitled. As a result, by putting their applications on indefinite hold or rejecting them for unfounded reasons, thousands of law-abiding immigrants have had their dreams of citizenship and other immigration status dashed, without ever being told why their applications were treated differently than others."[10]

In 2008, USCIS implemented a covert program, the Controlled Application Review and Resolution Program, to "ensure that immigration benefits are not granted to individuals and organizations that pose a threat to national security."[11]

———

Tamerlan had been identified as a threat to national security. He had spent his entire time in the United States collecting public assistance and when he died, his death certificate stated, "Never worked."[12] But months after his trip to a terrorist hotbed where he had met with Islamic militants and prayed at a mosque that displayed the black flag of jihad outside, he was taking a test for citizenship. Maybe it was a coincidence that many of those militants he had met ended up dead. But that was unlikely.

All that stood between him and US citizenship was a supervisor's approval, which was required, and a final swearing-in ceremony—the one that came after the October date had somehow been scuttled. Then everything went wrong. Tamerlan fully expected the USCIS agent to check the box that read: "Congratulations! Your application has been recommended for approval." Instead the agent checked the next box, which read, "A decision cannot yet be made about your application," as noted in the 2014 report from the Office of the Inspector General.

"A USCIS officer interviewed Tsarnaev on January 23, 2013, but did not adjudicate his naturalization after the interview because USCIS had not received the court records relating to his 2009 arrest," the report stated. Tamerlan's arrest for slapping his girlfriend in the face had triggered the disqualifying "moral turpitude" clause (discussed in a previous chapter).

Tamerlan's request to become a citizen was not being denied. It was being delayed—again. And he was furious. He demanded a name-change application and filled it out, requesting that his name be legally changed to Muaz, the name he had used in Russia. To him the name honored a slain Chechen rebel. In the section where the form asked for an explanation for the name-change request, Tamerlan wrote, "The Russian people have been terrorizing my home country for all these years."[13]

It wasn't entirely a surprise that Tamerlan wanted to adopt the moniker he had used in Dagestan. He had long been fascinated by aliases and spy craft. An Amazon wish list in his name listed the books *How to Make Driver's Licenses and Other ID on Your Home Computer; Voice Power: Using Your Voice to Captivate, Persuade and Command Attention; Document Fraud and Other Crimes of Deception;* and *How to Win Friends and Influence People.*

After angrily scribbling his new name, Muaz Tsarnaev stormed out of the John F. Kennedy Federal Building in Boston's Government Center and headed back to Cambridge.

Days later, on February 6, 2013, he drove to Phantom Fireworks, in Seabrook, New Hampshire, where he asked the clerk to help him find the "biggest and loudest" pyrotechnics in the emporium. He spent $200 on two "lock and load mortar kits."[14] Later that same month, on February 23, he went to Macy's in Downtown Crossing, according to an FBI search warrant affidavit, where—with his wife, investigators believe—he bought "five kitchen appliances." As noted above, Macy's is the only department store in the country that sells Fagor brand pressure cookers. FBI bomb experts would later testify that the bombs used at the Boston Marathon had been constructed inside two six-quart Fagor pressure cookers. The FBI also recovered seven issues of Al Qaeda's *Inspire* magazine on Tamerlan's computer, including one that contained the article "How to Build a Bomb in the Kitchen of Your Mom."

On March 6, 2013, Tamerlan drove around New Hampshire to buy bomb parts. Investigators analyzed the GPS in the Tsarnaevs' car and learned that it had been at the Walmart in Manchester, where he purchased two boxes of BB ammunition, containing a total of 6,000 copper-head BBs. Two hours later, investigators placed Tamerlan at the Walmart in Amherst, where two more boxes of BB ammunition were purchased. Next, there was a stop at the Walmart in Hudson, where more BBs were purchased. Then, on April 11, just four days before the bombing, prosecutors said the brothers visited Stateline Guns, Ammo and Archery in Plaistow. Investigators said they purchased $40 worth of ammunition there.

Investigators also found a stack of anarchist newspapers, including the *Sovereign*, whose headlines blared "New Muslim Group Takes On Islamaphobia in Tea Party" and "Senator Slams Department of Homeland Security for Wasteful, Frivolous Spending."[15]

What the FBI didn't find, however, was the location where the bombs were built.

The fireworks that Tamerlan purchased wouldn't have provided enough gunpowder for a pipe bomb, never mind a pressure-cooker explosive like the sophisticated bombs used in Boston. "Certain states sell mortars. They can contain up to maybe 30 grams or more of explosive material within them. So if you're looking for a pound, 30 grams, 454 grams in a pound, you would need dozens of those mortars just to create a pound of explosive material," FBI explosives expert David McCollum testified. He then described the "small grains of black powder" recovered along with smudges on surgical gloves found at 410 Norfolk Street. The lack of evidence would become an issue with prosecutors.[16]

"Mr. McCollum, you testified that there may have been pounds of low explosives that were used in this case?" Assistant US Attorney Aloke Chakravarty asked.

"Correct."

"And you testified that it's an extremely messy process to create those low explosives?"

"Yes."

"And as far as you know, with regards to the trace amounts of low explosives that Mr. Watkins asked you about, you found them on some gloves, and you found some in some vacuum filters from 410 Norfolk Street?"

"Yes."

"And that's the only trace amounts that you found in this case; is that fair to say?"

"Yes."

"And unlike trace amounts of explosive product, there was actually intact fireworks found in the dorm room in Pine Dale Hall, isn't that right?"

McCollum answered, "If it was submitted to the laboratory coming from there, I analyzed it, so, yes, there were."

"And in the landfill, there was a bag containing intact amounts of low-explosive, pyrotechnic mixture?"

"Yes."

"Did you ever find a location, a single location, where there was a production facility for these IEDs?"

Before McCollum answer Dzhokhar's defense lawyers objected, and the judge sustained that objection. It didn't matter—the message was clear. To this day, the FBI has no idea, or if they do, they're not telling, where the bombs were built, even if the government's own court filings suggested investigators believed, and probably continue to believe, the Tsarnaevs had help. The point would be repeated on the stand over and over, in the trials of Dzhokhar and of his college buddies.

22

MAXIMUM HARM

It was March 4, 2015, the first day of Dzhokhar Tsarnaev's trial, and the swagger with which he had walked into the same courthouse for his July 10, 2013, arraignment was gone. So were the cast and his youthful appearance. Being held in a solitary cell had already aged him. Instead of the orange prison jumpsuit he had worn the first time he appeared in court, he had on a black blazer and dress pants. The beard he had seemingly been trying to grow on that day in July when he showed his middle finger to the security camera in his holding cell was fuller, and his hair was cut shorter. Before the proceedings began he joked with his attorneys. Victims of his attack on the city nearly two years before stared at the back of his head, willing him to turn around and look them in the eye.

An eerie silence filled the courtroom as the clerk announced "All rise," and US District Court Justice George O'Toole took his seat on the bench. O'Toole would be the presiding judge for the duration of the trial. The government was ready to present its case—in fact, its attorneys were eager to do so. Assistant US Attorney William Weinreb stood up. With a new haircut and wearing an appropriately dapper but not flashy suit, he turned to the jury before he began. In front of him were the twelve jurors—seven women and five men from all over Massachusetts who had been painstakingly selected. Only one lived in Boston; the rest were from suburban towns scattered across the Commonwealth: Dartmouth, Franklin, Ipswich, Malden, Marlborough, New Bedford, Osterville, Peabody (the home of two jurors), Scituate, and Woburn. Six alternates sat nearby.

Weinreb took a breath and began, using Dzhokhar's American nickname, "Jahar" (as would often be done throughout the trial):

"Nearly two years ago, on Marathon Monday, the defendant, Jahar Tsarnaev, rounded the corner onto Boylston Street and began walking towards the Boston Marathon finish line. It was about 2:30 in the afternoon. The race had started about six hours earlier, and the sidewalks were packed with spectators. The Red Sox game had just ended, and people were pouring out of Fenway Park, making the crowds even bigger. There were people from all over the world and all walks of life—men, women, boys, and girls—all loudly cheering on the runners. And because Marathon Monday falls on Patriots' Day, the school holiday, there were plenty of families enjoying the special day with their children.

"But the defendant wasn't there to watch the race. He had a backpack over his shoulder, and inside that backpack was a homemade bomb. It was the type of bomb favored by terrorists because it's designed to tear people apart and create a bloody spectacle. It was a sealed pressure cooker about this wide and this high, and it was filled with explosive powder and thousands of pieces of tiny shrapnel: nails, tacks, and little BBs. The purpose of that type of bomb is to shred flesh, shatter bone, set people on fire, and cause its victims to die painful, bloody deaths and permanent disfigurement. The defendant's goal that day was to maim and kill as many people as possible, so he took his time figuring out where to plant his bomb. He began walking slowly down towards the finish line with his brother, Tamerlan, who was also carrying a bomb in his own knapsack. They walked a little ways together, and then they split up.

"Tamerlan continued all the way down to the finish line and planted his bomb there in a crowd of people. The defendant waited a bit and then started walking in the same direction. He decided to stop in front of a crowded restaurant called Forum, and to place his bomb right behind a row of children who were standing on a railing by a curb—the curb watching the race.

"One of those children was an eight-year-old boy named Martin Richard who was watching the race with his family. No one noticed the defendant plant the bomb because there was nothing out of the ordinary to see. He just got there, slipped his backpack onto the ground, and stood there looking at the backs of those children. He pretended to be a spectator, but he had murder in his heart, although you wouldn't have known it just to look at him.

"The defendant looked and acted like a typical young adult, but the evidence will show that he wasn't. He had a side to him that he kept hidden, even from his closest friends.

"When he was with his friends, he hung out and played video games. But when he was by himself, he read terrorist writings and listened to terrorist lectures. Those writings and lectures convinced him that he should kill innocent Americans in order to punish the United States for mistreating Muslims in other countries. And by doing so, he thought he would earn a place in paradise, which explains what happened next.

"The defendant stood there for nearly four minutes directly behind the row of children who were watching the race. Dozens of people stood around him, and dozens more were behind him in the Forum restaurant enjoying a meal with friends, cheering on the runners, or just enjoying the day. Then when the defendant had given his brother, Tamerlan, enough time to get into place, he called Tamerlan on the phone and spoke to him for about 20 seconds. About ten seconds later, Tamerlan detonated his bomb. A few seconds after that, the defendant walked briskly back the way he had come, leaving his own bomb behind him on the ground. When he was a safe distance away, he detonated the bomb by remote control.

"The explosions from the two bombs were terrifying. They made a deafening roar and created fireballs several stories high. The air filled with the smell of burning sulfur and people's screams. Pieces of the pressure cookers and thousands of pieces of tiny shrapnel were propelled with huge force in every direction. Some of them landed hundreds of feet away.

"The defendant's bomb exploded in the middle of a crowd of people. Pieces of the pressure cooker and bits of shrapnel tore through them, shredding their flesh and severing their arteries. The explosion deafened many of them and set others on fire. Some of them were blinded. Many had a leg or a foot blown off their bodies, and some bled to death on the pavement while the defendant ran away.

"One person the defendant murdered that day was Martin Richard. As I said earlier, he was one of the children standing on the railing watching the race. Martin was eight years old. He was at the marathon with his father, Bill

Richard; his mother, Denise; his six-year-old sister, Jane; and his 11-year-old brother, Henry. They were all standing together waiting for a family friend to cross the finish line.

"The bomb tore large chunks of flesh out of Martin's body. As the smoke cleared, Denise Richard found her little boy lying on the ground and tried to comfort him. She could only half see him because the bomb had permanently blinded her in one eye. Martin bled to death on the sidewalk as she looked helplessly on. Bill Richard, who had been blown into the street, came back to the curb and reached out to Jane to pick her up off the sidewalk. When she tried to stand up, she fell down again because her leg was no longer attached to her body.

"Another person the defendant murdered that day is Lingzi Lu, a student at Boston University. She was a 23-year-old known for her kindness and her passion for music. She was at the marathon with her friend, Danling. They just happened to be walking by the Forum restaurant when the bomb went off. That blast knocked Danling to the ground. When she opened her eyes, she saw a man in front of her missing his leg. She looked down to see if her own legs were still there, and she saw that her insides were coming out of her stomach, so she used her hands to push them back in. She looked around to find her friend and saw her lying a few feet away. Lingzi was screaming in pain and terror, but Danling couldn't hear her because the bomb had deafened her. Danling never saw her friend again because Lingzi, like Martin Richard, bled to death on the sidewalk.

"A third person the defendant murdered that day was Krystle Marie Campbell. Krystle was 29 years old. She was at the finish line with her good friend, Karen Rand. They were there to cheer on Karen's boyfriend, who was running the race. Krystle was killed by the bomb that the defendant's brother set off. It burned her skin, filled her with shrapnel, and opened gaping wounds in her legs and torso. It also knocked her friend, Karen Rand, to the ground and blew off Karen's leg. Karen held Krystle's hand tight as the life drained out of her body.

"Now, even though the defendant's brother set off the bomb that killed Krystle Campbell, the defendant is still responsible for her death. That's because he and his brother were partners in crime. They planned these crimes together, and they carried them out together. The defendant knew that his brother's bomb was going to kill people, just like he knew his own bomb was. That's exactly what he wanted to have happen.

"As soon as those bombs went off, Boylston Street erupted into chaos. The wounded lay on the sidewalk in pools of their own blood, wondering if they were going to live. Others fled the scene. But in the midst of the chaos, some people sprang into action. Police officers, medical personnel, family members and friends of the dead and dying, many of them jumped in to offer aid. There were a lot of heroes that day, and you'll hear from some of them.

"What was the defendant doing while people were frantically trying to save the wounded from bleeding to death on the street? We know the answer because he was caught on a surveillance tape. Just 20 minutes after he set off that bomb on Boylston Street, while paramedics were still giving CPR to Martin Richard in a futile attempt to try to save his life, the defendant drove to the Whole Foods in Central Square and purchased a gallon of milk. You'll see him on the surveillance tape walking into the Whole Foods, going over to the milk counter, shopping for the milk, choosing which one to buy, going back to the counter, calmly paying for it, and walking out of the store. You'll even see him come back a minute later and decide to exchange that milk for a different type of milk.

"And what did he do after that? While victims of the bombing lay in the hospital and learned that they would have to have their limbs chopped off to save their lives, the defendant pretended that nothing had happened. He went back to UMass Dartmouth, where he was enrolled as a sophomore. He hung out with his friends and partied. He went to the gym and played video games. He posted a message on Twitter that said, 'I'm a stress free kind of guy.' He acted like he didn't have a care in the world.

"The defendant acted that way because he believed that what he had done was good, was something right. He believed that he was a soldier in a holy war against Americans and that he had won an important victory in that war by killing Martin Richard, Lingzi Lu, and Krystle Campbell. And he also believed that by winning that victory, he had taken a step toward reaching paradise. That was his motive for committing these crimes.

"How do we know that? We know it in part because the defendant wrote out an explanation of why he committed these crimes. The police found that writing when they arrested him, and you will see it later on in court. This is part of what the writing said: 'I ask Allah to make me a shahied to allow me to return to him and be among all the righteous people in the highest levels of heaven. Allah Akbar.' 'Shahied' means martyr, and 'Allah Akbar' means God is great.

"The defendant wrote, 'The U.S. government is killing our innocent civilians, but most of you already know that. I can't stand to see such evil go unpunished. We Muslims are one body. You hurt one, you hurt us all. The ummah is beginning to rise. We are promised victory, and we will surely get it.' 'Ummah' is a word that people with the defendant's beliefs use to describe the Muslim people.

"The defendant wrote, 'Now, I don't like killing people. It is forbidden in Islam. Stop killing our people, and we will stop.' The defendant carried out an attack on the Boston Marathon because he believed that the United States government is the enemy of the Muslim people. He believed that punishing America by killing innocent young women and children would cause America to stop targeting Muslim terrorists overseas and help win him a spot in heaven. And you will hear evidence of how he acquired that belief. He acquired it by reading books, listening to songs, and watching videos that were created by other terrorists, and they convinced him that he should become a terrorist too.

"The defendant's transformation into a terrorist took place over a year or two. In 2011, he started reading terrorist writings and posting online messages about the persecution of Muslims. In 2012, he started listening to terrorist lectures and songs. He told one of his friends that he had a plan to reach paradise. In 2013, he created an online identity that he used to spread radical Muslim ideas. He said that people don't take notice when Muslims die over there, meaning overseas, but if something happens over here, meaning in America, then everybody takes notice. He also said that he knew how to make a bomb.

"You will hear that the defendant had terrorist writings, videos, and lectures on his laptop computer, on his iPod and on CDs in his car. We will show you many of those writings and videos during the trial, and you'll hear evidence that reading those kinds of writings and listening to those lectures, watching those videos, is a common way that young adults like the defendant turn into terrorists themselves.

"One of the things the defendant had on his computer was a virtually complete set of *Inspire* magazine. That is a magazine published in English by a group that calls itself al-Qaeda in the Arabian Peninsula. The goal of *Inspire* magazine is to do just that: to inspire young men like the defendant to become terrorists and to encourage them to attack western countries, regardless of whether they're associated with a terrorist organization.

"It's filled with stories of terrorists who punished America by killing innocent people, and it treats them as glorious heroes. It gives instructions on the best way to commit attacks so as to terrify people and kill as many people as possible.

"One of the issues in *Inspire* magazine that the defendant had on his computer contained instructions for making a bomb out of a pressure cooker filled with explosive powder and shrapnel. It recommends placing it in a crowded area to maximize its deadly effect. The defendant and his brother began accessing those instructions around Christmas of 2012. Later, the defendant's brother bought pressure cookers to hold the explosive powder and remote-control cars that were turned into remote-control detonators. They filled the bombs with explosive powder emptied from ordinary fireworks, as well as nails, tacks, and BBs to make them more deadly.

"A few months before the marathon bombing, the defendant got a 9-millimeter handgun. He told a friend of his named Stephen Silva that he needed a gun, so Silva got him a Ruger semiautomatic pistol with the serial number filed off. Silva will be a witness in this case, and he'll testify about giving the Ruger to the defendant.

"It is clear that the defendant intended to use the Ruger because on March 20th, 2013, just about a month before the marathon attack, he and his brother drove to the Manchester firing range in New Hampshire to practice shooting. The defendant rented two 9-millimeter pistols, just like the Ruger, and purchased four boxes of ammunition, and then he and his brother spent about an hour on target practice.

"After bombing the marathon on April 15th, the defendant maintained his double identity. He acted normal around his friends. He pretended to them that he hadn't even been at the Boston Marathon, and he continued reading the terrorist writings and listening to the terrorist lectures on his computer. For example, you'll hear evidence that on April 16th, the day after the bombing, the defendant opened up the copy of *Inspire* magazine on his computer that contained instructions for building pressure cooker bombs and pipe bombs; and then you'll hear that a few days later, he and his brother exploded several pipe bombs and another pressure cooker bomb, this time in Watertown.

"Now, I want to go back to April 15th and talk about what happened after the bombings over the next few days on Boylston Street. As soon as the bombs exploded, police officers halted the marathon midway and everyone—made everyone leave the scene. Bomb technicians began checking for additional bombs. Ambulances came and took the wounded to hospitals. And then the long, painstaking process of gathering evidence began.

"Three consecutive blocks of Boylston Street were roped off and treated as a crime scene. FBI agents and hundreds of other federal, state, and local law enforcement officers donned special clothing and began scouring the area for evidence. Among all the blood and human remains, they found shredded cloth from the backpacks, pieces of the exploded pressure cookers, and wires and batteries from the remote-control devices used to detonate them.

"And they found hundreds of pieces of shrapnel, little nails, tacks, and BBs. They found them on the street, they found them inside buildings, on the tops of roofs, and ER doctors found them on the bodies of the victims they were treating at the hospital, in their hair, in their clothing, and in their bloody wounds. The police also collected surveillance tapes from businesses on Boylston Street and elsewhere, and photos and videos from members of the public who had been there watching the race.

"Now, as I said earlier, the defendant exploded his bomb right in front of a restaurant called Forum, and that restaurant has a surveillance camera that is right over the door of the restaurant, and it happened to be pointing directly at the place where the defendant placed his bomb. The surveillance tape shows the defendant walk up to that spot. He's got a backpack slung over his shoulder. And the moment he gets there, he dips his shoulder, and after that, you never see the backpack on his back again. But photographs show that it's at his feet.

"It [the tape] shows him stop right behind Martin Richard and the other children who are lined up on the railing watching the race. It shows him standing there looking at them and looking over their heads at the runners.

Then it shows him make the phone call to his brother. A few seconds later, everyone in the Forum snaps their head to the left, towards the finish line, as the first bomb explodes. Almost immediately, the defendant begins walking rapidly in the other direction. As soon as he reaches a safe distance, his bomb explodes.

"That video revealed that the defendant was one of the bombers, but the FBI didn't know who the defendant was. They had a face but not a name. So they started looking at all the other surveillance tapes, seeing if they could find him walking up to that spot. And they did find him, and they found him walking with another man, who turned out to be the defendant's brother, Tamerlan. Tamerlan also had a backpack on. So now the FBI had two suspected bombers. They had two faces but still no names.

"Three days passed while the FBI and other law enforcement officers worked around the clock trying to identify who the two men in the video were. At the end of three days, they decided it was time to ask the public for help. So on Thursday, April 15th [*sic*], at 5 p.m., almost exactly three days after the bombings occurred, the FBI published some of those still photos from the surveillance videos on its website, and they had a press conference where they asked members of the public to call in if they had any idea who those two men were.

"News stations broadcast those videos and those photos all around the country and around the world. A few hours later, at 8:45 p.m., the defendant got a text from his good friend, Dias Kadyrbayev. Dias texted, 'You saw the news?' The defendant texted back, 'Yeah, bro, I did.' Dias texted, 'For real?'

"The defendant texted back, 'I saw the news. Better not text me, my friend. LOL.' Dias texted, 'You saw yourself in there?'"

"The defendant didn't answer directly. He just texted back, 'If you want, you can go to my room and take what's there.' That's exactly what Dias did. He and two of the defendant's friends went to his dorm room at UMass. They searched it, and they found a backpack containing fireworks that had been partially emptied of their explosive powder. They took that backpack, and they threw it into a Dumpster to get rid of the evidence, but fortunately the police later were able to recover it. They also took the defendant's laptop computer and brought it back to their apartment in New Bedford.

"Meanwhile, the defendant and his brother went out in search of another gun. They drove by the MIT campus, which was close to their apartment, and they saw a police officer sitting in his cruiser next to a building. The police officer was named Sean Collier. He was a 27-year-old from Somerville. Students loved him because he was a friendly guy and took an active role in campus life.

"A surveillance video shows what happened next. Now, unfortunately, the surveillance camera that took this video was very far away. It was on top of a very high building, the distance from where the car was, and it was so far away that the human figures in it appear tiny. It's impossible to see their faces or exactly what they're doing with their hands. Even so, it shows enough for you to be certain, in conjunction with other evidence that I'll tell you about, that the defendant and his brother killed Officer Collier.

"The video shows two men walk through the courtyard and round the corner where Sean Collier is sitting in his cruiser. So they round one corner, walk all the length of the building, walk around the corner right to the cruiser. As soon as they reach the car, they open the door.

"A few seconds later you can see a young man ride his bicycle right by the cruiser. The man on the bike was an MIT graduate student named Nate Harman. He'll testify that as he rode by, he saw a man leaning into the driver's side of the cruiser, and he startled him. The man looked up in surprise and looked directly into Mr. Harman's face, and Mr. Harman's description of the man matches the defendant exactly.

"At the same time the video shows the two men standing by the side of the car, a student working in an office that had a window right above where the cruiser was parked called MIT's version of 911 and reported hearing six possible gunshots from below. Shortly after the call was made, the video shows the two men, the defendant and his brother, run away from the car back the way that they came. Five minutes later, fellow officers responded to the scene and found Officer Collier dead in his cruiser.

"The evidence will show that the defendant and his brother used the defendant's Ruger, the one that he had gotten from his friend, to execute Officer Collier by shooting him in the head at point-blank range twice in the side of his head and once right between the eyes. They also shot him three times in his right hand. Then they tried to steal his gun from his holster, but they couldn't get the holster lock to open, so they gave up, and they fled the scene.

"You'll know they tried to steal his gun from his holster because the holster had a two-stage lock to prevent the gun from being pulled out by someone else. The first stage is easy to open, but the second one isn't, especially if you're not the person wearing the holster. When other officers found Officer Collier in his cruiser, they saw that the first stage of the lock had been opened, but the second was still closed, and they also saw that the gun and the holster were covered with blood, as if somebody had been yanking at it, while the rest of his utility belt was clean.

"Now, because the surveillance camera was so far away, you can't see the defendant and his brother do the actual shooting. So the video doesn't reveal whether the defendant pulled the trigger, whether his brother pulled the trigger, or whether they both did, but it doesn't matter. They both murdered him. And other evidence, which I'll talk about in a few minutes, leaves no doubt that they are the ones who killed Officer Collier and that they did it with the defendant's gun.

"After murdering Officer Collier, the defendant and his brother got back into their Honda Civic, which was loaded with additional bombs, another pressure cooker bomb, like the one that had exploded on Boylston Street, and at least four pipe bombs. Their plan was to drive to New York City, but they needed a different car, one that couldn't be traced back to them or the murder of Sean Collier, so they drove in to Boston to find one.

"About 20 minutes later, they found what they were looking for: a young Chinese man named Dun Meng, who was sitting in a leased Mercedes SUV next to the AutoZone in Brighton reading a text message on his cell phone. The defendant and his brother drove up in their Honda Civic, and the defendant's brother got out. He went over to the passenger side of Mr. Meng's car, and he knocked on the window, and he signaled to Mr. Meng to roll it down. When Mr. Meng did, the defendant's brother reached inside, opened the lock, opened the door, and got into the car, and then he pointed the defendant's gun in Mr. Meng's face.

"He demanded that Mr. Meng give him all of his money, and Mr. Meng did, but he only had $40 on him. The brothers wanted more, so the defendant's brother told Mr. Meng to start driving, and the defendant followed in the Honda Civic. A nearby surveillance camera captured both cars driving away from the scene.

"They kept driving until they got to a quiet block in Watertown, and then they parked, one behind the other. The defendant got out and transferred all of the bombs from the Honda into the trunk of the Mercedes. Then he, himself, got into the backseat of the Mercedes, and the three of them drove to an ATM in—a Bank of America ATM in Watertown Square. When they got there, the defendant took Mr. Meng's ATM card, demanded his password, and robbed him of $800 by using the ATM machine to withdraw it from Mr. Meng's bank account. That $800 was still inside the defendant's wallet when he was arrested the next day.

"After robbing Mr. Meng, the defendant and his brother drove Mr. Meng to a Shell station on Memorial Drive in Cambridge. They got there about 12:15 a.m. The defendant and his brother had murdered Sean Collier less than two hours earlier, and their terrified carjacking victim was still inside the car. Even so, the first thing the defendant did when they got to the gas station was to leave his brother inside the Mercedes with Mr. Meng and go inside the Shell station to buy snacks. You'll see him shopping for those snacks on the Shell station video. He takes his time. He's not concerned. He makes sure he's getting exactly what he wants.

"But then things took a bad turn for the defendant. While he was inside the Shell station shopping for snacks, Mr. Meng realized that this might be his last chance to escape before the defendant and his brother have no longer [had] any use for him. So in a flash, while the defendant's brother's hands were occupied programming the GPS, Mr. Meng undid his seatbelt with one hand, opened the door with the other, jumped out of the car, and sprinted across the street to the Mobil station. You'll see him on a surveillance camera sprinting across the street and entering the Mobil station. And when he gets there, you'll see the terrified look on his face, and you'll hear it [terror] in his voice on the 911 tape.

"After Mr. Meng called 911, the police responded to the Mobil station and they interviewed Mr. Meng. They got all the information about the Mercedes, and they began tracking its location in real time using the GPS system in the car. By that time, the defendant and his brother had driven back up to that block in Watertown where they had left the Honda Civic. The defendant had gotten back into the Honda Civic, his brother remained in the Mercedes, and they had begun driving back in the direction of Boston in the two cars.

"The GPS tracking system in the Mercedes revealed that it was moving south on Dexter Avenue, which is a quiet, residential street in Watertown. A Watertown police officer named Joe Reynolds heard on his police radio that the Mercedes was wanted in a carjacking, and he began driving north on Dexter Avenue. He had no idea that the two people driving the cars were the Boston Marathon bombers.

"As Officer Reynolds drove north on Dexter, the defendant and his brother were driving south. The defendant was in the Honda. He was in the lead. The defendant's brother was in the Mercedes. He was following. As the two cars drove past Officer Reynolds, Officer Reynolds made a U-turn and began following them.

"The defendant decided to turn onto Laurel Street, which is another quiet residential street in Watertown, and his brother followed him. It was nearly one in the morning. The houses lining both sides of the street were dark and quiet. The street wasn't well lit. The defendant stopped his car in the middle of the street and got out, and his brother followed his lead and did the same. As soon as Officer Reynolds turned onto Laurel Street to follow them, they fired a bullet through his windshield, trying to kill him. Officer Reynolds backed up a short distance, got out of his car, and began shooting back.

"Another Watertown police officer, Sergeant [John] MacLellan, was on the street within seconds. As soon as he turned onto Laurel Street, the defendant and his brother tried to kill him too. They shot at him with the defendant's gun while he was still in his car. Rather than back up, he put his car into drive, got out, and let it roll slowly down the street towards the brothers so that he and Officer Reynolds could take cover behind it. And that's what they did. They walked behind it, shooting as they went.

"The defendant and his brother did everything in their power to kill those two officers. They shot at them with the defendant's Ruger, and they began throwing pipe bombs at them. Two of those bombs exploded within feet of the officers. Two others failed to detonate. Eventually, the defendant hurled a pressure cooker bomb at the officers. It exploded with a thunderous boom and created a massive fireball. Shrapnel rained down on the officers and blew in the homes on Laurel Street where the residents were cowering in terror.

"A third Watertown police officer, Sergeant Jeffrey Pugliese, arrived on the scene. He ran around the backs of some houses to get as close to the defendant and his brother as he could. The defendant's brother saw Sergeant

Pugliese in the side yard of the house and began shooting at him. Sergeant Pugliese just stood there and shot back. Eventually, the defendant's brother ran out of ammunition. He began walking rapidly down the street towards Officer Reynolds and Sergeant MacLellan. Sergeant Pugliese ran after him. He tackled him and tried to handcuff him. Officer Reynolds and Sergeant MacLellan jumped in.

"While they were doing that, the defendant got back into the Mercedes, which was pointing away down the street, turned it around, and began driving at the three officers at top speed trying to mow them down. He must have known they were trying to arrest his brother, but he cared more about killing them than he cared about his brother's life.

"Officer Reynolds and Sergeant MacLellan saw the car coming. They jumped off and took cover and told Sergeant Pugliese to do the same, but Sergeant Pugliese didn't. He grabbed the defendant's brother by his belt and tried to drag him out of the way of the coming Mercedes. At the last possible second, when the Mercedes was almost on top of him, Sergeant Pugliese rolled to the side. The defendant ran right over his brother and dragged his body about 50 feet down the street. He sideswiped Officer Reynolds' cruiser, which shook his brother's body loose, and continued driving away at top speed. As he sped by, other officers who had responded to the scene and were waiting down there at the end of the street, began shooting at the Mercedes. One of them was an MBTA officer named Richard Donohue. Officer Donohue was shot in the thigh by a stray bullet. It severed an artery, and he began bleeding heavily. Other officers tried to stanch the flow of blood, but it was impossible. Officer Donohue lost so much blood that he stopped breathing and nearly died. Fortunately, paramedics arrived, quickly got him to a hospital where doctors were able to save his life.

"The defendant drove a few more blocks and then ditched the Mercedes in the middle of the street. He made his way through the quiet, sleeping neighborhood to a house with a dry-docked boat in the backyard. The boat was a good size. It was about 22 feet long, about 8 feet wide, and it was up on a trailer, and it was covered with a tarp. It was still the end of winter, and it was covered with a tarp to protect it from the elements. It must have struck the defendant as a good place to hide out while the police searched for him.

"Although the defendant had been shot and was bleeding, he still had his wits about him. He smashed the cell phone that he had used to call his brother right before they detonated the bombs. He also smashed his other cell phone. By smashing those phones, he destroyed some of the evidence of what he had done, such as text messages between him and his brother that were stored on his phone. He also made it impossible for the police to use the GPS devices in the phones to figure out his location. Once he had smashed the phones, he took out Dun Meng's ATM card, which he still had, and he tried to hide it, along with the smashed phones, in a kind of ditch by where the boat was. But, again, the police searched the area and found it later. Once he had destroyed and hidden the evidence, he climbed into the boat and hid.

"Meanwhile, the police cordoned off a whole section of Watertown where they knew the defendant might be hiding, and they searched all night and all the next day, but they couldn't find him. When they finally decided to call off the search for the day, David Henneberry, the man who owned the boat, went outside to check on it. Mr. Henneberry saw that the tarp covering the boat was loose, and he climbed a short ladder to investigate. When he lifted the tarp to look inside, he saw the defendant lying there, so he went back into his house and called 911.

"The police showed up quickly and surrounded the boat. Several officers saw what they considered suspicious movement and fired on it. That triggered a barrage of shots at the boat. Then hostage negotiators arrived and tried to talk the defendant into surrendering. Eventually they succeeded. The defendant climbed out of the boat, and the police arrested him.

"That's when the police found the writing I mentioned earlier, the one where the defendant explained that he had bombed the marathon to punish America for mistreating Muslim people. He had written that explanation in pencil on an inside wall of the boat while he was hiding inside of it, and you will see the writing itself, the pencil he used to write it, and other evidence that was found in the boat.

"Meanwhile, officers had been combing Laurel Street and Dexter Avenue for evidence. One of the first places they looked was the Honda Civic that the defendant had been driving. When the defendant escaped from Laurel Street in the Mercedes, he left the Honda Civic behind. On the floor of the Civic, on the driver's side, right beneath the defendant's feet where he had been driving, officers found two bloody white gloves. DNA analysis shows that the blood on those gloves came from Officer Collier. That is one of the ways you will know that the defendant and his brother are the ones who killed Officer Collier.

"Another piece of evidence found in the Honda was the defendant's key ring, which had a UMass Dartmouth tag on it, and his car key, the same key he had used to drive the Honda to Laurel Street. Those items also were bloody, and once again, DNA analysis shows that the blood came from Officer Collier. That's yet another way you'll know that the defendant helped kill Officer Collier that night.

"Officers also found the defendant's Ruger, a BB gun that looks exactly like a Ruger, and 54 spent Ruger casings, meaning shells from bullets that had been fired from the Ruger. All of the Ruger casings were matched by a ballistics expert to the defendant's Ruger.

"Now, six Ruger casings were also found at the MIT crime scene, three inside the cruiser and three outside of it. A ballistics expert examined those, and they also matched the defendant's Ruger. And that's yet another way you will know that the defendant and his brother murdered Officer Collier that night using the defendant's gun.

"You're going to see all of the ballistics evidence, you'll hear from the ballistics expert, and you'll hear from the DNA expert who examined the gloves and the key ring.

"Shrapnel from the bombs the defendant used on Laurel Street and pieces of the pressure cooker were found everywhere. They were inside people's cars, on their front lawns, in their backyards, on their roofs, even inside their homes. Slugs from the Ruger were also found inside people's homes, some of them embedded in their—in their interior walls. We will show you maps, diagrams, photographs of them.

"Now, you've heard me talk a lot about the defendant's brother, Tamerlan, but you won't be seeing him in the courtroom. That's because the defendant killed him by running him over with this Mercedes. Tamerlan's bullet wounds also contributed to his death. But even though Tamerlan won't be in the courtroom, this case involves him too. That's because he and the defendant were partners. They agreed to do these crimes together, and they carried them out together.

"The judge will instruct you that when two people agree to commit a crime together, they're guilty of conspiracy. And the defendant is charged with three counts of conspiracy: conspiracy to use a weapon of mass destruction, conspiracy to bomb a place of public use, and conspiracy to destroy property with explosives.

"The defendant is also charged with many substantive counts of using a weapon of mass destruction, arming a place of public use, and destroying property with explosives. And he's charged with many counts of using guns and explosives to commit violent crimes. Even though he and his brother played different roles in each of these crimes, they are both equally guilty of committing them because they carried them out as partners.

"Now, what do I mean when I say they were partners? I don't mean that they did exactly the same thing. That's not required for the defendant to be guilty under the law. What I mean is that each one played a role in committing the crime. For example, the defendant—the defendant planted one bomb at the marathon, and his brother planted the other one. The defendant got his—got a gun from his friend, Stephen Silva, and his brother stuck it in Dun Meng's face. The defendant took Dun Meng's ATM card and password and robbed him of $800.

"The defendant's brother told Dun Meng where to drive. The defendant threw bombs at the police in Watertown and handled the ammunition while his brother fired shots at the officers. And both brothers together murdered Officer Sean Collier and tried to steal his gun.

"So even though Tamerlan Tsarnaev is not here, we will be offering evidence about his role in these crimes, but the focus is going to be on the defendant. That's because this is his day in court. He's the one the government has to prove guilty, not his brother. It's important for you to hear all the evidence against the defendant so that at the end of the trial you have what you need to find him guilty. It's far less important for you to hear all the evidence against the defendant's brother. In the end, it doesn't matter what role each of them played, so long as you find that they were partners and carried out these crimes together.

"Now, as you can tell from what I've said, there's a lot of evidence in this case. Some of the witnesses are just going to talk about how and where things were found. Others will simply testify that things are what they appear to be. We need to call those witnesses because you need to have confidence in the evidence, but we'll do our best to streamline its—its introduction into evidence and make that go as fast as possible, if we can.

"I want to conclude just by telling you a bit about the order in which we're going to present the government's case. We'll start with the marathon bombings and the collection of evidence at the marathon crime scenes. We'll show you some of the surveillance video, photos and—photos from the people who were at the—the marathon before the bombs went off that the FBI used to identify the defendant and his brother as suspects in the bombing. Then we'll put on evidence of what the defendant did in the days after the bombings and of the manifesto he wrote on the inside wall of the boat. Next we'll put on evidence of the events on April 18th and 19th, how the FBI published photos of the defendant and his brother on their website and held the press conference; how the defendant and his brother then murdered Officer Collier, carjacked, kidnapped, and robbed Dun Meng, and tried to kill police officers in Watertown with gun—with a Ruger and with bombs.

"After hearing about all the events that led up to the defendant's arrest, you'll hear about all the evidence that was collected from the Watertown crime scene and analyzed by the experts, including the bloody gloves, the bloody car keys, the Ruger, and all the ballistics evidence. You'll also hear about evidence collected from the defendant's residence in Cambridge and from his dorm room at UMass Dartmouth.

"One of the most important pieces of evidence is the defendant's laptop computer, the one that his friends took from the dorm room. The police got that computer and analyzed it. As with a lot of people, the defendant's computer is a window into his life, especially into the part of him that he kept mostly hidden from his friends.

"You'll hear a lot of evidence about all of the terrorist materials that were on his computer and the other digital devices that he owned. And you'll hear about other things that the defendant said and wrote that shed light on the sources of his terrorist beliefs. Some of those are papers he wrote for school, and some are things he wrote to friends and emails and text messages and posted on social media.

"You'll also hear from the medical examiners who examined the bodies of the four people the defendant murdered."[1]

Weinreb stopped here and showed jurors photos of the dead. Martin Richard, the little boy described as having a smile that could "light up Fenway Park," by the Boston mayor.[2] Lingzi Lu, the Boston University student with the bubbly personality and love for all things Disney. Krystle Marie Campbell, her daddy's princess. And Sean Collier, just weeks away from realizing his childhood dream of becoming a Somerville police officer. Then Weinreb continued:

"Each of the medical examiners who examined the people who died in this case will be testifying. And they'll tell you that Sean Collier was killed by multiple gunshot wounds to the brain. Krystle Campbell had blast injuries to her head, neck, body, and limbs. Her back was burned red; and her head, body, and legs were filled with shrapnel. There were gaping wounds in her legs that had drained virtually all of the blood from her body. Lingzi Lu was cut, battered, and bruised. The bomb that the defendant detonated blew large perforating holes in her legs that caused her to bleed to death.

"Martin Richard was only 4 feet, 5 inches tall, and he weighed only 70 pounds. Because of his size and height, the bomb damaged his entire body. The defendant blew large holes into Martin's chest and abdomen, exposing his ribs and organs and eviscerating his bowels. He blew Martin's arm nearly entirely off his body, burned his skin, and drove BBs and nails into his legs. Martin lost so much blood that he had virtually none left in his body by the time he was brought to the morgue. He died at the scene from his wounds.

"In the end, the evidence will prove to you beyond a reasonable doubt that the defendant committed all 30 crimes that he is charged with. He murdered Martin Richard, Lingzi Lu, Krystle Campbell, and Sean Collier. He used weapons of mass destruction at the Boston Marathon to terrorize the country and to influence American foreign policy. He used guns and bombs in Watertown to continue his campaign of terror, and he did it all because he believed that America needed to be punished for killing Muslims overseas. He did it to advance a cause that he believed in. And he did it because he thought it would help secure him a place in paradise. That is why, at the end of the case, we will ask you to find him guilty of all 30 counts in the indictment. Thank you."

The facts of the case were well known by then. The tragic stories of the victims had been told all over the world. But to hear them together as Weinreb had presented them traumatized spectators and victims. Two jurors wiped their eyes. The color had drained from the faces of other jurors. The crimes were evil, unimaginable. Even for the victims who had suffered, even for the witnesses of the carnage, the recounting was hard to take.

23
IT WAS HIM

Judy Clarke, as usual, put a comforting hand on her client's shoulder. Then she stood up to begin her attempt to save his life. Her opening statement included a startling admission: "It was him." She began:

"We meet in the most tragic of circumstances, tragedy in the lives of the victims of the bombings, lives that were lost and torn and shattered: the loss of a precious eight-year-old boy, whose smile captured all of our hearts; a young woman who—with an infectious laugh, who was always there for her friends and her family; a young graduate student whose passion for music was so clear, and she embraced Boston as her home away from home; and a very fine young police officer whose lifelong dream was to protect and serve. The circumstances that bring us here today still are difficult to grasp. They're incomprehensible. They're inexcusable. You just heard about the devastation, the loss, and the unbearable grief, and we're going to see it, feel it, and agonize with every witness who comes to talk about what they saw, they felt, and they experienced and what happened to them and to those that they love.

"For the next several weeks, we're all going to come face to face with unbearable grief, loss, and pain caused by a series of senseless, horribly misguided acts carried out by two brothers: 26-year-old Tamerlan Tsarnaev and his younger brother, 19-year-old Jahar. The government and the defense will agree about many things that happened during the week of April 15th, 2013.

"On Marathon Monday, Tamerlan Tsarnaev walked down Boylston Street with a backpack on his back, carrying a pressure cooker bomb, and put it down in front of the Marathon Sports near the finish line of the marathon. Jahar Tsarnaev walked down Boylston Street with a backpack on his back carrying a pressure cooker bomb and placed it next to a tree in front of the Forum restaurant.

"The explosions extinguished three lives. They unalterably injured and devastated many others. After their pictures were on television and on the Internet, Tamerlan and Jahar went on a path of devastation the night of April the 18th, leaving dead in their path a young MIT police officer and a community in fear and sheltering in place. Tamerlan held an unsuspecting driver, Dun Meng, at gunpoint, demanded his money and compelled him, commanded him, to drive while Jahar followed behind.

"The evening ended in a shootout. You've heard about it. Tamerlan walked straight into a barrage of gunfire, shooting at the police, throwing his gun, determined not to be taken alive. Jahar fled, abandoned a car, and was found hiding in a boat.

"There's little that occurred the week of April the 15th—the bombings, the murder of Officer Collier, the carjacking, the shootout in Watertown—that we dispute. If the only question was whether or not that was Jahar Tsarnaev in the video that you will see walking down Boylston Street, or if that was Jahar Tsarnaev who dropped the backpack on the ground, or if that was Jahar Tsarnaev in the boat—captured in the boat, it would be very easy for you:

"It was him." She paused for emphasis, then continued.

"So you might say, why a trial? Now, you've heard several instructions, and when we sat in this courtroom at the table—you may remember that—the judge talked to you about how this is a capital trial. The government has elected to seek the death penalty, and in a capital trial there are two phases—one in which the jury makes a determination of guilt and one in which the jury makes the determination of the appropriate penalty. The indictment in this case is not that simple. It's 30 counts. You heard the counts described. It's 74 pages long. There are complicated federal charges involved. And there will be much for you to analyze and decide.

"But the essence of the charges are four sets of criminal acts: the bombings at the marathon that killed three people and injured many others, the murder of Officer Collier, the carjacking, and the shootout in Watertown. We do not and will not at any point in this case want to attempt to sidestep Jahar's responsibility for his actions, but the indictment alleges, and the prosecutor talked with you about why, and we think the question of why is important, and this is where we disagree.

"We have a different answer to this question: What took Jahar Tsarnaev from this"—she turned and pointed to a picture of Dzhokhar and his brother—"to this"—and she pointed at an image of Dzhokhar and Tamerlan on Boylston Street, backpacks slung over their shoulders.

"The government has told you their answer to the question of why, and we ask you to look further. Clearly, Tamerlan Tsarnaev became obsessed with violent Islamic extremism. He became increasingly religious in a radical way. He traveled to Russia in—for six months in 2012 and explored violent jihad with people over there. He became aggressively obsessed with talking about Islam because of his radical views and his insistence that people accept them and agree with them. He disrupted services at the mosques here in Boston where he once fit in. It was Tamerlan Tsarnaev who self-radicalized. It was Jahar who followed him.

"The evidence will show that Tamerlan planned and orchestrated and enlisted his brother into these series of horrific acts. Tamerlan Tsarnaev did the Internet research on the electronic components, the transmitter and the receiver you'll hear more about, for the two bombs, and he bought them. Tamerlan Tsarnaev had the Russian-translated version of how to build a bomb on his computer. Tamerlan bought the BBs that were in the shrapnel that were in the pressure cooker and the pipe bombs. Tamerlan bought the pressure cookers. Tamerlan bought the fireworks that went into making the bombs. Tamerlan bought the ammunition. Tamerlan bought both of the backpacks. Rubber gloves with explosive residue on them were found in Tamerlan's car. Tamerlan led the way down Boylston Street. Tamerlan shot and killed Officer Collier. Tamerlan pointed the gun at Dun Meng, demanded his money, commanded him to drive away, telling him, 'I just killed a police officer.'

"You'll hear evidence about computers and the electronic devices, phones, hard drives that were seized in this case, and it will show that Tamerlan spent much of his time on the Internet in [looking at images of] death and destruction and images of carnage in the Middle East. Make no mistake, Jahar Tsarnaev's computer had many of the materials that the prosecutor told you about: *Inspire* magazine, "Join the Caravan," a number of extremist materials that you'll hear about. But there will not be any evidence that Jahar downloaded those materials as if he were searching the Internet to find them.

"The earliest traces of any extremist materials go back to a thumb drive, a jump drive. You know what I'm talking about? You stick in the computer and you transfer files. The earliest traces of the extremist materials traced back to this thumb drive that has never been found, but forensics can tell you about it. The last traces of attachment—when you stick it into the computer and pull it out, the attachment into the computer—were into Tamerlan's laptop, Jahar's laptop, and a desktop computer that was at the Norfolk Street apartment where Tamerlan and his wife and daughter lived, where the family had lived. The last known attachment was, then, the day that Tamerlan left for Russia for six months in 2012.

"So as you hear the computer evidence, please ask: What's the source of the document? Where else was it? Who else had it? Where did it come from? Can I know by the fact that it's on there who put it there and why?

"An analysis of the computer evidence will, at baseline, show that both Tamerlan and Jahar's computers had this library of extremist materials, but the evidence will also show you that, while Tamerlan Tsarnaev was looking [at] and immersed in death and destruction and carnage in the Middle East, Jahar spent most of his time on the Internet doing things that teenagers do: Facebook, cars, girls. The evidence will also help point you in the direction of understanding the flow of the materials: who got what first, who got the most, and who had the most.

"The evidence will not establish, and we will not argue, that Tamerlan put a gun to Jahar's head or that he forced him to join in the plan, but you will hear evidence of the kind of influence that this older brother had."[1]

At the mention of Tamerlan, the government's attorneys bristled. The court had ruled in the weeks after Dzhokhar was indicted that Tamerlan was not on trial and that mentions of his name would be kept to a bare minimum (all of the written rulings were among the sealed records, which remain sealed today). There would be no testimony about Tamerlan's dealings with government officials, or the questions about his travel raised by members of Congress and investigators within the intelligence community. There would be no questions about why Tamerlan was recording conversations with his mother's cousin, the leader of an Islamist group, during his time in Russia and downloading those talks onto his laptop. There would be no discussion of his bizarre immigration history or how he had been able to travel in and out of Logan Airport while on two terrorist watch lists.

The FBI was not on trial either, so the question of whether the FBI did or did not respond to the FSB's 2011 inquiry would not be answered. But Dzhokhar was on trial, and the government's attorneys were hellbent on making sure the court's order regarding Tamerlan would be followed. Assistant US Attorney William Weinreb jumped up to object but was overruled by the judge because Clarke had not overstepped the mark. Yet. Clarke then continued. Dzhokhar stroked his chin pensively as she talked, using his nickname, Jahar, throughout her opening statement:

"During the period of time when Tamerlan was becoming more radical and traveling to Russia and identifying with violent jihad, the evidence will show you what was happening with Jahar. His parents: his dad, Anzor; his mother, Zubeidat—"

This time the judge interjected: "I think this is—yeah, I think the family history is not appropriate, as I previously indicated."

Clarke continued: "His parents left and moved back to Russia. He was a student at UMass Dartmouth, but things were not going very well. His grades were plummeting; he wasn't going to class; and he was in danger of failing out of school. And Jahar, in one of those tough times of adolescence, as we all know, became much more vulnerable to the influence of someone that he loved and respected very much: his older brother."

Weinreb objected again but was overruled once more.[2]

"You'll see from the evidence that Tamerlan had a special kind of influence dictated by his age, their culture, and Tamerlan's sheer force of personality. They committed the acts in April of 2013 that led to death and destruction, and they are inexcusable and for which Jahar must be held responsible. But he came to his role by a very different path than suggested to you by the prosecution: a path born of his brother, created by his brother, and paid by his brother. And unfortunately and tragically, Jahar was drawn into his brother's passion and plan, and that led him to Boylston Street.

"The government talked to you about writings that were in the boat where Jahar was found hiding and where he had found a pencil, and those writings are very important to read in their entirety. And you'll see them. You'll get to read them. But essentially what Jahar wrote was, first, he expressed that he was jealous of his brother who had achieved martyrdom and his wish that he would as well. He wrote that he perhaps guessed that he was alive so that he could shed some light on their motives, and he wrote words that he had read and heard that the United States was responsible for the suffering of Muslims around the world.

"We ask you to carefully evaluate the testimony—and there will be testimony about these writings, not just the writings themselves—but about the writings inside the boat, where they came from, and how deeply rooted they may or may not be.

"And at the end of this first phase of the case, we think that you will have the evidence that you need to make the decisions about the 30 counts, about the four sorts of—essence of the criminal charges. We think that you will have the evidence that you need to weigh and analyze and make the decision in the first phase. But there will be questions that we cannot answer now. There will be questions that we ask you to carry over to the second phase, as the judge has explained.

"When we talked to you in voir dire around this table centered in the courtroom, the government, the defense, the Court was here. Most of you acknowledged that you knew something about this case. And most of you said—or many of you said that you knew, that you had seen images of devastation. But none of you would be sitting here today, had you not convincingly and with conviction told us that now, you can remain open through this phase, that you can hold your questions throughout the trial, and that you can remain open—your hearts and minds open to thinking about the evidence all the way.

"Witnesses—many witnesses are about to start to be called, some who work in forensics, some police officers who risked their lives, a number of first responders who cared for victims, a number of victims who were injured, and survivors, eyewitnesses, people that lost loved ones. We're all going to see and listen to their testimony with heavy hearts. Holding your assurances to us that you can hold your minds open to not only listening to the who, what, where, and when, but to the how and why, those assurances are going to be tested and going to be very difficult promises to keep. Holding the questions that you have that can't be answered in this phase, holding them open—your hearts and minds open until the second phase will not be an easy task, but that's what you promised when you swore your oath as jurors. That's what the judge expects. That's what our system of justice expects. It's going to be a lot to ask of you to hold your minds and hearts open, but that is what we ask. Thank you."

Clark sat down. It was the victims' turn to face the monster for the first time, their chance to take the witness stand to talk about their suffering. They had waited a long time for this day.

24

THE LION KING

Jessica Kensky ran for the last time in the morning of the day she lost her legs. She didn't run in the Boston Marathon but ran a smaller race in another town. However, she still wanted to be part of the biggest race in the country, so she met her husband, Patrick Downes, and they went to Boylston Street together: "I remember being happy. I remember feeling sunlight on my face. I remember feeling really free. I remember holding each other." Then came the booms. "I didn't see anything. I didn't feel anything. I just felt like I was on a rocket, shot straight into the air."[1]

When she hit the ground she saw that her husband's foot and part of his leg was completely detached: "I went into my nurse mode. I remember shifting myself to block his leg. This was a war zone." She tried to use her purse straps to tie a tourniquet around Patrick's mangled leg. Then she heard a man tell her, "Ma'am, you're on fire." He cut my clothes off. It feels really bizarre to be on a city street and have people removing your clothing. I wasn't even aware that I was on fire. I released control at that point."

Behind her in Marathon Sports Shane O'Hara, the store's manager, heard what sounded like "a big cannon blast" and saw smoke engulfing the store. Then came the smell of gunpowder, burned hair, and sulfur—followed by bloodcurdling screams for help. He opened the door of the store and ushered people inside. Someone fell to the floor bleeding, a lower limb ruined. O'Hara was captured on his store's video camera as he tore a pair of shorts from a display to use as a tourniquet. Other customers inside the store followed suit, tearing apart clothes to tie off the gushing wounded limbs of victims outside. O'Hara's voice shook with anger as he described on the stand how he is still haunted about the terrible decisions he was forced to make that afternoon, decisions ordinarily made by soldiers on the front lines in a combat zone, not store managers on a busy urban street. The entire scene was like something out of *Saving Private Ryan*, O'Hara remembered: "The things that haunt me the most is making those decisions . . . who needed help first, who needed more." He would try to comfort one injured victim and see someone in worse shape. As he tried to move where he was needed most he heard endless pleas of, "Stay with me. Stay with me."[2] He said that he could still hear those urgent, desperate cries in his sleep.

Those same agonizing memories nag at BPD Officer Frank Chiola, a former Marine who had seen combat in Iraq. He heard the explosion and then was overcome with the white smoke: "People were running, screaming, crying. You couldn't tell who was alive, who was dead." One woman was in terrible shape. For some reason he remembered that she was wearing blue eye shadow and had pretty eyes. "I later found out her name was Krystle. She had a friend near her calling out her name."

He tried to stem the bleeding, applying compression to her chest. When he did, "smoke came out of her mouth." His voice shook as the memory came back: "I helped her best I could. She was suffering. She was in pain. She was in shock. From the waist down it's really tough to describe, complete mutilation. That's as far as I want to say."

Roseann Sdoia remembered "two flashes of white light exploding at my feet." Then came nothing but excruciating pain: "I looked down and fortunately my leg was tucked under me. All I could see is blood pouring out of me, sort of where my knee should be. I looked on the ground and saw a foot and [it] had a little sock on it. In my mind I had to ask, did I have a sock on my foot? My answer was no. It was somebody else's foot in front of me." She tried to get up but failed—her other leg had been torn off below the knee: "I couldn't get up. I didn't have a leg. I knew it was bad. I knew I was bleeding out. I need[ed] to stay calm and stay conscious because if I didn't, I would die. I told myself I didn't want to live as an amputee . . . but then I thought I couldn't die."[3]

Lynn firefighter Matt Patterson said the bomb released an energy that felt like someone was "punching you square in the chest." He had been enjoying lunch at a steak house, Abe & Louie's, but the windows had been blown out.

He climbed through the glass, hopped over a barricade, and raced to help a little girl whose hair was on fire. Her leg was gone. He would learn later that her name was Jane Richard. Her little brother was dying behind her, and she was losing a lot of blood. Patterson's own belt was too big to use as a tourniquet, so he yelled at a smaller man to take his belt off, and he tightened that around what was left of Jane's leg to stop the gushing blood. He picked her up and carried her to an ambulance, with the stranger whose belt he used running alongside him to hold it tight around her ruined leg. It was a horrifying memory even for a first responder used to gore. "It was open. It was charred," Patterson said. Her flesh looked like "meat through a grinder."[4]

During all of this heart-wrenching testimony, Dzhokhar Tsarnaev showed no emotion—not for the maimed victims or the weeping relatives of the little boy, the two women, and the beloved cop he had killed. He didn't flinch as videos of the bloody aftermath of his bomb were played in court that showed anguished screams twisting the faces of innocent people who had been enjoying a Boston tradition. He didn't respond when BPD Super-intendent Willie Gross mumbled "maggot" under his breath as he passed the defense table. Gross had been on Boylston Street when the bombs went off, one of the hundreds who will have to deal for the rest of their lives with the agonizing images of the carnage forever etched in their brains. One after another, victims took the stand to talk about the burns and the trauma and the surgeries and the lost wages and the apartments that had to be abandoned because of the staircases. There was the evidence that he had killed his own brother and his friends had turned on him. Girls he dated took the stand. His old teachers talked about what a loving little boy he had been, his wrestling coach testified about his athletic prowess, and a representative of a charity praised him for his patience. No evidence—whether against him or in his favor—fazed him. He doodled on a legal pad and stroked his beard and giggled with his attorneys. He couldn't have cared less about the victims' pain. Rebekah Gregory took the stand on a prosthetic leg made to fit a high heel, all glamour and fiery temper as she stared down the man who forever altered her life and health. When she implored him "look at me" from the stand, he didn't even look up. It wasn't until his mother's sister and other Russian relatives took the stand in a last effort to save Dzhokhar's life that he reached for a box of tissues and dabbed at tears.

The tears came when his aunt, Patimat Suleimanova, had to be removed from the witness stand after she began weeping uncontrollably, her chest heaving, her sobs echoing through the courtroom. One after another, his aunts and cousins took the stand, crying. They had come to the country under "hotel arrest" and were wearing electronic bracelets that were monitored by the FBI around the clock. It wasn't a vacation. They wanted Dzhokhar's life to be spared.

Until that day none of Zubeidat's relatives had seen Dzhokhar since his family left Russia for the United States in 2002, when he was eight years old—the same age as the marathon attack's youngest victim, Martin Richard. All of the relatives cried as they looked at him from the stand. His female cousins called him "brother."

"I am seeing my brother for the first time in so many years and it is not easy," Naida Suleimanova, an ICU nurse at a hospital outside of Moscow, said through tears.[5] Her mother is one of Zubeidat Tsarnaev's seven siblings.

Defense attorneys used the relatives' testimony as an opportunity to show the jury a series of Tsarnaev family photos taken in Dagestan. There were pictures of Dzhokhar as a baby in a cousin's arms, him as a boy smiling as he finished his homework, and him smiling as he washed dishes. Naida said there was "never an occasion when there wasn't a smile on his face."

When Dzhokhar's gray-haired aunt Shakhurzat Suleimanova took the stand, she rocked back and forth with a handkerchief clutched to her face, stealing glances at her nephew. "He was a good boy," she said, "a very quiet boy"—so shy that if someone asked him a question, he would turn his face away.[6] Another cousin, Raisat Suleimanova, said Dzhokhar "was a sunny child. . . . If you looked at him, you would want to smile, even if you didn't feel good at that time. I could only say good things about Dzhokhar." She also cried, remembering that Dzhokhar was a sensitive child who wept watching "Simba's father die," in the movie *The Lion King*. "One would want to hug him and not let him go. He was an unusual child."[7]

Defense attorneys used the women's testimony in an attempt to portray a child raised by a matriarch—Zubeidat—whose grip on sanity appeared to be slipping, and whose care had been left largely to his older brother, Tamerlan, who appeared to be radicalized during his last trip to Dagestan in 2012. During that trip Tamerlan argued with a relative—a tape of the conversation was played in court—and said in Russian, "I have this rage of hatred inside me."[8]

The relatives testified that Zubeidat went from being a fashionable, fun-loving woman with a penchant for fancy fur-trimmed coats and hats to wearing black hijabs and dark clothing that covered her entire body in 2010. "When she came like that, we were in shock," Shakhurzat said, referring to her sister's suddenly taking up the practice of covering. Their family, she said, was Muslim but not in any way radical. "We prayed. We fasted. No people like that."[9]

For all the tears, a spurt of terse words came from assistant US Attorney William Weinreb as he cross-examined Raisat, who recalled Dzhokhar crying at *The Lion King* and said that "his kindness made everyone around him kind."

Weinreb asked her, "You would agree that the bombing of innocent people is not an act of kindness?"

The question led to an objection from Dzhokhar's defense attorneys, which was sustained by the judge.

Weinreb rephrased the question: "You would agree that a person who cries at the death of a cartoon character but was indifferent to the suffering and deaths of hundreds of people—"

Before he could finish the sentence, he was cut off with another objection, which was also sustained.

25

AIN'T NO LOVE

It was a shocking moment. For an entire summer Dzhokhar Tsarnaev had sat through his trial looking bored and impassive, even after he was found guilty in the first phase of his trial and even after he was sentenced to death, a sentence that shook the city that he had torn apart. Now he stood up and began to speak, the first time since the trial began that anyone had heard his voice, other than his lawyers and his spiritual advisor—the nun Sister Helen Prejean, on whom the movie *Dead Man Walking* was based. He mumbled softly in his heavy accent:

"Thank you, your Honor, for giving me an opportunity to speak. I would like to begin in the name of Allah, the exalted and glorious, the most gracious, the most merciful, 'Allah' among the most beautiful names. Any act that does not begin in the name of God is separate from goodness. This is the blessed month of Ramadan, and it is the month of mercy from Allah to his creation, a month to ask forgiveness of Allah and of his creation, a month to express gratitude to Allah and to his creation. It's the month of reconciliation, a month of patience, a month during which hearts change. Indeed, a month of many blessings. The Prophet Muhammad, peace and blessings be upon him, said if you have not thanked the people, you have not thanked God.

"So I would like to first thank my attorneys, those who sit at this table, the table behind me, and many more behind the scenes. They have done much good for me, for my family. They made my life the last two years very easy. I cherish their company. They're lovely companions. I thank you. I would like to thank those who took time out of their daily lives to come and testify on my behalf despite the pressure. I'd like to thank the jury for their service, and the Court. The Prophet Muhammad, peace and blessings be upon him, said that if you do not—if you are not merciful to Allah's creation, Allah will not be merciful to you, so I'd like to now apologize to the victims, to the survivors.

"Immediately after the bombing, which I am guilty of—if there's any lingering doubt about that, let there be no more. I did do it along with my brother—I learned of some of the victims. I learned their names, their faces, their age. And throughout this trial more of those victims were given names, more of those victims had faces, and they had burdened souls.

"Now, all those who got up on that witness stand and that podium related to us—to me—I was listening—the suffering that was and the hardship that still is, with strength and with patience and with dignity. Now, Allah says in the Qur'an that no soul is burdened with more than it can bear, and you told us just how unbearable it was, how horrendous it was, this thing I put you through. And I know that you kept that much. I know that there isn't enough time in the day for you to have related to us everything. I also wish that far more people had a chance to get up there, but I took them from you.

"Now, I am sorry for the lives that I've taken, for the suffering that I've caused you, for the damage that I've done. Irreparable damage. Now, I am a Muslim. My religion is Islam. The God I worship, besides whom there is no other God, is Allah. And I prayed for Allah to bestow his mercy upon the deceased, those affected in the bombing and their families. Allah says in the Qur'an that with every hardship there is relief. I pray for your relief, for your healing, for your well being, for your strength.

"I ask Allah to have mercy upon me and my brother and my family. I ask Allah to bestow his mercy upon those present here today. And Allah knows best those deserving of his mercy. And I ask Allah to have mercy upon the ummah of Prophet Muhammad, peace and blessings be upon him. Amin. Praise be to Allah, the Lord of the Worlds. Thank you."[1]

It was a four-minute speech, and those in the courtroom strained to make out his words. The stunning apology came on the same day the judge affirmed that his capital punishment would go forward with a quote from Shakespeare.

"The evil that men do lives after them," US District Court Justice George O'Toole said. "The good is oft interred with their bones. So it will be for Dzhokhar Tsarnaev."[2]

Dzhokhar received six death sentences, twenty sentences of life in prison and four more sentences of seven to twenty-five years, but the verdict hardly meant that the ordeal for the Boston Marathon victims was actually over. Appeals could take years, if not decades, to make their way through the courts, which is why some victims—like the Richard family—did not want the death penalty imposed.

Prosecutors and many victims insisted the apology meant nothing. Dzhokhar was remorseless, selfish—a narcissistic child who didn't show a single emotion until his aunt took the stand and testified about a cartoon. Assistant US Attorney Steve Mellin was still incensed by Dzhokhar's actions on the night of the marathon attack:

"He got on the Internet and tweeted to his friends, 'ain't no love in the heart of the city. Ain't no love in the heart of the city.' Hours after he fled the carnage that he had unleashed in Boston, he had the gall to tweet, 'Ain't no love in the heart of the city.' As to that, he couldn't have been more wrong. As the defendant sat at home drinking his milk and tweeting his glib commentary, the heartbreaking love of a mother comforting her dying child played out in the heart of Boston.

"Also on display were the bravery, the strength, the efforts of strangers trying to help those who had been injured, injured by the bomb planted by this defendant. He failed miserably in trying to blow apart the fabric of society.

"Make no mistake: Love prevailed in the heart of Boston on April 15th. But his true character was on display that night. It was on display in his words, in his callousness in that tweet. The next day, April 16th, while victims awoke in cold, antiseptic hospitals to the new reality that they were amputees, the defendant went to the gym and worked out. An hour later, he tweeted this: 'I'm a stress-free kind of guy.'

"He's stress free, April 16th. Then on April 18th, while Dun Meng, terrified, sits in the SUV with Tamerlan Tsarnaev, the defendant walks into that ATM and coolly withdraws money from Meng's account like it's any other day. Later at the gas station, he slowly takes his time buying snacks for that trip to New York where he wants to unleash even more havoc.

"And then finally, on July 10th, 2013, three months after the bombings, the defendant comes into court to be formally charged with murdering a little boy, murdering two women and murdering a police officer. He has had months to reflect on the pain and suffering that he has caused. But when he's put in that holding cell, you cannot see a trace of remorse on his face. He paces, he fluffs his hair, and he makes obscene gestures at the marshals watching over him and watching over the surveillance cameras.

"Who is capable of being so stress free after committing the crimes he committed? Who is capable of showing so little remorse? Only a terrorist, someone who had no reason for remorse because he believed that he had done something brave and something good. Someone who had set out to make a political statement, to commit a political crime and then firmly believed in the righteousness of what he had done."[3]

26

AMERICA'S WORST NIGHTMARE

It came as no surprise that Dzhokhar Tsarnaev was convicted, especially after Judy Clarke's startling admission that her client had committed the bloodletting that had been described in court by victims for weeks by then, and even after the Allah-laced apology Dzhokhar made to the jury in his halting English. In addition to the seventeen capital counts he was convicted of that carried the death penalty, he was also convicted of conspiracy to use a weapon of mass destruction resulting in death, use of a weapon of mass destruction resulting in death, conspiracy to bomb a place of public use resulting in death, bombing of a public place or place of public use resulting in death, malicious destruction of property resulting in personal injury and death, and possession and use of a firearm during and in relation to a crime of violence resulting in death.

Now it would be up to his high-priced defense team to keep Dzhokhar from receiving the death penalty during the penalty phase of the trial, which began on April 21, 2015. The prosecution would go first. The twelve jurors and six alternates would now have to deliberate about each one of the capital convictions separately. US District Court Justice George O'Toole addressed them before the second phase of the trial began: "It is impossible for me to overstate the importance of the decision before you. The appropriateness of sentencing another human being to death . . . it is not a mechanical process. You are never required to return a verdict of death. This decision, the question of life or death, is an individual decision. All twelve jurors must agree that death is the appropriate sentence."

The sentence would not just be about the victims. Jurors also had to determine whether Dzhokhar had "followed his brother down Boylston Street," as Judy Clarke had said in her opening statement, or made his own decision to become what Assistant US Attorney Nadine Pelligrini referred to as "America's worst nightmare,"[1] a man motivated by deliberate, calculated cruelty.

"You know how they died," Pelligrini told the jurors, motioning to photos of the dead that were posted on giant easels and also also displayed on tiny monitors in front of each of the jurors, "people who had time to feel pain, to become terrified as they took their last breaths, and to know that they would not be able to say goodbye. Now you need to know how they lived.

"The deaths committed by Dzhokhar Tsarnaev were deliberate, intentional and cruel. You know how Krystle, Lingzi, Martin, and Sean died. Now you need to know how they lived. You need to know and understand why their lives mattered. You will begin to know Krystle Campbell and understand what it meant to lose the young woman that her father, Bill Campbell, nicknamed 'Princess.' You'll hear more about Lingzi, and you will understand what it meant to lose the young woman that her father, Jun Lu, remembered as a jolly girl.

"You'll see Martin Richard who so resembles his dad, and see him in photos that will remind you of what an eight-year-old boy's life is like. Should be like. And you will know Sean Collier, the officer who inspired these words spoken to those who mourned him: 'Live long, like he would. Big hearts, big smiles, big service. All love.'

"These young women, this young man and this little boy, all of them were loved and they loved in return. This is how we should know them, because they weren't always just the victims of Dzhokhar Tsarnaev. Before he murdered them in some of the cruelest ways imaginable, they were sons, they were daughters, they were grandchildren, they were brothers and they were sisters. And all of them had rich and fulfilling lives even at their young age.

"But now these beautiful faces are memories and memorials. They're symbols, even, of loss, when all their families would want is to have them back one more time to be their son, their daughter, their best friend. When all they want is to have them come home one more time. For Lingzi, that would mean home to China, as she's pictured here, so that her parents could tell her that they kept their promise, they kept her beloved music collection safe when she left China to travel halfway around the world to come to Boston to study.

"One more time just to see them laugh and joke, like Krystle here celebrating after a wedding that she had successfully planned and pulled off on Spectacle Island. Just to watch them smile proudly, like Sean here at a family wedding. And just to see Martin decked out in green beads one more time for one more St. Patrick's Day. Their families had every right to expect they would live out their lives and realize the potential of these young lives, but Dzhokhar Tsarnaev took them all away, in the most painful and brutal ways possible. They were all beautiful, and they're all now gone.

"And there are others who, while they survived, found their lives dramatically, irrevocably changed in an instant by Dzhokhar Tsarnaev: Jessica Kensky, Roseann Sdoia, Karen McWatters, Jeff Bauman, Rebekah Gregory. They're just a few of the victim survivors. Roseann, Karen, and Rebekah each suffered the amputation of one leg; Jessica and Jeff have now lost both legs. You heard and you saw what they went through, what they suffered through and the terrible injuries inflicted by Dzhokhar Tsarnaev.

"And, yes, when they testified, they were brave, they were resilient and they were open. They faced you, as they still face life, with great humor and good grace. But now you need to know the full story of all of them, of all of the survivors. You need to know how close they came to death as a result of the actions of Dzhokhar Tsarnaev; how close they came and others came, and how close others still might be. The question of guilt has been answered, and the question of sentence remains."

The government tried to address the biggest question, the one that might never be answered otherwise: why? And Pelligrini warned the jury that the defense team planned to blame Dzhokhar's older brother:

"You may hear about family dynamics, family history, family dysfunction. But many people—millions of people, one would venture—face troubles throughout their lives. Who among them murders a child with a bomb? You may see photos of Dzhokhar Tsarnaev at family gatherings, school events, dances, at camp, playing the drums. That might tell you he had the advantages of a good education at schools; that he led others, like those on his wrestling team; that he was taken care of, and that he was educated.

"But nothing will explain his cruelty and his indifference. Nothing will, other than his own character. And everything you know and will know about Dzhokhar Tsarnaev and the crimes that he committed will reinforce [the fact that] he simply is callous and indifferent to human life. These personal characteristics are what set him apart, and it's his character that makes the death penalty appropriate and just.

"It's not that hate and callous indifference to human life are anything new. Sadly, they're not. But neither are the notions of jihad or radicalization. Those didn't start with Dzhokhar Tsarnaev, and they certainly didn't start with Tamerlan Tsarnaev, and it is tempting to look elsewhere when one's beliefs and actions are so fundamentally different than what you would expect from another human being."

Pellegrini even quoted Shakespeare to make her point:

"So when Shakespeare wrote that 'The fault, dear Brutus, is not in our stars but in ourselves,' he was reminding us that we have to look inward. We have to look towards the person in whom the fault lies. No alignment of the heavens will explain or excuse Dzhokhar Tsarnaev.

"The evidence presented and to be presented will show a person whose cruel character can be found in the way that he murdered and in his own reactions to those murders, his own beliefs, and his own motivations. It's the lines that he was so willing to cross that make him fundamentally different. And it may have been hard to imagine that an individual would have such feelings and then act upon them in such a way, but you no longer have to imagine. You've seen it. If you want to understand Dzhokhar Tsarnaev and what he did, you don't have to look to the heavens for an answer. You can look for the man who walked alone down Boylston Street, knowing that his brother had taken up his own place at another location. You can look for the man who stood alone behind the Richard family for almost four minutes. You can look for the man who then walked off alone, leaving behind a bomb that would kill Lingzi and Martin; who, without his brother, got back to the UMass Dartmouth campus and three days later came back.

"Look for the man who alone got the gun that killed Sean Collier; who alone went into the bank and used the debit card of a terrified carjacking victim to get money; and who drove alone down Laurel Street trying to mow down Watertown police officers; who escaped alone; and who then, alone with his own thoughts, wrote in his own words—wrote and carved his manifesto into the inside of that boat on Franklin Street, declaring his beliefs and righteousness of his own actions."

Pellegrini wanted to convince the jury of one thing—that Dzhokhar had made his own decisions with a single goal in mind, saying: "His destiny was determined by him, and he was determined and destined to be America's worst nightmare."[2]

The government repeatedly insisted that Dzhokhar had always had a dark side. He was just better at hiding it then his older brother was. The government pointed to Dzhokhar's own Internet activity that revealed his inner mujahedin. He maintained two twitter accounts including one, @J_Tsar, that he used to tweet "Ain't no love in the heart of the city, stay safe people," at 5:04 P.M. April 15, 2013, roughly two hours after he detonated the pressure cooker bomb that prosecutors said killed Lingzi Lu and Martin Richard—the same night he had dinner with his brother and a friend. A tweet that he sent from that account a year earlier—on April 16, 2012—was more ominous. It was written on the same day the Boston Marathon runners made their way toward the finish line without incident, something that his tweet suggested would not happen the next year. It read: "They will spend their money and they will regret it and then they will be defeated."[3]

Dzhokhar's second Twitter account was under the name @Ghuraba, which can be loosely translated as the Arabic word for strangers, and his profile shot was a picture of Mecca. The FBI said he used that account to write: "Dua is truly the weapon of the believer, pray for the oppressed it is your duty." Another insisted, "It's our responsibility my brothers & sisters to Allah to ease the hardships of the oppressed and give us victory over kufr [kaffirs]," as noted in a previous chapter. Those tweets were clearly written without Tamerlan's input, since at that time his big brother was in Russia meeting militants and recording meetings with their mother's second cousin.

Assistant US Attorney William Weinreb described Dzhokhar's secret life this way: "The defendant looked and acted like he was a typical young adult. But the evidence will show that he wasn't. He had a side to him that he kept hidden, even from his closest friends."[4]

Some of those closest friends and some of Dzhokhar's childhood teachers would tearfully take the stand, desperate for a glimpse of the old Jahar, the goofy boy who had smoked weed and flirted with them, the floppy-haired teen with the shy lopsided smile who had a way with dogs. That Jahar seemed to have evaporated into the black smoke that exploded over Boylston Street nearly two years earlier. He barely looked at them: not the woman who ran the Best Buddies charitable program at Cambridge Rindge and Latin, Jennifer Callison, who took the stand to describe how "kind" and "respectful"[5] Dzhokhar was as a high school student; and not the math teacher, Eric Traub, who testified that Dzhokhar "got along great with his peers" and brought "kind of a fun energy to the classroom."[6] Traub testified that Dzhokhar and other Muslim students had prayed in an empty classroom but added he didn't think Dzhokhar harbored any anti-American sentiments. In fact. Traub had written him a college recommendation "with enthusiasm" and described him as a student with "good nature and positive spirit." Traub was visiting family overseas in South Africa when Dzhokhar was identified as one of the marathon bombers: "I was shocked when I saw his picture on TV. And then his name was there. In fact, I didn't even believe it was him at first because it just didn't make sense to me and it took me a while to absorb that it was him and that, you know, it wasn't a misunderstanding."

Through all this testimony Dhzhokhar never looked up, not once. Not even when Rosa Booth—his close friend, one of the many giggling girls who testified that they had smoked pot with him—took the stand. By then she had become a college student at the Massachusetts College of Art and Design. She had sat next to him in math class at Cambridge Rindge and Latin.

"I had a crush on him then," she told the court, smiling. Dzhokhar asked her to the prom but she said no, too shy to actually talk to the boy she had secretly liked for so long. After the bombing she had posted a picture of a backyard BBQ she had attended with Dzhokhar. In it he was laughing and patting another friend's dog, Dempsey.

"What was Dempsey's relationship like with Jahar?" Miriam Conrad asked.

"He really liked Jahar," Rosa answered.

"And so can you tell from that photograph if he's looking at Jahar because Jahar's eating something or just because he likes Jahar?"

"He was eating something," Rosa admitted.

Then she was asked about Dzhokhar and why she liked spending time with him. She answered: "He had a sweetness about him. Maybe a little shy. I was very shy."[7]

One after another, witnesses for the defense took the stand—many of them crying—and described a sweet boy who cried watching *The Lion King* and peed in the kitchen sink for a laugh. Experts talked about his crazy father and his overbearing mother.

Inexplicably, most testimony about his brother Tamerlan was prohibited by the court, and his name came up only in the context of his relationship with Dzhokhar and the crimes the brothers committed during their April 2013 rampage of terror. There was video of the brothers at the Firing Line in Manchester, New Hampshire, a month before the blasts, practicing on rented guns like the one that Dzhokhar had borrowed from his friend Stephen Silva, the one that had been linked to the Portland, Maine, drug crew. There were graphics, maps and GPS coordinates, and text message transcripts about the trips Tamerlan took to New Hampshire to buy BBs, and receipts for toy car parts and fireworks were entered into evidence. But Tamerlan's relationship with the government before the bombings was never brought up, despite the defense team's earlier assertion—in writing—that the FBI wanted Tamerlan to become an asset, a mole in the Muslim world.

Defense attorneys instead relied on using Tamerlan's intimidating stature and his radical history to paint a picture of an easily influenced teenager, their client, who was forced by his big brother into the crimes he had admittedly committed. The attorneys showed a video of Tamerlan, Dzhokhar, and the missing Chechen witness, Magomed Dolakov, at Wai Kru the Friday before the bombings—highlighting a scene where Tamerlan threw equipment at his little brother, who seemed to cower a little. Dzhokhar needed to be punished, his defense team admitted, by being forgotten about in the world's most secure prison, ADX Supermax—the remote Colorado facility where terrorists like Richard Reid, the failed shoe bomber, and the Unabomber, Ted Kaczynski, had been held without incident since their convictions.

In fact, it was Judy Clarke who had saved Kaczynski, and many others, from being sentenced to death. She had a perfect record in death penalty cases. She had helped convince juries to spare the lives of some of the sickest individuals on the planet: Susan Smith, the mother who strapped her two small boys into car seats and then drove them into a lake and watched them drown so that her lover, who didn't want kids, wouldn't break up with her; Eric Rudolph, the unapologetic racist and Christian zealot who set off a bomb in Atlanta during the 1996 Summer Olympics, an attack that killed 2 people and injured 150 more; and Jared Lee Loughner, who opened fire in a parking lot near Tucson, Arizona, in 2011, shooting Representative Gabrielle Giffords through the head and killing six others. Even Zacharias Moussaoui, the Al Qaeda operative accused of helping to plan the 9/11 attacks was alive only because of the ferocious defense he had received from Clarke. Over and over again the media pundits and death penalty experts declared that it would be unlikely that Dzhokhar—a teenager so cute, as the Jaharians liked to say, that he was put on the cover of *Rolling Stone* magazine looking like Jim Morrison, the lead singer of the Doors—would be sentenced to death with Clarke in his corner.

Clarke used her opening statement in the guilt phase of Dzhokhar's trial in an attempt to save yet another mass murderer from an eventual lethal injection. She was no dummy. The testimony from the victims had been beyond heart wrenching, and her client's seeming indifference to their suffering had certainly been noted. Some victims, like the Richard family, were vehemently opposed to the death penalty, but their views would not be made available to the jury. Others, like Liz Norden, whose two sons had lost legs in the bombings, wanted Dzhokhar to die—and sooner rather than later. Clarke had her work cut out for her. But it was another defense attorney, David Bruck, who made the opening statement in the penalty phase of the trial where jurors would decide whether Dzhokhar would live or die.

"We are asking you to punish Jahar by imprisoning him for the rest of his life. And for the next few minutes, I'd like to tell you some of the reasons why and about some of the evidence that you will be hearing in this phase of the case. The choice might be easier if you only had to consider the evidence of these awful crimes. But the man who conceived, planned, and led this crime is beyond our power to punish. Only the 19-year-old younger brother who helped is left. So the question of what makes most sense, death or a lifetime of unrelenting punishment, is more complicated than just the crimes themselves. Now, you've all probably realized by now that no punishment, no punishment, could ever be equal to the terrible effects of these crimes on the innocent people who were killed and hurt or on their families. There is no evening the scales. There's no point in trying to hurt him as he hurt because it can't be done. All we can do, all you can do, is to make the best choice. And if there's one thing to remember through all of this, it is that Jahar will be severely punished either way. Your guilty verdicts have already guaranteed that. One punishment is over quickly, although after more media attention and fame and notoriety. The other will last for years and decades while he is locked away and forgotten.

"No matter what Jahar does now, no matter what regrets he feels, no matter how much he matures, no matter what amends he may wish to make, his last chance came when he was 19, and he will never be given another. We'll bring you evidence about that, and we'll let you see how the government will ensure that Jahar will be securely locked away, safely and securely, where he can never hurt anyone or even be heard from ever again if any of you choose to punish him with life imprisonment.

"Now, maybe we could have shown you this and stopped. He goes here and he's forgotten. No more spotlight like the death penalty brings. His legal case will be over for good. And no martyrdom. Just years and years of punishment, day after day, while he grows up to face the lonely struggle of dealing with what he did. And all the while society is protected. That might be—that should be—enough to vote for life for Tamerlan Tsarnaev's younger brother. But each of you said that you'd want to know everything about Jahar as well as about the crime before you made this decision. Whether you realized it or not, each of you persuaded Judge O'Toole that you meant it, and that is why you were found to be qualified to sit on this jury.

"No one is going to argue that Tamerlan forced Jahar to help him commit these crimes. When Tamerlan decided that it was time, his little brother went with him. And once he did, he was all in. But the evidence will show that, if Tamerlan hadn't led the way, Jahar would never have done any of this no matter what was on his computer and no matter what kinds of songs he listened to. How do we know that? First, because Tamerlan's motivation to commit this attack was so much stronger and had existed for much longer; secondly, because their personalities were so different; and, third, because Tamerlan had power over Jahar."[8]

Of course it was Dzhokhar who was ultimately responsible for his big brother's death when he ran Tamerlan over on that night in Watertown, a fact he seemed to wipe from his memory when he kept asking the FBI agents who questioned him in the hospital, "Where is Tamerlan? Is he alive?"[9]

27

OH, MY GOD, HE'S SO YOUNG

"Before you met with Jahar, did you know that he was Muslim?"[1]

That was the first question defense attorney Miriam Conrad asked the gray-haired Roman Catholic nun with the fireplug build as she took the stand, a silver cross around her neck. She was a witness whom prosecutors had wanted to keep from testifying, a woman who was so famous that her life had been featured in a movie—*Dead Man Walking*. Her name was Sister Helen Prejean, and on the stand she wore street clothes and smiled at the victims in the courtroom, many of whom were Catholic. Prejean had met with Tsarnaev five times, either at Fort Devens or in the holding cell at the federal courthouse. She told the court that she had begun to read about Islam to prepare for those encounters. The first meeting had been "pleasant," she remembered.

"Well, I'm not sure he had ever met a nun before, but he was very open and receptive. He was, it was pleasant. He was good," Sister Prejean told the court.

"What do you remember about that meeting? Without telling us anything that he said, but what do you remember about that first meeting with him?" Conrad asked.

"It's just, I walked in the room and I looked at his face and I remember [thinking], 'Oh, my God, he's so young,' which he is. And it just had that kind of spontaneity to it that you have with young people, because young people are open and more, you know, responsive. I sensed he was very respectful and that we easily—I felt it was pretty easy to establish a rapport."

"What kinds of things—without telling us again what was said, but what kinds of topics did you discuss, not just in that first meeting, but through the course of all five meetings?"

"I told him a little bit about being a nun, that I was dedicating my life to God. And one of the things I did know about Islam is [that] to try to do the will of God is the goal of your life. I talked about being a Catholic, serving the people, the kind of stuff I've done, growing up in Louisiana. A little bit about what it means to be a Cajun. And then we did get into the whole thing of the death penalty in the United States, told him what my work was and what I—"

Prejean had already gone too far. Conrad stopped her even before the government attorneys could object. She asked a question that did not address the death penalty directly: "Did you talk about some of the differences and similarities between Catholicism and Islam?"

"They kind of naturally emerged. Like I talked about how in the Catholic Church we have become more and more opposed to the death penalty—"

The government attorneys immediately raised an objection, which was sustained. Conrad went back to general religious "disagreements," as Prejean described them between her and Dzhokhar, and Prejean said: "Well, I think some of it revolved around the God of love."

"At some point did he express to you his feelings about what happened to the victims in this case?" Conrad asked. "What did he say to you about the victims?"

Prejean took a breath and answered firmly: "He said it emphatically. He said, 'No one deserves to suffer like they did.'"

"How did you perceive his sincerity?"

"As absolutely sincere," Prejean answered. "His response was so spontaneous, and it's not like he was hedging or it's not like he was trying to—he just simply said, 'Nobody deserves to suffer like that.' And I had every reason to believe that it was sincere."

"How would you describe his expression when he said that?" Conrad asked.

"Well, he—his face registered it, and he kind of lowered his eyes."

"Would you tell the jury he was sincerely remorseful if you did not believe that?" It was Conrad's last question.

"No I would not."

Sister Prejean's testimony would not sway the jury. Nor would Dzhokhar's crying aunts and former teachers and the girls who had smoked weed with him. On May 15, 2015, an eerie quiet settled over the federal courthouse in Boston as victims and relatives of those killed in the Boston Marathon bombings heard a jury condemn Dzhokhar Tsarnaev to death. The last execution in the Commonwealth of Massachusetts had been in 1947, and the state had outlawed the death penalty in 1984. He would be the second defendant in a federal case in Massachusetts since then to be sentenced to death. The first was spree killer Gary Sampson, who is still on death row.

Liz Norden, who wanted him to get the death penalty for detonating the bomb that left two of her sons amputees and their bodies forever burned and scarred, cried quietly when the jury decided that the twenty-one-year-old should die for his crimes. Bill and Denise Richard, who strongly advocated against capital punishment for the murderer of their eight-year-old son, Martin—the youngest victim killed in the horrific attack—sat stone faced as the verdict was read.

The jury forewoman had walked into the court just after 3:00 P.M. wearing a pink button-down shirt, taken an audible deep breath, and handed a sealed manila envelope containing the verdict to the judge's clerk, Paul Lyness. It took more than thirty minutes to read through the various factors the jury legally had to consider before it became clear that Dzhokhar would be sentenced to death. The jury found death an "appropriate" punishment for six of the seventeen capital counts he was facing after his conviction in the previous month.

Inside Courtroom 9 the jurors—seven women and five men—stood as the verdict was read, as did Dzhokhar. One juror removed his eyeglasses and wiped his eyes with a tissue, leaning his body against the rail of the jury box as if to prop himself up. Two female jurors, their cheeks flushed red, sipped from water bottles. Another woman had her arms crossed in front of her.

Dzhokhar never looked toward the jury box, not even when it became clear that those men and women had decided he should be put to death. One of his defense attorneys, Miriam Conrad, covered her mouth with her hand. Once the verdict had been read, police officials in court—including Watertown Police Chief Ed Deveau and BPD Commissioner Bill Evans, who continued to run in the Boston Marathon and has raised money for the Richard family—exchanged glances.

The mood in the courtroom was heavy and subdued. Before the jury verdict had been read, Lyness had admonished those assembled there that "any outbursts" would be treated as contempt of court. There were none. Karen Brassard, who had been injured in the bombing, put a comforting hand on Liz Norden's shoulder as they filed out of the courtroom after hearing the verdict.

Assistant US Attorney Steve Mellin, who had delivered the closing arguments about the "river of blood"[2] that Dzhokhar left on Boylston Street on April 15, 2013, hugged a victim to his chest as they bumped into each other leaving. Dzhokhar watched as the jurors filed out of the courtroom. Then, wringing his handcuffed fingers in front of him, he was escorted out a side door by a US Marshal. His attorneys were stunned. The verdict marked Judy Clarke's first failure to keep a client from receiving the death penalty.

Before he was transported out of the federal courthouse for the last time and before his eventual transfer to federal death row at a prison in Terre Haute, Indiana, Dzhokhar was allowed to say goodbye to his legal team, in the presence of security officials assigned to the courthouse.

A court officer, who cannot be named because he is still employed by the US District Court, described what happened next with utter contempt. "Everyone was crying and hugging each other. Hugging him. It was despicable," he remembered. "I'll tell you who wasn't crying. That piece of shit Jahar." Another officer still employed by the court would recall becoming nauseous and biting his tongue as he watched what transpired: "They were all weeping, every single lawyer, even the paralegals. It was disgusting. What were they crying about?"

But Dzhokhar didn't shed a tear. He was twenty-one years old, and he would be spending years and years in a solitary cell waiting to die.

EPILOGUE

Dzhokhar might be crying now, in his eighty-seven-square foot cell in what is referred to as the "Alcatraz of the Rockies," ADX Supermax. Among his fellow prisoners in that facility are Richard Reid—the failed shoe bomber, who was convicted in the same building where jurors sentenced Dzhokhar to death; Ted Kaczynski, the Unabomber; and Zacarias Moussaoui, who helped hijack one of the planes used in the 9/11 attacks. Judy Clarke had saved those three men from the death penalty, but not Dzhokhar.

The death sentence, especially in a state like Massachusetts, remains controversial to this day. In June 2016 Dzhokar's new defense team argued in court records that all of their travel expenses relating to their attempts to save his life should be sealed. "The fact that he is financially unable to pay for counsel on appeal should not be allowed to result in any potentially distracting public discussion about the travel and funding authorization," Gail Johnson, a federal defender in Colorado, and David Patton, a New York death penalty attorney, wrote in a brief submitted to a federal appeals court. Clarke, now a consultant on the case, also signed it. She also refused to submit any accounting for the bills that her defense team racked up during Dzhokhar's trial, not even the cost of her hotel rooms at the Intercontinental or her flights from California to Boston—a refusal that prompted the *Boston Globe* to sue for access to the final price to the taxpayers for the convicted bomber's defense. In September 2016 the judge issued another ruling denying any reporters access to the bills from Dzhokhar's defense team.

The death sentence brought no comfort to the parents of Martin Richard. In an opinion piece published in the *Boston Globe,* Bill and Denise Richard, who are still strongly entrenched community activists in their Dorchester neighborhood, argued for the government to sentence Dzhokhar to life in prison instead, "to end the anguish" for their family. "As long as the defendant is in the spotlight, we have no choice but to live a story told on his terms, not ours," they wrote. "The minute the defendant fades from our newspapers and TV screens is the minute we begin the process of rebuilding our lives and our family."[1]

Others involved in the marathon case have started the process of rebuilding their lives. Many have started their own charitable organizations, like the Martin Richard Foundation, which raises money to carry on his message of "no more hurting people" by investing in education, athletics, and community activities like youth sports. BPD Commissioner Bill Evans ran one of his many races wearing MR8—Martin's Little League number—on his back to raise funds.

As of this writing, the parents of Tamerlan and Dzhokhar Tsarnaev have never returned to the United States from Russia, where they have made statements critical of the US government, while insisting on their sons' innocence. Although they have kept a low profile since Dzhokhar's trial, his sisters, Bella and Ailina, were known to be living with Katherine Russell, Tamerlan's widow, in an apartment in New Jersey.

Dzhokhar's friend Stephen Silva, the convicted drug dealer who had boasted to cops that "my best friend is the bomber,"[2] and who loaned the gun used to execute Sean Collier and in the gun battle in Watertown to the Tsarnaev brothers, was released from prison after serving time on federal drug trafficking charges in 2015 and vowed not to get in trouble again. Azamat Tazhayakov, Tsarnaev's college pal, was released from a federal prison after serving time for lying to investigators in May 2016. Dias Kadyrbayev, also convicted of lying to investigators, is being held at a low-security prison in northern Texas and will be released in July 2018. Robel Phillipos, despite testimony pleading for mercy from former Massachusetts Governor and Democratic presidential candidate Michael Dukakis, was sent to a minimum-security prison in Pennsylvania. Khairullozhon Matanov, the taxi driver, was sentenced to thirty months in federal prison for lying to investigators and destroying evidence, and immigration officials are expected to eventually deport him to his native Kyrgyzstan.

After a nearly unprecedented two-year stay for a psychological evaluation in a mental institution (especially surprising in Massachusetts, where beds for the mentally ill are extraordinarily scarce)—Daniel Morley was released and as of this writing continues to live in Massachusetts, either with his mother in Topsfield or his father in Melrose. Wounded MBTA officer Dic Donohue returned to work but retired in early 2016. A memorial to Sean Collier was erected at MIT. There is still no marking on Boylston Street to remind people of the horror other than one: Before new cement near Marathon Sports dried, someone scrawled a message for one of the dead on it. The message reads: I love you Krystle.

Epilogue

ACKNOWLEDGMENTS

The gathering of evidence is a long, steep road, and some people close to me argued that trying to wangle answers out of members of the federal intelligence community would prove exhausting and thankless. I will admit it was a tremendous undertaking, and I could not have done it without the support of countless law enforcement sources, both on and off the record; court employees (they know who they are); and those who trusted me enough to slip me the sensitive information that helped connect some dots. Most importantly, however, two people believed in this project since the beginning: my doggedly determined literary manager, Sharlene Martin, and my talented and tireless editor, Stephen Hull. I owe them both my utmost gratitude. Amanda Dupuis, the managing editor of University Press of New England, thank you for your help during the editing process.

I am humbled to work alongside the best investigative journalists in the country at the ABC News Brian Ross Investigative Unit. Working with Brian Ross and his vaunted team of investigative journalists has made me a better reporter, and its leaders, Brian Ross and Rhonda Schwartz, have become trusted mentors and friends. There are so many producers, editors, and camera crew colleagues who steered the stellar ABC News coverage of the Tsarnaev trial alongside me at ABC News—including David Reiter, Wendy Fisher, Gregory Croft, and Santina Leuci—who are deserving of mention that I am afraid I could not list them all, but I hope everyone involved knows they have my respect. I do need to give a special thanks to Team Boston: Tom Llamas, Tina Chen, Carlos Boettcher, and the Tom Manning crew. And, of course, there were those who made the long wait for the jury to return the verdict bearable, including Hilary Sargent, then at *Boston.com*, and Patrick Radden Keefe of the *New Yorker*, along with WBUR's Bruce Gellerman and Emily Rooney, a longtime friend and mentor.

Many of the brave law enforcement officers from every police department in the Commonwealth of Massachusetts, federal prosecutors, defense attorneys, federal agents, and first responders from the Boston Fire Department and EMS who not only saved countless lives that day but also assisted in the reporting, cannot be named. Some can for the guidance they gave me or the Freedom of Information Act requests they answered: BPD spokesman Lieutenant Detective Mike McCarthy and his staff, Massachusetts State Police department spokesman David Procopio, FBI spokesperson Kristen Setera, former Watertown Police Chief Ed Deveau and current Watertown Police Chief Ed Long, Cambridge Police Department spokesman Jeremy Warnick, US Attorney's Office spokeswoman Christina Sterling, US Marshals Service spokesman Kevin Neale, retired Somerville Police Chief Tom Pasquarello, Massport firefighter Michael Ward, and others who I hope know my gratitude, especially the late Mayor of Boston Thomas M. Menino, whom I adored, and his staff, among them Dot Joyce.

Writing any book is a complicated task, and I leaned on a lot of people, most of all my boss; my friend; *mo anam cara*; the co-owner of the phenomenal radio station 1510 WMEX in Boston, where I have hosted a radio show from 3:00 to 7:00 P.M. since June 2, 2015; and the person who stayed up countless hours editing behind me, as I worked on past the morning side of midnight to meet deadlines. Mary Remmer, I love you. To Mary's husband Henry Remmer and the rest of the family at 1510 WMEX, including Bryan Berner, Tom Quinlan, and Ryan Nichols, thanks for putting up with me as I wrote my book and planned my show simultaneously for months. Of course to my girl Diane MacNamara, Di Mac, a special nod.

My family has always pushed me to write, since I was a little girl scribbling notes in my little locked diary. To my sisters Erin Donovan and Shannon Thompson; my godparents, Joan and Dick Dennis; and my father, Bruce, thank you. You all knew that my nosy nature might come in handy one day, especially you Erin. I also want to acknowledge my friends, among them Rob and Raquel, Andrea Ducharme, Noelle Spinosa, Lisa Cappuccio and so many others who patiently listened to my unrelenting theories for three years and pushed me to uncover the truth.

I dedicate this book to the victims: Martin Richard, Krystle Marie Campbell, Lingzi Lu, and Sean Collier, who died at the hands of the Tsarnaev brothers, the seventeen victims whose limbs were torn from their bodies and yet overcame, continuing to inspire all of us to turn tragedy into triumph; and the loved ones whose lives were turned upside-down caring for their critically injured family members. I must also mention the ones who have become honored friends: Rebekah Gregory-Varney, Liz Norden, and Roseann Sdoia.

And, finally, TJF.

NOTES

AUTHOR'S NOTE

1. Lorenzo Vidino and Seamus Hughes, "ISIS in America: From Retweets to Raqqa," accessed September 18, 2016, https://cchs.gwu.edu/sites/cchs.gwu.edu/files/downloads /ISIS%20in%20America%20-%20Full%20Report_0.pdf.

2. Brian Ross, Michele McPhee, and Cho Park, "Boston Cop's Son, an Accused Terrorist: ISIS Is a Good Thing," *ABC News*, July 15, 2015, accessed September 18, 2016, http://abcnews .go.com/US/boston-cops-son-accused-terrorist-isis-good-thing/story?id=32464662.

3. House of Representatives Homeland Security Committee, *The Road to Boston: Counterterrorism Challenges and Lessons from the Boston Marathon Bombings*, March 2014, accessed August 9, 2016, https://homeland.house.gov/files/documents/Boston-Bombings-Report.pdf.

4. United States v. Dzhokhar Tsarnaev defense motion filed on March 14, 2014.

5. Boston medical examiner's death certificate for Tamerlan Tsarnaev, dated April 19, 2013.

6. Stephen Silva testimony, transcript from the trial of Dzhokhar Tsarnaev, March 17, 2015.

7. The report noted: "Indeed after 19 hijackers demonstrated the relative ease of obtaining a U.S. visa and gaining entrance to the United States, border security is still not considered a cornerstone of national security. We believe, for reasons we discuss in the following pages, that it must be made one" (National Commission on Terrorist Attacks upon the United States, "9/11 Commission Report" [Washington: Government Printing Office, 2004, 168]).

PROLOGUE PATRIOTS' DAY

1. According to the "Action Report for the Response to the 2013 Boston Marathon Bombings" released by the Massachusetts Emergency Management Agency in December 2014.

2. Author interview with BPD Sergeant Dan Keeler, May 27, 2016.

3. Steven Woolfenden testimony, transcript from the trial of Dzhokhar Tsarnaev, April 23, 2015. All quotes attributed to Woolfenden are taken from his trial testimony.

4. BPD Officer Thomas Barrett testimony, transcript from the trial of Dzhokhar Tsarnaev, March 5, 2015. All quotes attributed to Barrett are taken from his trial testimony.

5. According to the "Action Report for the Response to the 2013 Boston Marathon Bombings" released by the Massachusetts Emergency Management Agency in December 2014.

6. Boston EMS Chief James Hooley testimony, transcript from the trial of Dzhokhar Tsarnaev, March 9, 2015. All quotes attributed to Hooley are taken from his trial testimony.

7. Danling Zhou testimony, transcript from the trial of Dzhokhar Tsarnaev, March 9, 2015. All quotes attributed to Zhou in the prologue are taken from her trial testimony.

8. BPD Officer Thomas Barrett testimony, transcript from the trial of Dzhokhar Tsarnaev, March 5, 2015.

9. William Richard testimony, transcript from the trial of Dzhokhar Tsarnaev, March 5, 2015. All quotes attributed to Richard in the prologue are taken from his trial testimony.

10. Adrianne Haslet-Davis testimony, transcript from the trial of Dzhokhar Tsarnaev, March 9, 2015. All quotes attributed to Haslet-Davis in the prologue are taken from her trial testimony.

11. Karen Rand-McWatters testimony, transcript from the trial of Dzhokhar Tsarnaev, March 5, 2015. All quotes attributed to Rand-McWatters are taken from her trial testimony.

12. The photograph was a government exhibit shown to the jury but not released publicly during the trial of Dzhokhar Tsarnaev.

13. Rebekah Gregory testimony, transcript from the trial of Dzhokhar Tsarnaev, March 9, 2015. All quotes attributed to Gregory are taken from her trial testimony or multiple author interviews conducted with Gregory in 2015 and 2016.

14. Nicole Gross testimony, transcript from the trial of Dzhokhar Tsarnaev, March 9, 2015. All quotes attributed to Gross are taken from her trial testimony.

15. Gillian Reny testimony, transcript from the trial of Dzhokhar Tsarnaev, March 4, 2015. All quotes attributed to Reny are taken from her trial testimony.

16. Celeste Corcoran, testimony, transcript from the trial of Dzhokhar Tsarnaev, April 21, 2015. All quotes attributed to Corcoran—including the quotes she attributed to her husband—are taken from her trial testimony.

1 THESE MOTHERFUCKERS ARE HERE

1. Assistant US Attorney Steven Mellin, closing argument, transcript from the trial of Dzhokhar Tsarnaev, May 13, 2015. All quotes attributed to Mellin in this chapter are from that transcript.

2. Multiple author interviews with BPD Commissioner William Evans in 2014-16. Evans, a BPD deputy superintendent at the time of the bombings, was promoted to commissioner in 2014.

3. Federal Bureau of Investigation, "A Byte Out of History: 1975 Terrorism Flashback: State Department Bombing," January 29, 2004, accessed September 18, 2016, https://archives.fbi.gov/archives/news/stories/2004/january/weather_012904.

4. David Abel, "Apologetic in the End, William Gilday Dies," *Boston Globe*, September 16, 2011, http://archive.boston.com/news/local/massachusetts/articles/2011/09/16/william_lefty_gilday_dies_at_82/.

5. Author interview with retired BPD Captain Frank Armstrong in June 2016.

6. Homeland Security Secretary Janet Napolitano, testimony at a Senate Judiciary Committee hearing on April 23, 2013.

7. I was at the FBI press conference, covering it for ABC News.

8. ABC News special report, "Five Days: The Hunt for the Marathon Bombers," an ABC Ross Investigative Unit web series with multiple producers including the author, Michele McPhee. The series was posted in a five-day sequences beginning on April 15, 2016.

9. Letter from Senator Charles E. Grassley to FBI Director Robert Mueller on October 15, 2013. (I was given a copy of the letter.)

10. FBI, "Joint Release from Massachusetts Law Enforcement Agencies," October 18, 2013, accessed September 20, 2016, https://archives.fbi.gov/archives/boston/press-releases/2013/joint-release-from-massachusetts-law-enforcement-agencies.

11. According to the "Action Report for the Response to the 2013 Boston Marathon Bombings" released by the Massachusetts Emergency Management Agency in December 2014.

2 GET ON IT

1. "Five Days: The Hunt for the Marathon Bombers," an ABC News special report.

2. From the transcript of my notes from the prayer service.

3. Multiple author interviews with FBI Special Agent Vincent Lisi, the agent in charge of the bureau's Boston field office in 2012, 2014, and 2015.

4. MIT Police Chief John DiFava testimony, transcript from the trial of Dzhokhar Tsarnaev, March 11, 2015. All quotes attributed to DiFava are taken from his trial testimony.

5. 911 call placed to MIT Police Department played in court at the trial of Dzhokhar Tsarnaev, March 11, 2015.

6. MIT Police Sergeant Clarence Henniger testimony, transcript from the trial of Dzhokhar Tsarnaev, March 11, 2015. All quotes attributed to Henniger are taken from his trial testimony.

7. Medical Examiner Renee Robinson testimony, transcript from the trial of Dzhokhar Tsarnaev, March 12, 2015.

8. Aaron Swartz, "Guerilla Open Access Manifesto," July 2008, accessed September 18, 2016, https://archive.org/stream/GuerillaOpenAccessManifesto/Goamjuly2008_djvu.txt.

9. United States of America v. Aaron Swartz, September 12, 2012, accessed September 18, 2016, https://archive.org/stream/UsaV.AaronSwartz-CriminalDocument53/UsaV.AaronSwartz-CriminalDocument53_djvu.txt.

10. Carmen M. Ortiz, "Statement of United States Attorney Carmen M. Ortiz Regarding the Death of Aaron Swartz," January 16, 2013, accessed September 18, 2016, https://www.justice.gov/usao-ma/pr/statement-united-states-attorney-carmen-m-ortiz-regarding-death-aaron-swartz.

11. Josiah Ryan, "Anonymous Hacks MIT Website to Avenge Reddit Founder's Suicide," Campus Reform, January 24, 2013, accessed September 18, 2016, http://www.campusreform.org/?ID=4573.

12. Rebecca Baird-Remba, "Anonymous Threatens to Leak Sensitive Records If the Feds Don't Reform an Anti-Hacking Law," *Business Insider*, January 28, 2013, accessed September 18, 2016, http://www.businessinsider.com/anonymous-hacks-us-sentencing-commission-2013-1.

13. MIT News Office, "Israel Ruiz Writes to MIT Community Regarding Recent Hoax," March 1, 2013, accessed September 18, 2016, http://news.mit.edu/2013/letter-to-the-community-ruiz-0228.

14. Quoted in Milton Police Department Deputy Chief Charles Paris statement, March 16, 2013.

15. Statement by US Attorney Carmen Ortiz released by her spokesperson, Christina Sterling, March 16, 2013.

16. Quoted in United States v. Swartz government motion, filed March 23, 2013.

17. United States v. Swartz government motion, filed March 23, 2013.

18. Dun Meng testimony, transcript from the trial of Dzhokhar Tsarnaev, March 12, 2015. All quotes attributed to Meng in this chapter are taken from his trial testimony.

3 GOOD JOB, BOY. GOOD JOB

1. Dun Meng testimony, transcript from the trial of Dzhokhar Tsarnaev, March 12, 2015. All quotes attributed to Meng in this chapter are taken from his trial testimony.

2. The law enforcement officers agreed to an interview with the author but did not want to be identified.

3. 911 call from the clerk at the gas station played in court at the trial of Dzhokhar Tsarnaev, March 12, 2015.

4 BOLO

1. Transcript of Cambridge Police Department transmission over police radios.

2. BPD Officer Michael Nickerson testimony, transcript from the trial of Dzhokhar Tsarnaev, March 12, 2015.

3. Watertown Police Department Officer Joseph Reynolds testimony, transcript from the trial of Dzhokhar Tsarnaev, March 16, 2015. All quotes attributed to Reynolds in this chapter are taken from his trial testimony.

4. Watertown Police Department Sergeant John MacLellan testimony, transcript from trial of Dzhokhar Tsarnaev, March 16, 2015. All quotes attributed to MacLellan in this chapter are taken from his trial testimony.

5. Watertown Police Department Sergeant Joseph Pugliese testimony, transcript from the trial of Dzhokhar Tsarnaev, March 16, 2015.

6. Multiple author interviews with Watertown Police Department Sergeant Jeffrey Pugliese and his testimony, transcript from the trial of Dzhokhar Tsarnaev, March 16, 2015.

7. Watertown Police Department Sergeant Jeffrey Pugliese testimony, transcript from the trial of Dzhokhar Tsarnaev, March 16, 2015. All subsequent quotes attributed to Pugliese in this chapter are taken from his trial testimony.

8. BPD incident summary report on the injuries suffered by Officer Dennis Simmonds, April 19, 2013.

9. Letter MSP Trooper Chris Dumont wrote about his actions in Watertown on April 18-19, 2013, and sent to his superiors (copy on file), corroborated by author interviews with MSP officials.

10. Heather Studley testimony, transcript from, the trial of Dzhokhar Tsarnaev, March 16, 2015. All quotes attributed to Studley in this chapter are taken from her trial testimony.

11. Michael Sullivan testimony, transcript from the trial of Dzhokhar Tsarnaev, April 29, 2015.

12. Boston medical examiner's death certificate for Tamerlan Tsarnaev, dated April 19, 2013.

13. Multiple author interviews with FBI Special Agent Vincent Lisi, the agent in charge of the bureau's Boston field office, and the assistant agent in charge, Special Agent Kiernan Ramsey, in 2014 and 2015.

14. MSP Trooper David Cahill, testimony, transcript from the trial of Dzhokhar Tsarnaev, March 24, 2015.

15. "Action Report for the Response to the 2013 Boston Marathon Bombings," released by the Massachusetts Emergency Management Agency in December 2014.

16. Transcript of press conference held by Massachusetts Governor Deval Patrick, April 19, 2013.

17. "Saudi Similar to [Boston] Marathon Speaks about Raid on His Apartment," *Saudi Today*, April 25, 2013, accessed September 19, 2016, http://www.alarabiya.net/ar/saudi-today /2013/04/25/%D8%B3%D8%B9%D9%88%D8%AF%D9%8A-%D8%B4%D8%A8%D9%8A %D9%87-%D8%A8%D9%85%D8%AA%D9%87%D9%85-%D8%A8%D9%88%D8%B3%D8% B7%D9%86-%D9%8A%D8%B1%D9%88%D9%8A-%D9%82%D8%B5%D8%A9-%D9%85% D8%AF%D8%A7%D9%87%D9%85%D8%A9-%D8%B4%D9%82%D8%AA%D9%87-%D9% 88%D8%A7%D8%B3%D8%AA%D8%AC%D9%88%D8%A7%D8%A8%D9%87.html.

18. Author interview with retired Somerville Police Department Chief Thomas Pasquarello, June 2016.

5 FACES BUT NO NAMES

1. United States v. Dzhokhar Tsarnaev indictment filed on June 27, 2013.

2. Multiple author interviews with BPD Lieutenant Detective Michael McCarthy in 2013-16.

3. Multiple author interviews with FBI Special Agent Kieran Ramsey, the assistant agent in charge of the bureau's Boston field office. Some of the contents of those interviews appeared in the ABC News special report, "Five Days: The Hunt for the Marathon Bombers."

4. Multiple author interviews with Roseann Sdoia in 2013-16.

5. Jessica Kensky testimony, transcript from the trial of Dzhokhar Tsarnaev, May 13, 2015.

6. Frank Chiola testimony, transcript from the trial of Dzhokhar Tsarnaev, March 5, 2015.

7. Sydney Corcoran testimony, transcript from the trial of Dzhokhar Tsarnaev, March 4, 2015.

8. Jeffrey Bauman testimony, transcript from the trial of Dzhokhar Tsarnaev, March 5, 2015.

9. Multiple author interviews with Carlos "the Cowboy" Arredondo in 2013-15.

10. Author interview with FBI Special Agent Jeffrey Rowland in March 2016. All quotes attributed to Rowland in this chapter are taken from this interview, which appears in "Five Days: The Hunt for the Boston Marathon Bombers."

6 *SLIP AWAY II*

1. Robert McCarthy testimony, transcript from trial of Dzhokhar Tsarnaev, March 18, 2015. All quotes attributed to McCarthy in this chapter are taken from his trial testimony.

2. Edward Knapp testimony, transcript from the trial of Dzhokhar Tsarnaev, March 26, 2015.

3. David Henneberry testimony, transcript from the trial of Dzhokhar Tsarnaev, March 17, 2015.

4. Multiple author interviews with BPD Commissioner William Evans in 2014-16.

5. Transcript of police radio scanner feed, recorded during the hunt for Dzhokhar Tsarnaev in Watertown, April 18-19, 2013.

6. Multiple author interviews with Revere Police Department Chief Robert Cafarelli in September 2016.

7. Transcript of police radio scanner feed, recorded during the hunt for Dzhokhar Tsarnaev in Watertown, April 18-19, 2013.

8. Transcript of police radio scanner feed, recorded during the hunt for Dzhokhar Tsarnaev in Watertown, April 18-19, 2013, and multiple author interviews with BPD Commissioner William Evans in 2014-16.

9. Multiple author interviews with Everett Police Department Officer Matt Cunningham in September 2016.

10. Laura Lee, testimony, transcript from the trial of Dzhokhar Tsarnaev, April 29, 2015. All quotes attributed to Lee in this chapter are taken from her trial testimony.

11. FBI 302 report, July 9, 2013, containing proffer notes from interviews between Khairullozhon Matanov and federal investigators (Assistant US Attorney Aloke Chakravarty; FBI Special Agent John Daly, assigned to the Joint Terrorism Task Force; MSP Trooper Joel Gagne, assigned to the still unsolved triple homicide investigation in Waltham for the Middlesex District Attorney's Office). Also present was Matanov's attorney, Paul Glickman.

12. BPD Tweet posted April 19, 2013, accessed September 19, 2016, https://twitter.com/bostonpolice/status/325413032110989313.

13. I attended this April 19, 2013, press conference where the arrest of Dzhokhar Tsarnaev was announced.

14. Author interview with BPD Commissioner William Evans in 2016.

15. United States v. Tsarnaev motion to suppress statements filed by federal prosecutors on May 7, 2014.

7 GROWING UP TSARNAEV

1. Raisat Suleimanova testimony, transcript from the trial of Dzhokhar Tsarnaev, May 4, 2015. All quotes attributed to Suleimanova in this chapter are taken from her trial testimony.

2. House of Representatives Homeland Security Committee, *The Road to Boston: Counterterrorism Challenges and Lessons from the Boston Marathon Bombings*, March 2014, accessed August 9, 2016, https://homeland.house.gov/files/documents/Boston-Bombings-Report.pdf.

3. Sam Lipson testimony, transcript from the trial of Dzhokhar Tsarnaev, April 28, 2015. All quotes attributed to Lipson in this chapter are taken from his trial testimony.

4. Graham E. Fuller, "About," accessed September 21, 2016, http://grahamefuller.com/about/.

5. Author e-mail exchange with Graham E. Fuller in June 2016.

6. House of Representatives Homeland Security Committee, *The Road to Boston: Counterterrorism Challenges and Lessons from the Boston Marathon Bombings*, March 2014, accessed August 9, 2016, https://homeland.house.gov/files/documents/Boston-Bombings-Report.pdf.

7. This quote is from Tamerlan Tsarnaev's US Citizens and Immigration Services Alien File, a DHS record of all paperwork pertaining to his asylum request and naturalization processing, obtained by the author through a Freedom of Information Act request in 2016.

8. Multiple author phone interviews with Ruslan Tsarni in 2013 and 2014. All quotes attributed to Tsarni in this chapter are taken from these interviews.

9. Lauren Sher, "Marathon Bombing Suspects' Uncle: 'We Are Ashamed,'" ABC News, April 19, 2013, accessed September 19, 2016, http://abcnews.go.com/blogs/headlines/2013/04/marathon-bombing-suspects-uncle-we-are-ashamed/.

10. According to court records filed in Middlesex District Probate and Family Court.

11. BPD incident summary report by Detective Robert Kenney filed in South Boston District Court pertaining to a charge that Ailina Tsarnaeva refused to cooperate with investigators in connection with a counterfeit money case.

12. Quoted in criminal complaint filed by Manhattan District Attorney's office in August 2014 after Ailina Tsarnaev was accused of threatening the father of her youngest child's ex-girlfriend.

13. I was present at Ailina Tsarnaev's hearing in South Boston District Court for and heard this statement in the hallway.

14. Cambridge Police Department incident report pertaining to the arrest of Tamerlan Tsarnaev on a domestic battery charge dated July 10, 2009.

15. Amanda Ransom testimony, transcript from the trial of Dzhokhar Tsarnaev, April 27, 2015.

16. Judy Russell testimony, transcript from the trial of Dzhokhar Tsarnaev, April 27, 2015. All quotes attributed to Russell in this chapter are taken from her trial testimony.

17. Author interview with Imam Taalib Mahdee from the Masjid Al-Qur'aan mosque in Boston 2013.

18. The quote is from notebooks recovered from 410 Norfolk Avenue during execution of search warrants and entered into evidence in the trial of Dzhokhar Tsarnaev by the government.

19. Author Michele McPhee, "Boston Bomb Suspect Eyed in Connection to 2011 Triple Murder," *ABC News*, April 22, 2013, accessed September 19, 2016, http://abcnews.go.com /Blotter/boston-bomb-suspect-eyed-connection-2011-triple-murder/story?id=19015628.

8 IT LOOKS LIKE AN AL QAEDA TRAINING VIDEO IN HERE

1. National Commission on Terrorist Attacks upon the United States, *The 9/11 Commission Report* (Washington: Government Printing Office, 2011).

2. *New York Times*, "The 9/11 Tapes: The Story in the Air," September 7, 2011, accessed September 19, 2016, http://www.nytimes.com/interactive/2011/09/08/nyregion/911-tapes .html?_r=0.

3. "Rest in Peace Brendan Mess," January 12, 2012, accessed September 19, 2016, http:// www.youtube.com/watch?v=-ampMMBT7j4.

4. Author interview with friends of Brendan Mess on background, 2013.

5. United States v. Safwin Madarat, transcript of preliminary hearing, May 13, 2011.

6. US Attorney's Office, District of Massachusetts, "Individuals Charged with Federal Drug, Extortion and Money Laundering Charges: Former Watertown Officer Charged with Impeding a Federal Investigation," May 24, 2011, accessed September 20, 2016, https://www .justice.gov/archive/usao/ma/news/2011/May/MadaratiSafwan.html.

7. US Customs and Immigration Enforcement, "Former Massachusetts Police Officer Named in Federal Indictment," May 24, 2011, accessed September 20, 2016, https://www.ice .gov/news/releases/former-massachusetts-police-officer-named-federal-indictment.

8. Cambridge Police Department incident report pertaining to the 2010 arrest of Brendan Mess on charges of aggravated assault and battery, resisting arrest, and disorderly conduct on August 10, 2010.

9. The quote is from an off-the-record author interview.

10. I was on the scene when the neighbor spoke to reporters.

11. Michele McPhee, "What Happened on Harding Avenue," ABC News, September 2011.

12. Michele McPhee, "Boston Bomber Suspect Eyed in Connection to 2011 Triple Murder," April 22, 2013, accessed September 20, 2016. http://abcnews.go.com/Blotter/boston-bomb -suspect-eyed-connection-2011-triple-murder/story?id=19015628.

13. Background author interview.

14. Transcript of Middlesex District Attorney Gerry Leone's press conference, September 12, 2011. All quotes attributed to Leone in this chapter are taken from this transcript.

15. Author phone interview with Waltham City Councilor Gary Marchese, September 2011.

16. Author interview with Scott Wood, April 2013.

17. Author interview with Dylan Mess, April 2013.

9 MUAZ IN THE MOTHERLAND

1. Author interview with Congressman William Keating after his return from Russia on June 2, 2013.

2. Unclassified summary of information handling and sharing prior to the April 15, 2013, bombings, prepared by the inspector generals for the Central Intelligence Agency, Department of Justice, and DHS, released April 10, 2014.

3. Unclassified summary of information handling and sharing prior to the April 15, 2013, bombings, prepared by the inspector generals for the Central Intelligence Agency, Department of Justice, and DHS, released April 10, 2014.

4. Department of Homeland Security, "Privacy Impact Assessment Update for the TECS System: CBP Primary and Secondary Processing (TECS) National SAR Initiative," August 5, 2011, accessed September 21, 2016, https://www.dhs.gov/xlibrary/assets/privacy/privacy -pia-cbp-tecs-sar-update.pdf.

5. Unclassified summary of information handling and sharing prior to the April 15, 2013, bombings, prepared by the inspector generals for the CIA, Department of Justice, and DHS, released April 10, 2014.

6. Defense motion filed on behalf of Dzhokhar Tsarnaev in US v. Tsarnaev Case #: 1:13-cr-10200-GAO-1 on March 28, 2014.

7. Boston FBI field office press release, "2011 Request for Information on Tamerlan Tsarnaev from Foreign Government," April 19, 2013, https://archives.fbi.gov/archives/news /pressrel/press-releases/2011-request-for-information-on-tamerlan-tsarnaev-from-foreign -government.

8. Boston FBI, "Aafia Siddiqui Sentenced in Manhattan Federal Court to 86 Years for Attempting to Murder U.S. Nationals in Afghanistan and Six Additional Crimes," September 23, 2010, accessed September 20, 2016, https://www.fbi.gov/newyork/press-releases/2010 /nyfo092310.htm.

9. Boston FBI, "Tarek Mehanna Sentenced in Boston to 17 Years in Prison on Terrorism-Related Charges," April 12, 2012, https://archives.fbi.gov/archives/boston/press-releases /2012/tarek-mehanna-sentenced-in-boston-to-17-years-in-prison-on-terrorism-related -charges.

10. Paul Peachey and David Connett, "British Dissident Investigated over Colonel Gaddafi Plot to Assassinate Saudi King," *Independent*, March 25, 2016, accessed September 20, 2016, http://www.independent.co.uk/news/uk/crime/british-dissident-investigated-over-colonel -gaddafi-plot-to-assassinate-saudi-king-a6952756.html.

11. Quoted in transcript from the trial of Dzhokhar Tsarnaev, April 29, 2015.

12. Nadia Suleimanova testimony, transcript from the trial of Dzhokhar Tsarnaev, May 4, 2015.

13. Michael Reynolds testimony, transcript from trial of Dzhokhar Tsarnaev May 5, 2015. Reynolds is associate professor of Near Eastern Studies at Princeton University.

14. Elmirza Khuozhugov testimony via video from the US Embassy in Almaty, Kazakhstan, transcript from the trial of Dzhokhar Tsarnaev, May 6, 2015.

15. Jamestown Foundation, "Jamestown Foundation Responds to False Izvestia Article About Tsarnaev Link," April 26, 2013, accessed September 21, 2016, http://www.jamestown.org/single/?tx_ttnews%5Btt_news%5D=40797&tx_ttnews%5BbackPid%5D=381#.V-Oh2 PArLIV.

16. Brian Glyn Williams website, accessed September 21, 2016, http://www.brianglynwilliams.com/.

17. Steve Urbon, "UMass Dartmouth Professor: 'I Hope I Didn't Contribute,'" *South Coast Today*, April 19, 2013, accessed September 20, 2016, http://www.southcoasttoday.com/apps/pbcs.dll/article?AID=/20130419/NEWS/130419860.

18. Alexander Niss testimony, transcript from trial of Dzhokhar Tsarnaev, May 5, 2015. All quotes attributed to Niss in this chapter are taken from this transcript.

19. Quoted in BPD incident summary report, August 8, 2009.

20. The client agreed to an author interview but did not want to be identified.

21. Elmirza Khuozhugov testimony, transcript from the trial of Dzhokhar Tsarnaev, May 6, 2015.

22. Quoted in transcript from the trial of Dzhokhar Tsarnaev, April 29, 2015.

23. Stephen Silva testimony, transcript from the trial of Dzhokhar Tsarnaev, March 17, 2015.

24. "Yahoo Emails between Dzhokhar and Tamerlan Tsarnaev," exhibit filed in the trial of Dzhokhar Tsarnaev.

25. Quoted in transcript from the trial of Dzhokhar Tsarnaev, April 29, 2015.

26. United States v. Dzhokhar Tsarnaev, transcript of sidebar conversation between Tsarnaev's defense team and federal prosecutors, April 27, 2015.

10 INTO THE FORESTS

1. Simon Shuster, "The Boston Bomber Trail: Fresh Clues in Rural Dagestan," *Time*, April 29, 2013, accessed September 20, 2016, http://world.time.com/2013/04/29/picking-up-the-boston-bomber-trail-in-utamysh-russia/.

2. Stewart Bell, "The Canadian Who Converted to Islam: Boxer Turned Militant Killed in Dagestan," *National Post*, August 20, 2012, http://news.nationalpost.com/news/canada/dagestan.

3. FBI Director James Comey, Statement before the Senate Committee on Homeland Security and Governmental Affairs, Washington, D.C., "Threats to the Homeland," October 8, 2015, https://www.fbi.gov/news/testimony/threats-to-the-homeland.

4. FBI Director James Comey speech about ISIS given to the National Association of Attorneys General, February 25, 2015, available online at https://www.washingtonpost.com/posttv/world/national-security/comey-extremists-exist-in-all-50-states/2015/02/25/8bb6a716-bcfd-11e4-9dfb-03366e719af8_video.html.

5. Stewart Bell, "Canadian Jihadist's Disturbing Video Shows Fanaticism of Rebels Who

May Have Inspired the Boston Bomber," *National Post*, May 1, 2013, http://news.nationalpost
.com/news/canadian-jihadists-video-may-have-been-inspired-boston-bombings.

6. Ibid.

7. National Commission on Terrorist Attacks upon the United States, *The 9/11 Commission Report*.

8. Anton Troianovski, "Lost Son," *Wall Street Journal*, May 24, 2013, http://www.wsj.com
/articles/SB10001424127887323975004578501360359119672.

9. This statement and story were posted on Kavkaz.org. After the death of founder Doku
Umarov, the site was taken down. http://www.kavkaz.org.uk/eng/content/2012/07/16
/16472.shtml.

11 THE INFORMANTS

1. Simon Shuster, "A Dead Militant in Dagestan: Did This Jihadi Meet Tamerlan Tsarnaev,"
Time, May 1, 2013, accessed September 20, 2016, http://world.time.com/2013/05/01/a-dead
-militant-in-dagestan-did-this-slain-jihadi-meet-tamerlan-tsarnaev/.

2. Representative William Keating and others, testimony to the House Homeland Security
Committee, July 10, 2013.

3. Video of standoff between Mahmoud Nidal and Russian counterterrorism officials,
posted by UmaraskmaM on May 22, 2012, https://www.youtube.com/watch?v=nEt3k2Pgryg.

4. Representative William Keating testimony, transcript from a Homeland Security Committee hearing on the Boston Marathon attacks, July 9, 2010.

5. Author interview with Joanna Herlihy, June 2013.

6. "Tsarnaevs' News Conference: A Transcript," *New York Times*, April 26, 2013, http://
www.nytimes.com/2013/04/26/world/europe/tsarnaevs-news-conference-a-transcript.
html?_r=0.

7. Unclassified summary of information handling and sharing prior to the April 15, 2013,
bombings, prepared by the inspector generals for the Central Intelligence Agency, Department of Justice, and DHS, released April 10, 2014.

8. Transcript of DHS Secretary Janet Napolitano, testimony before a Senate Committee
on immigration reform, April 23, 2013.

9. Tamerlan Tsarnaev Department of Homeland Security U.S. Citizenship and Immi-
gration Services A-file posted on DHS reading room website February 2016 pursuant to a
Freedom of Information Act Request, https://www.uscis.gov/sites/default/files/USCIS
/About%20Us/Electronic%20Reading%20Room/A-Files%20of%20Interest%20-%20
Static%20Files/Tamerlan_Tsarnaev.pdf

10. Department of Homeland Security, "Janet Napolitano, Homeland Security Secretary
2009-2013," accessed September 21, 2016, https://www.dhs.gov/janet-napolitano.

11. Transcript of phone calls between Omar Mateen and Orlando Police Department's Cri-
sis Negotiation Team released by Orlando Police Department September 23, 2016, after a court
order prompted by multiple Freedom of Information Act requests by news media outlets.

12. Unclassified summary of information handling and sharing prior to the April 15, 2013, bombings, prepared by the inspector generals for the Central Intelligence Agency, Department of Justice, and DHS, released April 10, 2014.

13. Unclassified summary of information handling and sharing prior to the April 15, 2013, bombings, prepared by the inspector generals for the Central Intelligence Agency, Department of Justice, and DHS, released April 10, 2014.

14. Tamerlan Tsarnaev Department of Homeland Security U.S. Citizenship and Immigration Services A-file posted on DHS reading room website February 2016 pursuant to a Freedom of Information Act Request: https://www.uscis.gov/sites/default/files/USCIS/About%20Us/Electronic%20Reading%20Room/A-Files%20of%20Interest%20-%20Static%20Files/Tamerlan_Tsarnaev.pdf.

15. Quoted in United States v. Dzhokhar Tsarnaev indictment filed on June 27, 2013.

12 RATS

1. US House hearing, "The FBI's Controversial Handling of Organized Crime Investigations in Boston: The Case of Joseph Salvati," May 3, 2001, https://www.gpo.gov/fdsys/pkg/CHRG-107hhrg76507/html/CHRG-107hhrg76507.htm.

2. House of Representatives Homeland Security Committee, "Bipartisan Support in Congress to Counter Violent Extremism," July 17, 2015, https://homeland.house.gov/press/bipartisan-support-congress-counter-violent-extremism/.

3. Quoted in United States v. Alexander Ciccolo, motion to detain, July 15, 2015.

4. Quoted in United States v. Alexander Ciccolo, indictment, July 23, 2015.

5. Author interview with BPD Commissioner William Evans in July 2015.

6. City of Boston press release regarding Department of Homeland Security grant of $17.7 million posted February 17, 2016, a reduction from $18 million in fiscal year 2015, http://www.cityofboston.gov/news/Default.aspx?id=20520.

7. Author interview with Rene Fielding, Boston Office of Emergency Management, and Boston Mayor Marty Walsh in February 2016.

8. Columbia University Law School "Illusions of Justice: Human Rights Abuses in US Terrorism Prosecutions," 2014, accessed September 21, 2016, https://www.hrw.org/sites/default/files/reports/usterrorism0714_ForUpload_0_0_0.pdf

9. American Civil Liberties Union, "Fact Sheet: The NYPD Muslim Informant Program," accessed September 21, 2016, https://www.aclu.org/other/factsheet-nypd-muslim-surveillance-program.

10. New York Police Department, "Radicalization in the West: The Homegrown Threat," 2009.

11. United States v. Dzhokhar Tsarnaev, defense motion, filed March 28, 2014.

12. United States v. Dzhokhar Tsarnaev, defense motion, filed March 28, 2014.

13. United States v. Dzhokhar Tsarnaev, defense motion, filed March 28, 2014.

14. Unclassified summary of information handling and sharing prior to the April 15, 2013,

bombings, prepared by the inspector generals for the Central Intelligence Agency, Department of Justice, and DHS, released April 10, 2014.

15. Letter from Senator Charles E. Grassley to FBI Director Robert Mueller on October 15, 2013.

13 MAYBE, MAYBE NOT

1. Braintree Police Detective Matt Heslam report detailing interview of Khairullozhon Matanov on April 19, 2013.

2. FBI 302 proffer reports between federal investigators and Khairullozhon Matanov.

3. FBI 302 proffer reports between federal investigators and Khairullozhon Matanov.

4. Dzhokhar Tsarnaev April 15, 2013, Tweet entered into evidence by US Attorney's Office Trial Exhibit.

5. Author interview with Edward Hayden, attorney for Khairullozhon Matanov, in September 2014.

14 VASELINE, FIREWORKS, BACKPACK

1. FBI Special Agent John Walker testimony, transcript from trial of Dzhokhar Tsarnaev college friend Robel Phillipos, May 14, 2014.

2. FBI Special Agent John Walker testimony, transcript from trial of Dzhokhar Tsarnaev college friend Robel Phillipos, May 14, 2014.

3. Transcript of Dzhokhar Tsarnaev text messages entered into evidence by US Attorney. Trial exhibit.

4. FBI Special Agent John Walker testimony, transcript from trial of Dzhokhar Tsarnaev college friend Robel Phillipos, May 14, 2014.

5. Transcript of text messages sent and received by Dias Kadyrbayev and Azamat Tazhayakov entered into evidence by US Attorney. Trial exhibit in trial of Dzhokhar Tsarnaev.

6. Azamat Tazhayakov testimony, transcript from trial of Robel Phillipos, October 8, 2014.

7. Azamat Tazhayakov testimony, transcript from trial of Robel Phillipos, October 8, 2014.

8. Author interview with retired Somerville Police Chief Tom Pasquarello in September 2016.

9. FBI Special Agent Stephen Kimball testimony, transcript from the trial of Dzhokhar Tsarnaev, March 10, 2015.

10. Mark Preble, Chief Financial Officer at University of Massachusetts/Dartmouth testimony, transcript from trial of Dzhokhar Tsarnaev, May 24, 2015. Copy of form entered into evidence by US Attorney's Office. Trial exhibit.

11. Elizabeth Zamparelli testimony, transcript from trial of Dzhokhar Tsarnaev May 5, 2015.

15 BETTER TO BE A DOG THAN THE YOUNGEST SON

1. Author obtained exclusive photo of note Dzhokhar Tsarnaev wrote on the *Slip Away II*. Michele McPhee, "Image Shows Dzhokhar Tsarnaev's Last Message Before Arrest," *ABC*

News, April 17, 2014, http://abcnews.go.com/Blotter/image-shows-Dzhokhar-tsarnaevs
-message-arrest/story?id=23335984.

2. FBI Special Agent John Walker testimony, transcript from trial of Dzhokhar Tsarnaev college friend Robel Phillipos, May 14, 2014.

3. Receipt from Target store in Watertown for two backpacks purchased April 14, 2013, entered into evidence by US Attorney. Trial exhibit in trial of Dzhokhar Tsarnaev.

4. Defense brief filed in US Appellate Court Memoranda in Support of Motion to Dismiss April 11, 2014, in US v. Robel Phillipos.

5. US Magistrate Justice Marianne Bowler at bedside arraignment of Dzhokhar Tsarnaev, transcript filed in US v. Dzhokhar Tsarnaev, April 23, 2013.

16 DEAD MEN TELL NO TALES

1. FBI Special Agent Tim McElroy testimony, transcript from detention hearing and arraignment of Khairullozhon Matanov in US District Court, June 4, 2014.

2. Michele McPhee and Aaron Katersky, "Mystery Aircraft Spied on Mass. Man After Bombing," *ABC News*, June 4, 2015, http://abcnews.go.com/blogs/headlines/2014/06/mystery-aircraft-spied-on-mass-man-after-boston-bombing/.

3. Michele McPhee, "Boston Bomb Suspect Eyed in Connection to 2011 Triple Murder," *ABC News*, April 22, 2013, http://abcnews.go.com/Blotter/boston-bomb-suspect-eyed-connection-2011-triple-murder/story?id=19015628.

4. FBI 302 proffer reports between federal investigators and Khairullozhon Matanov.

5. Author interview with Dylan Mess, some of which was contained in on-air piece by Michele McPhee, "What Happened on Harding Ave," *WCVB TV ABC News* affiliate, September 12, 2011.

6. Press release from Nixon Peabody law firm, "Middlesex Massachusetts District Attorney to Join Nixon Peabody LLP," March 19, 2013, http://www.nixonpeabody.com/Middlesex_District_Attorney_Gerry_Leone_Joins_Nixon_Peabody.

7. Michele McPhee, "Mounting Evidence Boston Bombers Involved in 2011 Triple Murder," *ABC News*, May 10, 2013, http://abcnews.go.com/Blotter/mounting-evidence-boston-bombers-involved-2011-triple-murder/story?id=19151271.

8. Ed Hannon, "DA tells Nashoba Grads: Exceed Your Potential," *Lowell Sun*, June 3, 2012, http://www.lowellsun.com/rss/ci_20772373/da-tells-nashoba-grads-exceed-your-potential.

9. FBI 302 proffer reports between federal investigators and Khairullozhon Matanov.

10. FBI 302 proffer reports between federal investigators and Khairullozhon Matanov.

11. FBI 302 proffer reports between federal investigators and Khairullozhon Matanov.

12. Office of the Florida State Attorney General Jeffrey Ashton report on investigation into fatal shooting of Ibragim Todashev released on March 25, 2014.

13. Office of the Florida State Attorney General Jeffrey Ashton report on investigation into fatal shooting of Ibragim Todashev released on March 25, 2014.

14. Boston Police incident report dated February 11, 2010 (copy on file).

15. Office of the Florida State Attorney General Jeffrey Ashton report on investigation into fatal shooting of Ibragim Todashev released on March 25, 2014.

16. Ibragim Todashev Department of Homeland Security U.S. Citizenship and Immigration Services A-file posted on DHS reading room website February 2016 pursuant to a Freedom of Information Act Request, https://www.uscis.gov/sites/default/files/USCIS /About%20Us/Electronic%20Reading%20Room/A-Files%20of%20Interest%20-%20 Static%20Files/Ibragim_Todashev.pdf.

17. Office of the Florida State Attorney General Jeffrey Ashton report on investigation into fatal shooting of Ibragim Todashev released on March 25, 2014.

18. Office of the Florida State Attorney General Jeffrey Ashton report on investigation into fatal shooting of Ibragim Todashev released on March 25, 2014.

19. Office of the Florida State Attorney General Jeffrey Ashton report on investigation into fatal shooting of Ibragim Todashev released on March 25, 2014.

20. Kirit Radia, "FBI 'Bandits' Executed Friend of Boston Marathon Suspect, Dad Says," *ABC News,* May 30, 2013, http://abcnews.go.com/blogs/headlines/2013/05/fbi-bandits -executed-friend-of-boston-suspect-dad-says/.

21. Council on American-Islamic Relations press release, "Ibragim Todashev's Father Writes to Obama Over Son's Death in Connection to Boston Bombings," posted January 2, 2014, https://www.cairflorida.org/blog/ibragim_todashevs_father_writes_to_obama _over_sons_death_in_connection_to_boston_bombings.html.

22. Maria Sachetti, "FBI Shooter Had Stormy Record as Officer," *Boston Globe,* May 14, 2014, https://www.bostonglobe.com/metro/2014/05/13/fbi-shooter-had-stormy-record -officer/7zJ1ha78ZoSpfDeyoPBuJJ/story.html.

23. Council on American-Islamic Relations press release, "Cair-FL Says FBI Denied Todashev Friend the Right to an Attorney," March 11, 2015, http://www.cair.com/press-center /press-releases/12165-cair-fl-says-fbi-denied-todashev-friend-the-right-to-an-attorney.html.

24. Office of the Florida State Attorney General Jeffrey Ashton report on investigation into fatal shooting of Ibragim Todashev released on March 25, 2014.

17 ALLAH SENT HIM MONEY

1. Assistant US Attorney Aloke Chakravarty closing argument, transcript from the trial of Dzhokhar Tsarnaev, April 6, 2015.

2. FBI Special Agent Chad Fitzgerald testimony, transcript from the trial of Dzhokhar Tsarnaev, March 11, 2015.

3. Assistant US Attorney William Weinreb to court, transcript from trial of Dzhokhar Tsarnaev April 28, 2015.

4. Viskhan Vakhabov interview with FBI special agent Jeffrey Hunter conducted on April 20, 2013, at his Boston apartment, entered into evidence as defense exhibit, transcript from trial of Dzhokhar Tsarnaev, April 28, 2015.

5. FBI 302 proffer reports between federal investigators and Khairullozhon Matanov.

6. FBI 302 proffer reports between federal investigators and Khairullozhon Matanov.

7. FBI Special Agent Tim McElroy testimony, transcript of, during detention hearing and arraignment of Khairullozhon Matanov in US District Court June 4, 2014.

8. Magomed Dolakov interview with FBI special agents Timothy Brown and William Filbert conducted on May 21, 2013, at Dolakov's Cambridge apartment, entered into evidence as defense exhibit, transcript from trial of Dzhokhar Tsarnaev April 28, 2013.

9. Defense attorney Miriam Conrad sidebar conversation with US District Court Judge George O'Toole and prosecutors, transcript from trial of Dzhokhar Tsarnaev April 28, 2015.

18 HAVE TO ANSWER TO GOD FOR

1. Topsfield Police court filings pertaining to the arrest of Daniel Morley in June 2013 filed in the Newburyport District Court (copy on file).

2. FBI supervisory agent David McCollum testimony, transcript from the trial of Dzhokhar Tsarnaev, March 26, 2015.

3. United States v. Dzhokhar Tsarnaev government opposition to defense motion to suppress statements filed May 21, 2014. Unsealed in January 2016.

4. United States v. Dzhokhar Tsarnaev government opposition to defense motion to suppress statements filed May 21, 2014. Unsealed in January 2016.

5. Topsfield Police court filings pertaining to the arrest of Daniel Morley in June 2013 filed in the Newburyport District Court (copy on file).

6. Author interview with Daniel Morley associate Marc Pascuito, who recalled conversation, September 2014.

7. Gavin Aronsen, "N.H. City Wants a 'Tank' to Use against Occupiers and Libertarians," *Mother Jones*, August 6, 2013, http://www.motherjones.com/politics/2013/08/occupy-free -state-project-dhs-police-concord.

8. Evidence collected from the home of Daniel Morley after his June 2013 arrest included various Free State materials and printed propaganda (copy on file).

9. Author interview with David Bloss at his Topsfield home, September 2013.

10. Author interview with David Bloss at his Topsfield home, September 2013.

11. United States v. Dzhokhar Tsarnaev government opposition to defense motion to suppress statements filed May 21, 2014.

12. Statement released to author by Essex County District Attorney's Office in December 2014.

13. Multiple author interviews with Marc Pascuito in 2013–14.

14. United States v. Dzhokhar Tsarnaev court filing regarding evidence filed August 8, 2014.

15. United States v. Dzhokhar Tsarnaev indictment filed June 27, 2013.

16. Author interview with David Bloss in Topsfield, and interviews with law enforcement sources close to the case.

19 ONE-FINGER SALUTE

1. Michele McPhee, "Mom Comforts Two Sons Who Each Lost a Leg in Boston Bomb Blasts," *ABC News*, April 16, 2013, accessed September 21, 2016, http://abcnews.go.com/US /mom-comforts-sons-lost-leg-boston-blasts/story?id=18969625, and multiple author interviews with Liz Norden in 2013-16. All quotes attributed to Norden in this chapter are taken from these sources.

2. Arraignment of Dzhokhar Tsarnaev before US Magistrate Justice Marianne Bowler, transcript from July 10, 2013, initial appearance at US District Court.

3. I was present as Ed Fucarile addressed reporters outside of federal court, July 10, 2013.

4. Author interview with MIT Police Chief John DiFava, July 10, 2013.

5. US Marshal Kevin Roche testimony, transcript from the trial of Dzhokhar Tsarnaev, May 6, 2015.

6. Assistant US Attorney Nadine Pelligrini argument, transcript from the trial of Dzhokhar Tsarnaev, April 21, 2015.

7. Defense attorney Miriam Conrad cross-examination question to US Marshal Kevin Roche, transcript from trial of Dzhokhar Tsarnaev, April 21, 2015.

8. Roche testimony, transcript from the trial of Dzhokhar Tsarnaev, May 6, 2015.

20 FOOD FOR THE DOG

1. Stephen Silva testimony, transcript from the trial of Dzhokhar Tsarnaev, March 17, 2015.

2. Federal indictment of Stephen Silva filed by US Attorney Carmen Ortiz on July 14, 2014.

3. Stephen Silva testimony, transcript from the trial of Dzhokhar Tsarnaev, March 17, 2015. Subsequent quotes attributed to Stephen Silva in this chapter are from the transcript.

4. Federal indictment of Stephen Silva filed by US Attorney Carmen Ortiz on July 14, 2014.

21 KILL TO BE AN AMERICAN

1. Author interview with Congressman William Keating, October 2013.

2. United States v. Tsarnaev government motion arguing that Dzhokhar Tsarneav should be charged with violating his oath to America, August 16, 2015.

3. Motion to strike "Betrayal of the United States" as a nonstatutory factor filed by Dzhokhar Tsarnaev defense team, June 4, 2014.

4. National Commission on Terrorist Attacks upon the United States, *The 9/11 Commission Report.*

5. Unclassified summary of information handling and sharing prior to the April 15, 2013, bombings prepared by the inspector generals for the Central Intelligence Agency, Department of Justice, and DHS, released April 10, 2014.

6. Posted on the now-defunct Kavkaz.org.

7. Diantha Parker and Jess Bidgood, "Boston Marathon Bombing: What We Know," *New York Times*, January 1, 2015, http://www.nytimes.com/2015/01/02/us/boston-marathon-bombings-trial-what-you-need-to-know.html.

8. Unclassified summary of information handling and sharing prior to the April 15, 2013, bombings, prepared by the inspector generals for the Central Intelligence Agency, Department of Justice, and DHS, released April 10, 2014.

9. USCIS file for Tamerlan Tsarnaev released by the DHS pursuant to a Freedom of Information Act request in 2016.

10. ACLU of Southern California, Lawyers' Committee for Civil Rights, and Mayer Brown, "Muslims Need Not Apply: How USCIS Secretly Mandates the Discriminatory Delay and Denial of Citizenship and Immigration Benefits to Aspiring Americans," released August 2013, https://www.aclusocal.org/CARRP/.

11. Department of Homeland Security, "Refugee Processing and Security Screening," accessed September 21, 2016, https://www.uscis.gov/refugeescreening.

12. Boston medical examiner's death certificate for Tamerlan Tsarnaev, dated April 19, 2013.

13. USCIS file for Tamerlan Tsarnaev released by the DHS pursuant to a Freedom of Information Act request in 2016.

14. Author interview with Phantom Fireworks store assistant manager Megan Kearns, April 2013. Confirmed by multiple law enforcement sources.

15. Trial exhibits entered into evidence by federal prosecutors in trial of Dzhokhar Tsarnaev included photos of items seized from 410 Norfolk Street, including the items mentioned here.

16. FBI Supervisory Agent David McCollum testimony, transcript from trial of Dzhokhar Tsarnaev, March 26, 2015.

22 MAXIMUM HARM

1. Assistant US Attorney William Weinreb opening statement, transcript from trial of Dzhokhar Tsarnaev, March 4, 2015.

2. Boston Mayor Marty Walsh remarks at marathon tribute held at the Hynes Convention Center, April 15, 2014, http://www.cityofboston.gov/mayor/pdfs/walsh_marathon_tribute_remarks.pdf.

23 IT WAS HIM

1. Defense attorney Judy Clarke opening statement, transcript from the trial of Dzhokhar Tsarnaev, March 4, 2015.

2. Assistant US Attorney William Weinreb objection, transcript from the trial of Dzhokhar Tsarnaev, March 4, 2015.

24 *THE LION KING*

1. Jessica Kensky testimony, transcript from trial of Dzhokhar Tsarnaev, May 13, 2015.

2. Shane O'Hara testimony, transcript from trial of Dzhokhar Tsarnaev, March 4, 2015.

3. Roseann Sdoia testimony, transcript from trial of Dzhokhar Tsarnaev, March 5, 2015.

4. Lynn firefighter Matt Patterson testimony, transcript from trial of Dzhokhar Tsarnaev, March 9, 2015.

5. Naida Suleimanova testimony, transcript from trial of Dzhokhar Tsarnaev, May 4, 2015.

6. Shakhurzat Suleimanova testimony, transcript from trial of Dzhokhar Tsarnaev, May 4, 2015.

7. Raisat Suleimanova testimony, transcript from trial of Dzhokhar Tsarnaev, May 4, 2015.

8. Audio recording made by Tamerlan Tsarnaev during his trip to Russia in 2012, entered into evidence as trial exhibit by attorneys for Dzhokhar Tsarnaev and played in court on May 4, 2015.

9. Shakhurzat Suleimanova testimony, transcript from trial of Dzhokhar Tsarnaev, May 4, 2015.

25 AIN'T NO LOVE

1. Dzhokhar Tsarnaev addresses court, transcript from sentencing hearing June 24, 2015.

2. US District Court Justice George O'Toole to court, transcript from sentencing hearing of Dzhokhar Tsarnaev, June 24, 2015.

3. Assistant US Attorney Steve Mellin closing argument, transcript from trial of Dzhokhar Tsarnaev, May 13, 2015.

26 AMERICA'S WORST NIGHTMARE

1. Assistant US Attorney Nadine Pelligrini opening statement in penalty phase, transcript from trial of Dzhokhar Tsarnaev, April 21, 2015.

2. Assistant US Attorney Nadine Pelligrini opening statement in penalty phase, transcript from trial of Dzhokhar Tsarnaev, April 21, 2015.

3. Transcript of Dzhokhar Tsarnaev tweets entered into evidence as trial exhibits by US Attorney's Office in his trial.

4. Assistant US Attorney William Weinreb opening statement, transcript from trial of Dzhokhar Tsarnaev, March 4, 2015.

5. Jennifer Callison testimony, transcript from trial of Dzhokhar Tsarnaev, May 7, 2015.

6. Eric Traub testimony, transcript from trial of Dzhokhar Tsarnaev, May 7, 2015.

7. Rosa Booth testimony, transcript from trial of Dzhokhar Tsarnaev, May 9, 2015.

8. David Bruck defense attorney opening statement in penalty phase, transcript from trial of Dzhokhar Tsarnaev, April 27, 2015.

9. Defense motion to suppress statements in trial of Dzhokhar Tsarnaev filed May 4, 2014, under seal. Court unsealed motion in February 2016.

27 OH, MY GOD, HE'S SO YOUNG

1. Defense attorney Miriam Conrad questions Sister Helen Prejean, transcript from trial of Dzhokhar Tsarnaev, May 11, 2015.

2. Assistant US Attorney Steve Mellin closing argument, transcript from trial of Dzhokhar Tsarnaev, May 13, 2015.

EPILOGUE

1. Bill and Denise Richard, "To End the Anguish Drop the Death Penalty," *Boston Globe*, April 16, 2015, https://www.bostonglobe.com/metro/2015/04/16/end-anguish-drop-death-penalty/ocQLejp8H2vesDavItHIEN/story.html.

2. Michele McPhee, "'I Smoke a Lot of Weed Everyday because My Best Friend Was the Bomber,'" *ABC News*, July 23, 2014, http://abcnews.go.com/Blotter/smoke-weed-day-best-friend-bomber/story?id=24680223.

INDEX

313

Teken, Raphael "Rafi," 96–100. *See also*
Waltham triple murder

terrorism: attacks after marathon bombing,
132–33; war on, and racial profiling, 108,
130

terrorists, homegrown: authorities'
awareness of, ix; number of in US, 120;
Tsarnaev brothers as, ix

terrorist watch lists, Tamerlan Tsarnaev on,
104, 105, 106–7, 110, 128–29, 130, 229

Todashev, Abdul-Baki, 180–81

Todashev, Ibragim: death of, 179–80; father's
complaints about death of, 180–81; FBI
interrogation of, 174–80; FBI suppression
of details of death, 181; FBI surveillance
of, 175–76; flight to Florida, 102, 133, 168,
170, 174; investigations into death of, 175,
181–82; Matanov and, 168–69, 187; as
mixed martial arts fighter, 175, 181–82; and
Prospect Street mosque, 172–73; Russian
warnings about, 226–27; short temper of,
175–76; and Tamerlan Tsarnaev, 98, 133,
174; and Waltham triple murder, 102, 133,
168–69, 177–78, 183

Tsarnaev, Ailina (sister): birth of, 82; on
Dzhokhar's innocence, 89; at Dzhokhar's
trial, 209; and family migration to US, 83,
85; life in US, 67, 87–89, 116, 285; ties to
extremists, 113

Tsarnaev, Anzor (father): beating suffered
by, 114–15; as boxer, 86; on burial of
Tamerlan, 230; character of, 86; divorce
of, 115; emigration to US, 83; fake law
degree of, 92; FBI and, x, 106, 107, 141,
142; as "holiday" Muslim, 111; life before
migration to US, 82–83; marriage of,
81, 82, 86, 115; Matanov on, 151; as never
employed in US, 86; psychological
problems of, 85–86, 114–15; residence
of, 67; return to Russia, 115; on sons'

innocence, 285; on Tamerlan's passport,
129

Tsarnaev, Bella (sister): birth of, 82; at
Dzhokhar's trial, 209; and family
migration to US, 83, 85; life in US, 67,
86–87, 116, 285; ties to extremists, 112

Tsarnaev, Dzhokhar: account of bombing to
police, 163–64; activities after bombing,
76, 147, 148–49, 154, 157, 184–85, 240, 269,
275; announcement of capture of, 77;
on brother, fate of, 69, 77–78; capture
of, viii, 72–76; and Chechen struggle,
114, 116–17, 160; childhood of, 82, 83; and
CIA, 113; college friends of, 116; college
friends' hiding of evidence, 157–58, 217,
244; concerns about suicide vest on, 70,
72–73; correspondence with Tamerlan
in Russia, 116–17; as drug dealer, 86,
93, 116, 159, 160; and Eritrean gang, xi,
116, 142, 143; and family migration to
US, 83; gun obtained by, x–xi, 116, 143,
218–20, 242, 245, 246, 252, 274, 277;
hiding in boat, viii, 69–70, 249–50; as
homegrown terrorist, ix; identification
as suspect, vii; interrogation of, 77–78,
87, 162–64, 194; lack of remorse, 167,
269–70; medical treatment after capture,
76–77; messages left in boat, 69–70,
162, 240–41, 253, 259–60, 274–75; and
Miranda rights, 162–63, 164; motive for
attack, 238, 240–41, 254; phones carried
by, 68, 70, 155, 184–85, 249–50; in prison,
284; response to news coverage, 149;
Tamerlan's efforts to convert, 93; ties to
radical mosque, 28; turn to radical Islam,
157–58, 159, 241–42, 242–43, 253, 257–58,
275; Twitter messages of, 149, 159–60,
240, 275; at UMass/Dartmouth, 93, 113,
116, 154, 159, 160, 183, 185, 240, 259; as US
citizen, ix, 227–28; Vakhabov family and,

Tamerlan, 259; opening argument, 236–54; and pre-trial hearings, 164, 210–11, 213–14; on trial secrecy, 167; on Vakhabov, 185–86

Weissman, Erik, 94–100. *See also* Waltham triple murder

West, Joe, 29, 32–33

Wood, Scott, 98–99, 101

Woolfenden, Leo, 1–3, 4, 8–9

Woolfenden, Steve, 1–3, 5, 8–9

World Association of Muslim Youth, 119, 122

Zhou, Danling, 5, 239